NARRATIVE THERAPY

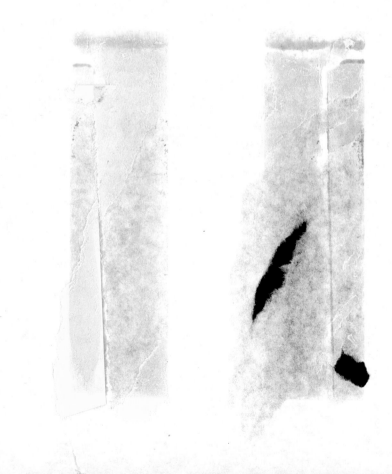

NARRATIVE THERAPY

Making Meaning, Making Lives

Catrina Brown
Dalhousie University

Tod Augusta-Scott
*Bridges-A Domestic Violence, Counseling,
Research, and Training Institute*

Editors

SAGE Publications
Thousand Oaks ▪ London ▪ New Delhi

For information:

Sage Publications, Inc.
2455 Teller Road
Thousand Oaks, California 91320
E-mail: order@sagepub.com

Sage Publications Ltd.
1 Oliver's Yard
55 City Road
London EC1Y 1SP
United Kingdom

Sage Publications India Pvt. Ltd.
B-42, Panchsheel Enclave
Post Box 4109
New Delhi 110 017 India

Printed in the United States of America

Library of Congress Cataloging-in-Publication Data

Narrative Therapy: Making Meaning, Making Lives/[editied by] Cartina Brown, Tod Augusta-Scott.
    p. cm.
Includes bibliographical references and index.
ISBN 1-4129-0987-2 (cloth)—ISBN 1-4129-0988-0 (pbk.)
    1. Narrative therapy. I. Brown, Cartina. II. Augusta-Scott, Tod.
RC489.S74N42 2007
616.89′165—dc22   2006008435

This book is printed on acid-free paper.

06   07   08   09   10   10   9   8   7   6   5   4   3   2   1

Acquiring Editor:	Kassie Graves
Editorial Assistant:	Veronica Novak
Production Editor:	Beth A. Bernstein
Copy Editor:	Carla Freeman
Typesetter:	C&M Digitals (P) Ltd.
Indexer:	Rick Hurd
Cover Designer:	Candice Harman

Contents

Acknowledgments

We would like to thank all of the contributing authors in this project for their thoughtful work. We also appreciate all that we have learned and continue to learn from our clients.

I (Catrina) want to thank Sarah Larsen, Shauna Melanson, and Elizabeth Stephen for the child care and support they offered during the work on this book. I want to acknowledge Zoe for her willingness to relinquish her mummy, however ambivalently, to this project. Special thanks to Tod for our many engaging conversations. Tod's graciousness, generosity, and flexibility allowed for the tremendous ease with which we were able to work together. Finally, I am thankful to my parents, who both demonstrated and encouraged thoughtful critical engagement with the world.

I (Tod) want to thank the many readers who reviewed my work for this project. Specifically, I appreciate the thoughtful feedback of Chris Augusta-Scott, Tionda Cain, Alan Jenkins, and Penny Moore. I especially want to thank Catrina for inspiring me with her intellect, rigor, and bravery, with which she disrupts dominant discourses.

I also want to extend my appreciation for those who have worked with Bridges, a domestic violence counseling, research, and training institute. Specifically, I want to extend my appreciation to my colleagues Marilee Burwash-Brennan, Art Fisher, and Sara Lamb, for their creativity and innovations in developing narrative ideas and practices in our work. Finally, I want to express my sincere gratitude to the volunteer board of directors at Bridges: Blanchard Atkinson, Dan Criss, Jeff Hunt, Nathalie Jamieson, Eric Johnson, Mark Scales, and Debbie Walker, for their vision and courage to support narrative ideas and practices in the field of domestic violence.

Introduction

Postmodernism, Reflexivity, and Narrative Therapy

Catrina Brown and Tod Augusta-Scott

Rooted in social constructionism and emerging initially from family therapy, narrative therapy emphasizes the idea that we live storied lives (White, 1995). Within this approach, we seek to make sense of our lives and experiences by ascribing meaning through stories, which themselves arise within social conversations and culturally available discourses. From this view, our stories do not simply represent us or mirror lived events—they constitute us, shaping our lives and our relationships. The narrative metaphor conveys the idea that stories organize, structure, and give meaning to events in our lives and help us make sense of our experiences. Stories are transmitted largely through socially mediated language and social interaction within specific cultural and historical contexts. The meanings that we attach to events are thus never singular, individual, or simply subjective, never outside the social, but have shared or intersubjective meaning within a cultural nexus of power and knowledge.

Influenced by feminist, postmodern, and critical theory, this book contributes to the field of narrative therapy by offering a critical discussion of the often unexamined epistemological contradictions evident in therapeutic work that remains, however ambivalently, positioned in modernism. Michael White's (1995, 2000a, 2000b, 2001; White & Epston, 1990) view that stories must not only be told and retold, but reconstructed, has shaped our approach to narrative therapy. A creator of narrative therapy, White (1994) is clear that there are no neutral stories. Not only are there no neutral stories, there is no neutral hearing of stories. He advocates a therapeutic alliance that is a partnership between active, embodied subjects, who together coauthor more helpful and less oppressive stories.

White's (1995, 1997, 2000a, 2000b, 2001, 2004a, 2004b; White & Epston, 1990) focus on the relationship between knowledge and power in the social construction of discourse and his belief that no stories exist that are independent of the social world is underscored in this book. In addition to White, other narrative therapists' attention to the political nature of social discourses has influenced this book. Madigan and Law's (1998) contribution to narrative therapy situates substantive issues within political discourse. Jenkins's (1990, 1996) work identifies the political context in which violence plays out in intimate relationships and which also shapes the alliance between the therapist and client. Hare-Mustin's (1994) postmodern analysis of "discourses in the mirrored room" elucidates the dangers of simply reinforcing dominant discourses, such as gender, in therapeutic conversations. Building upon these influential works, we will explore the important contributions narrative therapy makes to clinical practice, while also interrogating its unreconciled positioning within a modernist and postmodernist knowledge base.

This book was born out of our conversations about the politics of narrative practice within our respective fields, Tod Augusta-Scott working in the field of "domestic violence" and Catrina Brown working with the continuum of eating "disorders" women experience. We began to observe significant areas of overlap in these cultural articulations of gendered subjectivity or notions of self. It became clear to us that gender essentialism—taken-for-granted and often biological assumptions about gender—and modernist approaches to understanding power produced similar limitations in our respective fields of work. In the field of "domestic violence," dominant gender stories led people to essentialize or naturalize men as violent perpetrators who want only power and control. Similarly, in the field of eating "disorders," gender stories essentialize women as compliant victims of the social pressure to be thin. Both of these dominant social stories are "surface" descriptions. Paradoxically, in both instances, these stories are invoked with the intent to advance positive social change, yet they are constrained or limited by gender essentialism. Our observations of these inadvertent limitations within our predominantly gendered fields of practice inspired this project's focus on a reflexive postmodern narrative practice.

In bringing these chapters together in this book, it is our intention to contribute to a narrative therapy that resists essentializing or naturalizing the subject—and by extension the experiences, emotions, knowledge, identity, or stories of the self. Furthermore, we wish to avoid producing subjectivist (or individualizing) and depoliticized accounts of individuals' problems by writing out the social. Through a postmodern lens, this book challenges the "either/or," binary constructions that constrain our understanding of stories about individuals' problems and the creation of alternative realities, such as Black/White, male/female, heterosexual/homosexual, body/mind, and self/society. Recognizing that knowledge and power are joined in discourse challenges relativist (no position is taken; all ideas are treated as though they were equal) and, subsequently, depoliticized approaches to therapy. We also wish to avoid unwittingly reproducing or reifying dominant socially constructed practices by being reflexive about these ideas. This book attempts to illustrate that politicized, or anti-oppressive, practice necessarily takes a stance, is necessarily positioned—abandoning the fiction of neutrality and the limitations of relativism. To not unpack, or deconstruct, dominant stories is to leave dominant social discourses and social relations of power intact. Aligned with the philosophy of Michael White, it is our view that narrative therapy is, then, a political process. A self-reflexive narrative therapy will turn a postmodern lens back upon itself and be aware of how we put ideas into play through processes of thinking and talking. By putting ideas into play, we all participate in organizing and sustaining particular stories of social reality. Often, dominant stories or discourses prevail, maintaining particular versions of reality. Such taken-for-granted dominant discourses close off possibilities of other interpretations.

This book is organized into four sections, which build upon each other. We begin in Part 1, "Writing in the Social," by arguing for the need to challenge individualizing or subjectivist approaches to understanding the struggles individuals bring to therapeutic conversations. In Part 2, "Self- Surveillance: Normalizing Practices of Self," we examine the role of self-regulation, ways in which we observe and correct ourselves, as normalizing practices of self in culture. Part 3, "Challenging Essentialism," exposes the limitations of essentialist discourse in therapeutic conversations. Finally, Part 4, "Re-Authoring Preferred Identities," explores the creation of preferred identities within narrative therapy. Within this book, we illustrate a range of narrative styles of practice and, in so doing, emphasize that there is no one formulaic application of narrative therapy. Themes such as eating "disorders," trauma, depression, violence, and working with the family are addressed. The writers contend with central theoretical constructs in the process of illustrating their therapeutic work in these areas, including the problems of essentialism, binary constructions, situating knowledge and power, externalization, and highlighting the importance of agency and audience.

History of Narrative Therapy

Narrative therapy emerged from the lenses of cybernetics, interpretive anthropology, and postmodernism. Specifically, White (White, 1984, 1986,

1991; White & Epston, 1990) was influenced by the work of Gregory Bateson (1972, 1979), Edward Bruner (1986a, 1986b), Jerome Bruner (1986, 1987), Clifford Geertz (1973), and Michel Foucault (1973, 1980a, 1980b, 1984, 1988, 1995). Bateson's (as cited in White & Epston, 1990) interpretative method within the social sciences, which emphasized that "we cannot know objective reality, all knowing requires an act of interpretation" (p. 2), provided an early influence on White. As we cannot have direct knowledge of the world, narrative therapy is centered on "lived experience." White and Epston (1990) ask, "How do persons organize their stock of lived experience? What do persons do with this experience in order to give it meaning and to make sense out of their lives? How is lived experience given expression?" (p. 9). The therapeutic narrative metaphor originated for White through the work of both Jerome Bruner (1986, 1987) and Geertz (1973). Interpretive anthropologist Geertz shaped White's approach to the interpretation of story-making process within culture. From Geertz, White brought forward the idea of seeking "thick description" in therapeutic conversations in place of the often unhelpful thin descriptions that suppressed alternative story possibilities.

We make sense of our lives through stories, and, according to White and Epston (1990), "It is this storying that determines the meaning ascribed to experience" (p. 10). Jerome Bruner's (1986) approach to stories provided a temporal landscape for understanding the meaning of events across time. The reflexive questioning that links actions (landscape of action) and meanings or beliefs (landscape of consciousness or meaning) within the larger context of relationships and culture also reveals parallels with Milan and post-Milan family therapy approaches (Hart, 1995). From Foucault, White drew his understanding of the relationship between knowledge and power and the normalizing techniques of power often intrinsic to therapeutic practice, including the dividing practices and objectification of persons through diagnoses and labeling. Of tremendous significance, White (1984) adapted Foucauldian philosophy to therapeutic conversations through his development of "externalizing the problem." His emphasis became less pragmatic or solution focused as he shifted toward emphasizing the externalization of stories of the self and internalized cultural discourses (Hart, 1995). These externalizing conversations subsequently enabled a process of reconstructing or re-authoring identities (Hart, 1995). Not only are subjugated knowledges resurrected through the articulation and thickening of alternative stories, dominant cultural stories are challenged. In this way, White offers to narrative therapy attention to the discursive mechanisms by which power is woven throughout people's stories of self within culture.

Through the influence of these thinkers, White extended his training as a family therapist, shifting from a cybernetic approach to a narrative metaphor (Freedman & Combs, 1996, Hart, 1995; Parry & Doan, 1994). Since White's narrative work surfaced in the late 1980s, many other postmodern therapy texts have emerged, including Anderson (1997); Epston (1989, 1998; Epston & White, 1992); Freedman and Combs (1996); Gilligan and Price (1993); Gremillion (2003); Hoyt (1998); Jenkins; (1990); Madigan and Law (1998); Maisel, Epston, and Borden (2004); Parry and Doan (1994); Strong and Paré (2003); White (1991, 1995, 1997, 2000a, 2000b, 2004a, 2004b); White and Denborough (1998); Monk, Winslade, and Crocket (1996); and Zimmerman and Dickerson (1996). While narrative therapy is undoubtedly influenced by postmodern philosophy, it is not a homogeneous field. As such, narrative therapy approaches differ epistemologically in their specific blend of modern and postmodern conceptualizations and practices. Thus, there are significant distinguishing features within narrative therapy, and, correspondingly, some are more likely to reify dominant social reality (Brown, 2003).

While narrative therapy is distinct from other approaches to practice, it is often compared to the collaborative work of Harlene Anderson (1997) and the solution-focused work of Steven de Shazer (de Shazer, 1991, 1993; de Shazer et al., 1986; Molnar & de Shazer, 1987). White and Anderson are both influenced by postmodern theory, but they follow different paths: Anderson leans toward relativism, while White argues for the importance of recognizing the politics of therapy. Whereas Anderson advocates that the story should be told and retold, White argues that the story must often be told, retold, and rewritten. Neither Anderson nor de Shazer is concerned with disrupting dominant social discourses or uncovering alternative stories that resurrect the suppressed voice and support preferred realities. White and de Shazer are often conflated because they both follow "strengths-based" approaches, seeking solutions to problems and looking for, in the case of de Shazer, exceptions to the problem and, in the case of White, unique outcomes or stalled initiatives. Through the identification of these exceptions or unique outcomes, it is conceived that one is able to move past the problem. Beyond this description, however, there are marked differences in their theoretical foundations, which are evident at the level of practice and politics. Although de Shazer abandons the idea of the expert and the problem-saturated story, he advances a primarily modernist foundation, compared with White, who is significantly influenced by postmodernism.

One significant difference is White's exploration of the social organization and meaning of people's stories and de Shazer's arguably modernist pragmatic focus on behavior, goals, and solutions. Beyond this description, however, we see marked differences in practice and epistemology between de Shazer's solution-focused therapy and White's narrative therapy. As Hart (1995) notes, White focuses on "meaning, narrative and power," whereas de Shazer focuses on "behaviour, goals and pragmatics" (p. 5). Furthermore, White highlights a fluid relationship between past, present, and future, whereas de Shazer is largely disinterested in the past. He is thus uninterested in the construction of the story and only superficially interested in its disruption. The abbreviated approach to solution-focused therapy is strategic, pragmatic, and mechanical via its line of questioning in the search for solutions. The approach does not center on how the meaning of experience is constructed within a cultural context; and thus, as it is often pointed out, there is little attention given to the social and historical contexts that shape individuals' problems. There is no provision for the analysis of power within de Shazer's schema or for challenging dominant social discourses. De Schazer's work focuses on the individual, whereas White's work situates the individual within the larger social context (Chang & Phillips, 1993).

Furthermore, the influences of J. Bruner (1986, 1987), E. Bruner (1986a, 1986b), Gergen and Gergen (1984), Geertz (1986), and Foucault (1972, 1973, 1980b, 1988, 1995) create a very different sensibility within White's work. We see de Schazer's solution-focused therapy as grounded in a primarily modernist foundation, at least in part because there is no unpacking of concepts such as power, knowledge, self, or experience.[1]

Blending Modernism and Postmodernism

This book offers a blend of modernist and postmodernist approaches to knowledge and power (Brown, 2003; Payne, 2000; White, 1995). We continue to draw upon modernism's commitment to social critique and emancipatory projects, which can envision a more just society. Modernism thus allows us to continue to take a stance toward social justice and eradicating social oppression. However, we also rely upon a postmodern sensibility toward deconstruction and reflexivity, which means that no ideas are beyond inquiry or escape scrutiny. This blended form of narrative practice is then reflexive about organizing concepts of therapeutic practice such as experience, self, and identity, which are themselves discursive productions, representing socially and historically constructed stories. By *discursive productions*, we are referring to social processes of "talk" in which we make meaning. As we story or talk about experience, self, and identity, we create them: We form them as we speak them. We abandon the modernist reliance upon essentialism and binary thought and the postmodernist tendency toward relativism. Therefore, within narrative therapeutic conversations, not only clients' stories, which are situated within their social and historically specific contexts, need to be unpacked but also the discursive or socially constructed therapeutic conceptual tools used for understanding these stories.

A Postmodern Lens

Postmodern narrative therapy represents a fundamental divergence from modernist psychotherapy perspectives. Unlike psychotherapy grounded in modernist constructions of knowledge, power, truth, knowledge, experience, emotion, reason, self, and identity, the postmodern lens that shapes narrative therapy means these central foundational constructs to therapy are interrogated rather than taken as is. As Flax (1990) observes, modernist foundational assumptions about reason, truth, knowledge, and the self are destabilized by postmodernism. For postmodernism, there is no one truth, no one universal, discoverable truth that exists outside human existence. There is no stable, fixed, knowable, or essential self or identity, as self and identity can emerge only within linguistic, cultural, and relational practices. Truth is only ever partial, located, and invested. What we take for granted to be true, reasonable, and normative are in fact social constructions that emerge within social and historical contexts and cannot be separated from human meaning-making processes. Knowledge is thus never innocent, but always culture bound. When it comes to social life and human experience grounded in social life, all knowledge is interpretative, valued based, and woven into the matrixes of power that shape the organization of society itself. And while human beings are socially created, this is a dialectical process in which they are simultaneously produced by and produce the world in which they live (Berger & Luckmann, 1967; Gergen, 1985a, 1985b; Shotter, 1993).

Therapeutism

Therapy itself is a social construction with a particular kind of social agenda and role. "Therapeutism" is a dominant form of discourse that guides ways of living with the difficulties and conflicts of contemporary society (Epstein, 1994). It is an ideological discourse that focuses on individuals' emotional problems and promises to "do good," while performing the social roles of surveillance, regulation, and control of moral and appropriate social behavior (Epstein, 1994). According to Epstein (1994), the therapeutic idea is the preponderant influence on the composition of normative standards for how we conduct ourselves, how we judge people, how we decide who to get involved with, who to avoid, where we take a job, bring up children, deal with illness, our bodies, our minds, all our social relations. (p. 2)

In other words, the discourse of the therapeutic idea pervades daily life. Therapeutism, then, is a central discursive practice that organizes our social world, one that ensures people are socialized "into occupying the appropriate places in social structure and behaving in right ways" (Epstein, 1994, p. 6). For the most part, narrative therapy disrupts the modernist basis of the therapeutic idea—that the therapeutic is "transhistorical, scientifically objective, apolitical" (p. 3). Yet like most therapy, narrative therapy is likely to claim that "it is good for you" (p. 3). This is qualified, however, for while narrative therapy may suggest that it can be helpful in rewriting problem stories and re-authoring identities, a postmodern and reflexive approach within narrative therapy rejects the promise that therapy can provide self-emancipation or discovery of the "real" self.

White (1997, 2001) suggests that narrative therapy is not an avenue for discovering the emancipated self. Indeed, he refutes the idea of an emancipatory psychology, arguing that within this view, the self is naturalized and formulated as though it had escaped historical and social forces. In writing out the social, the transcendental subject produces a subjectivist, essentialist, depoliticized analysis (Smith, 1999). Having escaped social forces, the self just is. White (1997, 2001) critiques the idea that therapy can free people to live according to their true natures or real, authentic selves. Such emancipatory psychologies are predicated upon the idea of a fixed, immutable, essential self. We live in a culture absorbed by the creation of self, whereby through social processes of subjectification (Foucault, 1984), we turn ourselves into subjects, endlessly attempting to shape, manage, improve, and understand ourselves. Psychological discourses center on the internal private life—experience, need, emotion—as though it were separate from the external world. Embedded within social constructionism, narrative therapy views self-stories as interpretations of lived events and thus challenges essentialist (naturalized), subjectivist (individualized and decontextualized), and ultimately depoliticized views of the subject. Our reflection, our gaze, turns inward in subjectivist understandings of the self, permitting a focus on the individual that obscures social and political analysis. A reflexive postmodern narrative therapy recognizes ways in which all therapy participates in "therapeutism," while also seeing therapy as a potential social site of resistance through the challenging of internalized dominant social discourse and in coauthoring more helpful stories.

Therapy is, of course, for Foucault, a modernist strategy or mechanism of power. Therapy relies upon the modes of objectification of the subject delineated by Foucault, whereby under the gaze of science and classification, we come to understand ourselves "scientifically." Power and knowledge are not separate from the formation of the subject. Therapy is a socially legitimized arena for turning our gaze inward, disciplining the docile body, and ensuring we are self-constraining. Dividing practices of traditional therapy include medicalization, labeling, stigmatization, and pathologization. Systems of classifying and labeling individuals rely upon the nexus of truth and power, legitimized by "experts" such as therapists, and are often dividing practices or strategies of power that determine which people are normal or abnormal, good or bad, strong or weak, moral or immoral.

Taken together, these processes enable the governance of subjects. Yet, for Foucault, the process of subjectification involves both power as constraint and domination and power as productive and constitutive. Thus, in making ourselves into subjects within the context of culture, we are both constrained and creative. Within this process there are, then, sites of resistance. This can be said of discourse, and in particular, discourses of self. Narrative therapy exploits these sites of resistance, unpacking the constraining aspects of our self-stories and resurrecting the suppressed voice by recognizing and emphasizing the agency and creativity available to individuals in re-authoring their identities.

We believe that while therapy can indeed invoke conservatizing, normalizing, and regulating processes of self in its operation as a social strategy of power, it can also be an effort to challenge the discursive practices of power and knowledge that have become problematically embedded within people's lives. Within narrative therapy, it is believed that changing people's stories about their lives can help to change their actual lives. Furthermore, changing these stories often involves challenging larger social stories within people's problem-saturated stories about themselves and their lives. All individual stories are social stories: There is never a sole author. When social stories leave unquestioned dominant social relations of power, coexisting and prevailing assumptions of truth and power remain intact. Narrative therapy can disrupt those dominant discourses that operate in tandem with power and thus sustain dominant social reality, which benefits only a few. We agree with White (1997), however, that there is nothing revolutionary about these narrative practices—they do not stand outside of the discourses of culture (p. 231).

Part 1: Writing in the Social

We begin this book with a critical examination of dominant social discourses that often shape therapeutic work, in terms of their influence on both clients' stories about themselves and therapists' interpretations of these stories. These discourses often reveal naturalized, biological, individualized, and decontextualized explanations of people's problems. Taken-for-granted dominant accounts of addiction, eating "disorders," depression, and violence are themselves often constituted by larger organizing discourses that rely on assumptions about truth, knowledge, power, experience, the self, identity, and gender. Prevailing discourses such as these regularly find their way into therapeutic conversations and are, therefore, unpacked in this book. In this way, we wish to highlight the complex creation and transmission of stories within our culture (Shotter, 1993). Surface readings, thin descriptions or interpretations of stories that do not also unpack organizing concepts in stories such as those identified above, are likely to deconstruct only the surface story. Instead, like interpretive anthropologists, we are interested in discovering rich or thick descriptions of people's experiences (Geertz, 1973). Exploring the multiple, complex, and overlapping scaffolds that structure stories will not only enable a more extensive deconstruction of stories but also enable a richer redescription in the process of reconstructing more helpful stories (White, 2004b). We are not, however, invoking the traditional psychotherapy notion of uncovering the "deeper truths" that are taken to explain surface expressions of psychopathology (see White, 1997, p. 62).

The stories we tell about our experiences are not separate from the larger social stories that circulate as universal representations of truth while remaining largely unquestioned. For example, dominant stories often presume that alcoholism is a chronic primary disease that necessitates abstinence, that depression is a product of either biochemical imbalances in the brain or oppressive life circumstances, that eating "disorders" are caused either by the influence of media images of thinness or genetic vulnerability, or that men use violence because they want power and control. So embedded are these stories, clients often present them as truths woven into their accounts of their experiences, and therapists wishing to legitimize clients' experiences leave the foundational presumptions of these stories intact. What this means is that together, the client and therapist may inadvertently constrain the possibility for creating alternative stories.

The process of externalizing within narrative therapy, or separating a problem from the individual, is itself discursive. As such, it is a political process that requires the therapist to interpret and take a stance about the stories presented. The therapist, like the client, will have been exposed to many of the same dominant social stories about the problems individuals and families bring to therapy. As such, they have not escaped, and cannot escape, the meaning-making process of which they themselves are a part.

As well, these stories often hold onto deeply conservatizing processes of individualizing and pathologizing that strip people of agency and self-control. It is not just the need to deconstruct these larger social stories that becomes important to narrative conversations that seek to externalize people's problems, it is all the other organizing ideas that remain unchanged when stories are taken up at face value: the self, identity, and experience. Too often, revealing its modernist origins, therapy presumes there is a real or discoverable essential self. According to White (2001), this naturalizing of identity poses many hazards, as "these naturalistic accounts obscure the contexts of people's lives, including the politics of their experiences" (p. 44). If, for instance, therapy presumes that it will uncover the "real self" in conversations of sexual identity, it presumes an essentialized self, a discoverable, preexisting, and fixed entity—an essentialized sexual identity. When, similarly, therapy presumes that if it peels back the layers of gendered or racial oppression, for example, it will discover the real unencumbered self, it presumes there can be a "real self" outside the social world. In this case, therapy naturalizes and decontextualizes social categories of gender or race, presuming there is a "real woman" or a "real Black woman." The collection of chapters in this book illustrates narrative conversational approaches that attempt to not essentialize or leave intact foundational social categories. The "self," identity, and experience are taken up as fully social (Smith, 1999). We assume that accountable therapeutic conversations are reflexive about their grounding assumptions.

Social Constructionism

While we are created by social life, we also create social life (Durkheim, 1966; Marx, 1978; Mead, 1977; Smith, 1987, 1990a, 1990b, 1999). This view conflates with the narrative story metaphor, for while we live our stories, our stories live us; we create our stories and are created by them (White & Epston, 1990). Indeed, "stories make meaning" (E. Bruner, 1986a, p. 140). However, we do not, and cannot, create our stories by ourselves, as they can emerge only within a preexisting context of meaning. This context of meaning is always social, as meaning cannot exist independent of social life. The human capacity to produce meaning and to attach it to social events and experiences requires social interaction.

White (2001) emphasizes that our stories do not simply represent us or reflect back, like a mirror, a discernable reality; instead, our stories are active—they constitute us. The stories we tell are the stories we live. When we write new stories of our lives, we live new stories. By telling unhelpful or oppressive stories about our lives, we keep these stories alive, and with them, often misery, unhappiness, and injustice. According to Jerome Bruner (2002), "We gain the self-told narratives that make and re-make ourselves from the culture in which we live" (p. 87). Yet we are not simply products of our stories or of a culture from whence our stories are made possible, but cocreators of ourselves through the creation of our stories and our culture. The narrative process of therapeutic conversation, then, centers clients as active subjects, agents in their own lives. This therapeutic approach is one of possibility, of hope, enabling the rewriting and subsequent reliving of one's lives through more helpful stories.

The social constructionist approach is central to narrative therapy.[2] From this view, Berger and Luckmann (1967) maintain that human constructions are "real" as they take on the properties of a material world, in that they have an essence or existence of their own, with concrete social effects and an ability to shape behavior. Although stories begin as social constructions, they have real effects as people live them. For Berger and Luckmann, what is defined as *real*, is real in its consequences. As meaning does not exist in the external world, in and within itself, acts must be given meaning through the process of consciousness, language, and social interaction (Mead, 1977). Over time, that which is socially constructed becomes detached from human creation, and social objects are taken to originate in the nature of things independent of human creation (Durkheim, 1966). Meaning is presumed to be universal as it becomes sedimented in the cultural, whereby social life becomes naturalized, dehistoricized, and depoliticized. Through such processes, social reality is transmitted and reproduced.

Knowledge, Power, and Discourse

Narrative therapy leans on social constructionism as well as postmodern discourse analysis. Following de Saussure (as cited in Weedon, 1997), for example, "Meaning is produced within language rather than reflected by language" (p. 23). Meaning does not already exist, but comes into being through the use of language. The work of de Saussure (1974) takes apart modernist concepts of language, knowledge, and reality. He disrupts conventional notions of the signifier and the signified, language and reality, arguing that language is constitutive rather than reflective of social reality. Similarly, White and Epston (1990) argues that we live storied lives; our stories constitute us. From this view, we live our stories, and our stories live us. Discourse analysis means taking apart how meaning has been constituted through acts or practices of talk, through speech or text. According to

Foucault (1972), discourses are social "practices that systematically form the objects of which they speak" (p. 49). For Foucault (1980a), knowledge and power are joined through discourse.

Drawing on Foucault, White and Epston (1990) state, "We are subject to power through the normalizing 'truths' that shape our lives and relationships" (p. 19). While power is often understood as negative, repressive, or constraining, power is also formulated by Foucault as positive, productive, or constitutive. Thus, dominant discourses or normalizing truths shape the stories that clients bring to therapy. These stories, situated within cultural discourse, do not escape power and are indeed constituted by power, thus revealing power as both constraining and constitutive. While within our culture, there is a willingness to see power as repressive, there is much more reluctance to see the constitutive or productive effects of power, because this requires humans to confront how power is implicit in our very subjectivity, that which people wish to honor and privilege as individual, private, and outside the social (Foucault, 1995). As knowledge and power are inseparable, "a domain of knowledge is a domain of power, and a domain of power is a domain of knowledge" (White & Epston, 1990, p. 22). For Foucault, power produces knowledge: They "imply one another" (Redekop, 1995, p. 314). Yet while knowledge and power are co-implicated, they cannot be reduced to each other; knowledge is more than simply an instrument of power (Tanesini, 1999, p. 195).

As stories are discursive, the living and telling of them are inseparable. We form or constitute our experiences as we speak of them, and as we speak of them, we experience them. The narrative metaphor moves away from the idea of representationalism to one of constitutionalism and thus shifts from the idea that stories simply describe social life to the idea that stories create and reflect social life (White, 1995). Stories are not, then, simply factual representations of an external world outside of human creation. The "constitutionalist" perspective advanced by White (1993) informs this collection:

> The constitutionalist perspective that I am arguing refutes foundationalist assumptions of objectivity, essentialism and representationalism. It proposes that an objective knowledge of the world is not possible, that knowledges are actually generated in particular discursive fields. It proposes that all essentialist notions, including those about human nature, are ruses that disguise what is really taking place, that essentialist notions are paradoxical in that they provide descriptions that are specifying of life; that these notions obscure the operations of power. And the constitutionalist perspective proposes that the descriptions that we have of life are not representations or reflections of life as lived, but are directly constitutive of life; that these descriptions do not correspond with the world, but have real effects in the shaping of life. (p. 125)

In this first section of the book, "Writing in the Social," five chapters will explore the limitations of subjectivism: the individualizing, depoliticizing, and medicalizing of individuals' experiences. The chapters focus on the relationship between knowledge and power, depression among women, genetic accounts of eating "disorders," disease model accounts of addiction, and the tensions involved in practicing psychiatry from a narrative approach.

Catrina Brown argues in her chapter, "Situating Knowledge and Power in the Therapeutic Alliance," that rethinking power includes challenging the ways in which both practitioners and clients keep oppressive stories alive. In this chapter, Brown argues that the therapeutic re-authoring of alternative stories necessarily involves questioning the dominant discourses that shape unhelpful stories. In addition, therapeutic practices themselves rely on dominant discourses of knowledge, power, and the self. Therapeutic practices often reflect the modernist dualistic assumption that either one has knowledge or one does not and one either has power or one does not. Contemporary binary constructions of therapy seek to maximize clients' power through positioning the client as "expert," which often implicitly requires the practitioner to abdicate knowledge and power by adopting a "not-knowing" position.

For Foucault (1980a, 1980b), power operates in both constraining and constitutive ways, for example, through the ways people story their lives. From a narrative perspective, we can see this clearly in the way people internalize dominant social discourses as their own, when these stories contribute not to greater power and agency, but less. Relying on Foucault's view that knowledge and power are joined in discourse, this chapter argues that the "not-knowing" stance is not effective for challenging oppressive dominant discourses, deconstructing identity conclusions, or rewriting alternative preferred identities. A postmodern narrative approach to the therapeutic alliance accentuates that therapy is a partnership of active, embodied subjects who join knowledge in their work together.

In their chapter, "Re-Storying Women's Depression: A Material-Discursive Approach," Michelle Lafrance and Janet Stoppard elaborate on their work with women who suffer from depression, presenting an analysis grounded in a postmodern material/discursive approach. This chapter draws upon the authors' qualitative research on women's experiences of being depressed. The research is positioned within a feminist social constructionist perspective that recognizes the embodied character of depressive experiences. Based on a discursive analysis of women's accounts, the chapter presents an understanding of becoming depressed and moving away from depression as experiences that arise at the intersection of discourses on femininity and the practices of femininity that such discourses entail. Implications for the theory, practice, and policy of situating and understanding women's depression within this material-discursive framework are discussed. This approach suggests strategies for dealing with depression and sadness by moving beyond the mind/body and culture/biology binaries.

Karin Jasper's chapter, "The Blinding Power of Genetics: Manufacturing and Privatizing Stories of Eating Disorders," critiques limiting genetic stories that situate eating "disorders" within individuals and outside dominant discourses and their social and historical contexts. Through examining the genetic discourse on eating "disorders," Jasper illustrates the manufacturing and privatizing of this ubiquitous social problem faced by contemporary women. Jasper elaborates upon the blinding power of genetic discourse and demonstrates the way it disqualifies and renders invisible other interpretations and possibilities for understanding and working with women's struggles with these problems. She addresses this dominant discourse and its potential implications for prevention and treatment, demonstrating the value of alternative narrative-based strategies.

Colin Sanders exposes the disease metaphor of the dominant addictions discourse, which renders invisible other alternative interpretations and possibilities for treatment, in his chapter, "A Poetics of Resistance: Compassionate Practice in Substance Misuse Therapy." Taken-for-granted, disease-based ideas about addiction are often reproduced within modernist frameworks. He discusses the continuing influence of the disease model discourse regarding substance misuse practices and proposes a perspective that evolved from 1989 to 2003 in his work at "Peak House," a coed, 8-week residential treatment program for young persons struggling with substance misuse and their families. In this chapter, Sanders recounts and remembers influences and inspirations contributing to what he refers to as a "poetics of resistance," a compassionate practice arising in response to the pathologizing discourse associated with the disease model metaphor. A poetics of resistance represents a counterstory to the story of hopelessness and self-doubt associated with the disease metaphor. Influenced by White and Epston (1990), Sanders's work at Peak House moved away from deficit-pathologized identities toward re-authored identities, including a re-visioning of difficult and demeaning experiences and the surfacing of preferred, more hopeful stories.

Normand Carrey's chapter, "Practicing Psychiatry Through a Narrative Lens: Working With Children, Youth, and Families," explores the tensions that emerge in his efforts to blend psychiatry and narrative therapy; and, in doing so, he challenges the dominance of biological explanations of people's problems. He combines a narrative approach with the three traditional stages of psychiatric intervention: "the psychiatric interview," "the diagnosis," and "treatment." As he seeks to work collaboratively with families, he emphasizes the language they use to describe their lives, rather than using only psychiatric language. Specifically, narrative practice assists him to move away from traditional notions of his role as "the expert," particularly through the traditional use of diagnostic labels, toward a more collaborative approach with families. Through case examples, he illustrates how psychiatric intervention from a narrative perspective can help children, youth, and families coconstruct alternative and more helpful stories and preferred identities.

Part 2: Self-Surveillance: Normalizing Practices of Self

Narrative therapy is indebted to French philosopher and historian Michel Foucault and his work that demonstrates the relationship between knowledge and power and the ways in which normalizing processes of self-surveillance have the effect of regulating and homogenizing human behavior, shaping our thoughts, preferences, and values. For Foucault, culture is regulated through strategies or techniques of power that regulate or discipline its members through the construction and internalization of dominant truths or discourses.

Such strategies of power engage individuals in active self-surveillance and in processes of normalization of the self. In other words, people primarily regulate themselves. For the most part, force is not required in regulating the populace, so committed are people to self-management.[3] A primary means of accomplishing this is through the stories they tell about themselves and their lives. Jerome Bruner (2002) highlights the balancing act of the self-story,

> A self-making narrative is something of a balancing act. It must, on the one hand, create a conviction of autonomy, that one has a will of one's own, a certain freedom of choice, a degree of possibility. But it must also relate the self to a world of others—to friends and family, to institutions, to the past, to reference groups. But the commitment to others that is implicit in relating oneself to others of course limits our autonomy. We seem virtually unable to live without both autonomy, and commitment, and our lives strive to balance the two. So do the self-narratives we tell ourselves. (p. 78)

Perhaps the most important contribution of narrative therapy is its belief that new or different stories, accounts, or representations are always possible. The process of unpacking and exposing unhelpful stories through the way they have been put together over time enables the discovery of alternative stories that have been disqualified or rendered invisible. Within narrative therapy, there is, then, no simple binary between the known and the unknown.

Discourses of the Self

Within a postmodern narrative therapy, the self is fully social; there is no transcendental subject. A postmodern lens reveals that the daily and ongoing reproductions of self-stories are not sacred or untouchable: They are, in fact, implicated in power. Following Foucault (1980a, p. 11), when we talk of ourselves, we put ourselves into discourse and, in so doing, draw on culturally available meanings. The social reproduction of dominant social discourse requires our participation, and one powerful vehicle is through our self-stories. At the same time, we are not without agency. We can disrupt these discourses. According to Foucault (1980a),

> Discourse transmits and produces power; it reinforces it, but also undermines and exposes it, renders it fragile and makes it possible to thwart it. In like manner, silence and secrecy are a shelter for power, anchoring its prohibitions, but they also loosen its hold and provide for relatively obscure areas of tolerance. (p. 101)

We are reminded that the telling of self-stories is flawed and circumscribed. The stories are not, and cannot be, perfect accounts or representations of "what is" or "what was." Thin descriptions of life experience, or self-stories, are interpretative and, as such, are necessarily incomplete or partial. In narrative therapy, the pursuit of thicker description recognizes this idea. Reflecting Foucault's view, postmodern narrative therapy is aware that there is no binary between what is told and what is untold. There is a distinct and complex relationship between the dominant self-stories people tell about themselves and those they disqualify. Narrative therapeutic conversations unpack what is said and are deeply curious about what is not said, that which has not made it into the story. Foucault (1980a) observes,

> Silence itself—the things one declines to say, or is forbidden to name, the discretion that is required between different speakers—is less the absolute limit of discourse, the other side from which it is separated by a strict boundary, than an element that functions alongside the things said, with them and in relation to them within over-all strategies. There is no binary division to be made between what one says and what one does not say; we must try to determine the different ways of not saying such things, how those who can and those who cannot speak of them are distributed, which types of discourse are authorized, or which form of discretion is required in either case. There is not one but many silences and they are an integral part of the strategies that underlie and permeate discourses. (p. 27)

Stories of the self are creations involving selective information about what is included and what is excluded. They are, therefore, only ever partial. Rather than actually representing an essential self, stories of self are constitutive.

In the second section of the book, "Self-Surveillance: Normalizing Practices of Self," the authors focus on the process of self-surveillance in society and how subsequent self-regulation is part of normalizing practices of self in which the self is a vehicle of social power. The section begins with Catrina Brown's exploration of the tension between discipline and desire that under-scores performances of self within our culture and how socially constructed normalizing processes of self and associated internalized negative identity conclusions are often at the heart of clients' stories. In her chapter, "Discipline and Desire: Regulating the Body/Self," Brown explores ways in which women regulate themselves as social subjects. Influenced by Foucault's notion of the "docile body" and of "disciplining the body," Brown examines the way women use their bodies as an illustration of one cultural form of self-regulation, illuminating the tension between the discipline of and capitula-tion to desire and need in contemporary culture. The body is not stable, constant, asocial, ahistorical, or "natural." It is, as Foucault suggests, in "the grip" of cultural practices, including relations of power. Abandoning the tendency to naturalize the body, this discussion of women's struggles with eating and body size serves as an example of normalization processes of the self. Challenging the oppressed/oppressor modernist formula of power, this analysis concedes that practices of power are often centered in such practices of self-regulation or "self-surveillance and self-correction to norms" (Bordo, 1993, p. 27) rather than conspiracies of power or coercion. Women's active use of the body is, then, situated within the context of gender, power, and cultural practices. Women's self-regulation or disciplining of desire is socially organized as part of the organization of a disciplined social body. Controlling their bodies can be seen as both compliance and resistance to cultural hegemony. As such, the body tells stories of women's struggles in culture.

In his chapter, "Watching the Other Watch: A Social Location of Problems," Stephen Madigan illustrates the process of self-surveillance in which one watches oneself through the eyes of others. In this way, self-surveillance is never solitary or private, as it always involves the judgment of an imagined social audience. People's views about themselves as persons, including how people conceptualize and where they locate "psychological" problems, are influenced through many institutional and professional discourses. People's relational conversations with themselves, "speaking" to themselves, are subject to the act of internal self-surveillance (looking, monitoring, and judging). A narrative therapy practice of counterviewing, therapeutic letter campaigns, and the creation of communities of concern are investigated as sites of resistance to dominant cultural and professional discourse about persons and problems, a means of "re-membering" alternative selves, and crucial for a dialogue of hope to respond and replace a dialogue of despair.

Glenda Russell draws on the analogy of the Mobius strip to illustrate the inseparability of the person and the social in her chapter, "Internalized Homophobia: Lessons From the Mobius Strip." Self-surveillance and the normalization practices of self are illustrated through Russell's discussion of internalized homophobia. She addresses the construct of internalized homophobia from two perspectives. The first and more standard perspective represents internalized homophobia as the psychic consequence of an individual's internalization of the *homonegative* attitudes in society at large. The construct in this form is almost always used in reference to lesbian, gay, bisexual, and transgender people and is often regarded in pathological or quasi-pathological terms. The second perspective offers a postmodern understanding of internalized homophobia. This perspective suggests that homophobia (and, by extension, internalized homophobia) cannot be understood as resident within individuals. Rather, homophobia in the world and internalized homophobia or, more aptly, homonegating processes, flow inexorably and inevitably between persons and their social worlds. The Mobius strip is used as an analogy to illustrate this inseparability of the person and the social. In this view, homonegating processes cannot be regarded as individual phenomena, but must be understood in reference to social context. All people, whatever their claimed sexual orientations, participate in incorporating and transmitting homonegating processes. Russell discusses both client- and therapist-initiated explorations of internalized homophobia and offers a therapeutic case that illustrates her postmodern perspective.

Part 3: Challenging Essentialism

Narrative therapy approaches reflect the social constructionist position that experience is always social (Smith, 1999). However, therapy that has simultaneously sought to avoid the therapist as expert and the pathologization of the client has often found its remedy through reverting to the flip side of the equation. In this new schema, the client is the expert, and therapists self-consciously avoid any exercise of power for fear it marks them as oppressive. Experience, or "first-voice" stories, have subsequently been privileged as authoritative truth. For narrative therapy influenced by postmodernism's destabilizing notions of truth, experience, and self, there is a pivotal, irreducible tension between the need to respect and value experience and the simultaneous desire to situate the self as fully social, as socially and historically constructed. This tension within postmodern narrative practice offers new possibilities for exploring alternative approaches to experience.

Although individuals are active participants in the creation of their stories, these stories draw upon available social discourses and therefore consist of both subjugated and dominant knowledges. Importantly, as our experiences exist within a field of knowledge and power, no story is outside power (Foucault, 1980a; White & Epston, 1990). Self-stories of experience are constructed through a selective process, including what information is left out. Influenced by larger stories around us, self-stories of experience are unable to embody the full complexity of lived life, its gaps, contradictions, and silences. First-voice stories or self-stories, then, are not inherently "truer" than other stories and thus cannot be privileged as beyond inquiry. Therapy, like most social processes, is constantly and actively involved in meaning making, but its assigned task is to also make sense of the self-stories that clients tell that not only do not work, but that often reinforce both negative identity conclusions and dominant social discourses. Taking a neutral stance to such stories is likely to further reinforce negative identity conclusions and dominant social discourse.

As narrative therapy grows out of a social constructionist approach to understanding social reality, the self, experience, and identity are all seen as social constructions, and as such they are not inherently true or real. Resurrecting the subjugated voice of the oppressed, marginalized, and even traumatized means bringing the suppressed voice into view. Uncovering subjugated or disqualified knowledges or experiences often means having to deconstruct the "thin descriptions" that reinforce dominant social stories and taken-for-granted, everyday discourses that are often organizing threads of people's own self-stories. There is no transcendental self-story, just as there is no transcendental subject. In other words, there is no self outside the social world. As the self is at all moments social, there is no experience that has not been socially organized. Experience is always "ideologically cast" (Fuss, 1989, p. 114). There are, therefore, no inherently legitimate or true stories, no self-legitimating stories. A postmodern and constructionist approach to knowledge necessitates this position. Yet this in no way suggests that all stories are equal.

This third section of the book, "Challenging Essentialism," focuses on challenging essentialism in therapeutic discourse. In her chapter, "Dethroning the Suppressed Voice: Unpacking Experience as Story," Catrina Brown deconstructs the essentialized and decontexualized conceptualization of experience as it is commonly taken up in therapy. Such approaches to experience treat experiences as though they were truth (i.e., "It's my experience, so it must be true"). Doing so includes taking apart routinized assumptions in practice that naturalize emotions and privilege and authorize and decontextualize clients' experiences, separating them from their social construction. Drawing on the work of Joan Scott (1992) and Dorothy Smith (1990a, 1990b, 1999), experience is deeply problematized, as is, subsequently, the privileging of the suppressed voice within practice. Within this work, experience is seen as an interpretation that needs interpretation. While resurrecting the suppressed voice is critical in developing alternative stories, it is argued that the suppressed voice reflects both subjugated and dominant knowledges. The suppressed voice does not represent or lead us to the "real self." Along with White (1997, 2001), Brown argues that narrative therapy is not a process for discovering the real or authentic self. Experience stories are not self-legitimizing and are not inherently more true. As experience does not escape the social, it must, like all other stories, be unpacked and new more helpful stories reconstructed. If we wish to move beyond the limitations of subjectivism, experience must be taken up in narrative work as fully social (Smith, 1999).

In his chapter, "Conversations With Men About Women's Violence: Ending Men's Violence by Challenging Gender Essentialism," Tod Augusta-Scott deconstructs gender essentialism in his conversations with men who abuse their partners. The essentialist gender construction that holds that women are not strong or powerful enough to perpetrate abuse is often held by men in counseling for perpetrating physical violence and by the domestic violence field itself. For those men who are abused by their female partners, acknowledging these experiences can help men take responsibility to stop their own abuse. Augusta-Scott illustrates how this process can challenge excuses and justifications that influence men's choices to perpetrate abusive behavior, challenge gender essentialism, and create conversations with men that are respectful to both men and their partners.

In the next chapter, "Challenging Essentialist Anti-Oppressive Discourse: Uniting Against Racism and Sexism," Tod Augusta-Scott explores the limitation of essentialist understandings of race and gender. He unpacks anti-oppressive discourse to find ways of uniting people from across various social locations to address issues of racism and sexism. He de-essentializes race and gender by describing a process of identifying differences in people's experiences from various social locations as well as their common values and aspirations to address issues of injustice. Then, within this context, people are invited to explore the oppressive practices they employ that lead them away from these values. People also explore the effects of these oppressive practices to develop the motivation to change.

These interventions to address racism and sexism involve deconstructing anti-oppressive discourse that leans upon essentialist constructions of race and gender (Bell, 1992; Cose, 1993, 1997; McIntosh, 1998; Tatum, 1997; West, 1993; Wiley, 1993). As well, this process involves working in a helpful manner with issues of shame, pride, and anger as people address oppressive practices. Finally, in therapy groups and workshops to address racism and sexism, Augusta-Scott uses an invitational approach rather than engaging people with oppositional confrontational practices.

Section 4: Re-Authoring Preferred Identities

Narrative therapeutic conversations involve a process of deconstructing unhelpful problem-saturated stories, reconstructing alternative stories, and re-authoring preferred identities. As this approach centers on the meanings attached to people's stories, it resists linear, mechanical, or formulaic interpretations that focus on technique. The process of deconstruction involves externalizing the problem and the socially constructed discourses that shape the problem, and it helps the client take a position on these stories. Toward this end, unique outcomes or stalled initiatives (times when the problem story has not dominated people's experiences), are identified as an entry point for creating alternative stories.[4]

Restructuring or re-authoring identity stories supports people's preferred identities. A process of re-authoring preferred identities also involves historicizing unique outcomes by tracing or mapping the history of these exceptions. White and Epston (1990) draws upon Jerome Bruner's (1986) idea that narratives emerge within a temporal landscape that includes both the events or experiences that occur and the meaning that we ascribe to them. Intertwined, these dual landscapes include a *landscape of action* and a *landscape of consciousness,* in which the knower and the known are inseparable (Bruner, 2002, p. 27; White, 1995, p. 31). The narrative form, according to Jerome Bruner (2002), is not only interactive: "Storytelling becomes entwined with, even at time constitutive of cultural life" (p. 31). Dependent on language and social convention, storytelling is necessarily intersubjective, both reflecting and reproducing shared social meanings.

White and Epston (1990) state, "I have been interested in how persons organize their lives around specific meaning and how, in so doing, they inadvertently contribute to the 'survival' of, as well as the 'career' of, the problem" (p. 3). Experience and meaning questions first map out the landscape of action or the history of events. The landscape of action describes what has happened: the sequence of events and incidents and the who, what, where, and when of a story. In the landscape of action, the experience is relived and retold.

The landscape of meaning (or consciousness/identity), in contrast, refers to the meanings we attach to experiences or events. Narrative therapy wishes to not only explore the historical map of events as they unfold and contribute to conclusions about the problem and identity but also reflect on the meaning of these events. E. Bruner (1986a) suggests,

> Stories give meaning to the present and enable us to see that present as part of a set of relationships involving a constituted past and future. But narratives change, all stories are partial, all meanings incomplete. There is no fixed meaning in the past, for with each telling the context varies, the audience differs, the story is modified. . . . We continually discover new meanings. (p. 153)

Reflective questions are asked about what the landscape of action means, what it says about a person, what it reveals about a person's desires, values, beliefs, intentions, and motives. While landscape of action questions reveal what happened, landscape of meaning questions allow for deeper exploration about the meaning of these events for people and how they have been significant in shaping their consciousness and identities.

Deconstructing the Story

The concept of externalizing conversations in therapy was developed by Michael White (see White, 1984, 1986). White and Epston (1990) proposed that externalizing

> is an approach to therapy that encourages persons to objectify and, at times, to personify the problems that they experience as oppressive. In this process, the problem becomes a separate entity and thus external to the person or relationship that was ascribed as the problem. (p. 38)

Deconstructing begins with externalizing the problem, which includes ideas, feelings, problems, practices, and interactions. Often this process focuses upon externalizing negative identity conclusions. The process of separating the person from the problem often separates the person from problematic identity conclusions and dominant social discourses. Externalization or externalizing turns the problem into an object outside the person, emphasizing that the person is not the problem. Narrative therapists often use metaphors as a way to turn the problem into an object, for instance, "The Depression," "The Anger," or "The Robot."

The objectified problem is then located in discourse by identifying the ideas and practices that strengthen and weaken the "problem." Conversations will explore where particular ideas were learned and uncover the effects of the discourse. Externalizing affects people's views of themselves and impacts upon their views of relationships, emotions, social, work, and life. The process of externalizing examines the influence of "the problem" on the person's past, present, and future. It explores how one is recruited into the story, as well as the cultural supports for the story. Exploring the history of the problem, one asks, how did the person learn the ideas that contribute to his or her story, and what events in the person's life have contributed to the story? The objective is then to uncover the influence of the problem on the person, the impact/effect of the problem on the person and his or her life, and then to move beyond problem saturation. It is important to uncover parts of the story not told by interrupting the dominant discourse and its ongoing performance.

Externalizing conversations unpack the dominant story or narrative about events or themes in people's lives and the meaning given to them. They, therefore, involve externalizing the internalized conversation. Externalization helps people separate from "truth" discourses and the notion of one universal or unitary knowledge. The problem is constructed as the performance of oppressive and dominant knowledge. The history of the effects of these truths can be explored in order to gain a reflexive perspective on one's life. New options can become available through challenging the "truths," and people may replace the stories into which they have been recruited with stories that work better for them. Through resurrecting subjugated, hidden, or obscured knowledges, the myth of a knowable, observable, universal knowledge is disrupted. Disqualified or alternative truth claims may emerge, making previous unseen conflict and struggle visible (White, 2001). Jerome Bruner (2002) explores the motives for studying the narrative, suggesting that one reason "is to understand it so as to cultivate its illusions of reality, to 'subjunctivize' the self-evident declarations of every-day life" (p. 11).

Externalizing the problem is at the center of deconstructing the problem and reduces the effects of labeling and pathologizing. It also helps to reduce guilt, shame, and blaming; contextualizes the problem; achieves separation from the dominant story; fosters a working relationship to resolve the problem story; and reflects an empowerment focus—shifting from inaction or being trapped by the story to active participation in re-authoring the story. The process of deconstruction will explore what events have occurred that support the dominant problem story and what events have challenged this story. There will be events in a person's life that helped to produce stories, such as "I am worthless," "I am unlovable," or "I am bad."

The following questions explore the history, influence, and effect of the problem on the person and are meant to be illustrative rather than read as is. All therapists must find ways of asking questions that are "genuine" to their own styles of working and speaking in the world. It is also important to ask questions in ways that are accessible, nonjargonistic, and avoid sounding detached:

- What brings you to therapy?
- What has been the effect of the problem on everyday life?
- How has the problem affected relationships with people you are close to?
- How has the problem affected how you see yourself?
- How have you been recruited into this way of seeing yourself?
- When do you remember the problem first occurring?
- Can you describe some of the times it has been present?
- How have others reinforced the problem?
- When has the problem been the strongest? The weakest?

After uncovering the history, influence, and effect of the problem on the person in a process of separating the person from the dominant story, options and choices begin to emerge. Relative influence questions explore when the problem was the weakest and when it was the strongest. From here, narrative therapy explores what people would prefer for themselves and their lives. This is called a *statement of position*. Statement-of-position questions explore the experience of the effect of problem and determine a preferred stance. According to White (1991),

> As persons separate themselves from the dominant or totalizing stories that are constitutive of their lives, it becomes more possible for them to orient themselves to aspects of experience that contradict these knowledges. (p. 29)

"Taking a position" on the problem story or negative identity conclusion requires a process of self-reflection on taken-for-granted ways of thinking in order to determine whether this is a preferred view of one's life and of oneself. White (1997) emphasizes that although preferred views do not exist outside culture, it is important to explore taken-for-granted assumptions as a way to produce alternative possibilities. This often involves "editing in" the context of the problem that has been "edited out" of the dominant story. This helps to thicken, or expand, the client's story.

Re-Authoring Alternative Stories

The process of deconstruction is ongoing in narrative therapy, making possible the reconstruction and re-authoring of unhelpful stories. Re-authoring explores how a person has influence on the problem rather than simply being influenced by the problem. The process of re-authoring an alternative story is based on curiosity and builds upon those events or experiences that fall outside or contradict the dominant story. Re-authoring, then, involves developing a more helpful story, one that allows for a life outside of the problem. In re-authoring or rewriting the story, the emphasis is on opening up other options and possibilities. While in the process of deconstructing the problem, narrative therapy uncovers the influence of the problem on the person; in the rewriting of more helpful stories, narrative therapy explores the influence of the person on the problem—in the past, present, and future. These events that contradict the problem-saturated story (often of the person's identity) are referred to as *unique outcomes*. Unique outcomes are the entry points for re-authoring alternative stories.

These unique outcomes, or exceptions to the problem stories, are at the heart of developing new life stories and help in the development of supports for the enactment or living of a preferred story. A term taken from Erving Goffman (1961), unique outcomes identify the parts of experience that "fall outside the dominant story" (White & Epston, 1990, p. 15) and are thus not oppressed by the problem. This aspect of experience is able to reveal protest and resistance to the problem. Furthermore, unique outcomes become a way to explore what a person values or stands up for. Through deconstruction and reconstruction, narrative therapy enables the resurrection of the alternative or previously disqualified story. The dominant story brought to therapy has the effect of rendering invisible other possibilities or other stories. Narrative therapy suggests that there are alternative stories attached to every unique outcome:

> In other words life experience is richer than discourse. Narrative structures organise and give meaning to experience, but there are always feelings and lived experiences not fully encompassed by the dominant story. (E. Bruner, 1986a, p. 143)

Only one unique outcome is needed to begin the re-authoring or reconstructed story process: It can be a fleeting thought. The unique outcome is identified by the client and invites the individual to notice intentions and/or actions that contradict the problem-saturated story. Unique outcomes can arise from a client's history or past, or they may emerge in the actual events of the session. The re-authoring process involves questioning clients in search of alternative interpretations necessary for rebuilding more helpful stories.

Narrative therapy questions will invite a client to make sense of unique experiences and produce dialogue about changes, turning points, and progress made in life. This will promote a history of struggle or protest against oppression by the problem. These questions come from the identification of a unique outcome. Identifying unique outcomes promotes a history of struggle, protest, or resistance against participating in constraining discourses:

- Tell me about a time that you stood up to, said "no" to, or resisted the problem?
- How was that situation handled differently?
- Have there been times recently when the problem has not played a role in your life?
- Can you think of any time in the past when the problem could have played a role in your life and it did not?
- Do you remember other times in the past when you have stood up to the problem?
- How did it feel when you stood up to the problem?
- How have you been able to keep the problem from getting worse?

Unique outcomes, events, or experiences outside the problem-saturated story are identified. Clients are then encouraged to analyze how these exceptions feel and to explore what they mean. Therapy develops the meaning and significance of the unique outcomes and unique accounts through a redescription of selves, others, and relationships. Furthermore, questions help people to be aware of experiences that nurture the alternative story. Questions explore how people feel or think about these revelations about themselves and their perceptions of how others may view them in relation to this reevaluation:

- What does it say about you that you were able to do this?
- What does it say about your future that you stood up to the problem?
- Who else knows this about you?

Building an Audience for the Preferred Story

As people begin to develop preferred stories about their lives and identities, it is important that these stories are circulated or shared with others in the world. This is very important for the life of the alternative story and helps to bring forward the preferred story, making it the "new reality". Seeking out an audience can reinforce and support a person's preferred story:

- Who would be least surprised that you stood up to the problem?
- What do they know about you that allows them to not be surprised?

- Who else knows?
- Who else should know that you were able to do this?
- What difference would it make to their attitudes toward you if they knew this?
- How could you tell them?
- What do you think this might reveal to me about what you value most?

Thickening the story involves developing an audience, circulating the new story, and beginning to understand how the new story might affect one's future life:

- What difference will this make in the future?
- As you continue to change, how will other people in your life respond to you?
- How would knowing this affect how you live your life?
- How would knowing this affect your future?

White (1997) developed the idea of "re-membering" practices to support the development of an audience for the preferred alternative identity stories. Re-membering practices involve inviting people to consider who from the past may have noticed their preferred identity stories and who might support the circulation of these stories. According to White (1997), "Re-membering practices provide the opportunity for persons to resist thin descriptions about their lives and to engage with others in the generation of rich descriptions of the stories of their identity" (p. 62).

In the final section of this book, "Re-Authoring Preferred Identities," three chapters illustrate narrative processes of unpacking unhelpful identity conclusions and the creation of preferred alternative identities. Jim Duvall and Laura Béres begin their chapter, "Movement of Identities: A Map for Therapeutic Conversations About Trauma," with their philosophical therapeutic position, followed by a map for guiding therapeutic conversations about the trauma of sexual abuse toward preferred story lines. The philosophical position advanced emphasizes the importance of giving voice to experiences of trauma, a respect for the "unknowable" aspects of others' experiences, and the recognition that both memories and hope are situated in the present. The conversational map comprises five elements: points of stories, backdrop, pivotal events, evaluating effects, and a summary and is illustrated through a case example.

In the chapter "Letters From Prison: Re-Authoring Identity With Men Who Have Perpetrated Sexual Violence," Tod Augusta-Scott illustrates his work with a man who sexually abused his daughter. He shares the correspondence this man has sent him from prison, which reflects on and illustrates the process of re-authoring identity. An important part of this process involves re-authoring his identity in a manner that highlights his agency, values, and preferences in relationships. The process of re-authoring identity reflects the postmodernist notion that identity is fluid and therefore moves away from static modernist notions of identity. This process also involves inviting him to study the effects of being victimized by violence and facing shame. Finally, the chapter also addresses the process of making amends, which, in turn, creates an audience for his re-authored identity.

In her chapter "Talking Body Talk: Merging Feminist and Narrative Approaches to Practice," Catrina Brown explores how a feminist approach may be blended with a narrative approach through a focus on women's struggles with eating and their bodies. Merging feminist and narrative therapy centers on rewriting women's identity stories to escape limiting cultural meanings and descriptions. The re-authoring of women's body talk involves a shift toward preferred stories that include women speaking about their experiences of conflict and distress in the world directly, rather than through their bodies. The feminist narrative approach to women's body talk presented here explores how women participate in normalization processes of the self through struggles with eating and the body. Together, feminist and narrative approaches enable an analysis and practice that address the construction and performance of gendered subjectivities through culturally available discourses. A feminist narrative approach to body talk acknowledges the ways in which women resource their bodies as forms of both compliance and resistance to dominant cultural ideas, including those of feminine subjectivity. Within this approach, the narrative process of externalization will move the story beyond the individual, locating these struggles within gendered cultural practices and discourses emphasizing the body as a site of both social constraint and protest. Brown's discussion of externalization underscores the importance of not reinscribing women to essentialist and pathologizing descriptions as weak, passive victims of social forces at the expense of acknowledging women's agency, power, and resistance (Ussher, 1989). This chapter illustrates the importance of recognizing agency, power, and resistance in re-authoring women's body talk.

Summary: Reflexive Narrative Practice

We begin this book with a focus on blending both modernist and postmodernist understandings of problems that incorporates a material-discursive sensibility into therapeutic conversations. The book seeks to conceptualize and work with social problems within a reflexive postmodern narrative framework. The first section of the book applies this narrative approach by emphasizing the importance of writing in the social (Smith, 1999) rather than treating depression, eating "disorders," and alcohol misuse as problems of individual pathology, in addition to exploring tensions in practicing narrative psychiatry through this lens. The next section of the book focuses on the practices of self-surveillance and the regulation of the self. Taken together, these chapters explore the inextricably interwoven matrices of knowledge, power, and culture in disciplining the self. The third section of the book involves unpacking the essentialism that often informs therapeutic work, specifically as it relates to modernist understandings of subjective experience, gender, and race. Finally, the last section of the book offers some examples of re-authoring people's identities in a manner that is informed by fluid, nonessentializing notions of identity, through focusing on working with those who have experienced sexual trauma, men who have perpetrated sexual abuse, and women who struggle with eating "disorders."

Notes

1. While Hart (1995) suggests that there are more similarities than differences between White (1995, 1997, 2004a, 2004b; White & Epston, 1990) and de Shazer (1991), we suggest, along with White (1993) and de Shazer (1993), that there are more differences, especially in White's later work.

2. While emanating from different traditions, there are overlaps between *constructionism* and *constructivism*. We are referring to *constructionism* and its clear position on the social construction of reality and knowledge, and we wish to avoid confusion with *constructivism*, which has more of a conservative tradition of focusing on the individual. In the case of radical constructivism, for example, reality is constructed in the mind rather than the culture. According to Anderson (1997), it emphasizes "the autonomy of the self and the individual as the meaning maker" (p. 43). In this approach, we are left with an emphasis on individual interpretation or subjectivist accounts of reality, rather than the relationship between the subject and culture emphasized in constructionism. Within constructionism, all knowledge is social.

3. Narrative therapy has been criticized for its use of reflection teams and the inadequately addressed issues of knowledge and power within this therapeutic practice (Luepntiz, 1992). Luepntiz (1992) suggests that as narrative therapy borrows heavily from Foucault's approach to knowledge and power, the use of the one-way mirror is problematic. She reminds us of Foucault's (1995) description in *Discipline and Punish* of prisons designed as "Pantopticons," whereby prisoners were never free from being watched, while also not being able to see those who watched them. Not only does the one-way mirror perform acts of control through observation, not unlike the "Pantopticon," the one-way mirror is an example of the ways in which individuals as "docile bodies" submit themselves to scrutiny, to the gaze of experts.

4. An unreflexive approach is evident in the therapeutic stance of "not knowing" (adopted by some postmodern narrative therapists). This stance is an effort to

distance oneself from the expert clinician model by emphasizing the client as expert. However, this invocation of a binary construction of knowing is only minimally reflexive. Within this formulation, the only options for "knowing" are to be all-knowing "experts" or to be "not knowing." The client's knowing position is essentialized and authorized in a decidedly not-postmodern manner through holding out a self-story of self-knowledge as though it were not discursive, as though it had escaped the social processes of construction. De Shazer adopts the same binary focus on clients' strengths exemplified by Saleeby's (1997) "strength perspective," which, like the concept "resilience," serves to virtually erase their struggles. Although strengths-based (Saleeby, 1997) and brief solution-focused social work (DeJong & Miller, 1995; de Shazer, 1991, 1993; de Shazer et al., 1986; Molnar & de Shazer, 1987) have emphasized strengths and solutions, we argue that little can be gained by simply supplanting problem talk with strength or solution talk when they clearly coexist. Furthermore, the formulation of "strengths and resilience" is often essentialized (White, 2001).

References

Anderson, H. (1997). *Conversation, language, and possibilities: A postmodern approach to therapy.* New York: Basic Books.

Bateson, G. (1972). *Steps to an ecology of mind.* New York: Ballantine Books.

Bateson, G. (1979). *Mind and nature: A necessary unity.* New York: Dutton.

Bell, D. (1992). *Faces at the bottom of the well.* New York: Basic Books.

Berger. P., & Luckmann, T. (1967). *The social construction of reality: A treatise in the sociology of knowledge.* New York: Anchor Books.

Bordo, S. (1993). *Unbearable weight: Feminism, Western culture, and the body.* Berkeley: University of California Press.

Brown, C. (2003). Narrative therapy: Reifying or challenging dominant discourse. In W. Shera (Ed.), *Emerging perspectives on anti-oppressive practice* (pp. 223–245). Toronto, Canada: Canadian Scholars' Press.

Bruner, E. (1986a). Ethnography as narrative. In V. Turner & E. Bruner (Eds.), *The anthropology of experience* (pp. 139–155). Chicago: University of Illinois Press.

Bruner, E. (1986b). Experience and its expressions. In V. Turner & E. Bruner (Eds.), *The anthropology of experience* (pp. 3–30). Chicago: University of Illinois Press.

Bruner, J. (1986). *Actual minds, possible worlds.* Cambridge, MA: Harvard University Press.

Bruner, J. (1987). Life as narrative. *Social Research, 54,* 1–17.

Bruner, J. (2002). *Making stories: Law, literature, life.* Cambridge, MA: Harvard University.

Chang, J., & Phillips, M. (1993). Michael White and Steve de Shazer: New directions in family therapy. In S. Gilligan & R. Price (Eds.), *Therapeutic conversations* (pp. 95–111). New York: Norton.

Cose, E. (1993). *The rage of a privileged class.* New York: HarperCollins.

Cose, E. (1997). *Color-blind: Seeing beyond race in a race-obsessed world.* New York: HarperCollins.

DeJong, P., & Miller, S. (1995). How to interview for client strengths. *Social Work, 40*(6), 729-736.

de Saussure, F. (1974). *Course in general linguistics* (W. Baskin, Trans.). London: Fontana/Collins. (Original work published 1916)

de Shazer, S. (1991). *Putting difference to work.* New York: Norton.

de Shazer, S. (1993). Commentary: De Shazer & White: Vive la difference. In S. Gilligan & R. Price (Eds.), *Therapeutic conversations* (pp. 112–120). New York: Norton.

de Shazer, S., Kim Berg, I., Lipchik, E., Nunnally, E., Molnar, A., Gingerich, W., & Weiner-David, M. (1986). Brief therapy: Focused solution development. *Family Process, 25,* 207-221.

Durkheim, E. (1966). *The rules of sociological method.* New York: Free Press.

Epston, D. (1989). *Collected papers.* Adelaide, Australia: Dulwich Centre.

Epston, D. (1998). *Catching up with David Epston: A collection of narrative-based papers published between 1991 and 1996.* Adelaide, Australia: Dulwich Centre.

Epston, D., & White, M. (1992). *Experience, contradiction, narrative and imagination.* Adelaide, Australia: Dulwich Centre.

Epstein, L. (1994). *The therapeutic idea in contemporary society.* Unpublished paper presented at University of Toronto, School of Social Work Postmodernism Workshop, Toronto, Canada.

Flax, J. (1990). Postmodernism and gender relations in feminist theory. In L. Nicholson (Eds.), *Feminism/postmodernism* (pp. 39–62). New York: Routledge.

Foucault, M. (1972). *The archaeology of knowledge and the discourse on language* (A. Sheridan, Trans.). New York: Pantheon Books.

Foucault, M. (1973). *The birth of the clinic: An archeology of medical perception.* London: Tavistock.

Foucault, M. (1980a). *The history of sexuality: Vol. 1. An introduction.* New York: Vintage.

Foucault, M. (1980b). *Power/knowledge: Selected interviews and other writings 1972-1977.* New York: Pantheon.

Foucault, M. (1984). Space, knowledge, and power: In P. Rabinow (Ed.), *The Foucault reader* (pp. 239–256). New York: Pantheon Books.

Foucault, M. (1988). *Madness and civilization: A history of insanity in the age of reason.* New York: Vintage.

Foucault, M. (1995). (2nd ed.). *Discipline and punish: The birth of the prison.* New York: Vintage.

Freedman, J., & Combs, G. (1996). *Narrative therapy: The social construction of preferred realities.* New York: Norton.

Fuss, D. (1989). *Essentially speaking. Feminism, nature, and difference.* New York: Routledge.

Geertz, C. (1973). *Thick description: Toward an interpretive theory of culture.* New York: Basic Books.

Geertz, C. (1986). Making experiences, authoring selves. In V. W. Turner & E. Bruner (Eds.), *The anthropology of experience* (pp. 373–380). Chicago: University of Illinois Press.

Gergen, K. (1985a). The social constructionist movement in modern psychology. *American Psychologist, 40*(3), 266–275.

Gergen, K. (1985b). The social constructionist inquiry: Context and implications. In K. Gergen & K. Davis. (Eds.), *The social construction of the person* (pp. 1–18). New York: Springer-Verlag.

Gergen, M. M., & Gergen, K. J. (1984). The social construction of narrative accounts. In K. J. Gergen & M. M. Gergen (Eds.), *Historical social psychology.* Hillsdale, NJ: Erlbaum.

Gilligan, S., & Price, R. (Eds.). (1993). *Therapeutic conversations.* New York: Norton.

Goffman, E. (1961). *Asylums: Essays in the social situation of mental patients and other inmates.* New York: Doubleday.

Gremillion, H. (2003). *Feeding anorexia: Gender and power at a treatment center.* Durham, NC: Duke University Press.

Hare-Mustin, R. (1994, March). Discourses in the mirrored room: A postmodern analysis of therapy. *Family Processes, 33,* 19–35.

Hart, B. (1995). Re-authoring the stories we work by: Situating the narrative approach in the presence of the family of therapists. *Australian and New Zealand Journal of Family Therapy, 16*(4), 181–189.

Hoyt, M. (1998). *The handbook of constructive therapies: Innovative approaches from leading practitioners.* San Francisco: Jossey-Bass.

Jenkins, A. (1990). *Invitations to responsibility: The therapeutic engagement of men who are violent and abusive.* Adelaide, Australia: Dulwich Centre.

Jenkins, A. (1996). Moving towards respect: A quest for balance. In C. McLean, M. Carey, & C. White (Eds.), *Men's ways of being* (pp. 117–133). Boulder, CO: Westview Press.

Luepntiz, D. A. (1992). Nothing in common but their first names: The case of Foucault and White. *Journal of Family Therapy, 14,* 281–284.

Madigan, S., & Law, I. (Eds.). (1998). *Praxis: Situating discourse, feminism, and politics in narrative therapies* (pp. 35–64). Vancouver, Canada: Cardigan Press.

Maisel, R., Epston, D., & Borden, A. (2004). *Biting the hand that starves you. Inspiring resistance to anorexia/bulimia.* New York: Norton.

Marx, K. (1978). The German ideology. In R. Tucker (Eds.), *The Marx Engels reader* (pp. 146–200). New York: Norton.

McIntosh, P. (1998). White privilege: Unpacking the invisible knapsack. In M. McGoldrick (Ed.), *Re-visioning family therapy: Race, culture, and gender in clinical practice* (pp. 147–152). New York: Guilford.

Mead, G. (1977). *On social psychology.* Chicago: University of Chicago Press.

Molnar, A., & de Shazer, S. (1987). Solution-focused therapy: Toward the identification of therapeutic tasks. *Journal of Marital and Family Therapy, 13*(4), 349–358.

Monk, G., Winslade, J., & Crocket, K. (1996). *Narrative therapy in practice: The archeology of hope.* New York: Wiley.

Parry, A., & Doan, R. (1994). *Story re-visions*. New York: Guilford.

Payne, M. (2000). Ideas informing narrative therapy. *In Narrative therapy: An introduction for counselors* (pp. 18–41). Thousand Oaks: Sage.

Redekop, F. (1995). The "problem" of Michael White and Michel Foucault. *Journal of Marital and Family Therapy, 21*(3), 309–318.

Saleeby, D. (1997). (Ed.). *The strengths perspective in social work practice*. New York: Longman.

Scott, J. (1992). Experience. In J. Butler & J. Scott (Eds.), *Feminists theorize the political* (pp. 22–40). New York: Routledge.

Shotter, J. (1993). *Cultural politics of everyday life. Social constructionism, rhetoric and knowing of the third kind*. Toronto, Canada: University of Toronto Press.

Smith, D. (1987). *The everyday world as problematic: A feminist sociology*. Toronto, Canada: University of Toronto Press.

Smith, D. (1990a). *The conceptual practices of power: A feminist sociology of knowledge*. Toronto, Canada: University of Toronto Press.

Smith, D. (1990b). *Texts, facts, and femininity: Exploring the relations of ruling*. New York: Routledge.

Smith, D. (1999). *Writing the social: Critique, theory, and investigations*. Toronto, Canada: University of Toronto Press.

Strong, T., & Paré, D. (2003). *Furthering talk: Advances in the discursive therapies*. Boston: Kluwer.

Tanesini, A. (1999). *An introduction to feminist epistemologies*. Malden, MA: Blackwell.

Tatum, B. D. (1997). *Why are all the Black kids sitting together in the cafeteria? And other conversations about race*. New York: Basic Books.

Ussher, J. (1989). The *psychology of the female body*. New York: Routledge.

Weedon, C. (1997). *Feminist practice and poststructuralist theory*. Cambridge, MA: Blackwell.

West, C. (1993). *Race matters*. Boston: Beacon Press.

White, C., & Denborough, D. (Eds.). (1998). *Introducing narrative therapy: A collection of practice based writings*. Adelaide, Australia: Dulwich Centre.

White, M. (1984). Pseudo-encopresis: From avalanche to victory, from vicious to virtuous cycles. *Family Systems Medicine, 2*(2), 150–160.

White, M. (1986). Negative explanation, restraint, and double description: A template for family therapy. *Family Process, 25*(2), 169–184.

White, M. (1991). Deconstruction and therapy. *Dulwich Centre Newsletter, 3,* 21–40.

White, M. (1993). The histories of the present. In S. Gilligan & R. Price (Eds.), *Therapeutic conversations* (pp. 121–135). New York: Norton.

White, M. (1994). The politics of therapy: Putting to rest the illusion of neutrality. *Dulwich Centre Newsletter, 1,* 1–4.

White, M. (1995). *Re-authoring lives: Interviews & essays*. Adelaide, Australia: Dulwich Centre.

White, M. (1997). *Narrative of therapists' lives*. Adelaide, Australia: Dulwich Centre.

White, M. (2000a). *The narrative metaphor in family therapy. Family therapy: The field's past, present, and possible futures.* Adelaide, Australia: Dulwich Centre.

White, M. (2000b). *Reflections on narrative therapy.* Adelaide, Australia: Dulwich Centre.

White, M. (2001). Narrative practice and the unpacking of identity conclusions. *Gecko: A Journal of Deconstruction and Narrative Ideas in Therapeutic Practice, 1,* 28–55.

White, M. (2004a). *Narrative practice and exotic lives: Resurrecting diversity in everyday life.* Adelaide, Australia: Dulwich Centre.

White, M. (2004b, March). *Narrative therapy: New modalities of practice workshop.* Truro, Canada: Bridges (A domestic violence counseling research and training institute).

White, M., & Epston, D. (1990). *Narrative means to therapeutic ends.* New York: Norton.

Wiley, R. (1993). *What Black people should do now.* New York: Ballantine Books.

Zimmerman, J. L., & Dickerson, V. (1996). *If problems talked: Narrative therapy in action.* New York: Guilford.

PART I

Writing in the Social

1

Situating Knowledge and Power in the Therapeutic Alliance

Catrina Brown

The narrative process of re-authoring identities requires moving beyond simply telling and retelling stories to an active deconstruction of oppressive and unhelpful discourses. Unpacking unhelpful stories and creating alternative preferred stories involves recognizing the relationship between knowledge and power, as knowledge and power are joined through discourse (Foucault, 1980a). The postmodern sensibility of narrative therapy is contingent upon Foucault's insistence on the inseparability of power and knowledge and his efforts to study the way humans govern and regulate themselves and others through the production of truth. Narratives then, are "not only structures of meaning but structures of power as well" (Bruner, 1986, p. 144). Rethinking modernist approaches to knowledge and power challenges the ways in which both practitioners and clients may inadvertently keep oppressive stories alive.

Drawing upon Foucault's understanding of the inseparability of knowledge and power, I adopt the therapeutic stance that knowledge is never innocent and power is never just constraining. This therapeutic stance moves away from the binary idea that either one has knowledge or one does not and either one has power or one does not. Disrupting modernist binary constructions of knowledge and power recognizes both the therapist and client as active embodied subjects in the therapeutic process of coauthoring identities.

Rather than the traditional position of the expert, all-knowing therapist or its mirror twin, the "not-knowing therapist," I will argue that both the therapist and the client are "partial knowers." As such, both bring knowledge and agency to the conversation. While I agree with abandoning the idea of the "all-knowing" therapist and minimizing power differences in the therapeutic alliance, I argue that a "not-knowing" stance is not effective for challenging oppressive social discourses or, subsequently, for deconstructing negative identity conclusions or rewriting alternative identities.

I will argue for a conceptualization of power that moves away from the modernist formulation of power as simply negative, constraining, and repressive (Foucault, 1980a). From this position, I argue that narrative therapy acknowledges both the social constraints on subjective life and the individual agency and power within these constraints. In addition to illustrating the significance of Foucault's approach to knowledge and power for the process of unpacking the dominant social discourse evident in clients' stories and the creation of less oppressive, more helpful alternative stories, I will emphasize the importance of recognizing individuals' agency and power in the re-storying and living of their lives.

I begin by discussing the importance of narrative therapy in deconstructing dominant discourse and, in the process, challenge the normalizing truths of culture that often structure people's narratives. I then question the idea that either the therapist or client can be an expert knower and suggest that both are partial knowers. Next, I argue that therapists must be positioned, or take a stance in, their interpretation of clients' stories if they are to challenge internalized oppressive social discourses within clients' stories and be helpful in the creation of alternative stories. I explore the limiting conceptualization of knowledge and power in the therapeutic alliance and argue for a collaborative therapeutic relationship, in which both the therapist and client are seen as active embodied subjects who offer (partial) knowledge and power to the therapeutic conversation, through a conceptualization of power as both constraining (negative) and constituting (positive). This chapter emphasizes that people's narratives are both shaped socially and creations of their own agency. This view allows therapy to see humans not as simply social products, but as active subjects.

Deconstructing Dominant Discourse: Joining Knowledge and Power

In his work, Foucault (1980b) engages in the possibility of a new politics of truth and a new politics of power. Central to the practice of narrative therapy and the deconstruction of stories is Foucault's (1980a) idea that "it is in discourse that power and knowledge are joined together" (p. 100). In *Power/Knowledge,* Foucault (1980b) argues,

> There can be no possible exercise of power without a certain economy of discourses of truth which operates through and on the basis of this association. We are subjected to the production of truth through power and we cannot exercise power except through the production of truth. (p. 93)

It is Foucault's (1995) view that "truth is no doubt a form of power" (p. 45); power is thus constituting of knowledge (Tanesini, 1999, p. 188). Influenced by Foucault, White and Epston (1990) similarly suggest that we are "always participating simultaneously in domains of power and knowledge" (p. 29) and thus therapy practices are never benign. White (1992) maintains that "A domain of knowledge is a domain of power, and that a domain of power is a domain of knowledge" (p. 122). At the same time that Foucault and White argue that knowledge and power are always "mutually implicated" (Tanesini, 1999, p. 195), they do not suggest that one is "reducible to the other" (p. 195) or that knowledge claims are at all moments a means for masking power.

However, as our lived experiences exist within a field or web of power and knowledge, no story is outside power (White & Epston, 1990). Therefore, no telling or hearing of a story is neutral (White, 1989). Yet according to Foucault (1980a), "Where there is power, there is resistance, and yet, or rather consequently, this resistance is never in a position of exteriority in relation to power. . . . These points of resistance are everywhere in the power network" (p. 95). While this does not suggest that we are engaged in unconstrained choice, or "free play" (Butler, 1993; Foucault, 1991), it does leave space for agency, space for counterdiscourses. Foucault (1980a) suggests that "discourse can be both an instrument and an effect of power, but also a hindrance, a stumbling-block, a point of resistance and a starting point for opposing strategy" (p. 101). Discourses, then, like power, can be seen as both constituting and constraining.

Postmodernism has called into question how it is we know what we know; as such, objectivity has been exposed as a fiction (Flax, 1990). Through a postmodern lens, knowledge is multiple and only ever partial. Knowledge is understood to be socially and historically specific and inseparable from social relations of power. From a postmodern perspective, there are always competing stories of truth. For Bruner (1991), "Knowledge is never point-of-viewless" (p. 3).

A postmodern influence on narrative therapy is evident in its view that power and knowledge are inseparable and that humans govern and regulate themselves and others through the production of truth. In contrast, the modernist quest for objective knowledge has separated knowledge and power. To move beyond bias, interest, and power, modernist therapy has often upheld the need to be neutral or objective. Against neutrality, I argue for the necessity of being positioned, or of taking a stance. Reflecting White (White, 1995, 2001; White & Epston, 1990), I argue that we need to unpack and reconstruct clients' stories, rather than leaving them intact, as frequently the stories brought to therapy reflect dominant social discourses and relations of power (Brown, 2003). Thus, while modernists argue that the way out of bias is to be more objective, I argue that we will always be biased and thus we need to acknowledge our own biases and be clear and up-front about the positions we adopt. Rather than cloaking interest and/or power under the veil of objectivity and science, we need to examine how clients' stories have been put together, what ideas predominate, and what alternatives are rendered invisible within these stories. Narrative externalizing practices will shift unhelpful discourses and enable the creation of alternative or preferred stories.

Above and beyond recognizing power differentials between therapists and clients in therapeutic conversations, it is critical that we not censor power from the stories told or our interpretations of them (Flaskas & Humphreys, 1993). If therapists wish to challenge oppression, they must challenge those stories that are grounded in dominant discourse. Power cannot be left out of an approach to narrative therapy if it is to be accountable. In politicized work, practitioners are positioned in making sense of clients' stories. Practitioners on the side of social justice cannot take a neutral stance with regard to power (Brown, 2003; White, 1994; White & Epston, 1990). Thus, practitioners must actively deconstruct and re-author oppressive stories and, in turn, the power and power relations embedded within them (Brown, 2003; Fook, 2002; White, 2001; White & Epston, 1990). This means that we cannot adopt a neutral stance to these stories, but must help unpack them in order to create less oppressive stories. We will then interpret clients' stories through our own positioned narratives. Narrative therapy in this sense involves the deliberate shifting of oppressive, and often dominant, discourses and the reconstruction of counterdiscourses that are themselves sites of social resistance. This does not, however, involve simply erasing clients' stories and replacing them with narrative therapists' reconstructed accounts.

White describes therapy as a political process that recognizes that stories are constructed socially and historically within culturally available discourses. Narrative therapy, then, is interested in the construction of stories, rather than inherent truths. Clients' stories are multiple, shifting, discontinuous—not inherently real, true, or immutable. Within social life, people tell stories about themselves, which they tend to both experience as and treat as truths. Not only is the story experienced as truth, it is shaped by larger discourses also presumed to be truth. These stories are wrapped in layers of socially constructed truths, which are taken up as inherently real in and of themselves.

Clients often bring problem stories to therapy about themselves, their identities, and their lives. These stories often involve the internalization of dominant social stories, and, importantly, the stories themselves are often unhelpful. Thus, while we can study the real effects of stories, it is critical that we not treat the story itself as "real." Virtually every story told about oneself and one's experiences involves identity conclusions. Fixing stories as real and self-legitimizing forecloses the possibility of rupturing limiting identity conclusions. One must allow the story in all its layers, complexity, and contradiction to emerge. The story's fluidity, multiplicity, and changing shape are entry points to explore alternative understandings and to begin to develop stories that the storyteller prefers.

The narrative process of externalizing the story begins to unpack and socially locate the origins and history of the story being told. As such, stories cannot be separated from power and need to be situated as fully social. This process allows the client to see that the story itself is not fixed, or absolute, and that other possibilities exist. The problem story is deconstructed with an eye toward reconstructing more effective and less damaging, pathologizing, blaming, or oppressive accounts. Externalizing conversations will shift unhelpful discourses and enable the creation of alternative or preferred stories by examining how clients' stories have been put together, what ideas predominate, and what alternatives are rendered invisible within these stories. In White's (2001) language, re-authoring identities often involve " resurrecting" the disqualified or marginalized voice. The counterhegemonic and deconstructive process of externalizing internalized problem stories and the subsequent re-authoring of identity are political practices in therapy.

Knowing, Not Knowing, and Partial Knowing

Within collaborative-based therapies, therapists often adopt a "not-knowing" stance (Anderson 1997; Malinen & Anderson, 2004).[1] From this view, it is suggested that the client is the expert on content and the therapist is the expert on process (Anderson, 1997). Anderson (1997) argues as follows:

> A client brings expertise in the area of content: a client is the expert on his or her life experiences and what has brought that client into the therapy relationship. When clients are narrators of their stories, they are able to experience and

recognize their own voices, power, and authority. A therapist brings expertise in the area of process: a therapist is the expert in engaging and participating with a client in a dialogical process of first-person story-telling. It is as if the roles of therapist and client were reversed. *The client becomes the teacher.* (p. 95, emphasis in original)

This construction reveals an effort to grapple with the problem of therapists holding too much knowledge and authority in therapeutic conversations, while simultaneously recognizing the fiction of objectivity. The route out of this dilemma has been to adopt a not-knowing position, which seems to enable one to avoid problematic power imbalances between the therapist and client, as well as to avoid making false truth claims under the guise of objectivity. This strategy intends to decenter the therapist's knowledge and center the client's knowledge and experience. This "not-knowing" stance is described by Anderson (1992):

The therapist does not "know" a priori, the intent of any action, but rather must rely on the explanations made by the client. By learning, by curiosity, and by taking the client's story seriously, the therapist joins with the client in a mutual exploration of the client's understanding and experience. . . . To "not know" is *not* to have an unfounded or unexperienced judgement, but refers more widely to the set of assumptions, the meanings, that the therapist must bring to the clinical interview. The excitement for the therapist is in learning the uniqueness of each individual client's narrative truth, the coherent truths in their storied lives. This means that therapists are always prejudiced by their experience, but that they must listen in such a way that their pre-experience does not close them to the full meaning of the client's description of their experience. This can only happen if the therapist approaches each clinical experience from the position of not knowing. To do otherwise is to search for regularities and common meaning that may validate the therapist's theory, but invalidate the uniqueness of client's stories and thus their very identity. (p. 30, emphasis in original)

Well-known and influential among narrative practitioners, Anderson's work is located within a postmodern stance of "not knowing" and "multi-partiality." It advances a binary construction that accords expert status to clients over content and practitioners over process (Brown, 2003). While these binary constructions seek to maximize clients' power through positioning the client as "expert," they often implicitly require practitioners to abdicate their own knowledge and power. For example, Anderson (1997) admonishes that we must not involve ourselves in rewriting or editing clients' stories, as we are not "master storytellers."

The concept of clients as experts about their own lives leans heavily on the treatment of "experience" as uncontestable truth. Postmodern feminists have criticized this approach, as it separates experience from its social construction. When experience is separated from its social construction, it is not only decontextualized, but the focus of experience shifts to the individual. This subjectivist view often takes up experience as natural, individual, and apolitical (Alcoff, 1988; Fuss, 1989; Haug, 1992; Scott, 1992; Smith, 1990, 1999). Postmodern feminists argue, instead, that clients' stories about their experiences are always social, always political.

When stories are understood as social constructions embedded within social discourses and social relations, their self-legitimacy is more immediately questionable and dominant stories are more likely to be unpacked. In contrast, subjectivist approaches to clients' stories are likely to leave dominant and oppressive stories intact. This is at least in part because they have failed to acknowledge the relationship between knowledge and power in these stories. Through invoking a not-knowing position, many therapists today distance themselves from the strategies of power deployed by traditional hierarchical therapeutic practices. Oddly, clients' stories within this not-knowing stance appear to escape the social processes that make knowledge and power inseparable. Seen somehow to be outside of the influence of power, these stories can be taken up as is, as self-legitimizing. Yet clients' stories are no more inherently outside power than therapists' stories. The formulation of knowledge and power within this approach to therapy results in a focus on the individual, rather than social context and an attempt to discover the real unencumbered self, rather than to pursue emancipatory social practices and epistemology that acknowledge and challenge social power.

Creating Alternative or Preferred Stories: The Limitations of Relativism

Invoking the idea of "not knowing" in therapy suggests a potentially dangerous relativism in which all stories are considered equal. Such relativism is evident if not knowing is a way to avoid taking a stance, forming an opinion, developing an analysis, or being responsible for one's knowledge and power. I suggest that to do good work, we need to take a position: Anything does not go. One can argue that a moral and political relativism may result when client-directed sessions designed to avoid a therapist-controlled agenda result in "wandering here and there" (Malinen & Anderson, 2004, p. 68). When power is left unexplored, left intact, and obscured within the construction of clients' stories, therapy participates in its reification of dominant and often unhelpful stories.

The approach I adopt here draws upon the strengths of modernism and postmodernism, while abandoning their limitations. From modernism, I hold on to the possibility of an emancipatory social agenda or vision. From postmodernism, I take the idea that knowledge is always partial, located, and thus never neutral. Furthermore, the postmodern focus on deconstruction is useful to the adoption of a reflexive and ongoing critical analysis, especially in the process of unpacking clients' narratives. Taken together, this blend of modernism and postmodernism allows me to take a position without suggesting that it is objective. I can in this way be positioned and recognize my partiality.

I reject the modernist belief in objective, value-free knowledge and its subsequent totalizing, and often essentializing, truth claims. Instead, I adopt the view that all knowledge is socially constructed. I also abandon postmodernism's tendency toward relativism—the view from nowhere and everywhere—as this does not enable one to take a position and thus treats all positions or stories as if they were equal (Bordo, 1990). The relativist position "of being nowhere while claiming to be everywhere equally" (Haraway, 1988, p. 584) is evident in the "not-knowing" construction of therapists' knowledge in therapy. While this relativist stance is sometimes offered as an improvement over absolutism, which claims it can be "everywhere while pretending to be nowhere," Code (1996, p. 214) suggests neither will do. Bordo (1990) describes postmodern relativism:

> It may slip into its own fantasy of escape from human locatedness—by supposing the critic can become wholly protean by adopting endlessly shifting seemingly inexhaustible vantage points; none of which are "owned" by either the critic or the author of the text under examination. (p. 42)

> Deconstructionist readings that enact this protean fantasy are continually "slip-slidin' away" through paradox, inversion, self-subversion. . . . they often present themselves as having it any way they want. They refuse to assume a shape for which they must take responsibility. (p. 44)

Supporting Bordo, Haraway (1988) suggests that relativism, like objectivism, is a "god trick," promising a view from everywhere and nowhere simultaneously:

> Relativism is a way of being nowhere while claiming to be everywhere equally. The "equality" of positioning is a denial of responsibility and critical inquiry. Relativism is the perfect mirror twin or totalization of the ideologies of objectivity;

both deny the stakes in location, embodiment and partial perspective; both make it impossible to see well. Relativism and totalization are both "god tricks" promising vision from everywhere and nowhere equally and fully. (p. 584)

Therapy approaches on the side of social justice that take a stance against oppression and social inequity cannot arguably be relativist, as they require a vision. Being positioned, then, means recognizing that all positions are not equal. By blending modernist and postmodernist approaches, one can adopt a position and have a vision for social change without claiming to hold on to an absolute truth (Stanley & Wise, 1990).[2] This "both/and" position allows one to make truth claims, while acknowledging they are always socially constructed, located, and incomplete. Therapy that wishes to disrupt the dominant discourses that uphold and reify relations of social power cannot be relativist.

While I concur with the desire to not be overly directive in therapeutic work, the writing out of power seems misguided. Determined not to guide or direct her clients, Anderson (1997) ultimately presents a relativist approach to knowledge in therapy, stating,

> In my view, such attempts at modifying a client's narrative take the form of narrative editing—revising, correcting, or polishing. A therapist's task is not to deconstruct, reproduce, or reconstruct a client's story but to facilitate and participate in its telling and retelling.
>
> Narrative editing is a slippery slope. A narrative editor position requires the technical expertise to edit. This entails certain risks: It implies the assumption that a therapist has more credibility as a master of human stories than does a client. It assumes that a therapist can read a client like a text. It makes a therapist an archaeological narrativist who believes there is *a* story, with an imagined significance, that needs to be uncovered or retold (p. 96).

Walter and Peller (1996) are also emphatic that therapists should neither adjudicate clients' stories nor privilege their own narratives. Similarly, Parry and Doan (1994) argue that "each person's stories become self-legitimizing" (p. 26) and that "attempts by others to question the validity of such a story are themselves illegitimate. They are coercive, and to the extent that such methods are used to silence or discredit a person's stories, they represent a form of terrorism" (p. 27).

Alternatively, narrative therapy involves the coauthoring of more helpful stories. These new stories are also seen to be socially situated, nonneutral constructions that will change over time. Those who adopt the not-knowing stance allow themselves to claim they are not positioned: Their biases, underlying assumptions, and foundational concepts remain hidden. Just as there is no neutral telling or hearing of a story, there is arguably no neutral question. There are no neutral body languages, voice tones, facial expressions, head nods, styles of dress, or furnishings. We are present, situated, positioned, and embodied in our work. The question is not whether we are. The question is how we are, and our reflexivity about it.

Along with White (1994), I believe that we cannot waive responsibility and accountability for the influence of our own knowledge and power in the therapeutic work by claiming to "not know" or to be responsible only for "expert" knowledge about process. White (1997) advocates an egalitarian approach to therapy that is transparent and accountable—committed to deconstructing limiting descriptions of life, challenging abuses of power, and avoiding reproducing relations of power.

In contrast to Anderson's "not-knowing" position, White (1989) is emphatically positioned against moral relativism:

> The personal story or self-narrative is not radically invented inside our heads. Rather, it is something that is negotiated and disrupted within various communities of persons and in the institutions of our culture. . . . Our lives are multi-storied. No single story of life can be free of ambiguity and contradiction. No sole personal story or narrative can handle all of the contingencies of life. . . . The personal story or self-narrative is not neutral in its effects. . . . Different personal stories or self-narratives are anything but equal in their real effects. . . . The narrative metaphor is associated with a tradition of thought that rules out the possibility of "anything goes" moral relativism. . . . This tradition of thought encourages therapists to assume responsibility for the real effects or consequences of his/her interaction with persons who seek help. (pp. 3–4)

Surely, we can negotiate the terrain of knowledge and power with clients in such a manner that both voices are present in the conversation, without fear that our own knowledge and power makes us guilty of attempting to be master storytellers. In my view, it is far more dangerous to deny the presence of our own knowledge and power through efforts at sidestepping it. Foote and Frank (1999) remind us that we should be especially wary of those claims of being outside power.

Positioning Knowledge and Power in the Therapeutic Alliance

Modernist conceptualizations of knowledge and power are inconsistent with a postmodern narrative therapy. Foucault's analysis of power and knowledge suggests that the therapeutic task of unpacking socially constructed stories of self require both the therapist and client to be active embodied subjects, both holding knowledge, agency, and power. With a postmodern approach to the therapeutic alliance, knowledge is joined in the telling, hearing, and re-authoring of stories. From this view, there are multiple, coexisting positions of "knowing," positions that are always interpretive and partial.

It is commonly assumed that the therapist has more institutional power than the client within the therapy relationship and that the client is typically more vulnerable. Efforts to equalize the relationship by emphasizing clients' expert knowledge and maximizing their power has ironically imposed a kind of constraint upon therapists: the need to deny their own knowledge and power. The implicit assumption is that power in the hands of the therapist is oppressive. To construct power in the hands of therapists as inherently pernicious is problematically paradoxical within approaches that center on increasing clients' power and agency in the world. When power is "perceived as being contrary to the principles of equality and useful only for oppressing others" (Rondeau, 2000, p. 221), practitioners fear and conflate their own power with oppressing others. According to Rondeau, from this position, "All power is suspect" (p. 221).

Instead of acknowledging and skillfully deploying knowledge and power, therapists have sought to escape power through invoking the more comfort-able stance of "not knowing." Not only does this stance risk passivity, little active problem solving or analysis is required. In the first instance, expert knowledge and power, while practiced, are denied; and, in the second, the therapist is rendered virtually ineffective for fear of being too knowledgeable or too powerful. Both instances are responses to the therapist's fear that hav-ing "expert" knowledge or having power is inherently oppressive to the client. This is evident in Anderson's (1997) argument that editing, revising, or refram-ing clients' narratives is a "slippery slope." Conceptualized in this way, thera-pists' power, knowledge, and authority are either too present or too absent.

Yet according to Foucault (1980a), "There is no escaping power, that it is always-already present, constituting the very thing that one attempts to counter it with" (p. 82). Power is already present in a formulation of the therapeutic alliance predicated on a negative repressive notion of power, binary construc-tions of knowledge and power, separation of knowledge and power, and the authorizing of clients' stories as self-legitimizing and expert.[3] While power is present in the telling and hearing of therapeutic conversations, it is obscured in this not-knowing position. Not knowing is not a solution to power.

Flaskas and Humphreys (1993) observe that while some collaborative practitioners are concerned with the "toxicity of power" and the repressive effects of power in the therapeutic alliance, these therapists, ironically, censor power from the stories of people's lives. Thus, while the effort to minimize power differences among therapists and clients is enacted through minimizing the role of the therapist as expert, it has been observed that "there is a lack of engagement with the full realities of power in clients' lives" (Flaskas & Humphreys, 1993, p. 38). This is further articulated through the example of working with people dealing with histories of childhood sexual abuse, when adopting a neutral or not-knowing stance may have some troublesome ramifications. Critics suggest that "not naming" power in such instances is much more harmful than naming power.

Moving Beyond Modernist Binary Constructions of Power

To practice effectively, a therapist needs to have knowledge and power; the issue is how they are deployed. To construct therapeutic power as inherently destructive reflects a misguided belief in the idea that all power is negative. The modernist dualistic assumption that one either has knowledge and power or one does not is revealed in the not-knowing position. Therefore, accordingly, if the client is the expert and the client's power must be maximized, the practitioner cannot have knowledge and must deny his or her own power.

The position of politics is a constant tension in therapy. From my view, whatever therapists' politics and goals are, we have an ethical responsibility to the well-being of the client. Politics are always evident in how we interpret stories, how we construct alternatives, and how we choose to work with our clients. While clients can be politicized through dialogue, ethically, our politics or worldviews should not be imposed. Thus, we must be positioned without forcing our clients into our positions. Accepting one's positionality means acknowledging, not denying, therapists' knowledge and power. In acknowledging their knowledge and power, therapists are more likely to be accountable for them. Furthermore, this stance suggests that it is possible to negotiate the terrain of power in relationships. The therapist is then not masking his or her own knowledge and power in an effort to advance the client's; instead, the knowledge and power of both can be actively present.

White and Epston (1990) suggest that Foucault offers a valuable alternative explanation to those views of power that argue that power exists only in language or that "power really exists and is wielded by some in order to oppress others" (p. 1). Modernist approaches to power often focus on who has power and who does not, rather than also examining how power operates or what the strategies or mechanisms of power are (Foucault, 1995). Foucault's (1980a) analysis challenges the seemingly unquestioned belief in the "binary and all-encompassing opposition between rulers and ruled at the root of power relations" (p. 94) within modernist constructions of power. According to Foucault (1980b),

> In defining the effects of power as repression, one adopts a purely juridical conception of such power, one identifies power with a law which says no, power is taken above all as carrying the force of a prohibition. Now I believe that this is a wholly negative, narrow, skeletal conception of power, one which has been curiously widespread. If power were never anything but repressive, if it never did anything but to say no, do you really think one would be brought to obey it? What makes power hold good, what makes it accepted, is simply the fact that it doesn't only weigh on us as a force that says no but that it traverses and produces things, it induces pleasure, forms knowledge, produces discourse. It needs to be considered as a productive network which runs through the whole social body, much more than as a negative instance whose function is repression. (p. 119)

Power as Negative and Positive

Adopting Foucault's approach to power in narrative therapy allows us to get beyond the idea that either one has power or one does not. As a result, it not only allows us to understand the stories people tell as a conflation of knowledge and power but also enables narrative practitioners to interpret stories as evidence of both social constraint and social agency.[4] Individuals are never totalized as the absolute products of their circumstances. There is, in this approach, room to maneuver. After all, the creation of alternative stories is possible only if alternatives are possible. Refusing to conceptualize power and identity as fixed or static produces new possibilities and thus the possibility of new stories. For Foucault, power is always relational or interactive, rather than monolithic, unilateral, or repressive (see Flaskas & Humphreys, 1993). According to Flaskas and Humphreys (1993), "Resistance, like power itself, has no life outside the network of relationships in which it is occurring" (p. 42). They suggest that power

> is an intrinsic part of every social relationship, and so it cannot be taken away. From Foucault's position, if the effects of power are to be challenged, they can only be challenged from within the power relationship itself, and it is the idea of the always-present potential for resistance that offers some optimism for change in oppressive power relationships (p. 44).

Furthermore, in a repressive approach to power, power is only ever toxic; there is no room for productive power. Foucault (1980a) and, subsequently, White (1997) view power as both constraining and constitutive or productive. Power has both negative and positive potential, which is evident in everyday interactions, in the structuring of the relationships between people, in the physical use of space and architecture, in the actual disciplining of bodies, and in the creation of ways of thinking, forms of subjectivity, and forms of knowledge. Thus, power is always present, both in its restraining and in its productive effects. (Flaskas & Humphreys, 1993, p. 41)

Power, Agency, and Subjectivity

Foucault (1995) privileges questions about how power happens, how it operates, and what its strategies or techniques are, rather than who exercises power. His work explores how human beings are both made into and turn themselves into subjects within our cultures (Rabinow, 1984). Within narrative therapy, clients' identity stories are evidence of how human beings are both shaped socially and active participants in the creation of their own lives.

Fook (2002) undertakes a reformulation of modernist approaches to power, rejecting the idea that "power is invested in particular people, often by virtue of their position in the social structure. It is 'possessed' rather than 'exercised,' and thus is more fixed and less accessible to change" (p. 103). Fook fears that this modernist conceptualization of power may become "a tool to preserve existing power imbalances" (p. 103). According to Fook, we must consider how power is exercised, its real effects, as well as how people "exercise and create their own power" (p. 104). She suggests that "this includes an understanding of how they might participate in their own powerlessness as well as powerfulness" (p. 104).

A view of power that moves beyond the construction of power as subjective and intentional concedes to the more insidious ways power operates (Lukes, 1974; MacDonald & MacDonald, 1999). Recognizing that power relations are not driven simply by subjective intent allows us to uncover the subtleties of power evident when individuals "act against their own objective interests—they do what, without socialization and conditioning, they would not otherwise do" (MacDonald & MacDonald, 1999, p. 54). As such, individuals, albeit unwittingly, often participate in their own powerlessness (Fook, 2002; MacDonald & MacDonald, 1999). From a narrative perspective, we can see this clearly in the way people internalize dominant social discourses as their own, when these stories contribute not to greater power and agency, but less (Brown, 2003; Hare-Mustin, 1994; Sanders, 1998; White & Epston, 1990). People's stories often reveal both their lack of power and their capacity to exercise power. This "both/and" position is critical to the narrative re-authoring process, as it involves turning inside out the internalized problem conversations that are derived from dominant social discourses.

White (1995, 1997, 2004) and White and Epston (1990) describes how people are involved in the subjugation of their own lives through processes of power. Narrative therapy is interested in helping people resist certain practices of power, including the internalized problem stories, which often become totalizing in their lives. According to White (1995), "Internalizing conversations obscure the politics of experience, externalizing conversations emphasize the politics of experience" (p. 24). White's emphasis on the politics of experience holds on to individual agency and power. From this perspective, the problem is deconstructed through the externalizing process, allowing for greater distance from the influence of the problem and more likelihood of being able to live according to one's preferences. In his moves away from a regressive model of power, White adopts a nonessentialized or nonnaturalized approach to externalizing experience through his emphasis on the politics of experience. While White (1997, 2001) is clear that he is positioned in his work against abuses of power, he is adamant that he is not advancing a form of personal or psychological emancipatory therapy that promises the discovery of one's true or real self through being liberated or freed from the constraints of social repression. This idea of psychological emancipation relies upon not only a problematic essentialism of the self but also a limited repressive model of power.

Foucault (1980a) refutes a negative representation of power, a model of power based on repression for it requires obedience. He suggests,

> It is a power that only has the force of the negative on its side, a power to say no; in no condition to produce, capable only of posing limits. . . . This is the paradox of its effectiveness: it is incapable of doing anything except to render what it dominates incapable of doing anything either, except for what this power allows it to do. (p. 85)

While he refutes this negative model, Foucault suggests it is the widely accepted view because it, in fact, masks, or hides, the complexity and insidiousness of how power operates. He argues, "Power is tolerable only on condition it masks a substantial part of itself. Its success is proportional to its ability to hide its own mechanisms" (p. 86). Viewed as repression, power is more tolerable: It is less tolerable when we are seen as active participants in our own subjugation.

Thus, Foucault's approach to power shifts our understanding from classical models, where power is conceived of only as repressive, negative, and constraining. His work is a significant departure from this understanding, as it focuses our attention on how people themselves are recruited as vehicles for power, requiring their everyday active participation regardless of their social location. Normalizing truths specify forms of individuality that are vehicles of power (White & Epston, 1990). White (2004) describes this process:

> This is a power that recruits people's active participation in the fashioning of their own lives, their relationships, and their identities according to the constructed norms of culture—we are both a consequence of this power, and a vehicle for it. By this account, this is a system of power that is particularly insidious and pervasive. It is a power that is everywhere to be perceived in its local operations, in our intimate lives and relationships. (p. 154)

When we move beyond a negative approach to power, it becomes possible to recognize that people can both have power and be constrained by power. From this perspective, externalizing people's stories can allow for recognition of the subjugated and the dominant knowledge within the story. Acknowledging subjugated knowledge in tandem with individual agency is an essential element for reconstructing alternative stories and re-authoring identities. When individuals are constructed only as victims or products, other aspects of the story are obscured, and disqualified. Resistance and action outside of dominant discourse seem more possible when human agency is underscored. Conversely, when people's stories are decontextualized, their lack of social power and the social context of their oppression are obscured. We can achieve a thicker description through the view that power can be both constraining and productive, through noticing powerlessness and power in people's stories without totalizing them to either subject position. White (1997) emphasizes that even the production of alternative knowledge and subjectivities do not escape power,

> Although we do not have to be unwitting accomplices in the reproduction of the subjectivities that have been imposed on our lives . . . alternative modes of life and thought exist in discursive fields—they are constituted of knowledges, of techniques of the self, of practices of relationship, and of the power relations of culture. (p. 232)

Foucault's approach is important to narrative therapy, for not only does it reiterate that the creation of the self is social but also that the self as social is inseparable from processes of knowledge and power, from power as a both a negative and positive force. In the process of subjectification, what is apparent is that the social formation of the self or the subject requires that human beings be active, not simply constrained. Human beings create themselves as subjects in part through the stories they tell about themselves. These stories arise from within culturally available social discourses and social relations of power through social interaction. White (1995) argues that our stories don't reflect or represent our lives; our lives are, rather, constituted through our stories, our narratives (p. 14). Furthermore, through stories, individuals put themselves and their lives into discourse. Not only do self-stories rely on social discourses of the self for their construction, the self is actually put into discourse through the stories one tells about oneself and one's life. Thus, the production of self is not separate from processes of discourse, knowledge, and power.

Conclusion

I have problematized the modernist constructions of knowledge and power in narrative conversations through drawing on Foucault's analysis of the nexus of knowledge and power. Foucault's insistence on the inseparability of knowledge and power and his study of the ways in which humans govern themselves and others through the production of truth are central ideas to narrative therapy. At the center of externalizing, deconstructing, and reconstructing dominant social discourses is an exploration of the relationship between knowledge and power. I have argued in this chapter that the "not-knowing" strategy for escaping power and position in therapy risks reifying dominant discourse. With Foucault, I have argued against a repressive model of power, for an approach that recognizes power as both constraining and productive. Taken together, I have argued for an approach that does not separate knowledge and power and that recognizes that the therapist and client contribute knowledge and are active constituting agents in the therapeutic conversation. It is my view that if we wish to avoid inadvertently reifying dominant social discourses and social relations, we need to be reflexive in our conceptual practices. Holding on to a politicized practice requires therapists to come to terms with their own knowledge and power.

Notes

1. Despite my critique of Harlene Anderson's "not-knowing position," I believe she provides an excellent discussion of self, experience, and the narrative metaphor (1997). While she doesn't call herself a "narrative therapist," she uses the narrative metaphor, adopts a postmodern perspective, and emphasizes a collaborative approach. The "not-knowing" approach she has made popular is taken up by narrative therapists in practice often in a manner that is relativist and essentializes experience.

2. While I draw on postmodernism in my analysis of knowledge and power in narrative practice, I also hold on to a modernist belief in the possibility of a social vision that supports social justice. This approach to power and knowledge is then grounded in a blended epistemology or fractured foundationalism.

3. Postmodern reformulations of power will challenge modernist constructions of power that authorize clients' stories as expert and self-legitimizing. Traditional conceptualizations of emotion and experience—pivotal elements of these stories, which are characteristically naturalized and undisputed—are contested. Emotion itself is rarely deconstructed or taken up as a social construction. An additional problem lies in reductionist approaches to diversity and difference. Some therapists seem to believe that if they acknowledge their social locations, they can overcome their biases and hence achieve a mythical neutrality. Just as the self, identity, and experience have to be denaturalized, so does the category of difference.

4. As the conceptualization of power is central to externalizing internalized negative identity conclusions and problem-saturated stories, it is important that a reflexive approach be taken toward power. Power is evident at these related levels, but not limited to them: (a) part of the way the problem is defined and internalized and in the social discourses that determine what constitutes a problem; (b) present in the social construction and context of people's experiences, including social location; (c) present in the interaction between the client and the practitioner despite efforts to equalize the relationship; and (d) part of achieving a sense of greater power and agency through a re-authored identity. Power can be seen as both constraining and constitutive in these instances. For example, social discourses are vehicles that reify power and constitute reality. Yet people are both constrained by and resist dominant discourses. In the creation of re-authored identity, power can be seen as constitutive and productive; however, this doesn't rule out that preferred identities may also be constrained by power.

References

Alcoff, L. (1988). Cultural feminism versus post-structuralism: The identity crisis in feminist theory. *Signs: Journal of Women in Culture and Society, 13*(3), 405–436.

Anderson, H. (1992). The client is the expert: A not-knowing approach to therapy. In S. McNamee & K. Gergen (Eds.), *Therapy as social construction* (pp. 25–53). Newbury Park, CA: Sage.

Anderson, H. (1997). A philosophical stance: Therapists' position, expertise, and responsibility. In *Conversation, language, and possibilities: A postmodern approach to therapy sociology of knowledge* (pp. 93–107). New York: Basic Books.

Bordo, S. (1990). Feminism, postmodernism, and gender skepticism. In L. Nicholson (Ed.), *Feminism/postmodernism* (pp. 133–156). New York: Routledge.

Brown, C. (2003). Narrative therapy: Reifying or challenging dominant discourse. In W. Shera (Ed.), *Emerging perspectives on anti-oppressive practice* (pp. 223–245). Toronto, Canada: Canadian Scholar's Press.

Bruner, E. (1986). Ethnography as narrative. In V. Turner & E. Bruner (Eds.), *The anthropology of experience* (pp. 139–155). Chicago: University of Illinois Press.

Bruner, J. (1991, Fall). The narrative construction of reality. *Critical Inquiry,* pp. 1–21.

Butler, J. (1993). *Bodies that matter: On the discursive limits of "sex."* New York: Routledge.

Code, L. (1996). Taking subjectivity into account. In A. Garry & M. Pearsall (Eds.), *Women, knowledge, and reality: Explorations in feminist philosophy* (pp. 191–221). New York: Routledge.

Flaskas, C., & Humphreys, C. (1993). Theorizing about power: Intersecting the ideas of Foucault with the "problem" of power in family therapy. *Family Process, 32,* 35–47.

Flax, J. (1990). Postmodernism and gender relations in feminist theory. In L. Nicholson (Ed.), *Feminism/postmodernism* (pp. 39–62). New York: Routledge.

Fook, J. (2002). Empowerment. In *Social work: Critical theory and practice* (pp. 103–114). Thousand Oaks, CA: Sage.

Foote, C. E., & Frank, A. W. (1999). Foucault and therapy: The disciplining of grief. In A. Chambon, A. Irving, A., & L. Epstein (Eds.), *Reading Foucault for social work* (pp. 157–187). New York: Columbia University Press.

Foucault, M. (1980a). *The history of sexuality: Vol. 1. An introduction.* New York: Vintage.

Foucault, M. (1980b). *Power/knowledge: Selected interviews and other writings 1972–1977.* New York: Pantheon.

Foucault, M. (1991). Politics and the study of discourse. In G. Burchell, C. Gorden, & P. Miller (Eds.), *The Foucault effect, studies in governmentality* (pp. 53–72). London: Harverster.

Foucault, M. (1995). Strategies of power. In W. Anderson (Ed.), *The truth about the truth: De-confusing and re-constructing the postmodern world* (pp. 40–45). New York: Tarcher/Putnam.

Fuss, D. (1989). *Essentially speaking: Feminism, nature, and difference.* New York: Routledge.

Haraway, D. (1988). Situated knowledges: The science question in feminism and the privilege of partial perspective. *Feminist Studies, 14*(3), 575–599.

Hare-Mustin, R. (1994, March). Discourses in the mirrored room: A postmodern analysis of therapy. *Family Processes, 33,* 19–35.

Haug, F. (1992). *Learning from experience: A feminist epistemology.* Paper presented at the Ontario Institute for Studies in Education, Ontario, Canada.

Lukes, S. (1974). *Power: A radical view.* London: Macmillan Press.

MacDonald, K., & MacDonald, G. (1999). Empowerment: A critical view. In W. Shera (Ed.), *Empowerment practices in social work: Developing richer conceptual foundations* (pp. 50–78). Toronto, Canada: Canadian Scholars' Press.

Malinen, T., & Anderson, H. (2004). The wisdom of not knowing: A conversation with Harlene Anderson. *Journal of Systemic Therapies, 23*(2), 68–77.

Parry, A., & Doan, R. (1994). *Story re-visions.* New York: Guilford.

Rabinow, P. (1984). *The Foucault reader.* New York: Pantheon Books.

Rondeau, G. (2000, July). Empowerment and social practice, or the issue of power in social work. *Social Work*, pp. 216–222.

Sanders, C. (1998). Substance misuse dilemmas. A postmodern inquiry. In S. Madigan & I. Law (Eds.), *Praxis: Situating discourse, feminism, and politics in narrative therapies* (pp. 141–162). Vancouver, Canada: Cardigan Press.

Scott, J. (1992). Experience. In J. Butler & J. Scott (Eds.), *Feminists theorize the political* (pp. 22–40). New York: Routledge.

Smith, D. (1990). *The conceptual practices of power: A feminist sociology of knowledge*. Toronto, Canada: University of Toronto Press.

Smith, D. (1999). *Writing the social: Critique, theory, and investigations*. Toronto Canada: University of Toronto Press.

Stanley, L., & Wise, S. (1990). Method, methodology, and epistemology in feminist research processes. In *Feminist praxis* (pp. 20–60). New York: Routledge.

Tanesini, A. (1999). *An introduction to feminist epistemologies*. Malden, MA: Blackwell.

Walter, J., & Peller, J. (1996). Rethinking our assumptions: Assuming anew in a postmodern world. In S. Miller, M. Hubble, & B. Duncan (Eds.), *Handbook of solution-focused brief therapy* (pp. 9–26). San Francisco: Jossey-Bass.

White, M. (1989). Narrative therapy: What sort of internalizing conversations? *Dulwich Centre Newsletter*, 1–5.

White, M. (1992). Deconstruction and therapy. In D. Epston & M. White (Eds.), *Experience, contradiction, narrative, and imagination: Selected papers of David Epston and Michael White, 1989–1991* (pp. 109–151). Adelaide, Australia: Dulwich Centre.

White, M. (1994). The politics of therapy: Putting to rest the illusion of neutrality. *Dulwich Centre Newsletter, 1*, 1–4.

White, M. (1995). *Re-authoring lives: Interviews & essays*. Adelaide, Australia: Dulwich Centre.

White, M. (1997). *Narratives of therapists' lives*. Adelaide, Australia: Dulwich Centre.

White, M. (2001). Narrative practice and the unpacking of identity conclusions. *Gecko: A Journal of Deconstruction and Narrative Ideas in Therapeutic Practice, 1,* 28–55.

White, M. (2004). *Narrative practice and exotic lives: Resurrecting diversity in everyday life*. Adelaide, Australia: Dulwich Centre.

White, M., & Epston, D. (1990). *Narrative means to therapeutic ends*. New York: Norton.

2

Re-Storying Women's Depression

A Material-Discursive Approach

Michelle N. Lafrance and Janet M. Stoppard

Depression is one of the most common mental health problems in North America and also one that is particularly prevalent among women (Culbertson, 1997; Lecrubier 1998; McGrath, Keita, Strickland, & Russo, 1990). North American and international studies have found that depressed women outnumber depressed men at a fairly consistent rate of approximately 2 to 1, with prevalence rates of depression for women ranging as high as 25% (American Psychiatric Association, 2000; Cabral & Astbury, 2000). These findings suggest that gender-related influences need to be considered in any attempt to understand depression in women.

Currently, there are two culturally available ways of understanding depression. In the first, depression is viewed as a medical illness, the result of biochemical problems in the brain (Bebbington, 1996; Fuller & Sajatovic, 2000; Kaplan & Sadock, 1998; Russell, 1995). According to this medicalized view, the cause of depression resides within the body and is best treated biochemically, with psychotropic drugs (Essom & Nemeroff, 1996; McGrath et al., 1990). From this biological perspective, depression in women is explained in the same way as depression in men, and the social inequalities in women's lives are ignored. The focus is on women's bodies, and no attention is paid to social and political gender-related issues.

The second approach points to women's lives as a primary source of depression (e.g., Belle & Doucet, 2003; Cabral & Astbury, 2000; Stoppard &

McMullen, 2003). From a *women's-lives* perspective, depression is explained as being a consequence of the gendered power imbalances in patriarchal society, rather than as a product of chemical imbalances in the brain (Stoppard, 2000). Higher prevalence rates of depression among women are considered to reflect the overrepresentation of women among those who are poor, victims of abuse, and overburdened by the stressors of caregiving. This approach, developed within feminist scholarship, offers a view of depression that encompasses individual, social, and political factors. From this feminist perspective, therapy for depressed women should involve support for women in making changes in their lives coupled with action by therapists to address social inequalities that contribute to women's depression (Greenspan, 1993; Laidlaw & Malmo, 1990; Sturdivant, 1980; Worell & Remer, 1992).

Although the medicalized approach to women's depression remains dominant, it has been critiqued by feminists and others as reductionistic, individualistic, and gender-blind (Nicolson, 1998; Pilgrim & Bentall, 1999; Stoppard, 2000). By focusing on biochemical dysfunction within the individual, not only is gender ignored, but so are the social contexts of people's lives. Accordingly, medical interventions such as drugs point to the individual as the site of pathology, leaving interpersonal, social, and political inequalities unaddressed. The second approach to depression, which attends to women's lives, avoids the limitations of the medical approach and is better able to account for gender-related differences in rates of depression. However, although an understanding of depression rooted in the social and political realities of women's lives may help to explain feelings of demoralization and hopelessness that are part of being depressed, this framework is unable to account for aspects of depressive experience that involve physical changes. For instance, the so-called vegetative signs of depression, which include sleep and appetite disturbances and persistent lack of energy, are hard to explain from a women's-lives perspective. When women are troubled by experiences that may be perceived as indicating changes in their physical health, a medicalized approach is the only culturally sanctioned route available for understanding and addressing their distress.

Attempts to develop feminist approaches to understanding women's depression are likely to remain marginal (and therefore to have little impact on women's lives) unless the embodied character of women's experiences of depression can be theorized. At the moment, women appear to be offered a "forced choice" between their bodies (biomedical approach) and their lives (feminist-informed approach) as an explanation for their depressive experiences. At the same time, the intertwined subjective-embodied nature of women's depressive experiences cannot readily be validated in terms of either the medically oriented or feminist-inspired discourses available to them. Although a woman may ask herself, "Why am I depressed?" the process of arriving at an answer to this question involves negotiation of seemingly irreconcilable explanatory strategies. Postmodern scholars have argued that mainstream formulations are unequal to the task of theorizing the richness and complexity of experiences such as illness and distress, and they have encouraged a move away from essentialist and dualist thinking (e.g., Burr, 2003; Gergen, 1992; Miller, 2000; Ussher, 1997). Thus, women's difficulties in achieving a satisfactory understanding of their depressive experiences may reflect limitations in contemporary theories, rather than women's status as "lay knowers," expected to defer to the expertise of mental health professionals (see Stoppard, 1997).

Understanding Women's Depression: Exploring a Material-Discursive Alternative

One alternative for bridging the body-mind form of duality characterizing current theorizing about women's depression is offered by adopting a "material-discursive" perspective (Ussher, 1997; Yardley, 1996, 1997). Beginning from a postmodern perspective, a material-discursive approach enables us to avoid being trapped by limiting dichotomies such as body-mind and individual-social. Yardley (1997) has summarized the guiding assumptions of a material-discursive approach as follows:

> Because we are intrinsically social *and* embodied beings, the material dimension of human lives is always socialized—mediated by language and consciousness and modified by social activity—while the discursive dimension is inevitably physically manifested, in our speech and behavior, institutions and technology. (p. 15, emphasis in original)

A material-discursive approach addresses the problem of overcoming the body-mind divide by reconceptualizing embodiment within a cultural perspective.[1] From this culturally informed perspective, the body is understood as an organism that is immersed in culture, rather than being neutral with respect to cultural influences. Thus, the body is conceptualized as being both naturally (materially) and culturally (discursively) produced (see Bordo, 1993; Lock, 1993).

In our research, we have endeavored to develop an understanding of depression that is grounded in women's accounts of their depressive experiences, while being attentive to the material and discursive production of women's lives. That is, based on our own research with women who have been depressed, we have endeavored to "re-story" women's depression in a way that attends to both materiality and discourse. In the course of our research, we have interviewed women who self-identified as being depressed ($N = 60$) or as having recovered from depression ($N = 20$).[2] Research participants were recruited from urban and rural communities in a province in eastern Canada. The women we spoke with came from a wide range of personal, educational, and economic backgrounds, and they also differed in their contact with mental health professionals and the degree to which these interventions were considered helpful. We spoke with women who ranged in age from their early 20s to late 60s. They were single and married, with and without children, employed outside the home, working inside the home, unemployed, on disability insurance, and students. When we talked to women about their experiences of depression, most often their accounts revolved around their day-to-day lives as women. For instance, the following two excerpts are from interviews with women who combined being mothers and wives with full-time employment[3]:

> I get up in the morning, I get my daughter ready, we are off to work. My lunch hours are spent running around the malls to pay bills or to pick up this or whatever. I get home, I cook supper, I do homework and then there is the bath. Then there is quality time of playing and she [my daughter] is off to bed. Then I'm in the bedroom ironing. . . . And the next thing [I] have to go to bed because I have to get up early again the next morning and start all over again. . . . And now my husband, his aunt, she has got Parkinson's and she is suffering from depression herself, so she is having a hard time coping, so I am paying her bills, and I am doing her laundry, and I am doing his father's laundry.

> I looked after my family, plus my husband's family. Whenever anybody got sick, they always called [me]. . . . [I] would never say no. . . . I used to do fifty things at once. I look back and see, not that I want to get back to that person, but even if I could do five things at once I'd be happy.

These women, like many of the other women we have interviewed, told stories of their daily lives consumed by domestic practices and governed by the needs of others. Their lives seemed to be organized in relation to an unarticulated backdrop of what it means to be a "good woman," an identity enacted through an endless daily cycle of cooking, cleaning, and caring that, in turn, depletes women's physical and emotional resources. More or less taken for granted, these "practices of femininity" remain invisible as a possible source of women's depression. Moreover, women do not appear to question that they should continue to engage in these practices, even when depressed and incapacitated. For instance, in the following excerpt, a woman recounted how, when depressed, she maintained her work within the home even though she struggled to continue her work outside the home:

So they [family members] did not see a whole lot of change in me except that I couldn't work, because I worked around here [home]. I still did my daily activities. . . . You know, had supper ready, had dinner ready, had their lunches ready. Did the wash. But none of that had ceased, you know. But I did it because . . . well, you do it.

Rather than viewing practices of femininity as implicated in their depression, very often women spoke of struggling to maintain these practices despite being depressed. Instead, their deficient performance as women served only to compound their feelings of distress:

I try to become this super person that does everything, and I feel guilty for not doing it. And I think it still goes back to just wanting to make sure they are happy with me, that I am a good person.

So maybe that one week a month, I am going to scream and yell at my kids. And then I thought, well maybe I should never have had children, maybe I just am not a good mother.

But at times it's like, you know, everything seems to be so couple oriented, and if you don't have kids and you don't have a family, there is something wrong with you, especially when you are twenty-nine and thirty years old.

Indeed, feelings of inability to be a "good woman" may mark the low point of a woman's depression:

I remember saying to my husband when it was real bad, I remember saying, "Honey maybe you should just divorce me or like put me in a hospital or like an institute or something and divorce me, and then you can go and get married, find somebody nice whose going to be a better mother to [child] and a better wife for you, because I clearly can't do it." And I remember really believing that was the only solution.

When women who had been depressed talked about their lives, they drew on culturally pervasive "discourses of femininity" in their descriptions of the multiple roles and responsibilities that shaped their lives as mothers, daughters, and wives. Discourses of femininity can be viewed as sets of shared cultural beliefs that converge to define what it means to be a "good woman" (Bordo, 1993; Jack, 1991; Stoppard, 2000; Ussher, 1991). What is apparent in these women's accounts is that their sense of self draws heavily on activities oriented around family relationships and caring for others. Thus, one way to understand women's depression is as experiences that arise in the space where "discourses of femininity" and "practices of femininity" intersect. That is, women's everyday activities and sense of self are regulated discursively by the socially constructed figure of the "good woman" *and* enacted physically by means of the finite material resources of the female body. From this perspective, discourses are not simply "ideas," but have direct effects on women's bodies, as living life as a "good woman" taxes the body. Moreover, practices of femininity such as caregiving and running a household are taken for granted and devalued in Western society, making women's situations all the more oppressive.

Women's depression, then, can be viewed as one outcome of daily struggles by women to reconcile the cultural imperatives of the socially constructed "good woman" with their materiality as embodied beings and the social circumstances of their lives. This process is exacerbated by an individualistic cultural climate in which people are held personally responsible for solving their problems in living (Kitzinger, 1992; Stearns, 1993). In the face of these dilemmas, when a woman's body is no longer able to keep up with the demands of practices of femininity, the body provides a temporary respite. Effectively, the body goes "on strike" and shuts down, and, as a result, the woman in the body can no longer fulfill the mandate of the "good woman." Women's depression, then, can be understood as a response to the material and discursive contradictions that are part of the fabric of women's lives and that are rooted in a patriarchal sociocultural context.

Women's Recovery From Depression: A Material-Discursive Analysis

As with their accounts of being depressed, women's talk about overcoming depression revolved around discourses and practices of femininity. A common narrative drawn on by women was a story of having become overwhelmed by demands and expectations and, through the recovery process, learning to let go of practices of femininity. For instance, the woman mentioned in the previous section who identified her feelings of being incapable of being a good mother and wife as the lowest point in her depression also linked these feelings to the turning point, when she started to recover. In the next excerpt, she describes the personal transformation she experienced:

> My makeup was good, my hair was good, my house was tidy, my car was clean, just all of that really superficial stuff so that if anybody looked at me, everything would look just fine. . . . I used to wash my baseboards. . . . It was just one of those things that I would have done that would have been important to me at the time. . . . One of the really big parts of that [recovery] was realizing you don't need to have clean baseboards. That there are other things in life that are more important than that.

As this excerpt illustrates, women's recovery narratives often drew on an individualized way of accounting in which women constructed themselves as having been unrealistically concerned with domestic perfection, at times referring to themselves as having been perfectionists or "control freaks." Interrupting their prioritization of "good-woman" practices and beginning to attend to their own needs were central aspects of their recovery narratives:

> My priority list starts with me, instead of Mom, Dad [husband, work], return-ing those ten phone calls. Me used to be way down there. I don't even think it was on page one.
>
> I care for others, like the people that are important in my life, I am still a very loyal person, faithful person. I would never do anything to any other people that I truly love. I would never intentionally hurt anybody. But when it comes down to it, I think about what I want. I always stop and think, how do you feel about this? And I reflect a lot more now.

The "good woman" attends to others' needs and expectations, not her own. However, according to our research participants' accounts, neglecting their own needs in the past was, at least in part, something that led to their becom-ing depressed. At the same time, participants' accounts reflected a discursive bind whereby relinquishing practices of femininity and engaging in self-care were often discussed as central to their wellness but threatening to their iden-tities as women. Giving priority to one's own needs was seen as incompatible with being the "good woman," and women struggled with the implication of selfishness if they took time for themselves. As one young woman said,

> How I've changed is that I think this is for the better, but I sometimes feel inse-cure about this because I feel like it's not always a good thing. . . . I'm not, I shouldn't say "selfish," but I call it selfish because I think it's kind of like I think that's something that's built into me when I was young that thinking of yourself is like a selfish trait.

In addition to discursive impediments to women's recovery from depres-sion, there are also material constraints. Women's attempts to reduce and set limits on their involvement in practices of femininity occur in the contexts of their family relationships, access to resources (e.g., money, child care), and the institutions and organizations with which they are involved (e.g., work-place, schools, the health care system). A woman may endeavor to relinquish practices of femininity, but the extent to which she can do so will depend on the material context of her life. The following excerpt illustrates the mater-ial, as well as discursive, impediments faced by depressed women when they try to resist engaging in practices of femininity. This quote is taken from the interview with a woman who was married with children and caring for her terminally ill mother, as well as being primary caregiver for her toddler grandchild.

> Just a lot of little things that just . . . piled on top of each other. . . . I felt I had to solve all these problems, there was nobody else to do it. So it was just an accumulation and, you know. My doctor asked me once, she said, "Have you ever thought of committing suicide?" I said no, but I dream about a time when I could wake up in the morning and for two weeks everybody would have disappeared off the face of the earth. . . . It was all the pressures, all the demands, even making breakfast for your husband. It was like everything got piled on top of the other, you didn't want to do any of them. Yet it bothered you that you didn't do them.

This excerpt illustrates how the material and the discursive are inextricably linked. This woman's everyday activities were prescribed by the "good-woman" identity; at the same time, however, her activities were depleting her body's resources. While she may have wanted to resist enacting the "good-woman" ideal, at the material level, there was no one else to take responsibility for solving the problems she faced. Thus, this analysis implies that therapy with a depressed woman would need to address both social and practical impediments to changes in her life. For example, the practical problems she faced would need to be acknowledged and addressed (e.g., helping her to access resources in the community), while also exploring the meaning of her identity as a woman with the goal of reducing the guilt she feels about not living up to the "good-woman" ideal. Although the woman from whose interview the previous extract is taken felt overwhelmed and wanted to escape family demands ("I dream about a time when I could wake up in the morning and for two weeks everybody would have disappeared off the face of the earth"), her experiences were still regulated by discourses of femininity ("You didn't want to do any of them. Yet it bothered you that you didn't do them"). As this extract illustrates, the social meaning of a woman's activities needs to be taken into account in understanding her distress. From a material-discursive perspective, discourses of femininity construct the "good woman" as an identity position that, if embraced, can lead to both physical and emotional exhaustion when the demands of engaging in practices of femininity become excessive.

Implications of a Material-Discursive Understanding of Women's Depression

By attending to taken-for-granted facets of women's lives, we have come to see depression as one result of the depletion of women's bodies through their enactment of their lives as women, regulated by cultural discourses of femininity within a patriarchal sociocultural context. That is, the "good-woman" identity, while culturally revered, is also devalued and disadvantages women in relation to men. Resisting discourses of femininity by relinquishing "good-woman" practices and attending to one's own needs may be essential for a woman's recovery from depression; such a move, however, is likely to threaten a woman's identity. Thus, women who become depressed seem to be caught between the requirements of the culturally constructed "good-woman" ideal, on the one hand, and the limits of their physical embodiment, on the other (Stoppard, 1998, 2000). Our analysis points to the importance of continued social critique of the "good-woman" ideal coupled with exploration of alternatives to the "good woman" as identity positions for women.

Deconstructing the "Good-Woman" Ideal

Despite gains made by the feminist movement toward the goals of women's equality and empowerment and dismantling patriarchal structures, a focus on women, either collectively or individually, leaves unaddressed the cultural construction of women's lives. As our analysis of women's depression underscores, however, discourses of femininity are both pervasive and invisible. Discourses of femininity construct the "good-woman" ideal, which is central to women's accounts of being depressed, and shape the activities of women's everyday lives. Thus, when a woman surveys her life for sources of her distress, she may see that much of her time is taken up with caring work for others, but she may overlook these practices of femininity as a routine part of what women do on a daily basis. When the demands of the everyday become problematic, women are most likely to blame themselves and be blamed by others. Strategies are needed for deconstructing discourses of femininity that equate caring and other domestic work with women's work, while simultaneously devaluing women's caring work as a natural outgrowth of women's "caring nature."

Depictions of women as selfless caregivers (and of men as somehow less natural or competent caregivers) abound in media representations and in everyday talk about gender and are integral to the social construction of femininity (and masculinity) (Sunderland, 2002). The assumption that women should selflessly direct their energies toward caring for others remains taken for granted, and so is socially invalid as a legitimate source of women's distress. Moreover, when therapists' understanding of their clients is shaped by this perspective on women's lives, women's caregiving practices are unlikely to be questioned. Instead, women may be advised to reduce their involvement in activities outside the home (e.g., switching from full-time to part-time employment or scaling back educational goals) as a way to cope with stress, even though the implications of such changes are potentially disempowering (Stoppard & Gammell, 2003).

According to the women we interviewed, finding a way to "re-story" their lives such that they could relinquish "good-woman" practices was pivotal to their recovery from depression. Therefore, helping depressed women to shift self-narratives in order to allow them to reduce their engagement in activities signifying the "good woman" and to adopt self-care practices appears to be an important therapeutic goal. Opportunities for social critique of the "good-woman" ideal and representations of caring as women's work are offered by community-based initiatives such as self-help or women's groups. Deconstruction of the "good-woman" ideal could also form an important part of prenatal education and parenting groups. Such interventions would provide a context for encouraging acceptance and expression of a range of feelings and experiences associated with mothering, including exhaustion, distress, ambivalence, and depression. Challenging the construction of women as natural caregivers would also involve an emphasis on fostering fathers' involvement in child care.

In recent years, provision of care to elderly parents and other family members who are infirm or ill has increasingly become a private matter taking place in the home (so-called home care). The transfer of this caring work from hospitals and other institutions to the home has been accomplished largely through the unpaid labor of women (Grant et al., 2004). The notion of community-based care, often depicted as more humane than institutional care, usually translates into additional caring responsibilities for women, with the consequent demands on women's time and energy that such work entails. Feminist researchers and activists have identified the need for publicly funded home care services as an important health policy goal. Such efforts not only warrant political support but also provide legitimacy for challenges to the socially constructed ideal of the "good woman."

Constructing Alternative Identity Positions for Women

As Willig (1999) has pointed out, findings from discourse-analytic work can be used to design interventions that "facilitate empowerment through repositioning of the subjects" by opening up "spaces for resistance to limiting positionings and their associated practices" (p. 152). Therapy offers one avenue for exploring alternatives to the "'good-woman" ideal as an identity position for depressed women. In mainstream approaches to therapy, such as cognitive behavioral therapy (CBT) for depression, attention is focused at the individual level, and the social meaning of a depressed person's experiences is largely ignored. A potential drawback of approaches such as CBT is that a woman's ambivalence about replacing practices of femininity with practices that will facilitate her wellness (e.g., self-care) may be viewed by a therapist as irrational, resistant, or self-defeating. As our analysis reveals, however, relinquishing practices of femininity poses a threat to women who have been depressed, because such practices are not only central to the discursively constructed "good-woman" ideal but are also integral to women's sense of themselves as women. A narrative or discursive approach to therapy (e.g., Russell & Carey, 2004; White, 2004; White & Epston, 1990) enables women's experiences and sense of self to be re-authored and allows for more empowering understandings of the ambivalence and struggles faced by depressed women. Narrative therapists can work with women clients to attend to and deconstruct the larger cultural context that limits women's opportunities to re-story their lives in ways that are both positive and health promoting. Within this therapeutic approach, narratives of personal growth and change can be drawn upon to enable depressed women to develop alternative and more empowering ways of thinking about themselves and their situations.

Adoption of a material-discursive framework within a narrative approach would also provide a route for transcending the women's bodies/women's lives dichotomy that characterizes contemporary explanatory and therapeutic approaches to women's depression (Stoppard, 1997, 2000). Such a move would also help in resolving dilemmas faced by feminist therapists when feminist arguments that medicalization pathologizes women's distress are pitted against women's claims that medical interventions (e.g., antidepressant medication, electroconvulsive therapy) provide relief from their pain (see, for instance, Perkins, 1994; Stoppard & Gammell, 2003). In their feminist critique of medicalization, sociologists Findlay and Miller (1994) argue as follows:

> Perhaps the most important negative result of the medical perspective on women's lives is its tendency to individualize and depoliticize their problems . . . . The medical model tells women, "The problem is with you, so you must do the changing." As sociologists and as feminists, we find this approach myopic: it treats the female, but leaves dominant patriarchal conceptions of femininity untouched. (p. 300)

While acknowledging the validity of Findlay and Miller's assessment of medicalization, we hold the view that foreclosing on the use of potentially helpful medical interventions by individual women because of the political implications for women in general is an untenable position. Feminists may work toward social change in the long term without neglecting the suffering of individual women in the present. In our work as researchers and clinicians, we have found that women who are depressed often talk about and want to understand the embodied nature of their distress. Moreover, many women find relief in medical forms of intervention (Stoppard & Gammell, 2003). Thus, neither an exclusive focus on the body nor on the cultural context is theoretically satisfying, and, more important, neither perspective fits well with how women talk about their depressive experiences—as being both embodied and gendered. Most often, women's accounts of being depressed and overcoming depression reflect an interweaving of biological and social understandings. Thus, rather than viewing women's bodies and women's lives as opposing explanatory models, within a material-discursive framework, these approaches are understood as being both complementary and inextricably linked.

Conclusion

Addressing women's depression from the material-discursive perspective outlined in this chapter implies that change efforts should be directed toward both the material and discursive conditions that shape women's lives. Change in the material conditions of women's lives continues to be a feminist goal (e.g., pay equity, subsidized day care, changes to the legal system to better protect and defend victims of violence). Less often considered, however, is the need for change at the discursive level. Availability of alternative discourses, as Willig (1999) has argued, can open up new possibilities for practice, just as changes in institutions or technologies give birth to new ways of speaking. Thus, discourse and materiality operate in tandem. Accordingly, efforts to address women's depression and to promote recovery and wellness among women require simultaneous attention to these interlocking realms of experience. In the words of feminist psychologist Jane Ussher (1991), "We need to operate on the level of the political and of the individual: at the level of discursive practices, and individual solutions for misery. The two must go hand in hand if we are to move forward" (p. 293).

Notes

1. For discussion of a material-discursive approach to understanding women's depression, see Stoppard (1998).
2. See Lafrance (2003); Scattolon and Stoppard (1999); Stoppard and Gammell (2003); Stoppard, Guptill, and Lafrance (2000); and Stoppard, Scattolon, and Gammell (2000) for information on the original research.
3. All excerpts were taken from research interviews.

References

American Psychiatric Association. (2000). *Diagnostic and statistical manual of mental disorders* (4th ed., Text rev.). Washington, DC: Author.

Bebbington, P. (1996). The origins of sex-differences in depressive disorder—bridging the gap. *International Review of Psychiatry, 8,* 295–332.

Belle, D., & Doucet, J. (2003). Poverty, inequality, and discrimination as sources of depression among U.S. women. *Psychology of Women Quarterly, 27,* 101–113.

Bordo, S. (1993). *Unbearable weight: Feminism, Western culture, and the body.* Berkeley: University of California Press.

Burr, V. (2003). *An introduction to social constructionism* (2nd ed.). London: Routledge.

Cabral, M., & Astbury, J. (2000). *Women's mental health: An evidence based review.* Geneva, Switzerland: World Health Organization.

Culbertson, F. M. (1997). Depression and gender: An international review. *American Psychologist, 52,* 25–31.

Essom, C. R., & Nemeroff, C. B. (1996). Treatment of depression in adulthood. In K. I. Shulman, M. Tohen, & S. P. Kutcher (Eds.), *Mood disorders across the lifespan* (pp. 251–264). New York: Wiley.

Findlay, D. A., & Miller, L. J. (1994). Through medical eyes: The medicalization of women's bodies and women's lives. In B. S. Bolaria & H. D. Dickinson (Eds.), *Health, illness, and health care in Canada* (2nd ed., pp. 276–306). Toronto: Harcourt Brace Canada.

Fuller, M. A., & Sajatovic, M. (2000). *Drug information handbook for psychiatry* (2nd ed.). Hudson, OH: Lexi-Comp.

Gergen, K. J. (1992). Toward a postmodern psychology. In S. Kvale (Ed.), *Psychology and postmodernism* (pp. 17–30). London: Sage.

Grant, K., Amaratunga, C., Armstrong, P., Boscoe, M., Pederson, A., & Willson, K. (Eds.). (2004). *Caring for/caring about: Women, home care, and unpaid caregiving.* Aurora, Canada: Garamond.

Greenspan, M. (1993). *A new approach to women and therapy* (2nd ed.). New York: Sulzberger & Graham.

Jack, D. C. (1991). *Silencing the self: Women and depression.* Cambridge, MA: Harvard University Press.

Kaplan, H. I., & Sadock, B. J. (1998). *Synopsis of psychiatry: Behavioral sciences/clinical psychiatry* (8th ed.). Baltimore, MD: Williams & Wilkins.

Kitzinger, C. (1992). The individuated self concept: A critical analysis of social-constructionist writing on individualism. In G. M. Breakwell (Ed.), *Social psychology of identity and the self concept* (pp. 221–250). London: Surrey University Press.

Lafrance, M. N. (2003). *Struggling for legitimacy: Women's accounts of recovering from depression.* Unpublished doctoral dissertation, University of New Brunswick, Canada.

Laidlaw, T. A., & Malmo, C. (1990). *Healing voices: Feminist approaches to therapy with women.* San Francisco: Jossey-Bass.

Lecrubier, Y. (1998). Is depression under-recognised and undertreated? *International Clinical Psychopharmacology, 13*(Suppl. 5), S3–S6.

Lock, M. (1993). *Encounters with aging: Mythologies of menopause in Japan and North America.* Berkeley: University of California Press.

McGrath, E., Keita, G. P., Strickland, B. R., & Russo, N. F. (1990). *Women and depression: Risk factors and treatment issues.* Washington, DC: American Psychological Association.

Miller, L. J. (2000). The poverty of truth seeking: Postmodernism, discourse analysis, and critical feminism. *Theory & Psychology, 10,* 313–352.

Nicolson, P. (1998). *Post-natal depression: Psychology, science, and the transition to motherhood.* New York: Routledge.

Perkins, R. (1994). Choosing ETC. *Feminism & Psychology, 4,* 623–627.

Pilgrim, D., & Bentall, R. (1999). The medicalization of misery: A critical realist analysis of the concept of depression. *Journal of Mental Health, 8,* 261–274.

Russell, D. (1995). *Women, madness, and medicine.* Cambridge, UK: Polity Press.

Russell, S., & Carey, M. (2004). *Narrative therapy: Responding to your questions.* Adelaide, Australia: Dulwich Centre.

Scattolon, Y., & Stoppard, J. M. (1999). "Getting on with life": Women's experiences and ways of coping with depression. *Canadian Psychology, 40,* 205–219.

Stearns, C. Z. (1993). Sadness. In M. Lewis & J. M. Haviland (Eds.), *Handbook of emotions* (pp. 547–561). New York: Guilford.

Stoppard, J. M. (1997). Women's bodies, women's lives, and depression: Towards a reconciliation of material and discursive accounts. In J. M. Ussher (Ed.), *Body talk: The material and discursive regulation of sexuality, madness, and reproduction* (pp. 10–32). London: Routledge.

Stoppard, J. M. (1998). Dis-ordering depression in women: Toward a materialist-discursive account. *Theory & Psychology, 8,* 79–99.

Stoppard, J. M. (2000). *Understanding depression: Feminist social constructionist approaches.* London: Routledge.

Stoppard, J. M., & Gammell, D. J. (2003). Depressed women's treatment experiences: Exploring themes of medicalization and empowerment. In J. M. Stoppard & L. M. McMullen (Eds.), *Situating sadness: Women and depression in social context* (pp. 39–61). New York: New York University Press.

Stoppard, J. M., Guptill, A., & Lafrance, M. N. (November, 2000). *Understanding depression from the standpoint of women.* Paper presented at Feminist Utopias: Redefining Our Projects, inaugural conference of the Institute for Women's Studies and Gender Studies, University of Toronto, Canada.

Stoppard, J. M., & McMullen, L. M. (2003). *Situating sadness: Women and depression in social context.* New York: New York University Press.

Stoppard, J. M., Scattolon, Y., & Gammell, D. J. (2000). Understanding depression from the standpoint of women who have been depressed. In B. Miedema, J. M. Stoppard, & V. Anderson (Eds.), *Women's bodies/women's lives: Health, well-being, and body image* (pp. 82–102). Toronto, Canada: Sumach Press.

Sturdivant, S. (1980). *Therapy for women: A feminist philosophy of treatment.* New York: Springer.

Sunderland, J. (2002). Baby entertainer, bumbling assistant and line manager. In L. Litosseliti & J. Sunderland (Eds.), *Gender identity and discourse analysis* (pp. 293–324). Amsterdam: John Benjamins.

Ussher, J. M. (1991). *Women's madness: Misogyny or mental illness?* Amherst: University of Massachusetts Press.

Ussher, J. M. (1997). *Body talk: The material and discursive regulation of sexuality, madness, and reproduction.* London: Routledge.

White, M. (2004). *Narrative practices and exotic lives: Resurrecting diversity in everyday life.* Adelaide, Australia: Dulwich Centre.

White, M., & Epston, D. (1990). *Narrative means to therapeutic ends.* New York: Norton.

Willig, C. (Ed.). (1999). *Applied discourse analysis: Social and psychological interventions.* Buckingham, UK: Open University Press.

Worell, J., & Remer, P. (1992). *Feminist perspectives in therapy: An empowerment model for women.* Chichester, UK: Wiley.

Yardley, L. (1996). Reconciling discursive and materialist perspectives on health and illness: A reconstruction of the biopsychosocial approach. *Theory & Psychology, 6,* 485–508.

Yardley, L. (Ed.). (1997). *Material discourses of health and illness.* London: Routledge.

3

The Blinding Power of Genetics

Manufacturing and Privatizing Stories of Eating Disorders

Karin Jasper

In narrative therapy, the therapist engages with the client's own understanding of his or her problems and helps the individual to open and develop new possibilities through re-storying. This undertaking is guided by the ethic of being respectful of the client as a subject and is therefore opposed to therapeutic practices that objectify clients or reinforce stories that individualize their problems and pathologize them. Currently in the area of eating disorders, there is a biological narrative emerging that has the potential of eclipsing understandings developed over the last two or three decades. This new narrative features genetic research made possible by the Human Genome Project,[1] and there are good reasons to be concerned about how the findings from this research are being placed in the overall conversation about eating disorders. What is at stake is which narrative about eating disorders will dominate among mainstream clinicians and researchers. This has implications for how those with eating disorders are characterized as well as where responsibility for preventing eating disorders and treating them lies: Are they individual pathologies or understandable responses to a disturbing culture, and is preventing and treating them a private or social responsibility? In this chapter, the emerging genetic story about eating disorders and its implications will be tracked and questioned.

Genetic findings are the trump card of biological explanations because they are seen as establishing causal relationships between genes and their manifestations in characteristics or conditions. Such causal connections are integral parts of scientific explanations, and explanations that have been legitimated as scientific tend to disqualify competing or parallel accounts. We might expect, then, that as genetic explanations proliferate from the Human Genome Project, they will dominate the space previously occupied by sociocultural and other kinds of accounts.

For example, in a very recently published *Handbook of Eating Disorders and Obesity* (Thompson, 2004), the first section is devoted to "Etiology, Risk, and Prevention," and the first chapter is "Genetic and Biological Risk Factors." "Sociocultural Aspects of Eating Disorders" make their appearance in the last section of the book, a section that is marginalized both by its location in the book and by its title, "Special Topics." The lead paragraph of the book privileges biology and minimizes sociocultural understandings of eating disorders:

> Historically, sociocultural and family theories of etiology have dominated the scientific literature on eating disorders. There was certain sound logic to the belief that the pervasive emphasis on thinness as a symbol of beauty and control somehow "caused" eating disorders or that certain family interaction patterns were more likely than others to bring food and eating-related issues to the fore as a center of familial conflict. These explanations had considerable face validity—they seemed like common sense. However, they were not rigorously tested as true prospective risk factors. For decades, biological researchers have been working in the background of the scientific community of eating disorders. A small but dedicated group of researchers has continued to forge ahead with the notion that biology plays a substantial causal role in the etiology of anorexia nervosa (AN) and bulimia nervosa (BN). In this chapter, I address how research on genetic epidemiology and genetics of eating disorders is forcing us to refocus our understanding of the balance of the contributions of genetic and environmental factors to the etiology of anorexia and bulimia nervosa. (Bulik, 2004, p. 3)

While the passing away of sociocultural explanations is proclaimed and the nobility of biological research as "real" science is reinforced in the preceding paragraph, no specific, replicated genetic results have yet been found. This is particularly objectionable and underlines the dominating effects of genetic discourse in explanations of human behavior, because there are many significant findings in the area of sociocultural research that are simply submerged by statements such as those in the passage above.

Researchers like Anne Becker have shown that sociocultural characteristics can create increased vulnerability to eating disorders. A study conducted by Becker and colleagues in the Nadroga province of Fiji between 1995 and 1998 shows how its young women have become very vulnerable to Western women's preoccupations with weight and shape, due to Nadroga's transition from a traditional agrarian economy to an industrial economy that has imported Western cultural values (Becker, Burwell, Gilman, Herzog, & Hamburg, 2002). In Fiji, traditionally, a rounded body shape had been expected and valued in women, and up until 1995, dieting was rare. In 1995, television was introduced to Fiji for the first time, with a choice of two channels showing American, Australian, and British dramas, comedies, and advertising. By 1998, after 3 years of television, eating practices and weight-related attitudes had substantially changed among young women.

Sixty-nine percent of the 63 young women interviewed reported dieting to lose weight, and 74% reported feeling too big or too fat. Three times as many girls as previously had scored in the high-risk range for the development of eating disorders. While there had been no reports of self-induced vomiting in 1995, 12% of the young women reported this behavior in 1998. In their interviews, the young women said, for example, they did not want to be "fat" like their mothers; they felt fatter when watching television shows; and they wanted to have the lifestyles that went along with the body shapes they saw on the television shows they watched.

There is a plethora of other sociocultural research demonstrating, for example, increased body image dissatisfaction for women after viewing fashion magazines (Turner, Hamilton, Jacobs, Angood, & Dwyer, 1997); increased anger and negative mood after viewing fashion magazines (Pinhas, Toner, Ali, Garfinkel, & Stuckless, 1999); and increased eating-disorder symptomatology with increased viewing of fashion magazines—and the reverse, decreased eating-disorder symptomatology with decreased viewing of fashion magazines (Vaughan & Fouts, 2003); and there is evidence for a cumulative effect (over 2 years) of appearance-related TV commercials on body dissatisfaction and drive for thinness (Hargreaves & Tiggemann, 2003). Despite this research, the genetic model is successively moving the mainstream professional community in eating disorders from a biopsychosocial model that at least acknowledged a significant role for sociocultural factors (albeit with a rather superficial understanding of them) to a model that privileges the biological over the sociocultural and redescribes the psychological in terms of the biological.[2]

This process can be seen to be occurring in the area of eating disorders, where two versions of a *gene story* about eating disorders are present: a strong version and a weaker one. In its strong version, the genetic model is claimed to supercede the sociocultural, as in this quote from Cynthia Bulik, president of the Academy for Eating Disorders and the only endowed professor of eating disorders in the United States: "Socio-cultural factors are only important in that they might elicit an expression of someone's pre-existing genetic predisposition" (DeAngelis, 2002, p. 2); or "Historically, eating disorders have been considered to be primarily of socio-cultural origin. Over the past decade, this perspective has been resoundingly rebuffed by a systematic series of enlightening family, twin, and molecular genetic studies" (Bulik, Jordan, & Jordan, 2004, p. 1). In its weaker version, the genetic model claims only that "genes may play a role in the underlying vulnerability to developing an eating disorder" (Kaplan & Woodside, 2003, p. 1). Researchers in the area can be seen to vacillate between the two stories, using the weak version in more formal contexts and the strong version in less formal ones, but backing themselves up with the same research in either case.

This vacillation may reflect a change that has occurred in how genes are conceived scientifically, a change that has not yet been fully integrated into popular consciousness. As the possibility of mapping the human genome became more real, the assumption among geneticists was that human beings would be found to have more genes than any other species (the estimates ranged from around 90,000 to 150,000) because of the greater complexity of the human organism. This would be consistent with the view of the gene as a powerful determiner of traits and with the strong version of the gene story of eating disorders, the version with the most punch, which purports to say something really significant.

As it turns out, we have about 25,000 genes: fewer than the mouse and about the same number as the roundworm. Clearly, the complexity of our species cannot be explained by the sheer number of genes we have, nor can it be explained by some qualitative difference in our genetic material compared with those of other organisms, since all DNA is made up of the same chemical and physical components.[3] Genes, in fact, do not have the determinative power they were once credited with, and our characteristics are created through many-layered processes. As the psychologist David Moore states,

> Biologists no longer question the following two facts: (1) a bit of chromosome can do no more than provide information about the order of amino acids in a chain; and (2) traits are constructed in cascades of steps—many involving nongenetic factors—that lie between amino acid sequencing and final trait production. Given these facts, one conclusion is inescapable: genetic factors cannot themselves cause traits, even traits widely thought to be "genetic," such as hair color, eye color, or body type. . . . Just as no single domino in a series can be called *the* cause—or even the most important cause—of an outcome, neither can a genetic factor alone be *the* cause—or even the most important cause—of the development of a trait. Instead, genetic and nongenetic factors determine traits' appearances *collaboratively*. (Moore, 2001, p. 76)

This view of the role of genes is much more consistent with the weak version of the gene story at best, and possibly not with any currently existing version of a gene story about eating disorders.

Let's consider the following summary of the gene story about eating disorders (paraphrasing the point of view of various researchers) to look at its claims more closely:

We researchers noticed that there are more people with eating disorders in some extended families than in others. This could be because of the influence of family members on one another (learning), or it could be because of genes. Our comparison of identical twins (who share 100% of their genes) with nonidentical twins (who don't share more of their genes than any two siblings who are not twins) shows that more identical twins have eating disorders than do nonidentical twins. The relationship is strongest for anorexia nervosa but also strong enough to warrant believing there is a significant genetic contribution for bulimia nervosa. We estimate heritability to be in the range of 80% for both conditions (Bulik, 2004; Bulik, Sullivan, Wade, & Kendler, 2000).

We also looked for other psychiatric disorders in individuals with eating disorders and in their families. We looked for things like depression, substance abuse, obsessive-compulsive disorders and some personality traits like perfectionism and impulsiveness, and we found that there were more of these than is average. These shared characteristics made us think that probably some people have genes that make them more vulnerable to developing eating disorders than are people who don't have these genes. That would explain why only some people develop eating disorders when all of us share the same sociocultural environment. People with these genes might react to shared and nonshared environments in ways that people without them would not (Klump, Wonderlich, Lehoux, Lilenfeld, & Bulik, 2002; Lilenfeld et al., 1998).

So, out of 237 people and their family members who had eating disorders, we picked those who had specific characteristics—that is, we identified a phenotype. For anorexia nervosa, we picked the people who had been ill for at least 3 years and had always restricted their food intake, but had never binged or purged. For bulimia nervosa, to identify a phenotype, we picked the people who purged by vomiting only (Kaplan & Woodside, 2003; Price Foundation Collaborative Group, 2001).

We scanned samples of the DNA of each of the people in these groups to find out whether there were locations of linkage on particular chromosomes for each of the groups. We did find linkage on chromosome 1 for anorexia and on chromosome 10 for bulimia. It will take time to find the specific genes, because there are 300 genes just within the area of linkage on chromosome 1, but we already have some ideas about what kind of genes to look for. We asked geneticists and computer scientists to look for any genes having to do with appetite, eating, weight, and reward systems. That means looking at genes that control serotonin, dopamine, and opioids. We found some statistically significant connections, but we have not been able to replicate our findings. In the future, we will also be looking for genes that are linked to personality traits like perfectionism, impulsivity, and obsessionality (Bergen & Kaplan, 2004, Grice et al., 2002; Kaye et al., 2004).

There are many reasons—scientific, logical, and political—we should be skeptical about this narrative.

Scientific Issues: Heritability, Linkage, and Culture Mirrored in Nature

Heritability

Heritability is not the same as *inheritability*, but most readers unfamiliar with the limited field of behavior genetics will not be aware of this (Moore, 2001, p. 45), and researchers in the area of genes and eating disorders do not explain it. When researchers make heritability estimates, they are using a concept that originated with plant and animal breeding, which has a very specific meaning in that context (Joseph, 2004, p. 142). In plant and animal breeding, environment can be controlled so significantly that variation in the characteristics of organisms raised in a given environment can reasonably be understood as being genetic in origin. Since it is unethical to control human's environments to this extent, we can never have the same degree of certainty about the variation of human characteristics. Furthermore, heritability estimates are reliable only in relation to the population from which they originated: They are not applicable to organisms from populations that did not share the original environment, and they do not describe the importance of genetic factors as they relate to a particular individual (Joseph, 2004, p. 139; Moore, 2001, p. 44). Using the concept of heritability in contexts outside of plant and animal breeding, without contending with the implications of its use out of context and without explaining its specific meaning, will result in readers misunderstanding it.

Above, for instance, in the summary of the genetic narrative from current research, it would be reasonable for the general reader to assume that genetic factors contribute 80% of what causes eating disorders. Bulik states that it should actually be read as saying that approximately 50% to 85% of the variance in liability for eating disorders is due to genetic effects (Bulik, 2004, p. 6). What she doesn't say is that although this means that we may have some reason to believe that among the people who were studied, the variation in eating disorders is due to genetic effects, it does not mean that in any individual case, we can say that the person has an eating disorder because of some genetic factor or factors. Heritability is not the same as inheritability.

Linkage

A similar problem occurs with the idea of linkage. When genetics researchers report that they found linkage on chromosome 1, it sounds as though they found a definite connection between the genes in that area and anorexia nervosa. What the term *linkage* means within genetic discourse is that it is likely that when there is a certain characteristic (anorexia of the restricting type), there will also be another characteristic (a certain gene or genes). The linkage proves nothing about the nature of the relationship between these two things; it indicates only that in the population tested, they occurred together more often than chance would predict. To use the word *linkage* without explaining its technical meaning is to play on the general reader's understanding of linkage as indicating more than a statistical correlation. We would, for instance, say that smoking is linked with lung cancer, meaning that there is a causal relation between the two. Since most laypersons would still subscribe to the view that genes cause individual characteristics, it is likely that they would see "linkage" between a gene and a characteristic as a causal mechanism.

Culture Mirrored in Nature

Notice also in the summary story that there is a close connection between the genes that are being looked for and our psychological and psychiatric classification systems (e.g., personality disorders, mood and anxiety disorders, personality traits). Since this classification system is not even culturally universal, it seems a kind of hubris to assume that it will be mirrored on a molecular scale in nature. Yet researchers are proceeding as though these traits are good candidates with which to search for genes. All of these aspects of the gene story are legitimated by conclusions that are presented as authoritative, objective, and unequivocal and, being scientific, are treated as inherently real and independent of human construction or meaning making.

Logical Issues: The Notion of Susceptibility Genes

In its weak version, the gene story states that any gene found to be related to anorexia or bulimia will at best be of small-to-modest effect and will most likely be one of several contributory genes, which together will increase a person's *susceptibility to* developing an eating disorder, *given certain environmental conditions* (Bulik, 2004; Grice et al., 2002; Kaplan & Woodside, 2003). This is, of course, a much weaker claim than that of finding a gene for anorexia. But what sort of claim is it?

Janet Treasure (2003, p. 1) gives phenylketonuria (PKU) as an explanatory example of a hereditary condition in which the risks associated with having the condition become manifest in a certain environment. Those born with PKU have mutations on both alleles of a particular gene. Practically, this means that they lack a liver enzyme that is required to digest an amino acid commonly found in protein-containing foods, including breast milk. When babies who are born without this enzyme ingest such foods, they sustain brain damage. Brain damage is avoidable if the baby is diagnosed with PKU immediately after birth and the feeding "environment" is manipulated to eliminate certain protein-containing foods, that is, to eliminate the risk represented by having PKU. A person with PKU could be identified as such on the basis of the genetic mutation that constitutes PKU: Environment plays a role only in whether the risks of having PKU are made manifest or not.

Treasure (2003) also gives as an example "risk of diabetes in people of Asian and Native American ancestry, which becomes manifest in an environment when food is abundant" (p. 1). This is a more complicated example than PKU, because although about 10 loci in the human genome have now been found that seem to confer susceptibility to type 1 diabetes, we do not yet know all of the factors that contribute. We know something about how to keep people with diabetes healthy, but we don't know exactly what causes it and are postulating a combination of many genetic factors and some nongenetic factors.

Anorexia and bulimia are unlike either of these examples. We know they are unlike PKU in that there is no mutation such that if you have the mutation, you also have anorexia or bulimia and should therefore concentrate on avoiding the risks associated with them. In type 1 diabetes, the body's immune system mounts an immunological assault on its own insulin and the pancreatic cells that manufacture it. While the "mechanism" of how this happens is not yet understood, at least it makes some sense to think of there being a mechanism involved here, one that could be the result of a critical mass of genetic and nongenetic physical factors. On the other hand, to "qualify" as having either anorexia or bulimia, a person must have certain *attitudes,* for instance, attitudes reflecting body image disparagement and an extreme valuing of thinness. So, with anorexia and bulimia, we are bringing in the idea that certain attitudes must be present for the terms *anorexia* or *bulimia* to be correctly applied to any individual. Attitudes are not part of the diagnosis of PKU or diabetes. Attitudes are not in the same logical category as the factors in the gene story that are supposed to explain them. What sense does it make to think of these attitudes as somehow caused by a biological mechanism in concert with a particular physical environment? In other words, if we did happen to find a group of genetic factors that contribute to a person not eating, or vomiting after eating, would we have found genetic factors contributing to anorexia and bulimia—or to a syndrome that could be described and explained without requiring reference to attitudes? (For someone to have diabetes, for example, does not require that he or she have any particular attitudes or beliefs.) And what difference does it make when the environment that supposedly "triggers" the manifestation of the "illness" is a familial or cultural environment, not a physical one? The more we look at the ways that PKU and diabetes are different from anorexia and bulimia, the more it seems that the former are extremely limited sources of analogy for the latter.

Susceptibility to "Disease" or Normal Variation in a Problematic Context?

Suppose we think of a related genetic vulnerability that all of us have: For example, we will become unwell or die without appropriate types and quantities of nourishment. At any given time, there may be a lack of appropriate or sufficient food because of the natural, cultural, or political environment in which a person lives. A naturally occurring drought could result in there being little or no food available. A culturally significant social system, for example, a caste system, could limit access to quantity and variety of food for a segment of a population. A political situation, for example, a war, could slow down production and trade, with the result that there would be much less food for almost everyone. With human beings, of course, it is possible, and in fact likely, that all three types of environments could be operating at the same time. Drought conditions that make resources scarce increase the chances of war, and during war, those lower on the social hierarchy have more limited access to the few resources that are available. Some of the less privileged people have genetic dispositions that allow them to withstand conditions of deprivation for a longer period of time than others. Shall we privilege the role of genes when we tell the stories of their lives and deaths by saying that those who fell soonest were those whose genes left them most vulnerable?

The situation could perhaps be better likened to finding some genes that are not "for" any "disease," but are simply part of the ordinary variation that occurs among members of any species. That certain environments might turn these genes into vulnerability factors for a disease says more about the limits we should consider setting on the environments we create for ourselves to live in than it says about some genetically based disease entity. Perhaps we will soon hear researchers talking about the genes that are responsible for our requiring oxygen as though they are susceptibility genes for illness in an environment of poor air quality (Jasper, 2003).

While offering a newborn baby breast milk is usually in the baby's best interest and might arguably be described as a natural choice, it happens not to be a good choice for a PKU baby. This is a situation in which it makes sense to speak of susceptibility genes. The "environment" we provide for girls to grow into women—a cultural and political environment that inequitably values and devalues persons and *specifically generates intolerance toward women's bodies*—is not good for most girls and women. It doesn't make sense to speak of susceptibility genes here. Women's bodies tend to get fatter with puberty (Smolak & Levine, 1996, pp. 216–217), while men's bodies become leaner and more muscular with puberty (Thompson, Heinberg, Altabe, & Tantleff-Dunn, 1999, pp. 30–31). Fat is an object of disgust and is associated with many characteristics our Western culture disapproves of (MacInnis, 1993, pp. 70–71). It is in this environment that the vast majority of North American women have come to dislike their bodies (Maine, 2000, pp. 1–3) and in which a far greater number of females than males develop eating disorders[4] (Thompson et al., 1999, p. 30), a fact that is almost never mentioned in the scientific genes and eating-disorders literature.[5] Surely this is a paradigm example of a situation in which it makes most sense to speak of normal genetic variation in a problematic context, not of genetically based susceptibility.

Political Issues

Within dominant scientific discourse, cultural pressures are understood to be the same for all women, so they aren't seen as explanatory for why all women exposed to these pressures do not develop anorexia or bulimia. This picture discounts the many ways in which culture and its variants differentially affect women (Bordo, 1993, pp. 61–62), as well as the ways different families magnify, reinforce, or offer resistance to cultural pressures and the differences in how individual women relate to cultural ideas in the process of making meaning of their own lives. In its tendency to look for simple, linear, causal explanations, the reductionist scientific view also renders invisible the continuum of eating troubles and weight and shape preoccupation commonly experienced among women in Western and Westernized cultures (Brown, 1993, pp. 53–68). Nor does the gene story account for the predominance of eating problems among women, for the fact that among males, gay males are at higher risk for developing eating disorders, or for the fact that eating disorders are historically situated such that genetic changes in the population could not account for them.

Perhaps what makes the scientific gene story so attractive and worth manufacturing is that it avoids confrontation with the values of Western culture and all the economic and political interests involved, while appearing to be objectively founded on scientific "facts." There are, after all, serious financial interests in the many businesses that cater to weight loss and other "improvements" to appearance. The recently renewed attacks on fatness in response to the so-called epidemic of obesity also feed these business interests. As long as anorexia and bulimia are marginalized as individual pathologies, the connection between our culture's serious phobia with fat and the generation of widespread, troubled eating patterns among females need not put a damper on the anti-obesity business. The problem of eating disorders becomes an individual one, with a private-enterprise solution. At most, the cultural pressures on women are seen as triggering something that already existed within an individual prior to her contact with the culture. It is this "thing" within the individual that is targeted for correction, effectively neutralizing any collective sense of responsibility for prevention of eating problems.

Since the late 1970s, there has been a rise of right-wing governments and economic policies in Britain, the United States, and Canada. Such policies favor individualizing social problems and cheaper methods of dealing with them. The massively widespread use of pharmaceuticals, like "antidepressants," for a wide range of "illnesses" and the preferential funding of studies that look for biological causes are consistent with socially and economically conservative government. In this context, with regard to eating disorders, there is no apparent need to critically assess a pathogenic culture and less need to fund unwieldy and expensive prevention programs. The dream, no doubt, is to find pharmaceutical interventions.

There are ethical and practical concerns related to the few available ideas about how the genetic research will actually have an impact on prevention and treatment programs. Identifying the relevant genes will supposedly make possible early identification of those vulnerable to eating disorders. One researcher in the area of genes and eating disorders, Janet Treasure (2003), explains to the general public,

> [It may be] possible for people to adjust their environment so that unhelpful interactions between their genetic propensities and their ecological context are minimized, e.g., someone with high trait anxiety may choose to ensure that they have high levels of safety, a close support network, and low risk goals; others who are somewhat rigid will flourish best in an environment where the rules are predictable and unchanging. (p. 2)

So, one of the effects of the genetic endeavor may be the project of distinguishing people who are susceptible to developing eating disorders from those who are not, such that the former can be targeted for preventive treatment, whether that be pharmaceutical[6] or behavioral. An effect of this would be that girls (or boys) who are identified as carrying the susceptibility gene(s) could be seen as categorically different from those who are not. Girls (or boys) in this category could be treated differently from others in ways that could become discriminatory and disadvantageous.

Imagine explaining to a young woman in the "susceptible" or "vulnerable" category that unlike the other girls who are encouraged to try to "be the best they can be" and are told they can "be anything they want," she should choose low-risk goals and stay in environments that are predictable, "safe," and highly structured by rules. With Treasure's modest proposal in mind, it is interesting to return for a moment to the Fiji study. It seems that the young women of Fiji, whose eating-disordered attitudes have increased with exposure to Western culture, are simultaneously interested in a less highly structured "lifestyle" in which the young people are more "free" than in their traditional culture. Here are some things they and their parents have observed in relation to these issues:

> The rules that have been made by the village, they are not following it, [because] they are copying Western culture.

> They look good on the television, how they act and also how their body looks like when they . . . do some jobs, they are free to move around and do their jobs.

> I try to look at them change the way, my way, of dressing and also the ways of looking fit and look to lose weight.

> I like *Shortland Street* [an Australian drama] because of the many young adults involved with it. . . . I want to be like that, I want to imitate them—the way they live, the type of food they eat . . . it gives me ideas of how to solve problems when being in this world. (Becker et al., 2002, p. 513)

Treasure does not give us any suggestions for how we might persuade young women in Fiji or in North America to be happy with "lifestyles," identity projects, and body shapes that are unlike the ones that they are culturally induced to pursue. Clearly, the cultural forces that seem so neatly sidestepped by focusing on genes cannot be sidestepped after all.

It is not out of the realm of possibility to think that insurance companies might refuse to pay for treatment for, say, a young woman of 15 who was identified at the age of 6 as susceptible to developing an eating disorder because of her genetic makeup, but refused to take any of the preventive measures approved by and paid for by the insurance company. What supports and therapies will then be available to her?

It is obvious that much of the excitement about discovering genes for susceptibility to eating disorders is motivated by economics, just as it is in numerous other areas of medicine and psychiatry. The search for genes is being funded at unprecedented levels,[7] and scientists are increasingly affiliated with for-profit biotechnology firms rather than research institutes belonging to universities. The paradigm of genes as units that can cause characteristics and illnesses seems to thrive despite all the evidence there is to support the view that emphasizes the partnership of environment, both at micro- and macrolevels, in all developmental processes. As long as the role of genes is overstated, the tendency will be to act in terms of the genetics, because a "genetic approach" appears more likely to be effective, less expensive, apolitical, and objectively based.

Implications for Therapeutic Practice

A risk that comes with bringing genetic factors into therapeutic conversations about anorexia and bulimia parallels the risk of bringing them into theoretical discussions. Clients and therapists may allow the idea of genetic factors to replace or dominate other understandings about eating problems. Imagine scenarios that are something like the following.

The DeSousa-Jameson Family

Elena[8] is a 13-year-old girl who is an inpatient in a children's eating-disorders unit for the second time. Her parents Jack and Catalina are very frightened about her low weight and the fact that it does not seem to be getting any easier for her to eat. They have heard that of all psychiatric disorders, eating disorders have the highest mortality rate and are very difficult to treat. Elena recently read an Internet article in which experts reported that anorexia almost certainly has a genetic cause. She shows the article to her parents and says they should listen to her when she says the hospital treatment is not helping and is a waste of time. She sounds urgent when she tells them to take her home and promises that if they do, she will eat more than she did before, but she also says that if they make her stay in the hospital, she will make sure to lose any weight that she gains as soon as she does get home. Catalina, looking panicky, tells Elena that she may be able to come home very soon, and Jack mentions that a sister of his had an eating disorder. Catalina and Jack are wondering if the reason that Elena is not getting better may be that her illness is genetically based. They ask if there might be a genetic cure on the horizon.

Elena is terrified of eating and of gaining weight. Catalina and Jack are frightened by Elena's behavior and by how scared she is to eat, but they are also angry that she is making threats to lose weight if they don't do as she asks. They want to believe Elena's promise that she will eat more if they take her home, and they are seduced by the idea that taking her home could make all the uncharacteristic conflict among them disappear. This powerful mix of emotions and ideas creates a cloud of confusion in Catalina and Jack.

The genetic story is a welcome distraction from the emotion, conflict, and confusion that is characteristic in families trying to resist anorexia or bulimia. It dissolves confusions by appearing to reduce a multilayered, complex problem to a one-dimensional, material one, and it generates hope of a solution that would bypass interpersonal conflict. This hope is misplaced, since it rests on a misunderstanding of the nature of genes and of the possible role genetics plays in the development of anorexia and bulimia.

The risk is that clients and practitioners will be "blinded by science," that is, that the genetic explanation will first of all be misunderstood in terms of "classic" genetics and/or that it will be taken as "the real story," which will eclipse other important story lines, reducing the struggles a girl experiences to the material/genetic and implying that salvation resides in a manipulation of her material being. The latter, of course, echoes a practice that she is already convinced is necessary.

Whether or not there is a meaningful way in which we can say that certain genes represent risk factors for anorexia or bulimia, Catalina and Jack will need to find a way to help Elena face her fear of eating and gaining weight, because it is not a sustainable practice to avoid eating. Fear of eating is not like some fears, for example, the fear of spiders or of flying, because while a person could live a long and healthy life without ever making friends with spiders or flying in an airplane, it is not possible to avoid food (and weight gain) indefinitely. Fear of eating is also unlike the fear of, for example, staying in a burning building, where the fear of fire drives us to escape, ensuring our survival. Escaping eating rather ensures our demise. So, Elena's parents are in the difficult position of asking her to do something she is genuinely terrified of doing but which they know is necessary. This will involve discussing ways that they can support Elena in having regular adequate meals, at the same time understanding and caring that this is intensely difficult for her. She may be able to manage increased eating and weight only in stages, and this may take a long time. It could also include Jack and Catalina insisting on a longer hospital stay. Avoiding these aspects of supporting Elena colludes with her avoidance of food and weight gain.

Equally important is having Elena, Catalina, and Jack explore the ways in which resisting eating is important to Elena and the ways in which Catalina and Jack may be inadvertently supporting anorexia. This could involve many avenues of exploration. In what ways have Catalina and Jack themselves been affected by our culture's methods of generating body insecurity? Are there ways that they resist these cultural pressures? How might their body regulation and eating practices fuel or help resist anorexia? Can they find their way to helping Elena feel secure in a body of greater substance? Is Elena taking very little food as a way of punishing herself? If so, what aspects of her environment contribute to her sense that she should be punished?

Many other areas could be explored with Elena. Is Elena spending more and more time on her schoolwork, but not feeling satisfied with the results of her efforts? Might this be happening in the context of increased expectations from the teachers in her high school? Is talk of the difficulties of getting into a good university charging up her worries? Are worry and self-doubt making trouble for Elena as she sets about making new friends in her high school? Is Elena finding that she is not ready to bring her developing sexuality into relationships in the ways that her peers do seem ready for? Or is Elena ready, but finds herself stymied by her parents' worries? Is not eating or not gaining weight a way of resisting increased expectations or registering a vote against these expectations altogether? Would dominant stories about her be fractured if she needed help, wanted to shirk responsibility sometimes, or didn't feel confident? Would it provide an alternate identity in the face of her rejecting the ones that are offered at school or within her family? Would Elena prefer delaying declaring an identity, or does she need support in articulating or presenting one? The challenging and multifaceted work of developing an identity in a culture that generates personal and body insecurity while simultaneously demanding confidence (even of adolescents) cannot be avoided by reducing some adolescents' struggles in this area to stories about genes.

Paula

Paula[9] is a 30-year-old woman who has a history of many hospitalizations related to anorexia, some following near-death emergencies. She endured forced treatments several times, and medical complications have resulted in sustained damage to some of her internal organs. Nevertheless, she has now been doing well for over 2 years, is in a relationship, and has become pregnant by choice. An ultrasound reveals that the fetus is female. Paula recently read an article stating that the genes related to serotonin regulation and the genetic underpinnings of personality traits like perfectionism and novelty seeking are considered to be susceptibility genes for eating disorders. She is terrified at the thought that her daughter could go through experiences similar to those she has had. As she is in her first trimester, she is considering an abortion.

Paula has begun to think of her personality and brain chemistry as immutably flawed or defective and that these defective aspects of herself could be passed on to her daughter. The genetic story line thus encourages Paula to compare her personal characteristics with those of people who have not struggled with serious eating problems. She may be thinking that it would be better to have a baby with characteristics different from her own or that she is already a bad mother. In this way, the genetic story about eating disorders creates the idea that some psychological and chemical characteristics are defective, mirroring the culture-based judgment that certain body types are defective. Rather than encouraging an appreciation of natural and cultural variation that could encourage resistance to pressures to regulate our bodies, the gene story supports the rigid kind of thinking that gives eating problems an easier entry into our lives. In a narrative therapeutic conversation, Paula could be supported to deconstruct the gene story line so that the idea of genes as determining characteristics would be unraveled. She could also be encouraged to articulate the ways in which her personal characteristics have helped her ultimately to resist anorexia, thus challenging the idea of these characteristics as flaws or defects. Finally, Paula could be supported to recognize that she has insider knowledge of anorexia and that this knowledge provides a basis for strategies that would help protect her daughter in the future, giving her daughter an advantage rather than a liability.

The best impact that increasing knowledge about genetics could have for those with eating problems is to improve the specificity of medications that can play a role in supporting recovery from eating problems like anorexia. Currently SSRIs (selective serotonin reuptake inhibitors; predominantly fluoxetine [Prozac] for adolescents) and atypical antipsychotics (usually respiridone or olanzapine) are used to help ameliorate depression, anxiousness, and/or obsessiveness to a sufficient extent that the person is able to make use of other therapeutic supports. No research supports the view that any of these medications is sufficient when used without other therapies, nor does any research support the view that medications are always necessary; but research and clinical practice do support the view that medications can be helpful adjuncts to other therapies in many cases. Currently, there are undesirable effects (called "side effects") accompanying all of these medications, and sometimes a considerable amount of time-consuming and unpleasant experimentation is required before a useful medication is found for a particular individual. If genetic research were to make it possible to refine our understanding of, for example, the biological contributions to depression and to develop medications that target different variations of these, it is possible that more effective medications with fewer unwanted effects could be produced. These could play an important though time-limited role in the process of helping women to resist troubled eating.

A narrative approach is open and curious about the multiple experiences and meanings in women's lives that may support and assist in the resistance of troubled eating. It allows for many possibilities, and many forms of expression by individuals in their cultural contexts, which fits with the empirical fact that most women and girls are preoccupied with weight and that most associate being thin with status, self-esteem, power, and a sense of control. It also fits with findings that an individual woman might be dieting and preoccupied with weight at one time, anorexic at another, bulimic later on, and then, later yet, not particularly preoccupied with weight nor restrictive of food intake. Most important, those working from the narrative perspective are committed to respecting the agency of the client and working collaboratively to understand problems and develop solutions.

Conclusion

In the gene story, a pathogenic culture is recast as neutral or made invisible, and the nature-given, gender-irrelevant genes of a small percentage of the population are seen as causing vulnerability to a highly gendered disorder. This makes individuals responsible for fixing their culturally induced problems and leaves the economic and political interests that benefit from promoting a range of perfectionistic and obsessional body-regulating practices free to continue to do so without criticism. As these practices become more normative,[10] it becomes more difficult for people to question their effects and to see their costs. Manufacturing medical model, privatized accounts of eating disorders masquerading as objective scientific discovery depoliticizes and decontextualizes their development in cultures and in individuals.

The larger modernist quest to make the gene story part of mastery over our biology promises control over disease, aging, disability, and practically anything else we don't like, including what we call mental illnesses. It seduces us into the project of creating the perfect human being, who is seemingly very beautiful and never dies. This project may be conveyed as one that will benefit all of us, but it has historically required that some be sacrificed for the benefit of others, and access to its purported benefits has always been political. Even if genes are included in our understanding of eating disorders in a way that makes good theoretical sense, it will also be necessary to use this understanding in a way that makes good political and ethical sense.

Notes

1. A *genome* is an organism's complete set of DNA. When the Human Genome Project, undertaken by the U.S. Department of Energy in the 1980s, succeeded in drafting the human genome, it meant that geneticists had identified the approximate number of genes in human DNA (at the time, it was thought to be about 30,000, but more recent estimates are closer to 25,000, a number shared with the roundworm). It also meant that the particular side-by-side arrangement of bases along the human DNA strand could be described or sequenced (U.S. Department of Energy Genome Programs: http://www.ornl.gov/hgmis, p. 1).

2. Personality "traits" like perfectionism are now being described as "phenotypes," with the obvious implication that there are matching genotypes.

3. According to the U.S. Department of Energy Web site on the Human Genome Project, "The genetic key to human complexity lies . . . in how gene parts are used to build different products [proteins] through alternative splicing" and in the "thousands of chemical modifications made to proteins and the repertoire of regulatory mechanisms controlling these processes" (http://www.ornl.gov/hgmis/publicat/primer/, p. 3).

4. Although boys and men are increasingly subject to similar prescriptions to have a body that is "worked on" or otherwise made to fit an image that increases their social value, resulting in their being increasingly concerned with body image (Pope, Phillips, & Olivardia, 2000, p. 27), the current requirement for males in terms of body shape is to increase muscularity, which is consistent with the direction their bodies developmentally tend to take. This explains why the increase in concern with body image among males has not resulted in a corresponding increase in eating disorders among them.

5. The only exception I know of is Howard Steiger's (2004) article "Eating Disorders and the Serotonin Connection: State, Trait, and Developmental Effects" in the *Journal of Psychiatric Neuroscience,* in which he comments in passing that dieting is associated with more pronounced alterations in postsynaptic 5HT (serotonin) activity in women than in men (p. 23).

6. An entire issue of the journal *Current Drug Targets* was devoted to the subject of eating disorders in 2003 (see Tozzi & Bulik, 2003).

7. The value of the current National Institute of Mental Health (NIMH) grant funding the search for genes related to eating disorders is $10 million.

8. The "DeSousa-Jamesons" are a fictional family.

9. J. Hubert Lacey raised an example like this during a panel discussion on genetics and eating disorders at the 2005 International Eating Disorders Conference in Montreal, Canada.

10. In the October 2004 issue of *Harper's* magazine, it was reported that the town council of a city in northern Tuscany voted unanimously on a resolution by Mayor Sandro Donati to subsidize council members' expenses for cosmetic surgery, because the resulting improvement in council members' appearances and self-esteem could cash out in terms of "positive economic repercussions for the community" (Donati, 2004, p. 16).

References

Becker, A., Burwell, R. A., Gilman, S. E., Herzog, D. B., & Hamburg, P. (2002). Eating behaviors and attitudes following prolonged exposure to television among ethnic Fijian adolescent girls. *British Journal of Psychiatry, 180*, 509–514.

Bergen, A., & Kaplan, A. (2004, November). *Candidate gene analysis in anorexia nervosa.* Research seminar for staff of eating disorder programs at Toronto hospitals, Toronto General Hospital, Canada.

Bordo, S. R. (1993). Whose body is this? Feminism, medicine, and the conceptualization of eating disorders. In *Unbearable weight: Feminism, Western culture, and the body* (pp. 45–69). Berkeley: University of California Press.

Brown, C. (1993). The continuum: Anorexia, bulimia, and weight preoccupation. In C. Brown & K. Jasper (Eds.), *Consuming passions: Feminist approaches to weight preoccupation and eating disorders* (pp. 53–68). Toronto, Canada: Second Story Press.

Bulik, C. M. (2004). Genetic and biological risk factors. In J. K. Thompson (Ed.), *The handbook of eating disorders and obesity* (pp. 3–16). Hoboken, NJ: Wiley.

Bulik, C. M., Jordan, W. R., & Jordan, J. H. (2004, March 17–20). *The gene-environment nexus in eating disorders.* Abstract for Symposium on Diet and Eating Disorders at the International Association for Women's Health (IAWMH): Second World Congress on Women's Health, Washington, D.C.

Bulik, C. M., Sullivan, P. F., Wade, T. D., & Kendler, K. (2000). Twin studies of eating disorders: A review. *International Journal of Eating Disorders, 27*, 1–20.

DeAngelis, T. (2002). A genetic link to anorexia. *Monitor on Psychology, 33*(3). Retrieved March 6, 2006, from http://www.apa.org/monitor/mar02/genetic.html

Donati, S. (2004, October 16). The body politic (M. Krieger, Trans.). *Harper's Magazine*, p. 16.

Grice, D. E., Halmi, K. A., Fichter, M. M., Strober, M., Woodside, B., Treasure, J. T., Kaplan, A. S., et al. (2002). Evidence for a susceptibility gene for anorexia nervosa on chromosome 1. *American Journal of Human Genetics, 70*, 787–792.

Hargreaves, D., & Tiggemann, M. (2003). Longer-term implications of responsiveness to "thin-ideal" television: Support for a cumulative hypothesis of body image disturbance? *European Eating Disorders Review, 11*(6), 465–477.

Jasper, K. (2003). Reflections on genes and eating disorders. *National Eating Disorder Information Centre Bulletin, 18*(3), 1–4.

Joseph, J. (2004). *The gene illusion: Genetic research in psychiatry and psychology under the microscope.* New York: Algora.

Kaplan, A. S., & Woodside, D. B. (2003). Genes and eating disorders: Unraveling the mystery. *National Eating Disorder Information Centre Bulletin, 18*(2), 1–4.

Kaye, W. H., Devlin, B., Barbarich, N., Bulik, C. M., Thornton, L., Bacanu, S-A., Fichter, M. M., et al. (2004). Genetic analysis of bulimia nervosa: Methods and sample description. *International Journal of Eating Disorders, 35*, 556–570.

Klump, K. L., Wonderlich, S., Lehoux, P., Lilenfeld, L., & Bulik, C. (2002). Does environment matter? A review of nonshared environment and eating disorders. *International Journal of Eating Disorders, 31*, 118–135.

Lilenfeld, L. R., Kaye, W. H., Greeno, C. G., Merikangas, K. R., Plotnicov, K., Pollice, C., Rao, R., et al. (1998). A controlled family study of anorexia nervosa and bulimia nervosa: Psychiatric disorders in first-degree relatives and effects of proband comorbidity. *Archives of General Psychiatry, 55*(7), 603–610.

MacInnis, B. (1993). Fat oppression. In C. Brown & K. Jasper (Eds.), *Consuming passions: Feminist approaches to weight preoccupation and eating disorders* (pp. 69–79). Toronto, Canada: Second Story Press.

Maine, M. (2000). *Body wars: Making peace with women's bodies.* Carlsbad, CA: Gurze Books.

Moore, D. (2001). *The dependent gene.* New York: Henry Holt.

Pinhas, L., Toner, B., Ali, A., Garfinkel, P., & Stuckless, N. (1999). The effects of the ideal of female beauty on mood and body dissatisfaction. *International Journal of Eating Disorders, 25*(2), 223–226.

Pope, H. G., Phillips, K. A., & Olivardia, R. (2000). *The Adonis complex: The secret crisis of male body obsession.* New York: Free Press.

The Price Foundation Collaborative Group. (2001). Deriving behavioural phenotypes in an international, multi-centre study of eating disorders. *Psychological Medicine, 31,* 635–645.

Smolak, L., & Levine, M. (1996). Adolescent transitions and the development of eating problems. In L. Smolak, M. Levine, & R. Striegel-Moore (Eds.), *The developmental psychopathology of eating disorders* (pp. 216–217). Mahwah, NJ: Erlbaum.

Steiger, H. (2004). Eating disorders and the serotonin connection: State, trait, and developmental effects. *Journal of Psychiatric Neuroscience, 29*(1), 20–29.

Thompson, J. K. (2004). (Ed.). *The handbook of eating disorders and obesity* (pp. 3–16). Hoboken, NJ: Wiley.

Thompson, J. K., Heinberg, L. J., Altabe, M., & Tantleff-Dunn, S. (1999). *Exacting beauty: Theory, assessment, and treatment of body image disturbance.* Washington, DC: American Psychological Association.

Tozzi, F., & Bulik, C. (2003). Candidate genes in eating disorders. *Current Drug Targets—CNS & Neurological Disorders, 2*(1), 31–39.

Treasure, J. (2003). *Genetic research in eating disorders: What YOU need to know.* King's College London, Institute of Psychiatry Web site. Retrieved March 6, 2006, from http://www.iop.kcl.ac.uk/iop/Departments/PsychMed/EDU/Genetics.shtml

Turner, S. L., Hamilton, H., Jacobs, M., Angood, L. M., & Dwyer, D. H. (1997). The influence of fashion magazines on the body image satisfaction of college women: An exploratory analysis. *Adolescence, 32,* 603–610.

Vaughan, K. K., & Fouts, G. T. (2003). Changes in television and magazine exposure and eating disorder symptomatology. *Sex Roles, 49*(7/8), 313–320.

4

A Poetics of Resistance

Compassionate Practice in Substance Misuse Therapy

Colin James Sanders

Dedicated in loving memory to my brother, Kieran Gerard Sanders,
1959–2004

I n being invited to write this chapter, I have appreciated the opportunity
to gather together for the first time some of the philosophical, theological, and theoretical perspectives informing my therapeutic practice, particularly over the years 1989 to 2003, when I worked as the clinical director at Peak House, Vancouver, Canada.[1] Apart from several early formative influences and experiences, my work has been inspired by the ways in which persons suffering from substance misuse have variously interpreted their own experiences, including ways in which they have resisted labels, diagnoses, and the discursive power of prescriptive and normative identities. Foucault (2003) referred to this sort of resistance as representative of "knowledges from below . . . unqualified or even disqualified knowledges" (p. 7). It is this sort of knowing that is evocative of a poetics of resistance.

Challenging dominant discourses and the practices accruing from such discourses is relatively easy to do; replacing such discourses and practices with viable alternatives is something else entirely. In this chapter, I review the ongoing legacy of the disease model metaphor, as reflected in biochemical explanations for substance misuse practices. I also trace the varied tapestry of influences and inspirations that have culminated, over many years of practice, in the importance of a narrative imagination in evoking a poetics of resistance (Sanders, 1999). As well, I will discuss the evolution over almost 15 years of my work at Peak House, Vancouver, Canada, as this work relates to creating choice, fostering agency, and directly applying some postmodern ideas within a therapeutic practice directed toward expanding possibilities for those struggling with substance misuse.

Disease Metaphors, Biochemistry, and Delimiting Personal Agency

As a matter of fact, nothing has cured the human race, and nothing is about to. Mental ills don't work that way; they are not universal, they are local. . . . So when we are studying a particular illness, we are also studying the conditions that shape and define the illness, and the sociopolitical impact of those who are responsible for healing it.

—Cushman, 1995 (p. 7)

Only recently has there been a veering away from the predominant way of conceptualizing the etiology and treatment of substance misuse deriving from the discourse of a disease model metaphor. Despite shifting perspectives in Western European countries and in Canada, this discourse remains powerful in the United States (Fingarette, 1988; Levine, 1978, 1984; Musto, 1973). The tendency to locate the etiology of the addiction experience within a person's biochemistry is the latest, albeit most sophisticated, variant of the history of the disease metaphor.

Szasz (1992) suggests the "medical tutelage" (p. 303) of citizens of the United States was initiated over a century ago. Earlier than that, around 1784, the father of American psychiatry, Benjamin Rush (Breggin, 1991), initially proposed that habitual drunkenness represents a disease (Peele, 1989). Alexander (1990) further suggests Rush was "arguably the father of American temperance doctrine" (pp. 5–6), and the disease metaphor, in fact, became a basic tenet of the largely Protestant, predominantly female Temperance movement seeking to eradicate male drunkenness and shut down the sites in which this behavior largely occurred, chiefly saloons. (For a Canadian perspective on this movement, see Gray, 1995, and especially Heron, 2003.)

I suggest the research of physiologist Elvin Jellinek (1960) represents one of the earliest attempts at medicalizing the etiology of alcoholism. At the same time, Jellinek's attempt to medicalize problem drinking represented an advance over the early Temperance and Prohibition beliefs, which were largely moralistic, judgmental, and punitive.

Further consolidating its discursiveness regarding evolving treatment practices, Jellinek's disease model metaphor became successfully woven into the ideology of Alcoholics Anonymous (AA), and "by the 1970s, AA had become the model for all treatment groups and a linchpin in the provision of services for drinking problems in the United States" (Peele, 1989, p. 24). Yet the peculiar preoccupation with "medicalising the ordinary problems of everyday life" (Kelleher, Gabe, & Williams, 1994, p. xx) had commenced long ago, as myriad human foibles and idiosyncrasies became designated as diseases. Throughout the 1980s, the treatment industry became more psychopharmaceutical in its focus, and "with the advent of the *DSM-III* and the torrent of new medications pouring out of the pharmaceutical pipeline, psychiatry grew ever more inclined to define emotional and mental problems as purely medical illnesses reflecting biochemical imbalances in the brain" (Wylie, 2004, p. 33). The "diseasing of America" (Peele, 1989) was well under way. This tendency to mystify the sources and origins of substance misuse, particularly regarding sociocultural influences, and other dilemmas of the mind carries on. Recently, for example, I became aware of yet another disease-on-the-rise: "status anxiety."

Indeed, from the creation of the *Diagnostic and Statistical Manual of Mental Disorders (DSM)*, in 1952, "the official listing of all mental diseases recognized by the American Psychiatric Association (APA)" (Spiegel, 2005, p. 56), touted by some as an "scientific instrument of enormous power" (p. 56), a plethora of so-called disorders have been invented, named, and localized within the behaviors of individuals, with little attention being given to the sociocultural and socioeconomic contexts within which human beings experience difficulties and struggle. In fact, perhaps we have not really moved too far from Benjamin Rush's idea that "lying, murder, and political dissent were diseases" (Peele, 1989, p. 5), with no appreciation given to the context(s) in which such actions occur.

As a further example of the elusive hunt for certainty within biochemical explanation for social problems, Wittenauer (2004) reports, "Scientists say they have identified a gene that appears to be linked to both alcoholism and depression, a finding that may one day help identify those at higher risk for the *diseases* and guide new treatments for them" (p. 19, emphasis added). While scientists vying for research grants have been expressing such optimism for decades, so-called proof eludes description, and I am reminded of Bateson's (1979) opinion that "science probes; it does not prove" (p. 30).

While I would not be adverse to the possible discovery of such a gene, in the meantime, as a therapist, I will continue to listen to and collaborate with suffering others intent upon changing the material, psychological, and sacred conditions of their lives. As the late Jesuit activist and social psychologist Martin-Baro (1994) has pointed out,

> Even the *DSM-III* . . . has recognized, all behavior involves a social dimension . . . [and] the work of psychology cannot limit itself to the abstract plane of the individual but must also confront social factors, which form the arena for the expression of all human individuality. (p. 41)

When considering substance misuse practices and beneficial, effective interventions, reductionist biochemical hypotheses pay little regard to, and remain discouraging of, human agency and intention. R. D. Laing, in conversation with Evans, points out, "We know—at least we ought to know—that there is nothing more sensitive to social, psychological, communicational, and environmental influences than the chemistry of the body. The body chemistry is a contingency of unremitting resonance with its social environment" (Evans, 1976, p. 20). In the same conversation, Laing points out, "The original Hippocratic practitioner, in the tradition of Western medicine, was expected to take into account the politics when he visited a place to treat a person" (Evans, 1976, p. 21). A biochemical explanation for problem drinking ignores the context of a person's social matrix. Yet considering the sociocultural, socioeconomic, and sociopolitical contexts of a person's life remains imperative to an understanding of how best to collaborate with the individual and take action toward an evolving poetics of resistance. Bateson (1979) distinguishes between genetic determinism and the creative ability of human beings to comprehend and negotiate social context, noting, "Genes may perhaps influence an animal by determining how it will perceive and classify the contexts of learning. But mammals, at least, are capable also of *learning about context*" (p. 115, emphasis in original).

The discouraging practice in contemporary times of designating biochemical causes for the vagaries of human behavior and decision making remains part of the legacy of the disease metaphor. I was heartened recently to read an article by a physician challenging the reigning biochemical discourse as representing a "dangerous oversimplification" (Mate, 2004, p. 7). Mate writes, while "the dominant medical tendency in the past few decades has been to reduce illness to chemical imbalances in the brain . . . our interactions with the environment do much to determine our brain's chemistry" (p. 7). Echoing Laing above, Mate concludes, "This is especially true of the developing brains of young children and adolescents whose moods and mood disorders often reflect stresses in their immediate environment" (p. 7).

I am not antimedication; I am pro-choice and pro–informed consent where psychiatric medication is concerned. I accept and recognize there are times and circumstances within people's lives when they may wish to utilize pharmacology to manage disturbing and discomforting thoughts or difficult, debilitating circumstances. At the same time, I would argue that for a person experiencing suffering, making such a decision is representative of exercising personal agency. A part of the person's own poetics of resistance in making such a decision is that individual's intention to begin to demystify the context of his or her suffering and pain and to stand outside of discourses suggestive of stigma and blame as attached to psychological pain.

When the etiology of substance misuse is attached to biochemical explanation, opportunities for personal agency become diminished. The prospects for a hopeful outcome from one's actions appear restrained. Human beings, while biological beings, are also cogitating and contemplative beings, capable of intentionally reflecting upon the dialectic between self, other, and environment, and acting with purpose. Human beings are beings for whom it is possible not only to think and reflect consciously upon the creation and composition of identity but, moreover, to transform identity in purposeful and intentional ways, exercising personal agency. As the feminist adage goes, biology is not destiny. I have to agree with Simblett (1997), a psychiatrist, who writes, "People are made up of biochemicals as well as hopes, wishes, thoughts, feelings and spirits" (p. 146); and this consideration invites recognition for both compassionate social policies and therapeutic practices.

Harm Reduction as Compassionate Social Policy

I remain hopeful there will be a continuing acceptance and advocacy for practices related to reducing the harm associated with chronic and acute substance misuse. Harm reduction policy is predicated upon a nonmoralistic, nonjudgmental, compassionate, and pragmatic philosophy (Marlatt, 1998). This approach rejects the all-or-nothing "Just say no" discourse long dominant within addiction interventions, acknowledging that social policy initiatives are necessary in order to approach substance misuse as a social, not an individual, problem. By insisting it remains the person's individual responsibility to remove themselves from the predicament of substance misuse, the "Just say no" discourse further obfuscates the social, sociocultural, and familial experiences that contribute to dilemmas involving substance misuse. To a considerable degree, the ideology associated with the disease metaphor and the medicalization of substance misuse likewise succeed in alienating the subject from the social context contributing to these dilemmas.

Moving away from the belief that "alcoholism" is a primary disease requiring abstinence, harm reduction strategies for alcohol use dilemmas typically involve a choice of abstinence or controlled-use strategies. At Peak House, when we started to incorporate a harm reduction ideology, we were often challenged and, indeed, confronted on this paradigm shift by prospective consumers of our service, as well as by prospective referral sources and agencies. Our use of the words *substance misuse,* not *substance abuse,* occasioned numerous challenges prior to the more or less general acceptance by others working within the field that *use, misuse,* and *abuse* could entail significant differences, both in practice and in regard to appropriate treatment matching.

While Canada and several European countries promote compassionate social policy, situating substance misuse and the addiction experience within sociopolitical contexts, the disease metaphor remains the dominant discourse in the United States. Yet in Canada, despite a federal harm reduction position, many provincial and municipal programs do not adopt a harm reduction approach, and those that do often need to fine-tune the provision of these services to make choices around controlled use versus abstinence more acceptable. Many European countries have established needle exchange programs within prisons (e.g., Switzerland, Germany, Spain, Moldova, Kyrgyzstan, and Belarus). As well, in a controversial decision, Scotland recently decided to offer heroin injection kits to prisoners on a "no-questions-asked" basis, noting that 80% of convicted persons entering Scottish prisons use drugs, with 40% using heroin (Foster, 2004).

In the city of Vancouver, British Columbia, there is a significant history of employing practices promoting harm reduction and a recognition of substance misuse as a social, and sometimes political, dilemma. For example, Vancouver had the first needle exchange program in North America (created by John Turvey and others at the Downtown Eastside Youth Activities Society [DEYAS] program), and needle exchange programs now exist throughout the province of British Columbia. Most recently, the Vancouver City Council voted, albeit it unsuccessfully, to decriminalize all street drugs. Vancouver also possesses a long history of methadone maintenance clinics, acceptance for medicinal use of marijuana, and related initiatives; it has North America's first safe injection site for cocaine use, supported and financed by the municipal, provincial, and federal governments; and, as of January 2005, it has a community-based research program for heroin use, the North American Opiate Medication Initiative (NAOMI) project, on the city's downtown eastside. I am further encouraged by the increasing movement toward integrating psychotherapy, psychoeducation, and pharmacology within mental health, particularly with those suffering from mental illness and substance use.

Along with the implications of harm reduction for social policy, it is also worth noting the implications for therapeutic conversations with those misusing drugs and alcohol. The former predominant treatment strategies and practices are being increasingly challenged by an appeal to modernist science research into effective interventions in facilitating change (see Hubble, Duncan, & Miller, 1999). Lebow (2004) highlights some of the outcome findings deriving from two extensive research reports regarding the treatment for adults misusing substances. Among the findings highlighted, Lebow notes that the following were challenging and dissolving of the truth claims of disease metaphor practitioners and social policy:

> Therapy relationship factors are crucial in treating substance misuse. . . . Contrary to stereotypes, high levels of confrontation seldom result in better treatment outcomes. . . . Therapists with a personal history of overcoming substance abuse are no more effective than those without such a history. . . . No one substance abuse treatment is more successful than others. (p. 92)

Rather than challenging and confronting people to change, as an advocate for harm reduction, I think those who use alcohol or other drugs in an effort to attempt to manage pain and suffering often realize the benefits of moving beyond such practices and making changes in their lives when access to necessary resources is available or they have experiences leading to changes in their intentions.

In addition, many practitioners, not to mention the public, pass over or do not acknowledge the social knowledge and hard-won wisdom of experience that those struggling with substance misuse dilemmas experience. As noted by Robertson and Culhane (2005), this is especially so regarding women. These authors note that on the downtown eastside of Vancouver,

> Street life has its own dynamic history, its own set of rules, and social knowledge, most of which celebrate survival. . . . The women's daily routines include negotiations around access to shelter, clothing, telephones, laundry facilities, showers, and nutritious meals. Valued expertise includes the ability to perform effective cardio-pulmonary resuscitation, to manage relationships in the drug trafficking hierarchy, and to negotiate dangerous situations in the street-level sex trade. For the narrators in this book who are drug users, social knowledge extends to evaluations of drug purity and the risks inherent in particular practices relating to use. (p. 12)

The above social knowledge is indicative of the disqualified knowledges that are rendered invisible by labeling a person simply as a *junkie, drug addict,* or, for that matter, a *borderline person* or a *depressed person.*

The fascination with technique and strategy needs to continue to dissolve, and practitioners need to listen more to what clients are suggesting works best for them. As Lomas (1999) writes, and I agree,

Many family therapists are now recognizing the limitations of technique and developing an approach which is more obviously based on attitudes that are part of everyday living. My own experience of gifted family therapists leaves me with the impression that they rely on a substantial amount of common sense and ordinary wisdom. (p. 71)

Influences and Inspirations

R. D. Laing influenced my work at Peak House significantly. Laing (1967) introduced innovative and radical experiences in "re-visioning" psychiatric practice. Laing's radical thinking was exemplified in the experiment in anti-institutional, communal living established for those suffering from mental illness at London's Kingsley Hall. This experiment internationally influenced the ways of working within mental health homes and programs. Laing helped people begin to comprehend the struggles of, and collaborate with, those suffering from problems of the mind (see Thompson, 2000) in nonpathologizing ways. Among others, Laing's practices were pioneered in the Unites States by Loren Mosher (see Mosher & Burti, 1989), whose work also became decisive in what I was doing with therapeutic practices at Peak House.

Along with Laing and Mosher's work, I was significantly influenced by White and Epston's (1990) narrative, re-authoring therapy perspective. White and Epston folded together philosophy and anthropology, creating therapeutic applications of the ideas of Jacques Derrida, Michel Foucault, Rom Harré (1983; Harré & Gillet, 1994), Victor Turner (1969, 1974), and others. Inspired by their work, I "re-visioned" the interventions offered at Peak House as ones in which young persons, families, and the community of others with whom they share a sense of belonging may be invited to attend within a conversational domain, re-authoring difficult and demeaning experiences in preferred ways, re-visioning what may lie upon the horizon. Within a brief period of time, I initiated a shift away from practices of confrontation, discourses of "denial," a disciplinary structure of "level systems," and diagnosing any sort of substance use in adolescents as "chemical dependency" (Holcomb, 1994; see Sanders, 1997, 1998). No longer did we sit in "chemical dependency groups"— we sat in "re-authoring groups"; no longer did young persons "graduate" from Peak House—they "commenced" in ceremonies marking entrance back into the world beyond the liminal space of Peak House. My therapeutic practice at this point (1992) became rigorously intent upon facilitating a shift from deficit identity ("alcoholic," "addict") toward re-authored identities (Sanders, 1997; Saville, 1998) and nonregulative (Kaye, 1999), nonpathologizing agency practices evocative of the "narrative mind" (see Thomson, 1994).

Considering a significant population of young people entering Peak House were from First Nations cultures, we became challenged (largely as persons from the dominant culture) to discover ways to collaborate that were culturally accountable. We were guided in this challenge by the work of Charles Waldegrave and Kiwi Tamasese (1993) and others working at "The Family Centre" in New Zealand. We also began to examine our hiring practices, bringing in more persons from other cultures, exploring the utility of cultural consultants, sweat lodge ceremony and ritual, and so on. As well, when I was invited to present the work we were doing, I invited the resident experts of Peak House to copresent, compensating them for sharing their experiences, wisdom, and knowledge.

I began considering our work as a form of bearing witness to the suffering and pain of others. I thought of it as a theological experience within the family therapy process, "bearing witness to the lived experience of the dispossessed and the constraints of statutory mandates" (Kearney, Byrne, & McCarthy, 1989, p. 17). This awareness opened a space for adventuring into exciting, novel, witnessing practices at Peak House, especially the cultural witnessing practices initiated by Vikki Reynolds (Dennstedt & Grieves, 2004; Radke, Kitchen, & Reynolds, 2000; Reynolds, 2002; Sanders, 2000).

I continue to view my current therapeutic practice, and the practices at Peak House throughout my tenure there (1989–2003), as conceptualized within the domain of what Kearney et al. (1989) refer to as the "Fifth Province" metaphor. According to the history of the Fifth Province metaphor, McCarthy (2001) writes,

> The Fifth Province Approach takes its title from an ancient Celtic myth. According to this myth, a Druidic site existed at the center of Ireland where the still extant four provinces of the country met. It was believed that leaders and chieftains from the four provinces came to this site to settle conflicts through talking together. . . . *What appealed about this metaphor was that it referred to a domain where language and conversation was important in the negotiation of different viewpoints and realities. . . . The metaphor of the fifth province came to refer also to the possibility of holding together and juxtaposing multiple and often conflicting social realities. In this way it specified a domain of imagination, possibilities and ethics.* (pp. 258–259, emphasis added)

While postmodernist approaches in family therapy have been critiqued for their relativism (Held, 1995), I am not suggesting "anything goes." As an aside, I argue for a fractured foundationalism as a way to get past the limits of relativism, which postmodernism in its "pure form" would have a hard time escaping. In practice, this means I continue to draw on the emancipatory project of modernism and its commitment to being positioned. Byrne and McCarthy (1998) weave into the metaphor of the Fifth Province what Irish philosopher Richard Kearney (1996) refers to as an "ethics of the imagination"; they summarize Kearney's trinity of guiding principles in this way: "The first is the acceptance of the other. The second principle is the right of all to be heard and to have the testimony to their experiences witnessed. The final principle is the imagining of future possibilities" (Byrne & McCarthy, 1998, p. 389). Adherence to this ethic within practice allows me to not become captured by despair and to persevere in listening for threads of a hopeful narrative amid others' disenchantment.

Bearing Witness Within a Poetics of Resistance

According to the late philosopher Jacques Derrida (1995), "As soon as one utters the word 'drugs,' even before an 'addiction,' a prescriptive or normative 'diction' is already at work, performatively, whether one likes it or not" (p. 229). It is prescriptive and normative discourse, the addiction mythology (Sanders, 1994) that a poetics of resistance seeks to unravel and present as an alternative to a medicalized, disease-based perspective. A poetics of resistance becomes composed, formulated, and re-authored within the linguistic engagement occurring between therapists and others. A poetics of resistance, then, challenges the disease mythology, allowing for the creation of alternative stories and different understandings of the role played by substance use in contending with marginalization, suffering, and pain.

Accordingly, within a therapeutic context, a poetics of resistance may arise within therapeutic conversation as an antidote to the homogenizing effects of predominant medicopolitical disease model metaphors and wars against people masquerading as "wars against drugs."

A poetics of resistance will highlight actions and behavior promoting of personal agency, intention, and choice. A poetics of resistance highlights and encourages narratives other than those offered by normative descriptions, diagnoses, and labels, especially descriptions disconnected from sociopolitical, sociocultural contexts and pathologizing of the person. A poetics of resistance believes a person is always more than the sum of the diagnosis.

A poetics of resistance does not participate in the perpetuation of personal pathology and disease metaphor language. A poetics of resistance insists that ideological phrases such as "my addiction" can always be reconceptualized and renegotiated in terms of "the impact addiction has on my life is such that . . ." or "this relationship addiction has with me . . . " or "my response to the direction addiction wants for me is . . . " or "my resistance to the intentions of addiction within my life is such that . . . " and so on.

A poetics of resistance respectfully questions whether the confessional mode and public acknowledgment of defect is the most beneficial path toward rejection of the ways by which a person may choose to contend with suffering and the mediation of pain.

A poetics of resistance represents a counterstory to the story of hopelessness and self-doubt associated with the restraints of a genetic fundamentalism (Schwartz, 1997). Adhering to the idea that so-called genetic disposition toward particular behaviors is directing and ultimately shaping of one's life represents a limited worldview, a restraining perspective that needs to be respectfully questioned. From a sociobiological perspective, genetic fundamentalism represents a dangerous rational for all sorts of violent, destructive human behaviors. I believe that imagining a Fifth Province domain within therapeutic conversation allows for resistance to the primacy of genetic predisposition in the creation of an "addictive personality." This way of thinking needs to be resisted if space for personal agency and re-authoring possibilities is to emerge.

In the following, concluding section, I discuss some of the ways in which the influences and inspirations described above direct therapeutic conversations with suffering others.

Adam's Poetics of Resistance

I see this work as representative of a form of bearing witness to clients' "knowledges from below . . . unqualified or even disqualified knowledges" (Foucault, 2003, p. 7). Often, this form of witnessing entails unraveling the identity promoted by the problem discourse (for example, "I'm an addict," "I'm an alcoholic," "I'm depressed," "I'm bipolar," "I've got ADHD," etc.) and moving toward the composition of a refined, personable, accepting identity. This "other" identity forms a poetics of resistance to the debilitating, demoralizing, destructive identity of diminishing returns. To be sure, it is not always an easy, smooth task evoking alternative threads of identity and highlighting these threads with a person who has been suffering in the throes of an identity of diminishing returns. In practice, I diligently persevere, alongside the client, in offering up differing perspectives, thoughts, reflections, and possibilities—at the same time, checking with the person along the way, so as not to deter or disrespect his or her unique momentum and pace (see Bird, 2003, 2004).

Recently, I collaborated with a Caucasian man I will call "Adam," age 60. His father was second-generation Irish, his mother second-generation Scottish. Originally, his parents lived in Newfoundland, Canada, moving to

Edmonton, Canada, for employment with Adam and his older sister when Adam was an infant.

Adam initially consulted with me regarding his long-standing struggle with a devastating relationship with alcohol and other drugs, particularly heroin and cocaine. Adam described himself as a person who suffered significant violence and violation within the context of his life.

Adam's father died in an industrial accident when he was a child, and his mother was most often confined to bed, suffering from a debilitating, degenerative illness. Dislocated from his sister, Adam lived in a series of foster homes, where he was subjected to various forms of mistreatment, humiliation, and degradation, including sexual abuse perpetrated by the supposed caregivers.

Adam informed me he spent as much time away from these homes as possible, and, in the company of others, he began experimenting with various substances, including glue, gas, cigarettes, alcohol, marijuana, and methamphetamine. After several years of living in foster homes and running away from many, he lived in a residential institution. Adam claims this experience was a comfortable and encouraging one, and he stayed in this place until he was 17 years old, at which point he left Alberta, hitchhiking to Vancouver, Canada.

By his account, Adam endured a prolonged struggle with substance use over many years, exacerbated by experiences counselors and doctors told him represented "chronic depression." Adam now believes these experiences had more to do with how he came to accept being alone without being lonely and, more important, how he could move through being lonely without using drugs to contend. The so-called chronic-depression experience proved refractory to a variety of medications and other medical model interventions, including 23 experiences with electroconvulsive therapy (ECT). I asked Adam if, in his experience, these "treatments" had been beneficial. He responded, "Yeah, I forgot some things for a while, but then I started remembering them again (laughing)." Adam insists he is now capable of accepting the humiliating, exploitative violations that have occurred in his life without attempting to disappear or manage these memories with substances. He remarked, "I find it interesting, the more I tried *not to* accept suffering, the more I suffered!" Regarding the ECT, Adam now assures me that knowing himself in the ways he does now, he would never again acquiesce to such an invasive experiment.

Adam acknowledges he has accomplished significant changes in his day-to-day existence over the past year. He believes some of these changes have evolved from the decision he made to stay connected to his partner, Pam, of 1 year. Outside of two marriages, each lasting only months, maintaining this connection with Pam represents the longest period of time he has been in a companionship. Adam is clear this is a choice he now makes out of his desire to create a life with another human being rather than to continue to engage in the pseudo-relationship he experienced with drugs. Working diligently at maintaining this connection has proven beneficial, as Pam has been a witness to his victories over substance misuse and has been acknowledging of these struggles, encouraging the creative ways in which he now chooses to manage his life, especially through his painting and his musical poetics of resistance.

Adam informed me he not only was a painter but also played guitar, piano, and harmonica in his own blues band. We both laughed at the significance of this choice of career. However, on the intake form, under "Occupation," I noticed he had written "Clerk," and I asked him about this. He replied that no one ever took his musicianship seriously, and he had only recently accepted this passionate interest as a worthy occupation, an activity providing him with value and purpose. When he reflected upon this, he said that his guitar was the last thing he would ever have considered pawning in his days of destitution. Even at that juncture in his life, he considered his music as a form of grace.

Currently, at the time of this writing, Adam is designing a cover for a CD he is recording with his band. He and his band were playing at several clubs throughout the summer, rehearsing and refining original compositions, all composed by Adam.

I experienced delight and enchantment engaging with Adam in dialogue around what he believed constituted his own poetics of resistance, in response to the impact substance use and misuse exerted over his mind. He is extremely pleased regarding his choice not to drink alcohol and remains untroubled by his occasional use of marijuana. In no way does he consider marijuana as opening the door to other drug use, and he no longer considers himself "an addict." Adam recently curtailed his nicotine habit from two packs per day to 10 cigarettes per day, because smoking was creating obstacles for him when swimming. "Weird, isn't it!? Tobacco's the toughest drug to quit, tougher than smack [heroin]," he said.

Formerly, Adam was convinced alcohol, cocaine, and heroin were necessary for managing his lifestyle, particularly relations with others in the music industry. He mentioned, "I'm a different man in front of an audience." I asked him if he could imagine that audience staying with him, throughout his day-to-day activities. He thought he could experiment with this possibility, the notion of an appreciative, supportive, internalized audience.

Adam's existence is by no means perfectly comfortable. He accepts that while discomfort may enter into his experience, he can be accepting that the discomfort will also pass. For many years, Adam believed that the "addict" and "dually diagnosed" medicalized stories regarding his identity were constitutive of his life. Lately, he has started to be mindful of paying more attention to the threads of identity contradicting and showing the lie to the diseased, medicalized version of his life and identity. Adam no longer thinks a genetic disposition to debilitating, destructive practices is directing his life.

For a significant period of his life, Adam coexisted with difficulty in a negative relationship with his medicalized identity. On many occasions, he experienced doubt as to whether he could ever begin to unravel this deficit-laden way of experiencing his life. Adam had come to realize through his own hard work of resistance, and through collaboration with myself and others, that renegotiating this negative relationship was entirely possible.

I was careful to highlight with Adam some of the advances he himself had made prior to his conversations with me. I especially highlighted actions and decisions he had made that seemed indicative of determination, perseverance, courage, and hard work. In narrative therapy terms, I explained to Adam what re-authoring one's life entailed, and he intimated that he believed this was, in fact, what he had started to do. He then referred to me as "a specialist in hope," remarking he wished to stay in touch, checking in periodically, saying his re-authored considerations regarding who he was now would not be given up without resistance.

Conclusion

I have come to believe debilitating experiences such as substance misuse represents in part an attempt by people to remove themselves from subjective suffering and pain; however, and often unfortunately, such attempts often result in even more debilitating, despairing experiences. What commences as an attempt to experience more comfort and solace quickly escalates into some thing more horrific, or ultimately tragic; what begins as a journey to accept pain and manage pain can become deadening.

In this chapter, I have briefly outlined the history, legacy, and hegemony in the substance misuse field of the disease model metaphor. I have emphasized the inadequacy of the prevailing biochemical discourse in accounting for pathways both into and beyond substance misuse practices. In Canada and Europe, there are important examples of alternate social policies reflective and supportive of harm reduction practices. The alternative approaches are juxtaposed to the medicalized disease metaphor and blame-the-victim discourse dominant in the United States.

As a therapist, my hope is to be able to contribute toward a voluntary space within which stories of resistance may be fomented and cultivated, as described within my collaboration with Adam. This approach reflects and addresses some of the ethical considerations of my praxis, in my continuing effort to collaborate with suffering others struggling toward "the insurrection of subjugated knowledge" (Foucault, 2003, p. 7), as evidenced and documented by a person's own poetics of resistance.[2]

Notes

1. Peak House is a not-for-profit program of the Pacific Youth & Family Services Society, Vancouver, Canada. Codirectors Wendy Wittmack and Judy Connors may be reached at peakhouse@telus.net. My thanks to the many workers over many years who contributed to evolving emancipatory practices, and to the young persons and families who collaborated in this adventure.

2. Once again, I acknowledge my companion, Gail Marie Boivin; my children, Maya and Adrian; my eight siblings; and my mother, Noreen Farrell Sanders, for their love and encouragement in supporting my own poetics of resistance. As well, I invoke the memory of my father, "Rocky" Sanders, for turning me on to literature, philosophy, theology, and R. D. Laing.

References

Alexander, B. (1990). *Peaceful measures: Canada's way out of the "war on drugs."* Toronto, Canada: University of Toronto Press.

Bateson, G. (1979). *Mind and nature: A necessary unity.* New York: Dutton.

Bird, J. (2003). *The heart's narrative: Therapy and navigating life's contradictions.* Aukland, New Zealand: Edge Press.

Bird, J. (2004). *Talk that sings: Therapy in a new linguistic key.* Aukland, New Zealand: Edge Press.

Breggin, P. (1991). *Toxic psychiatry: Why therapy, empathy, and love must replace the drugs, electroshock, and biochemical theories of the "New Psychiatry."* New York: St. Martin's Press.

Byrne, N., & McCarthy, I. (1998). Marginal illuminations: A Fifth province approach to intercultural issues in an Irish context. In M. McGoldrick (Ed.), *Re-visioning family therapy: Race, culture, and gender in clinical practice* (pp. 387–403). New York: Guilford.

Cushman, P. (1995). *Constructing the self, constructing America: A cultural history of psychotherapy.* Reading, MA: Addison-Wesley.

Dennstedt, C., & Grieves, L. (2004). Unraveling substance misuse stories: Re-authoring and witnessing practices. In S. Madigan (Ed.), *Therapeutic conversations 5: Therapy from the outside in* (pp. 55–72). Vancouver, Canada: Yaletown Family Therapy.

Derrida, J. (1995). *Points . . . interviews (1974–1994)* (E. Weber, Ed.). Stanford, CA: Stanford University Press.

Evans, R. I. (1976). *R. D. Laing: The man and his ideas.* New York: Dutton.

Fingarette, H. (1988). *Heavy drinking: The myth of alcoholism as a disease.* Berkeley: University of California Press.

Foster, K. (2004, October 17). Heroin kits on demand for Scots prisoners. *Scotland on Sunday.* Retrieved March 7, 2006, from http://scotlandonsunday.scotsman.com/index.cfm?id=1207582004

Foucault, M. (2003). *Society must be defended: Lectures at the College de France, 1975–76.* New York: Picador.

Gray, J. H. (1995). *Booze: When whisky ruled the West.* Saskatoon, Canada: Fifth House Press.

Harré, R. (1983). *Personal being.* Oxford, UK: Blackwell.

Harré, R., & Gillet, G. (1994). *The discursive mind.* Thousand Oaks, CA: Sage.

Held, B. (1995). *Back to reality: A critique of postmodern theory in psychotherapy.* New York and London: Norton.

Heron, C. (2003). *Booze: A distilled history.* Toronto, Canada: Between the Lines.

Holcomb, H. W. (1994). Incorporating new treatment perspectives into a residential adolescent drug and alcohol program. *Journal of Child and Youth Care, 9,* 43–50.

Hubble, M. A., Duncan, B. L., & Miller, S. D. (1999). *The heart and soul of change: What works in therapy.* Washington, DC: American Psychological Association.

Jellinek, E. M. (1960). *The disease concept of alcoholism.* New Haven, CT: College and University Press.

Kaye, J. (1999). Towards a non-regulative praxis. In I. Parker (Ed.), *Deconstructing psychotherapy* (pp. 19–38). London: Sage.

Kearney, P. A., Byrne, N. O'R., & McCarthy, I. C. (1989). Just metaphors: Marginal illuminations in a colonial retreat. *Family Therapy Case Studies, 4,* 17–31.

Kearney, R. (1996). Narrative imagination: Between ethics and poetics. In R. Kearney (Ed.), *Paul Ricoeur: The hermeneutics of action* (pp. 173–188). London: Sage.

Kelleher, D., Gabe, J., & Williams, G. (1994). Understanding medical dominance in the modern world. In J. Gabe, D. Kelleher, & G. Williams (Eds.), *Challenging medicine* (pp. xi–xxix). London: Routledge.

Laing, R. D. (1967). *The politics of experience and the bird of paradise.* London: Penguin Books.

Lebow, J. (2004, March/April). Addictions treatment: Myth vs. reality: Effective interventions often don't match stereotypes. *Psychotherapy Networker,* pp. 91–93.

Levine, H. G. (1978). The discovery of addiction: Changing conceptions of habitual drunkenness in America. *Journal of Studies in Alcohol, 39,* 143–174.

Levine, H. G. (1984). The alcohol problem in America: From temperance to alcoholism. *British Journal of Addiction, 79,* 109–119.

Lomas, P. (1999). *Doing good? Psychotherapy out of its depth.* Oxford, UK: University Press.

Marlatt, G. (1998). Basic principles and strategies of harm reduction. In G. Marlatt (Ed.), *Harm reduction. Pragmatic strategies for managing high risk behaviours* (pp. 49–66). New York: Guilford.

Martin-Baro, I. (1994). *Writings for a liberation psychology.* Cambridge, MA: Harvard University Press.

Mate, G. (2004, August 21). Drugs are not enough. *Globe and Mail,* p. F7.

McCarthy, I. (2001). Fifth province re-versings: The social construction of women lone parents' inequality and poverty. *Association for Family Therapy and Systemic Practice, 23,* 253–277.

Mosher, L. R., & Burti, L. (1989). *Community mental health: Principles and practice.* New York and London: Norton.

Musto, D. F. (1973). *The American disease: Origins of narcotic control.* New Haven, CT: Yale University Press.

Peele, S. (1989). *Diseasing of America: Addiction treatment out of control.* Boston: Houghton Mifflin.

Radke, C., Kitchen, M., & Reynolds, V. (2000). *Witness, not gossip: The female gender group at Peak House.* Unpublished manuscript.

Reynolds, V. (2002). Weaving threads of belonging: Cultural witnessing groups. *Journal of Child and Youth Care, 15,* 89–105.

Robertson, L., & Culhane, D. (2005). *In plain sight: Reflections on life in downtown eastside Vancouver.* Vancouver, Canada: Talonbooks.

Sanders, C. J. (1994). Workshop notes: Deconstructing addiction mythology. *Calgary Participator, 4,* 25–28.

Sanders, C. J. (1997). Re-authoring problem identities: Small victories with young persons captured by substance misuse. In C. Smith & D. Nylund (Eds.), *Narrative therapies with children and adolescents* (pp. 141–162). New York: Guilford.

Sanders, C. J. (1998). Substance misuse dilemmas: A postmodern inquiry. In S. Madigan & I. Law (Eds.), *Praxis: Situating discourse, feminism, & politics in narrative therapies* (pp. 141–162). Vancouver, Canada: Yaletown Family Therapy/Cardigan Press.

Sanders, C. J. (1999). *Workshop notes: The poetics of resistance.* Unpublished manuscript.

Sanders, C. J. (2000). *Accountability practices, dominant male discourses, and the male gender group at Peak House, Vancouver.* Unpublished manuscript.

Saville, S. (1998). *Overcoming the problem of substance misuse: Adolescent experience in a narrative re-authoring program.* Unpublished master's thesis, University of British Columbia, Vancouver, Canada.

Schwartz, J. (1997). The soul of soulless conditions? Accounting for genetic fundamentalism. *Radical Philosophy: A Journal of Socialist and Feminist Philosophy, 86,* 2–5.

Simblett, G. T. (1997). Leila and the Tiger: Narrative approaches to psychiatry. In G. Monk, J. Winslade, K. Crocket, & D. Epston (Eds.), *Narrative therapy in practice: The archaeology of hope* (pp. 121–157). San Francisco: Jossey-Bass.

Spiegel, A. (2005, January 3). The dictionary of disorder. *New Yorker,* pp. 56–63.

Szasz, T. (1992). The United States v. drugs. In J. K. Zeig (Ed.), *The evolution of psychotherapy: The second conference.* New York: Brunner-Mazel.

Thompson, M. G. (2000). The legacy and future of R. D. Laing's contribution to contemporary thought [Special issue]. *Psychoanalytic Review, 87,* 4.

Thomson, G. (1994). (Ed.). Narrative mind and practice in child and youth care [Special issue]. *Journal of Child and Youth Care, 9,* 2.

Turner, V. (1969). *The ritual process.* Ithaca, NY: Cornell University Press.

Turner, V. (1974). *Drama, fields, and metaphor.* Ithaca, NY: Cornell University Press.

Waldegrave, C., & Tamasese, K. (1993). Some central ideas in the "just therapy" approach. *Australian and New Zealand Journal of Family Therapy, 14*(1), 1–8.

White, M., & Epston, D. (1990). *Narrative means to therapeutic ends.* New York: Norton.

Wittenauer, C. (2004, April 9). Gene linked to both alcoholism and depression. *Globe and Mail,* p. A19.

Wylie, M. S. (2004, September/October). Mindsight. *Psychotherapy Networker,* pp. 29–39.

5

Practicing Psychiatry Through a Narrative Lens

Working With Children, Youth, and Families

Normand Carrey[1]

N arrative therapy has been helpful to me in my work as a child psychiatrist with children, youth, and families. I have been trained in psychophar-macology, psychiatric diagnosis of the *Diagnostic Statistical Manual of Psychiatric Disorders (DSM)* (American Psychiatric Association, 1980), as well as family therapy and, specifically, narrative approaches. I have, how-ever, found combining the two worlds of psychiatry and narrative therapy challenging. Psychiatrists often speak the language of "the biopsychosocial model" (Engel, 1977) but are more individually oriented, while many of my narrative colleagues speak the language of social construction, "multiple perspectives," and "inclusiveness" but often diminish the importance of med-ical, developmental, and biological factors. Often the polarizing differences of the two fields are emphasized at the expense of looking at how they might complement each other in a manner that is helpful to clients.

Through adopting a postmodern philosophy, I realize the epistemological tensions that narrative-thinking psychiatrists face. The meaning of the stories generated through therapeutic conversations can be at cross-purposes with the dominant (medical) discourse expectations of both therapist and client.

I have struggled with the fact that, despite my narrative sensibility, psychiatrists are expected to adopt a traditional expert authority, diagnose people, and prescribe medication as expected by parents, the medical system, and the culture at large. If narrative psychiatrists do not conform to professional expectations, they may be ostracized from colleagues and parents. On the other hand, they may be shunned by narrative therapists because of the perception that all psychiatrists practice within the dominant biomedical discourse.

Sociology and ethnography have identified psychiatry among the medical specialties as particularly culture bound (Launer, 1999), occupying an uncomfortable "no man's land" between conventional medical science and the search for meaning, which may extend into political and religious domains. However, narrative medical clinicians stand at the intersection of the world of stories and the world of scientific categorization. Practitioners with a narrative orientation aim at working collaboratively with people to coconstruct or cocreate empowering stories about healing and coping with physical and mental illness. In this view, the doctor works with people to coconstruct a story that is helpful, while acknowledging that truth and knowledge are not absolute, but biographical and interpretive, rather than prescriptive and paradigmatic (Launer, 1999).

Social constructionism states that knowledges, including professional or expert knowledge, are stories that are negotiated among people, often as a means of exerting power (Foucault, 1980; Launer, 1999). To relieve people's suffering, in keeping with social constructionism, I invite them to deconstruct taken-for-granted assumptions about the problems they face (e.g., the idea that most problems can be fixed simply with medication or that a more accurate diagnosis will solve all problems). However, offering a family relief from suffering only through deconstruction is often not enough. Many families also benefit from re-authoring preferred stories as well as being prescribed medication. Psychiatric stories can be used as starting points and then built upon, into alternative, more empowering stories.

Medical narrative therapy draws on a blended epistemology—modernism and postmodernism—that accepts that physical and severe psychological problems (e.g., schizophrenia, mood disorders, severe anxiety, severe aggression, learning disabilities) are often both material or biological and embedded in a culturally based system of meaning (Greenhalgh & Hurwitz, 1999; Kirmayer, 2005). Material or biological brain "disorders" are interpreted, made sense of, and labeled within a cultural context. As such, there cannot be an understanding of "mental illness" outside of culture.

From this view, narrative therapists can draw on the knowledge claims of genetics, molecular biology, neuroimaging, psychopharmacology, and evidence-based medicine, while recognizing that these fields of science are not outside discourse. In this sense, the narrative psychiatrist must be "bilingual": versed in "brain disorders" as well as the art of translating this knowledge into a story that resonates with clients' own stories. Moreover, the narrative psychiatrist adopts a collaborative stance with those seeking help or relief from suffering.

By recognizing and using the power invested in medical practitioners by society and culture, a psychiatrist can help coauthor preferred narratives that provide meaning, context, and perspective for the child's, youth's, and family's predicaments. The psychiatrist may invite curiosity about the family and the social and historical origins of a problem, while also unpacking conventional biomedical stories.

Within the collaborative approach of narrative psychiatry, I constantly struggle to consolidate and re-create my professional identity as I navigate my relationship with parents, the medical system, and the cultural expectations of me as a medical authority—at the same time as I am trying to integrate narrative ideas and practices into my work. Navigating this territory has resulted in creative tensions as I integrate both narrative practices and traditional medical-oriented practices, such as "interviewing," "diagnosing," and "treating." These three stages of the traditional psychiatric interview involve "interviewing" families about the problem to determine a "diagnosis," which can then be responded to with "treatment."

Narrative ideas can enrich collaborative work with people and generate alternative meanings that can contradict and also complement traditional psychiatric practice. The collaborative approach recognizes the knowledge that children, youth, parents, and therapists have, thereby moving away from the more traditional conflicts that can emerge when a psychiatrist or parents compete to be the "expert" or clients uncritically accept expert knowledge. The story in this chapter is the distilled experience of my interactions working as a team with my family therapy colleagues over the course of 16 years.

This chapter is divided into three sections, in accordance with the three stages of the traditional psychiatric interview mentioned above, "interviewing," "diagnosing," and "treating." In the "Interviewing" section, I review the ways narrative ideas and practices can be used to create a collaborative approach to working with families that recognizes the values of both the psychiatrist's and the family's knowledges. Furthermore, I illustrate the importance of using people's own language, using genograms and reflecting teams to enhance this therapeutic collaboration.

In the next section of the chapter, "Diagnosing," I explore how diagnosing can be used with a postmodern sensibility that acknowledges the fluidity of identity while, at the same time, helping to mobilize people and community resources to assist those whose problems include a biological, material basis. Furthermore, I offer strategies for using diagnosis while at the same time recognizing a child's agency and empowering parents to deal with the problem.

Finally, the section on "Treatment" focuses on prescribing medication within a narrative framework. When I prescribe medication, I take into account the often significant meanings a family attaches to this form of treatment. I am also attentive to the influences, for example, of parents, schools, and pharmaceutical companies in determining which medications should be prescribed for children. I also illustrate the processes of collaboratively prescribing medication using therapeutic letters and documenting families' stories in a manner that does not objectify them.

I begin this chapter with a brief overview of the history of child psychiatry and demonstrate how it overlaps with the ideas and practices of the narrative therapy movement.

Historical Context

Historically, psychiatry has been invested in both deconstructing people's problems through unpacking "meaning" and engaging in the modernist practices of diagnosis and treatment (mostly through individual psychotherapy and prescribing medications). Some of this tradition of psychiatry overlaps with narrative ideas and practices. More recently, with the advent of the *DSM*, a descriptive classification model of mental disorders, psychopharmacology and evidence-based medicine, psychiatry has become dominated by a primarily modernist, biologically focused approach to people's problems. These developments in the field have regretfully distanced the field of child psychiatry from its own past and, in turn, from narrative therapist colleagues. I will highlight these historical developments and their implications for bridging postmodernism and modernism through narrative practices.

Aries (1962) was one of the first historians to look at the social construction of childhood and the family, noting that the recognition of childhood as a special stage of life did not appear until the late 18th and early 19th century. With industrialization and subsequent urbanization, the social construction of the category of the child emerged. Institutional responses to the changing status of the child (Jones, 1999) and social concerns about exploitive child labor practices resulted in child labor laws, compulsory schooling, the juvenile court, and child guidance clinics. This period cemented the view of childhood as a special stage of life as the child became the object of public concern and social policy (Skolnick, 1976).

By the end of the 19th century, child psychiatry emerged under the shadow of adult psychiatry, influenced by psychoanalysis, the predominant theory of the time (Freud, 1934). Among other things, Freud focused on the meaning and stories of people's lives by emphasizing dreams and childhood experiences in his work (Gomez, 1996). Freud's ideas were consonant with and helped shape Western cultural ideas of individuality and the growing preoccupation with introspection and mental life.[2] Freud understood that human mental life reflected the specific nature of the human brain and the social context of human psychological development. Together, brain function and cultural meaning-making processes produced mental life. Neither the brain nor culture by itself was sufficient for explaining human mental life.

In the 1950s, psychiatry's engagement with the meanings of people's stories through psychoanalysis underwent a paradigm shift toward a biological basis for mental distress through the discovery of powerful drugs. The drugs chlorpromazine, an antipsychotic; imipramine, an antidepressant; and lithium, a mood stabilizer, offered the first substantive breakthrough to relieve symptoms of psychosis and mood disorders, ushering in the psychopharmacology movement. Psychiatrists became more interested in carving out symptoms, disorders, and syndromes for which the psychoanalytic model was totally unsuitable. Psychoanalytic treatments seeking to explore the meaning of people's problems were considered time consuming, protracted, and ineffective for serious mood problems and psychosis. Consequently, the *DSM,* claiming to be atheoretical, scientific, and objective, was more in line with organic medicine and the neuropsychiatry tradition, which became the dominant psychiatric paradigm.[3] In its successive refinements, the *DSM* has been criticized by psychiatrists and nonpsychiatrists alike for decontextualizing people's lives and overemphasizing an individual (biological and reductionistic) approach (Jensen & Hoagwood, 1997; Kutchins & Kirk, 1997; Tomm, 1990). Both the psychoanalytic and biologic descriptive schemes have been criticized for their failure to distinguish between serious psychopathology (psychosis, bipolar mood disorders) and the everyday distress of life as society shifted toward both drugs and psychological therapy as cultural responses to mental and emotional distress.

In response to the individual trend in psychiatry, other practitioners (some of them psychoanalysts) began to develop alternative ways of working with children, adolescents, and parents through family therapy (Ackerman, 1980; Bowen, 1982; Minuchin, 1974). Family therapists critiqued the individualistic focus of psychoanalysis and biological psychiatry and began to think of the family as the unit that needed to be changed to address problems effectively (Haley, 1976). Family therapy was initially influenced by systems theory and cybernetics, with a shift from linear cause and effect to circular causality (Bateson, 1971). Family therapists emphasized relationships in people's lives, but the assumption shifted from the pathological individual to the pathological family, and interventions still relied on the traditional expert status of the therapist.

Later on, through solution-focused (de Shazer, 1985, 1988; O'Hanlon & Weiner-Davis, 1989) and narrative therapies (White & Epston, 1990), the field began to define problems and solutions in terms of a social constructionist philosophy, emphasizing strengths in families rather than deficiencies or problems and challenging the traditional professional stance of the therapist as the "expert" in possession of objective truth. In contrast, narrative therapy values the knowledge of clients as experts on themselves and "reality" as cocreated in conversations between therapist and client (Parry & Doan, 1994).

Several developments within the field of family therapy began to resonate with postmodern ideas. Specifically, narrative and solution-focused therapists were looking for metaphors that would be more helpful than those of organic disease. When applied to people's lives, the disease metaphor inadvertently reinforces helplessness and hopelessness. Furthermore, these more recent approaches try to be more transparent about the politics of the therapy process.

White and Epston (1990), the founders of the narrative approach, were influenced by French philosopher Michel Foucault's (1980) theory of knowledge and power, and they translated his ideas to the clinical arena. They contrasted the scientific analogy of positivistic sciences characterizing psychiatry and medicine to the text analogy of narrative therapy, in which clients are invited to re-author their lives according to a preferred richly storied life. Most psychiatrists and psychologists are trained in reductionistic models that decontextualize people's lives. However, current scientific metaphors about complex biological systems can have liberating possibilities.

In addition to the text analogy, there have been other therapeutic contributions from postmodern therapies. Gergen (1990a, 1990b) questions the use of "pathologizing language" in medicine and psychiatry, as it creates a language of deficiency, reinforces power imbalance in the therapy relationship, and perpetuates a sense of blame and failure in the client. Reflecting teams have been created as a therapeutic tool that embodies the philosophy of the collaborative healing dialogue between therapist and family (Andersen 1991, 1995). Anderson, Goolishian, and Winderman (Winderman, 1986; Anderson & Goolishian, 1988) suggest that therapists adopt a collaborative stance in which the client and therapist have mutually respectful roles in defining problems and solutions. Tomm (1987a, 1987b, 1988) focuses on reflexive questioning. Eventually, family therapists have extended their focus to include the larger cultural context of the family and, in particular, acknowledge the significance of gender and race within families (Caplan, 1995; Chesler, 1997).

The turn toward narrative therapy in family therapy resonates with those who have held on to the early (child) psychiatry tradition of focusing on stories and meaning through psychoanalysis. In a convergence of schools of thought, many psychoanalytically trained therapists have adopted and contributed to narrative ideas through a focus on language as the mediator of subjective experience. According to Gomez (1996), "The concept that language is a social phenomenon, and that humans exist in language and become human via conversations—sometimes becoming their conversations and sometimes generating the conversation they become—is not foreign to psychoanalysis" (p. 132).

The dualistic separation of biological and social discourses often negates the complicated relationships in which the embodied mind is at all moments both embodied and inseparable from social meaning-making processes. Rapid developments in genetics, neurosciences, psychopharmacology, and evidence-based medicine have the potential to further polarize the medical model against narrative approaches (although recent gene environment studies point to a complex interplay of reciprocal influences; Rutter, 2005). A heuristic model is needed that incorporates the effects of medical discursive practices within the context of our social discourses but at the same time acknowledges the painful reality of struggling with severe mental symptoms or early traumatic experiences.

Interviewing: Inviting Collaboration

I begin to work collaboratively with families by listening to their accounts of their difficulties and sharing with them the information I have received about them from collateral sources. In this initial process, there are often differences between working collaboratively with adults and working collaboratively with children. In work with adults, narrative psychiatrist Simblett (1997) increases his collaborative stance with adults by reading the referral information he receives about the client. This process helps to build a therapeutic alliance in which openness and collaboration are valued. Simblett deconstructs the technical terms used when doctors or therapists communicate professionally. In this manner, people do not have to worry about secret information or being "spoken about" by different therapists or professionals. Previous diagnoses and assumptions behind the diagnoses are explored for their potential to either limit or expand possibilities. During this process, Simblett resists getting distracted by judging previous therapists and interventions and, instead, focuses on whether those encounters were helpful or not.

Working with children and youth versus adults, however, may at times require a different stance. Often the child does not understand the purpose of our work together or, in the worst-case scenario, has not been told about the visit. Sharing the referral information with the parents in the child's presence may be shaming to the child or have the effect of encouraging the parents to focus on describing all of the child's problems. Instead, I explore what the child knows about the referral. I then introduce the reflecting team or the use of a family genogram and explain who we are, what our philosophy is, what our intention is, what we think is expected from us, how questions will be handled, and how the family can be helped. This establishes the context for a collaborative relationship.

For example, I may say to the family that while I have been trained in using medications and I have been doing therapy for many years, equally important to our conversations is the parents' knowledge about their family and child and the problem. In one instance, a parent, who felt empowered in most areas of her life, kept repeating, "But what do I know? I'm not the professional." I kept reiterating that her knowledge was different than mine and no less important. While families might expect such an approach from family therapists, they are often not familiar with doctors behaving in this manner.

Typically, during the initial clinical interview, a psychiatrist seeks to make an assessment and define the problem people have brought to therapy. The psychiatric interview determines the reason for the referral, the presenting problem, past history, and family-personal history and conducts a mental status examination.[4] The psychiatric interview is traditionally defined as a process in which the expert determines the objective truth of the person's problem. This approach has often emphasized deficiencies and problems rather than solutions and strengths (Gergen, 1990a, 1990b). Simblett (1997) has started to deconstruct the claims of objectivity in the psychiatric interview through revealing the privileging of dominant discourse over clients' stories—there is an assumption that a psychiatric history taken with sufficient skill will avoid the pitfall of the psychiatrist corrupting the development of objective truth. A postmodernist view of history taking, by contrast, accepts that the process is always subjective, always coconstructed (Simblett, 1997, p. 132).

Simblett (1997) demonstrates that each section of the conventional psychiatric interview (determining the reason for referral, presenting problem, past history, family-personal history, mental status examination) is often conducted in a manner that inadvertently invites people to focus on problems and deficiencies couched in the psychiatrist's language, rather than coconstructing with people alternative, more hopeful possibilities.

Mr. Potato Head

In interviews when I have privileged psychiatric language, meanings, and stories over those of the families I work with, I have inadvertently shut down possibilities, rather than opening them up. For example, in the first conversation I had with Kevin,[5] who was 8 years old, and his family, he held his hands over his ears for the entire hour to block out his mother's description of his temper problems at home and at school. My focus on Kevin's deficiencies in the first session reinforced a negative shameful story about himself as a failure. Kevin came into the second session expecting a repeat of the first conversation. I scrounged around the playroom to find a way to keep from repeating this unfortunate experience. "Mr. Potato Head" lay at the bottom of a toy drawer. He had helped me in the past collaboratively define problems using the child's own language. Would Kevin be interested in hearing Mr. Potato Head, who had helped me in the past listen to kids talk to adults about their problems? Kevin jumped at the possibility. Everything spoken in that session by the parents, Kevin, or myself had to pass through Mr. Potato Head, who was very knowledgeable but very shy. Mr. Potato Head talked in a nonblaming, nonshaming manner and used Kevin's language to collaboratively define the problem and its solution. For the first time, Kevin began to speak about what triggered his temper.

The conversation of that day was followed up by a letter to Kevin from Mr. Potato Head congratulating Kevin but also reminding him of the teamwork necessary for his family to conquer temper. Kevin's parents joined Mr. Potato Head in encouraging Kevin to look at solutions necessary to conquer temper. Through using Mr. Potato Head, I was able to engage Kevin by using his language and also honor his knowledge about the problem.

The dominant discourse within psychiatric and mental health training privileges the therapist's definition of the problem and solutions over people's own descriptions of their problems and solutions. The language of the dominant discourse can have an oppressive effect on children and adolescents, leading them to feel excluded and marginalized from the conversation, making them tune out the "adult talk." Parents, influenced by larger cultural trends of the biomedical individual model, often mimic or reflect the language of the dominant discourse as well. After years of training, I was professionally conditioned to neglect the clients' meaning of their stories because they were perceived as irrelevant to making an expert diagnosis within a deficiency model of pathology. Within the psychiatric discourse, I focused primarily on deficits and problems and was not encouraged to explore clients' stories, strengths, or possibilities for re-authoring identities.

Wrestling Temper

In contrast to traditional psychiatric discursive practices, I find it more helpful to work collaboratively with people to define their problems and subsequent solutions. One way of working collaboratively involves using the same metaphors and language that families, youth, and children themselves use to describe the problem. Michael White (1995b) refers to this practice as using "experience-near" language. Using people's own language and eliciting and enriching their stories and metaphors often helps mobilize them against the problem. For example, a child named Jodi came in, and I noticed he had the word "Wrestling" emblazed on the back of his jacket. When I inquired about this, he told me he had recently joined the school wrestling team and beamed with pride about this achievement. We were able to use his metaphor to work collaboratively to "wrestle" his hyperactivity and impulsivity to the ground. As well, I wanted Jodi to receive the message loudly and clearly that I was just as (if not more) interested in his accomplishments before we launched into a discussion about the recent difficulties that had brought him to my office.

Using language people are familiar with and metaphors supplied by children to describe their problems often leaves them feeling relieved that someone has listened and understood them and feeling more empowered to solve their problems. Using the traditional mental health approach (i.e., the therapist's solutions are best) reinforces people's dependency on external factors to solve their problems, which may lead them to feel less empowered and less in charge of their potential for change and growth in their lives. Consistent with the narrative approach, the language chosen in the therapeutic conversation not only conveys information but also actually coconstructs the reality between therapist and client. The language used to describe people actually speaks and writes them into the world in a manner that is either helpful or unhelpful to them.

I often externalize temper by personifying anger as "Mr. Temper." Some parents are reluctant to work metaphorically because they fear the child may escape accountability by blaming Mr. Temper for the misbehavior. Children are reminded that they have to take responsibility for kicking Mr. Temper out of their lives, that it can be difficult, but that they will be helped by their "anti–Mr. Temper team." Often the team is made up of the therapist, the parents, the teacher, coaches, and others. The conversations also explore how others can become part of the team of resisting Mr. Temper, including people who may have previously been defining the child as the problem—people under the influence of the problem.

We continued to use Mr. Potato Head and the team and coach metaphor to tame anger and temper; and despite my own initial reluctance, Kevin benefited from taking medication to help him overcome his overwhelming anxiety. Did the helpfulness of the medication mean that externalizing the problem had not worked? At first, I thought so; however, Kevin's parents reported that they found both approaches helpful, so we continued to work in this manner.

Enhancing Collaboration: Family Genograms

One tool that my colleagues and I have found useful to enhance collaboration is the family genogram (Carrey, Costanzo, Sexton, & Aspin, 2004). Initially used to map intergenerational family influences by structural and strategic family therapists (Bowen, 1982; McGoldrick & Gerson, 1985), genograms were limited by the modernist presumption of an objective truth about the family structure identifiable only through the therapist's expert knowledge. Genograms were often used to trace the family history of "problems" in people's lives. More recently, genograms have been used by solution-focused and narrative therapists (Hardy & Laszloffy, 1995; Kuehl, 1995). The use of genograms helps to enhance collaborative work with families to create opportunities across generations. Genograms can be used to highlight solutions rather than problems and help to discover unique outcomes (exceptions to the problems) and hidden family acts of strength. Genograms also ensure that vital information is not missed. For example, information about a suicide of an extended family member can have implications in terms of a susceptibility to a psychiatric disorder but also simultaneously act as a trauma shaping the family story.

Using family genograms is also a visual way of relating to younger children who may prefer to draw (McGoldrick & Gerson, 1985). The team I work with uses a broad sheet on which the therapist can write down information, and the child can draw with coloring pencils on the sheet at the same time. The whole family is invited to participate in this process. This creates a back-and-forth style of interaction with all family members. Different stories about extended family members overcoming adversity are brought forth, and a virtual community of caring is marshaled to overcome the influence of the problem. We keep the genogram sheet and bring it out at subsequent sessions as a way to document any moves forward in the family.

Enhancing Collaboration: The Reflecting Team

The reflecting team is a relatively new therapeutic tool that illustrates and embodies the technique and philosophy of collaborative healing dialogue between therapist and family (Anderson, 1991, 1995).[6] The reflecting team involves the supervisor, colleagues, and students (e.g., in social work, psychiatry, pediatrics, or psychology) being behind the one-way mirror while a therapist conducts an interview with a family. The team observes the interview without any dialogue between members so that each team member can offer reflections from his or her perspective, rather than a group consensus or the supervisor's perspective. In the first stage of the reflecting-team process, the therapist has a conversation with the family about their problem and the influence of the problem on the family's life.

In the second stage of the process, the therapist and family then reverse positions with the reflecting team and observe the reflecting team in dialogue about how the family is both burdened by the problem and escapes the influence of the problem. Team members situate and contextualize their comments in their own personal life experiences (White, 1995b). The team is careful to use language that takes into account each family member's developmental level. This "experience-near" level of discussion helps the family reflect on strengths and possibilities to engage in new patterns of change to defeat old patterns. The students are asked to emphasize change and growth metaphors rather than symptom and disease. Therapists are also asked to state their comments from a position of curiosity rather than certainty, offering reflections as possibilities rather than defined truths. In the third stage, the family and the therapist invited back into the room and are asked to reflect on the comments they have just heard about themselves. Finally, in the fourth stage, the family leaves, and the team members deconstruct their own experiences of the interview process, the reflecting team, and any previous (personal) issues that may have stimulated the team's reflections.

This idea of watching and being watched serves to remind therapists and trainees to use language that is more personal and helps therapists to resist the pull to hide behind professional language that distances them from families and asserts unhelpful power relationships (Anderson, 1995). For many families, hearing the reflecting team is the first time they hear others talk about them in such positive, intimate, and familiar terms. Most of our families report that they find reflecting teams are helpful.

While all family members may not be present in the conversations, collaborative family work often benefits from acknowledging all members of the family. After I initially meet the family, I offer children, adolescents, and parents the opportunity to see me on their own, while making it transparent that everyone will be treated equally and no secrets will be withheld from anyone. Often parents speak with me separately because they are afraid what they may say might hurt their child's feelings. As well, parents may want to talk without their child present to talk about tensions between themselves or other family secrets they do not feel the child is ready to hear. Parents' decision to speak with me without the child present is often motivated by their empathy and respect for the child, which strengthens my collaboration with the parents as important agents of change in the child's and their own lives.

Contrary to working collaboratively, psychiatrists are often initially reluctant to abandon the standard interview templates that they have learned during their training, the three-stage psychiatric interview of "interviewing," "diagnosing," and "treating." The standard interview template can reify the institution's and therapist's position in the power hierarchy: the psychiatrist "knows," and families do not. The dominant psychiatric discourse presumes that these templates for interviews are the objectifiable truth passed down from mentors and teachers, who are responsible for maintaining the discipline's tradition. These standard interview formats, which can function as guidelines, are too often mistaken as the truth about people and their lives. Narrative therapy helps therapists acknowledge the therapist's position of power, which, in turn, can be used to create a context in which they can resist automatically privileging their own voices over parents' and children's voices.

Diagnosing

For the narrative psychiatrist, the exercise of diagnosing and labeling represents challenges and opportunities. Narrative therapists are reluctant to label people because of the potential totalizing judgment (e.g., the person with schizophrenia becomes a schizophrenic) or because of the normative judgments involved, such as expert definitions of "normal" or "abnormal" behavior. As Launer (1999) points out, classifying people can become self-fulfilling prophesies. By compartmentalizing clients' narratives so that a category is divorced from its familial or social context, clinicians run the risk of amplifying the problem they are trying to solve. For example, Launer writes that once someone is labeled as *schizophrenic*, others may stop trying to have "normal" conversations with that person about his or her life, further contributing to the process of marginalization and isolation. When psychiatrists with a postmodern sensibility diagnose someone, however, they do so realizing the fluid nature of identity and of the psychiatric categories while, at the same time, recognizing the material, biological components of some people's problems.

Diagnosing people helps to mobilize people and communities against problems that have material, biological components. In some situations, making the diagnosis can create potential possibilities for children, youth, and their families. In our jurisdiction, children and youth who are diagnosed as autistic are privy to qualify for more therapeutic services. Children diagnosed with learning disabilities may also qualify for more school resources. Caring for children with these diagnoses can impose significant emotional and financial stresses on the family, and any help that they can receive (e.g., financial, social, educational) is often welcomed by the family. In children with severe developmental and/or psychiatric problems, some parents may need the initial "certainty" associated with diagnosis as a way to name the unknown. Parents want to know "what they are dealing with," while at the same time, I want to resist totalizing a child's identity with a label or diagnosis. Diagnoses of biological components to people's problems can have positive consequences because they can be used to enlist and recruit "antiforces" or teamwork to fight against the influence of the problem.

As psychiatry tries to align itself with the success of the organic model in medicine and the biomedical discourse, it is required to use the same language of "disorder" and "psychopathology," and hence everything that is labeled in the *DSM* (like disruptive behavior) is categorized as a disorder, obscuring potential psychosocial or developmental elements. Some of the behaviors labeled as disorders (shyness, oppositionality) are temperamental traits that have both positive and negative aspects to them. In addition, the "adaptability" of these traits is dependent on how the environment responds to them. Other disorders may prove to have more of an "organic" basis, such as autism and reading disabilities. For the profession and many parents, however, all diagnostic labels seem definitive and certain and imply a final judgment that only the expert can make and, in certain instances, unmake. Other labels are subject to diagnostic fads, as with the recent cultural preoccupation with pediatric bipolar disorder to explain all kinds of oppositional behavior in children and teenagers. As parents often believe in the biomedical labels, before we are able to explore other alternative understandings, I find it is important to reassure the child and parent that we are not missing any serious biological problems.

Diagnosis: Too-Darn-Smart-for-His-Own-Good

I find it helpful to be creative and playful with some diagnoses, especially in the service of liberating a child and a family from a label associated with an oppressive story. For example, I met a youth named Duncan prior to his being admitted to a residential facility after numerous interventions had failed. His foster parents, the social worker doing the preadmission, and myself, his outpatient psychiatrist, were present. In an effort to review the file, the social worker asked Duncan to confirm his previous diagnosis of attention-deficit/hyperactivity disorder (ADHD). Duncan's identity was being storied into the conversation through a narrative about his deficits. Duncan deflated and slid into his chair. I blurted out, "He also has a diagnosis of TDSFHOG, Too-Darn-Smart-for-His-Own-Good." Duncan brightened upon hearing this label that acknowledged he was very intelligent, which I found out had been celebrated before as one of his strengths. His foster parents appeared relieved. This act of relabeling served to re-story Duncan's identity according to an identity story he preferred.

I have found it useful to unpack the metaphors surrounding psychiatric disorders that imply deficiency. For example, in the case of ADHD, parents usually come in with the understanding that their child's condition is a neurobiological disorder. As a result of the dominant psychiatric discourse, parents often have a limited understanding of how other factors (e.g., social, cultural, or problem-saturated stories of people's identities) can impact the child's behavior. Many parents have had the child assessed by a psychologist or have visited the family doctor. Medical discourse invokes a disease metaphor to understand both physical and mental difficulties. For example, the medical discourse leads psychiatrists to approach fixing ADHD in the same way they would fix a broken arm that needs a cast or defective vision in need of eyeglasses or a diabetic who needs insulin. All of these medical metaphors to describe mental difficulties imply a deficit that needs to be corrected, invariably with medication.

Giving people a diagnosis often stories them according to possible deficits, and the label often precludes celebrating the wonderful talents and energies most children demonstrate as individuals (many of them with great coordination, energy, and superior visual-motor skills). Narrative therapy has allowed me to invoke labels and diagnosis in a tentative manner, while at the same time acknowledging the fluidity of these categories, the multiple factors that create such conditions (biological and otherwise), and the person's preferred identity.

Diagnosis: Consummate Multitasker

In working with parents of a child with ADHD, I usually start by extending the medical metaphor by suggesting, for example, that a person with diabetes also needs a good diet and exercise. By extending this metaphor, I emphasize the importance of the child's agency, contrary to what a simple disease metaphor infers. Then, I often suggest metaphors of excess or abundance rather than deficits: "Your child has a surplus of energy that I would like to bottle and sell"; or "Your child is creative to have so many thoughts"; or "Your child is the consummate multitasker." I then may suggest restraining metaphors to complement the abundance metaphors: "Your child's energy is like a team of wild horses. Do you think we can teach them to run in the same direction?" In addition, along with celebrating their child, I often find it helpful to give parents the opportunity to acknowledge frustrating and difficult moments as a result of the problem in the child's life; otherwise, the parents may feel that the therapist cannot relate to the stresses in their lives.

In working with families, I find it is important to be attentive to empowering parents (Suberri, 2004). While parents may initially define their child or youth as "the problem," I resist defining the parents as "the problem" for doing so. They often do not intend to blame the child; rather, they are often caught in a culturally normative ways of individualizing problems. I find it helpful to acknowledge the parents' caring for their child, recognizing that they are the ones requesting the service, as children do not typically have the verbal skills or psychological development to understand the impact of their behavior. Parents seeking help may also experience loss and guilt, because after a long search, the psychiatrist may confirm their worst fears. I often discuss all of these factors with the family before I seek to separate the problem from the person and propose an intervention such as externalizing the problem. My eagerness to wrestle the problem from the person and not spend time acknowledging the effects of it on the family often conveys the message to the parents that I am minimizing the seriousness of the problem.

I acknowledge hopefulness about change as well as the challenges children and youth with serious emotional difficulties and their families face with autism, extreme aggression, bipolar disorder, overwhelming anxiety, severe obsessive symptoms, and psychosis (see White, 1995a). Although "talk therapy" can help people contain overwhelming feelings, I am often faced with the limitations of what can be accomplished in these severe cases. At the same time, I am often in situations in which parents want to pursue *only* the "true" or underlying diagnosis. I resist being critical of this pursuit and realize parents are often their child's best advocates and supports. Thus, I find it helpful to see parents as consultants, rather than thinking I need to win them over to my point of view. Some parents, however, will remain diagnosis or medication driven, and I must work to enrich the story within this paradigm.

A narrative approach does not preclude comprehensive assessments of the child's cognitive and emotional level. In this instance, I find the distinction helpful that Suberri (2004) makes between biological problems within the child (e.g., severe cognitive or emotional limitations, such as autism and severe ADHD) and interpersonal, interactional, or transient developmental or traumatic difficulties. For example, children with mental retardation or with fetal alcohol syndrome may not benefit as much from narrative approaches compared with children with better cognitive function. These distinctions may be important to parents still trying to make sense of how to understand their child's problem and then how to help him or her. Sensitive comprehensive psychological assessments are often compatible with a narrative orientation. These assessments are different, however, from the computer algorithms generated as a result of filling out rating scales or symptom checklists. The latter often results in a decontextualized understanding of a person's life and circumstances.

Treating

The biomedical psychiatric tradition creates a linear cause-and-effect process in which people are assessed through the "psychiatric interview," "diagnosed," and then treated through the "treatment phase." Everything in the psychiatric assessment leads to a diagnosis, in the belief that once a definitive diagnosis is established, treatment naturally will follow, as in the medical model of pathology. In the "treatment phase," attention is given to medication and psychiatric stories. Focusing on psychiatric beliefs and perceptions about medication and reliance on medical expertise about treatment can crowd out alternative or complimentary possibilities that may enhance alternative solutions and enrich lives.

Although I believe *solely* relying on medications is often problematic, I also find medication can be helpful for many families. I have found prescribing medication with families can be opportunities for growth and rich story development, but, at the same time, there can be numerous minefields. Regretfully, often a prescription for medication signals the end of an interview, prematurely closing down potential helpful meanings that can be made of taking medication, rather than the start of an therapeutic alliance (Blackwell, 1973; Pruett & Martin, 2003).

How I relate with the people who consult with me during all stages of the interview is as important as what I actually offer them in terms of medication options or "treatment." Often the traditional psychiatric approach defines the helpfulness of a session only in terms of determining a correct diagnosis and "treatment." The helpfulness and importance of the psychiatrist's relationship with the family in creating change is often rendered invisible. Poor alliances lead people to terminate the therapeutic relationship, just as good alliances with people, in which they feel understood, lead to better outcomes. Along with Pruett and Martin (2003), I believe the relationship I have with families is more important than the pills prescribed. Regretfully, with children I have followed for a long time, out of habit, I ask the parents about the child's medication right away rather than asking them about their lives first. My training often leads me to assume that some other therapist is supposed to do that part of the work, or I forget that there is a person behind that prescription.

In a situation where medication is part of the treatment, the stories that psychiatrists and families cocreate are influenced by the effects of the medication, the therapeutic alliance, the person's developmental stage, the psychological-familial context in which the medication is prescribed, and the larger cultural understanding of drugs. Often medications change children's mood and behavior, which, in turn, leads children or young people to think their choices have no influence over the problem. This is especially so in children and youth forging their self-identities. How does the medication change the evolving story of a person's identity? Does it enhance it or diminish it? Often too much control is credited to the medication by the parents or the youth. Alternatively, how does the therapist balance the person finding medication helpful in relieving suicidal ideation, for example, and the person's perceived false sense of control over the problem? The crucial issues of the various roles that the child, the parent, the therapist, and the medication play in controlling the problem have significant implications for a child's or a young person's developing sense of identity.

The meanings associated with taking medications often change as children and youth develop. Medications can be storied as poisons, magic bullets, mind restraints, brain implants, or contraceptives. I codevelop helpful metaphors for taking medications by listening to and collaboratively working with families. Often dominant psychiatric discourse restrains psychiatrists from taking the time to have such conversations. I work at being a good listener, a decipherer and a translator, and not merely a doctor who needs to be obeyed and knows what is best for the client. Doctors in particular, by habit of training and cultural pressures on them, must resist prematurely reaching for the prescription pad.

Recommending medication without knowing the meaning the family attaches to taking medication can have devastating effects on the child or the family. Sometimes family members conclude that the doctor is giving up on them by giving in to medication. However, in other instances, I find parents are frustrated and have tried many solutions by the time they meet with me and are ready to consider medication. Such parents may feel relief when medication is suggested because of the affirmation of the seriousness and accuracy of their concern for the child's difficulties. They may also feel less judgmental and self-deprecatory about failures to date, seeing medication as a new lease on effective parenting, and be more hopeful about their child.

Alternatively, unexamined feelings of loss and grief over having a child so sick as to warrant a diagnosis and a trial of medication can be problematic if the therapist is not aware of parents' feelings and the meanings they attach to their child taking medication. Parents may perceive the acts of diagnosing and treating by the psychiatrist as the beginning of lifelong journey of what they think may be a chronic illness, and they may begin storying their child primarily in terms of "deficits," which, in turn, has serious implications for the child's developing story about herself or himself.

Prescription Politics

Apart from the opinion of the psychiatrist, diagnoses are often negotiated in conjunction with parents, schools, and indirectly through pharmaceutical companies. For most children, medication is prescribed to them and administered through the agency of their parents. Often parents operate from the dominant psychiatric discourse, which suggests with certainty that a child's problem is the result of a "chemical imbalance" and hardwired genetic influences. According to child psychopharmacologists Pruett and Martin (2003), the term *chemical imbalance* masks multiple meanings that need to be unpacked or deconstructed to distinguish between parents' legitimate requests for thoughtful diagnostic clarification and attempts to avoid investigation of personal or emotional issues. Parents may also have the impression that the study of genetics in psychiatry is far more advanced than the field actually is. Discussion of heritability questions in the context of a biomedical model of psychiatric diagnosis and treatment has the potential to exacerbate parents' guilt and shame for genetically "giving" their children problems, and it emphasizes deficiencies.

School officials may share in the delusion of precision (Gutheil, 1982), perceiving drugs as specific, concrete, and targeted agents that are uniformly effective. Teachers and administrators feel the urge to control children for reasons other than those related to the children, such as overcrowding, understaffing, and new meritocracies of mandatory testing with their norm-driven academic testing. Some parents work collaboratively with the schools, but others may grasp at solutions such as changing the teacher, classroom, or curriculum to solve their children's problems. I try to appreciate these larger issues within a dominant education discourse and resist resorting to the prescription pad because of these, at times, intense systemic pressures.

The process of diagnosing children is also influenced by the corporate interests of pharmaceutical companies, and, as a result, it has become more culturally acceptable to medicate children and solve their problems through chemical means. These corporations assert influence through academic institutions and by bombarding individual doctors and parents through direct advertising, with the biomedical paradigm of understanding people's problems. They influence the choice of solutions sought (individual and biological rather than social and communal). Direct marketing to consumers often results in requests from parents for specific medications, in the mistaken belief that a new product will cure their children, and distracts parents from exploring other possibilities that might be contributing to their children's problems (Carrey, 1999).

Collaborative Prescription Writing

Routine prescription writing can be enhanced by collaborative work. I find that I need relief from the many times a day I write prescriptions to renew children's medication. In psychiatry, prescriptions are often referred to informally as "scripts." Reenacting this ritual every day has made me want to become a more creative scriptwriter. This new script needs to acknowledge the helpfulness of medication while also honoring the agency and responsibility people take to overcome their problems. While not belittling the serious medical responsibility of prescribing medications, I want to reenvision how the usual routine phone conversation or brief meeting can both acknowledge the effect of medication and facilitate rich story development. I now try to "spice up" my routine phone calls for medication renewals by inquiring as to whether the parent has noticed any moves by the child in the right direction, and who is responsible for this change.

For example, Harry's mother called me for his 3-month renewal of a stimulant for his ADHD. (I had previously been engaged with the child and the family extensively for other issues related to family trauma in the past.) The mother did not volunteer, so I asked how Harry was doing. "Oh, he's been doing just great," she said, with pleasure in her voice. I asked what she attributed this change to. "To the medication," she replied. I then asked her whether she thought all the change was due to the medication or whether part of the change was due to his efforts. She replied, "Oh, of course, a lot of the change is him, he is much more thoughtful and mature now." She went on to tell me how much more responsible Harry was than before, and so forth. I ended the conversation by reinforcing my message for her to be on the lookout for more changes coming from him.

Therapeutic Letters

"Treatment" can also take the form of writing therapeutic letters. I find many families enjoy receiving these letters. They experience themselves as important by receiving a letter from what they perceive to be a "busy doctor." The letters personalize the relationship and diminish professional distance with children, teenagers, and families. David Epston (Epston, Lobovits, & Freeman, 1997; White & Epston, 1990) disciplines himself to write a letter after every session, and the letter becomes part of the official chart record. Letters are written in a conversational, age-appropriate tone and use the child's and family's own words and metaphors. The letters document change, alternative moves in the right direction, and possible next moves. Letters are not used to reinforce diagnoses or medication instructions. Letter writing creates reflexive loops that reinforce the family's ability to work on problems together without developing an overreliance on the therapist's solutions. Often letters reinforce solutions talked about in the office that may be forgotten once the client leaves.

Documentation

Another unintended consequence of the psychiatric interview and treatment is therapists constructing clients as objects of analysis through their systems of documentation. The documents created (medical notes and files) are archived in the hospital, reinforcing the idea that clients are under official scrutiny and that their lives are under the experts' control. The child sees the medical record and may conclude that the thicker it gets, the bigger failure he or she is. Epston et al. (1997) and Simblett (1997) subvert the medical-legal construction of the medical record. Simblett bypasses this practice of objectifying people by reviewing whatever he writes in the chart with the person's input, and in some instances, he recirculates the official chart document so that it creates a reflexive loop as coconstructed by the client and therapist. The documents thus created are live documents open to possibilities, rather than simply documents acting as constraints and reminders of dominate oppressive ideas. Similarly, my consultation reports are written so that the family, rather than other professionals, is the main intended audience for their reception. The family has a chance to review the report and send it back to me before it becomes part of the "official" hospital record.

Conclusion

Drawing on early child psychiatry and narrative therapy has enriched my work with families. Engaging the tensions and contradictions of invoking both narrative and psychiatric work has led to many possibilities in conversations with families. Specifically, by working collaboratively, I have increased my effectiveness in engaging in the traditional stages of the psychiatric interview: "interviewing," "diagnosing," and "treating." In the past, I have inadvertently limited exploration of people's alternative, more empowering narratives. As the psychiatric interview is designed to determine a diagnosis rather than alternative stories, it is often focused on the precision of delineating symptoms at the expense of collaborating with families by focusing on the meaning behind symptoms, on strengths, and on generating hopefulness.

Parents are anxious about their children not fitting in and not being equipped for the future and feel a great responsibility toward them. Some parents find narratives consistent with the dominant psychiatric discourse limiting, and they support the development of alternative views. Parents whose children have serious adaptation and emotional difficulties often find that narratives of hopefulness can help the family cope with enormous stresses. Working collaboratively in a transparent manner has helped the families and myself find solutions that emphasize their own knowledges and expertise.

As illustrated in this chapter, there are many psychiatric traditions; the field is not homogeneous. Along with narrative therapists, many within mainstream child psychiatry disagree with the current overemphasis on the biomedical model. Many psychiatrists, among them my mentors, work collaboratively and are respectful of clients' strengths. In addition, while based in a modernist framework, many current "talk therapies" (e.g., cognitive behavior therapy, interpersonal therapy) have similarities with narrative therapy approaches. The possibilities for synthesizing narrative therapy with other approaches is perhaps best summarized by narrative psychiatrist Glen Simblett (1997):

> Narrative beliefs and practices allow me to consider different views of problems and their effects on people. Instead of trying to marry dichotomy and difference, I use an alternative metaphor that views experience as an ecological system, with each part dependent on and influenced by the other. The biological and biochemical are neither ignored nor overemphasized. (p. 145)

Narrative ideas have given me permission to return to traditional child psychiatry practices of being creative and getting down on the floor and playing with children. With the diagnostic and psychopharmacological movement, one could argue that much of the fun has been taken out of child psychiatry. When I have been relegated to the role of "med checks," it has resulted in a professional pessimism and stifling of therapeutic creativity. More than anything else, the narrative philosophy has reintroduced *hope* into my vocabulary. A narrative approach has allowed me to become changed by the stories I have been privileged to hear, as the reciprocal shaping of identities happens between myself and families.

Notes

1. I want to thank Anne Sexton, MSW, for review and thoughtful discussion of the text and being a wonderful, supportive colleague throughout all the years.

2. It should be emphasized that there were many competing psychoanalytic ideas. Freud's Oedipal theory of the role of the father in male identity formation was emphasized in contrast to Otto Rank's more inclusive theory of character formation due the mother's, probably more important, pre-Oedipal role.

3. See Berrios (1996) for a history of psychiatry and Micale and Porter (1994) for a critique of the history of psychiatry and antipsychiatry movements.

4. While a formulation using the biopsychosocial approach is made, this information is reduced to a multi-axial system where the psychiatric diagnosis (axis 1), predominantly individualistically based, is given the most importance. For example, children may end up with a plethora of diagnostic acronyms on axis 1 (e.g., ADHD, ODD, and CD, or PDDNOS-) without consideration being given to how a child's difficulties may be created by her or his cultural, family, or institutional context.

5. All case names in this chapter are pseudonyms.

6. I appreciate Michael White's (1995b) development of the definitional ceremony and integrate some of these ideas into work with reflecting teams.

References

Ackerman, N. (1980). The family with adolescents. In E. A. Carter & M. McGoldrick (Eds.), *The family life cycle: A framework for family therapy.* New York: Gardner Press.

American Psychiatric Association. (1980). *Diagnostic and statistical manual.* Washington, DC: American Psychiatric Press.

Andersen, T. (1991). *The reflecting team: Dialogues and dialogues about the dialogues.* New York: Norton.

Andersen, T. (1995). Reflecting processes: Acts of forming and informing. In S. Friedman (Ed.), *The reflecting team in action.* New York: Guilford.

Anderson, H., & Goolishian, H. (1988). Human systems as linguistic systems: Preliminary and evoking ideas about the implications for clinical theory. *Family Process, 27*(1), 371–394.

Anderson H., Goolishian, H., & Winderman, L. (1986). Problem created system: Towards transformation in family therapy. *Journal of Strategic and Family Therapy, 5*(4), 1–11.

Aries, P. (1962). *Centuries of childhood.* London: Jonathan Cape.

Bateson, G. (1971). A systems approach. *International Journal of Psychiatry, 9,* 242–244.

Berrios, G. (1996). *The history of mental symptoms: Descriptive psychopathology since the nineteenth century.* New York: Cambridge University Press.

Blackwell, B. (1973). Drug therapy: patient compliance. *New England Journal of Medicine, 289,* 249–252.

Bowen, M. (1982). *Family therapy in clinical practice* (2nd ed.). New York: Jason Aronson.

Caplan, P. (1995). *They say you're crazy: How the world's most powerful psychiatrists decide who is normal.* Boston: Addison-Wesley.

Carrey, N. (1999). Making the grade. *Readings: A Journal of Reviews and Commentary in Mental Health, 14*(1), 6–12.

Carrey, N., Costanzo, L., Sexton, A., & Aspin, J. (2004, November). The Dalhousie Family therapy training program: Our six year experience. *Bulletin of the Canadian Academy of Child and Adolescent Psychiatry, 13,* 114–118.

Chesler, P. (1997). *Women and madness.* New York: Four Walls, Eight Windows.

de Shazer, S. (1985). *Keys to solutions in brief therapy.* New York: Norton.

de Shazer, S. (1988). *Clues: Investigating solutions in brief therapy.* New York: Norton.

Engel, G. L. (1977). The need for a new medical model: a challenge for biomedicine. *Science, 196,* 129–136.

Epston, D., Lobovits, D., & Freeman, J. (1997). Annals of the "new Dave." *Gecko: A Journal of Deconstruction and Narrative Ideas in Therapeutic Practice, 3,* 59–85.

Foucault, M. (1980). Truth and power. In *Power/knowledge: Selected interviews and other writings.* London: Harvester Press.

Freud, S. (1934). *A general introduction to psychoanalysis.* New York: Pocket Books.

Gergen, K. (1990a). Therapeutic professions and the diffusion of deficit. *Journal of Mind and Behavior, 11*(4), 107–122.

Gergen, K. (1990b). Therapeutic professions and the diffusion of deficit. *Journal of Mind and Behavior, 11*(4), 353–368.

Gomez, E. (1996). Radical constructivism and narrative. *Journal of American Academy of Psychoanalysis, 24*(1), 1–14.

Greenhalgh, T., & Hurwitz, B. (1999). Why study narrative. *British Medical Journal, 18,* 48–50.

Gutheil, T. (1982). The psychology of psychopharmacology. *Bulletin of the Meninger Clinic, 46,* 321–330.

Haley, J. (1976). *Problem solving therapy.* San Francisco: Jossey-Bass.

Hardy, K., & Laszloffy, T. (1995). The cultural genogram: Key to training culturally competent family therapists. *Journal of Marital and Family Therapy, 21*(3), 227–237.

Jensen, P., & Hoagwood, K. (1997). The book of names: *DSM-IV.* In *Context, Development, and Psychopathology, 9,* 231–249.

Jones, K. (1999). *Taming the troublesome child.* Cambridge, MA: Harvard University Press.

Kirmayer, L. (2005). Culture, context, and experience in psychiatric diagnosis. *Psychopathology, 38*(4), 192–196.

Kuehl, B. (1995). The solution-oriented genogram: A collaborative approach. *Journal of Marital and Family Therapy, 21*(3), 239–250.

Kutchins, H., & Kirk, S. (1997). *Making us crazy: DSM: The psychiatric bible and the creation of mental disorder.* New York: Free Press.

Launer, J. (1999). A narrative approach to mental health in general practice. *British Medical Journal, 318,* 117–119.

McGoldrick, M., & Gerson, R. (1985). *Genograms and the family life cycle: Genograms in family assessment.* New York: Norton.

Micale, M., & Porter, R. (1994). *Discovering the history of psychiatry*. New York: Oxford University Press.

Minuchin, S. (1974). *Families and family therapy*. Cambridge, MA: Harvard University Press.

O'Hanlon, W., & Weiner-Davis, M. (1989). *In search of solutions*. New York: Norton.

Parry, T., & Doan, R. (1994). *Story revisions: Narrative therapy in the postmodern world*. New York: Guilford.

Pruett, K., & Martin, A (2003). Thinking about prescribing: The psychology of psychopharmacology. In A. Martin, L. Scahill, D. Charney, & J. Leckman (Eds.), *Pediatric psychopharmacology: Principles and practice* (pp. 417–425). New York: Oxford University Press.

Rutter, M. (2005). Environmentally mediated risks for psychopathology. *Journal of Academy of Child and Adolescent Psychiatry, 44*, 3–18.

Simblett, G. (1997). Leila and the tiger: Narrative approaches to psychiatry. In G. Monk, J. Winslade, K. Crocket, & D. Epston (Eds.), *Narrative therapy in practice: The archeology of hope* (pp. 132–145). San Francisco: Jossey-Bass.

Skolnick, A. (1976). *Re-thinking childhood*. Boston: Little, Brown.

Suberri, K. (2004). Pediatric psychology with a postmodern twist. *Journal of Systemic Therapies, 23*(1), 21–37.

Tomm, K. (1987a). Interventive interviewing: Part 1. Strategizing as a fourth guideline for the therapist. *Family Process, 26*, 3–13.

Tomm, K. (1987b). Interventive interviewing: Part II. Reflexive questioning as a means to enable self-healing. *Family Process, 26*, 167–183.

Tomm, K. (1988). Interventive interviewing: Part III. Intending to ask lineal, circular, strategic or reflexive questions? *Family Process, 27*, 1–15.

Tomm, K. (1990). A critique of the *DSM*. *Dulwich Center Newsletter, 3*, 5–8.

White, M. (1995a). Psychotic experiences and discourse. In *Re-authoring lives: Interviews and essays* (pp. 112–153). Adelaide, Australia: Dulwich Centre.

White, M. (1995b). *Reflecting teamwork as definitional ceremony*. In *Re-authoring lives: Interviews and essays* (pp. 172–198). Adelaide, Australia: Dulwich Centre.

White, M., & Epston, D. (1990). *Narrative means to therapeutic ends*. New York: Norton.

PART II

Self-Surveillance: Normalizing Practices of Self

6

Discipline and Desire

Regulating the Body/Self

Catrina Brown

Influenced by Foucault's notion of the "docile body" and of "disciplining the body," I will examine the way women use their bodies as a form of self-regulation, illuminating the tension between the discipline of and capitulation to desire and need in contemporary culture. The body is not stable, constant, asocial, ahistorical, or "natural." It is, as Foucault suggests, in "the grip" of cultural practices, including relations of power. I will focus on women's struggles with eating and body size as an example of normalization processes of the self. Challenging the oppressed/oppressor modernist formula of power, this analysis concedes that practices of power are often centered in practices of self-regulation or "self-surveillance and self-correction to norms" (Bordo, 1993, p. 27) rather than conspiracies of power or coercion. Women's self-regulation through controlling the body and how they appear in the world is a vivid example of self-surveillance as a mechanism of social power.

In *Civilization and Its Discontents*, Freud (1962) argues that becoming social citizens compromises our freedom to do whatever we want, as we are responsible not just to ourselves but also to the collective. In regulating ourselves to meet the expectations of culture, we participate in the larger regulation of the social body. Being a member of society means learning the language, expectations, meanings, and values of the culture in which we live. Today, normalization processes of the self invoke the cultural logic of self-management (Gremillion, 2001, 2003). The widespread proliferation of eating "disorders" among women within Western culture beginning in the 1970s is an articulation of these normalization processes in the cultural context of self-surveillance and self-management. Anorexia, bulimia, and pervasive chronic dieting among women reflect intersecting cultural discourses of self-management, the body, and gender. According to Gremillion (2001),

> A resourcing logic is a logic informed by an understanding of nature and the body as "things" that are somehow quite separate from consciousness. Within a resourcing logic, the body becomes something one controls and manipulates to create a particular kind of self, a self that reflects a certain kind of power in consumer culture today. I believe that anorexia reveals some of the problems, contradictions and devastations of these ideas. (p. 143)

Women's active use of the body, then, is situated within the context of gender, power, and cultural practices. Women's self-regulation or disciplining of desire is socially organized as part of the organization of a disciplined social body. Controlling their bodies can be seen as both compliance and resistance to cultural hegemony. As such, the body tells stories of women's struggles in culture.[1] The body is "seen as demonstrating correct or incorrect attitudes toward the demands of normalization itself" (Bordo, 1993, p. 203). The imperative for self-management "becomes more elusive as it becomes more pressing," according to Bordo (p. 59).

In other words, as social demands for self-management intensify, so too must one's self-surveillance practices. As the demands for self-management intensify and become increasingly normative, they are taken for granted in day-to-day life. Failure to self-manage or discipline is interpreted not as a problem stemming from the cultural imperative itself, but as individual failure. People, therefore, become invested in practices of regulation, hoping to demonstrate to others and themselves their success at self-control and management, which holds significant cultural value, admiration, and reward.

Socially Constructed Normalizing Practices of Self

Stories we tell about the self are, according to Bruner (2002), a balancing act between culturally expected performances of self and individual agency in the making of self. Cooley's study of the self suggests that we see ourselves through the eyes of others. He describes this interactional process as the "looking-glass self" (see Turner, 1978). Similarly, Bruner (2002) reminds us that the self is always, also, the other:

> Besides, narrative acts of self-making are usually guided by unspoken, implicit cultural models of what selfhood should be, might be—and, of course, shouldn't be. Not that we are slaves of culture, as even the most dedicated cultural anthropologists now appreciate. . . . Yet, all cultures provide presuppositions and perspectives about selfhood, rather like plot summaries or homilies for telling oneself or others about oneself.
>
> But, these self-making precepts are not rigid commands. They leave ample room for maneuver. Self-making is, after all, our principal means for establishing our uniqueness, and a moment's thought makes plain that we distinguish ourselves from others by comparing our accounts of ourselves with the accounts that others give us about themselves. (pp. 65–66)

Bruner (2002) highlights the coexistence of individual agency and social determinism in the shaping of our self-narratives:

> Telling others about oneself is, then, no simple matter. It depends on what we think they think we ought to be like—or what selves in general ought to be like. Nor do our calculations end when we come to telling ourselves about ourselves. Our self-directed, self-making narratives early come to express what we think others expect us to be like. Without much awareness of it, we develop a decorum for telling ourselves about ourselves. . . . Self-narratives conform to a tacit pacte autobiographique governing what constitutes appropriate public story telling. We become some variant of it even when we are only telling ourselves about ourselves. In the process, selfhood becomes res publica, even when talking to ourselves. (p. 66)

The construction of self within culture involves the necessity to self-regulate or to self-discipline. The creation of self is, however, distanced from its social processes of construction and meaning making. Berger and Luckmann's (1967) detailed account of the social construction of reality maintains that the human creation and history of ideas is lost over time, and in the process of separating ideas from their creation, they become dehumanized and objectified. Thus, in everyday, taken-for-granted reality, we separate our assumptions from their social construction, treating them as real in and of themselves. These ideas or assumptions act back upon us and create narrowing normative processes that limit choice and control doubts. Social discourses of the self act in just this way, in that we are then able to take up social notions of the self as if they were real in and of themselves. We then lose sight of the history of the social construction of the self, which naturalizes and obscures its social construction.

Widespread social discourses of the self center on the notion of individualism. The celebration of individualism champions the capacity and achievement of the individual, allowing the subject to be separated from social context. The cultural emphasis on the unique and essentialized individual self implies that both individual successes and individual problems are individual. The atomized self, reduced to the individual, becomes, according to Ewen and Ewen (1982), "the vehicle for general conformity" (p. 265); it is "individualism as conformity."

Such modernist and humanist interpretation of the self may be called *subjectivist*. Subjectivist interpretations of the self emphasize individual consciousness and lived experience. An emphasis on individual consciousness and lived experience from this perspective tends to avoid addressing the "social and historical productions of consciousness" (Grosz, 1992, p. 410) and thus makes the practices of self-regulation and discipline even more effective as cultural practices of power. Practices of self-regulation are decontextualized and depoliticized when they are interpreted as simply individual creations or expressions of the self. When notions of failure and success are tied to individual efforts of will and discipline, they effectively mask self-regulation as cultural practices of power.

Foucault (1980a, 1980b) suggests that individuals are vehicles of social power through enacting and reifying normative practices of self. Normalizing truths about what it is to be a subject are taken for granted in everyday practices of self. Power is insidious, White (2004) suggests, as it "recruits people's active participation in the fashioning of their own lives, their relationships and their identities" (p. 154). Power is especially insidious, because while individuals see themselves expressing their individuality, their uniqueness, their "real" selves, they are in fact, enacting—and, of course, resisting—socially constructed discourses about what constitutes the self. Subjectivity is thus produced and specified within cultural knowledges and practices. However, these practices are not fully determining of subjectivity, as individuals negotiate social life, both complying and resisting to normative constructions of self. There is space for individuals to go against limiting discourses and constructions of self. Nonetheless, we cannot overlook how individuals are "being incited to reproduce their subjectivities that are specified by the 'truth' (of human nature)" (White, 1997, p. 225). Narrative therapy challenges the unexamined, taken-for-granted, everyday assumptions that often shape limiting stories of the self through the process of re-authoring identities.

As Foucault (1980a, 1980b) observes, people are not ruled so much by force, but by their own willing participation in ensuring that they conform to normalizing practices of the self. Through a process of subjectification, we turn ourselves into subjects, absorbed by the creation, improvement, management, and performance of self. This process turns our gaze inward, as we seek to cultivate and manage ourselves as individuals, and renders invisible the social and historical context in which the subject is made. In anticipating being seen and judged by others, we shape ourselves accordingly. For Foucault, governance of subjects enables governance of the social body. Disciplining the social body requires disciplining the "docile body." The docile body refers to the processes by which individuals participate in normalizing and disciplinary practices of the self (Foucault, 1984). Rather than being ruled by force, they "supervise their own disciplined behavior" (Tanesini, 1999, p. 198).

The process of subjectification involves both power as constraint and domination and power as productive and constitutive (Foucault, 1984). In making ourselves into subjects within the context of culture, we are both constrained and creative. This understanding permits a view of individuals both constrained by and resisting power and its effects. Although dominant discourses of self-management turn the gaze inward, disciplining the docile body, ensuring that individuals are docile or self-constraining, they are also sites of resistance. And similarly, we are reminded by Butler (1993) that while there is choice or "free play" in the performance of self, there are social limits or constraints on this performance. In short, the performance of self in culture involves both agency and self-determination and limitation and social constraint.

There is, according to Foucault (1984), an "'elegance' of the discipline" (p. 182) whereby,

> An art of the human body was born. . . . What was then formed was a policy of coercions that act upon the body, a calculated manipulation of its elements, its gestures, its behavior. The human body was entering a machinery of power that explores it, breaks it down, and rearranges it. A "political anatomy," which was also a mechanics of power. (p. 182)

The notion of self-regulation or self-discipline requires particular social constructions of the self that are tied to the body. Our presentation of self through the body reveals to others the degree to which we have succeeded at self-regulation and, subsequently, reveals the meanings attached to self-regulation in this culture. Thus, self-management involves both agency and constraint. Put another way, self-regulation requires our participation; it involves "self-determinism" and social control.

Bordo finds Foucault's conceptualization of power a more effective tool for understanding a reading of the slender body than the oppressor/oppressed formula of power. Women's efforts at controlling or regulating their bodies through conforming to social pressures to be thin is an example of how domination and subordination are not achieved so much through overt acts of authoritarianism, conspiracies of power, or coercion, but through "self-surveillance and self-correction to norms" (Bordo, 1993, p. 27). According to (Bordo 1993), Foucault's treatment of power is useful in unpacking women's relationship to their bodies:

> In my own work, they have been extremely helpful both to my analysis of the contemporary disciplines of diet and exercise and to my understanding of eating disorders as arising out of and reproducing normative feminine practices of our culture, practices which train the female body in docility and obedience to cultural demands while at the same time being experienced in terms of power and control. (p. 27)

This approach allows us to all see that where there is power, there is resistance. Women experience themselves as powerful when they establish control over their bodies, yet this desire for control suggests a perceived lack of control over their lives. Moreover, the meaning that they associate with controlling their bodies is a product of power relations. Their self-regulation or disciplining of desire is socially organized as part of the organization of a disciplined social body. Women controlling their bodies can be seen as both compliance and resistance to hegemonic gendered subjectivity and to the processes of subjectification that both produce and require the "docile body."

How do women come to associate controlling their bodies with a sense of personal control? How and why do they want to feel in control? How is this meaningful to them and to their perceived sense of self? How is this central to processes of self-surveillance?

Typically, the problems individuals bring to therapy are instances of perceived failure or difficulties in meeting cultural expectations of selfhood (White, 2004). The discourse of personal failure—incompetence, inadequacy, not being good enough—is pivotal to processes of subjectification and identity construction. Such struggles with self are, of course, struggles between who one perceives oneself to be, who one would like to be, and who one is expected to be. Discourses of failure ensure an ongoing monitoring and policing of oneself. However, self-regulation or management is not always straightforward, as individuals both conform to and resist culturally constructed normalizing practices of self. Eating too much, drinking too much, and gambling too much and being too angry, too sad, or too unproductive are typically taken up as failures of self. Stories people tell about themselves reflect discursive cultural constructions of the self. These stories reflect modernist cultural discourses of the self, which is presumed to be stable, fixed, unified, and essential. Furthermore, cultural discourses construct the self as unique, self-determined, independent, managed, contained, controlled, and responsible and are internalized as uncontestable truth. The logic of this pivots on the individual as an entity outside both cultural context and social relations of power. According to Foucault (1980b), "Now the phenomenon of the social body is the effect not of a consensus but of the materiality of power operating on the very bodies of individuals" (p. 55). Problematically, then, women struggling with eating "disorder" issues situate the struggle within themselves and are unable to see their normalizing practices of self as participation in social regulation.

Disciplining the Body: Paradoxes of Control and Power

I argue that eating "disorders" and weight preoccupation among women are culturally encoded normative practices; they are but one example of normalizing practices of the self that ultimately contribute to disciplining the social body. This self-regulation is a cultural imperative, but the specific articulation of women's talk through their bodies, the resourcing of their bodies to speak for them, to represent their struggles of self-regulation, is worthy of further exploration.

Narrative therapy helps to "refuse those subjectivities that are informed by practices in the calculated management of self" (White, 1997, p. 232). While this challenge to the calculated management of self is vital, striking a balance in the ways in which people have been constrained by and with which they resist oppressive cultural constructions of self is of fundamental importance. Throughout, I argue that anorexia, bulimia, and the entire spectrum of eating problems among women can be constructed not only as compliance to self-management as "docile bodies" but also as expressions of resistance.

According to Lawrence (1979), "When anorexics talk about control, they invariably mean the power to regulate, command and govern their own lives and actions" (p. 93). The terror of becoming or being fat or losing control over their desire for food is a surface telling of the source of terror. Furthermore, being in control is an imperative, and being out of control is equated with moral and personal failure. Lawrence (1979) was one of the first to identify anorexia as an issue of control. Anorexic women's internal lives are a struggle between satisfying themselves and satisfying their perception of others' expectations. An aspect of their own self-management involves how to reconcile the two.

Women who struggle with anorexia are often intolerant, violently self-critical of any transgression of self-regulation. They seem to have deeply internalized the cultural imperative of self-management; they must "tow the line," "buckle down," and "suck it up." The fragile sense of control over the experience of self, and of themselves in the world, seems to result in overabsorbing the cultural imperative to self-regulate. This strict self-policing and surveillance offers a sense of being in control. Reflecting dominant social discourses of the self shaped by the logic of self-management, individual control, management, and discipline is valued, whereas, alternatively, capitulating to desire or taking care of or responding to needs is devalued. Subsequently, one's emotional world is held hostage to the imperative of self-control and self-management. An opposition is instituted between "needs," desires, and the relaxing of one's self-surveillance and "shoulds," rules, and the intensification of self-management.[2] It is as though women hold large sticks over their own heads, ready to strike out at themselves when they imagine themselves to have stepped out of line.

This rigid and authoritarian form of emotional self-totalitarianism is a powerful example of Foucault's idea that people typically do not need to be forced to constrain themselves or to comply to social relations of power; power operates from within through such disciplining, normalizing practices of self. Anorexia, bulimia, chronic restrictive dieting, and relentless exercise take the social requirement of self-management to an extreme, and, in so doing, reveal, importantly, its very existence. These struggles are cultural articulations that expose the broader and more widespread cultural practices of power. Through unpacking the individual disciplinary practices of eating "disorders," we are given a glimpse into the mechanism of regulating and controlling the social body. These more extreme expressions of self-regulation are not separate from the normative expectations of self-regulation that are central strategies in the social practices of power.

According to Lawrence (1979), anorexic women, "exercise self-control, which we might understand as power turned inward. The battleground then becomes an internal one; the battle is fought within the individual rather than between the individual and the world" (p. 93). They wish to be confident, masterful, in control, special, and unique but are afraid of the expectation this will produce, afraid they cannot achieve this, and afraid others will not accept this version of them. They are concurrently afraid of achieving this strong expression of self and afraid of not achieving it. This fear is expressed as ambivalence. Lawrence goes on to say, "Controlling weight is used by many women as a substitute for controlling the real issues in their lives over which they feel they have no control" (p. 94). Self-control is a substitute for taking active and effective control through interacting with others in the social world. In the throes of struggling with eating "disorders," women absent themselves from the world, turning inward, making their bodies and their worlds very small, contained, manageable—almost invisible. They metaphorically attempt to disappear at the same time that they experience a powerful, seductive, and intoxicating sense of power and control over themselves through self-starvation and regulation of the body/self. Lawrence describes this as a "control paradox."

Within this control paradox, it is in feeling out of control—drowning in an incapacity to define herself in the world, to make a mark, and to matter, while holding onto a competing suspicion that she is somehow special, worthy, and capable of achievement—that the anorexic women is compelled to seek this fragile and dangerous sense of control. The paradox is that it is only in feeling so desperately out of control that one needs to establish this form of compensatory control. Hence, the internal struggle expressed through eating "disorders" is not simply an individual struggle, but a struggle to work out a satisfactory relationship between one's experience of self and one's environment. It is easier and less emotionally threatening for it to become an internal problem (Lawrence, 1979). Similarly, it is less culturally threatening for it to appear to be the woman's individual problem, as it does not then have to be taken up as a problem with the cultural logic of self-management or gendered cultural expectations.

Women's struggles with eating "disorders" protest and resist cultural expectation, in part by appearing to conform while also indirectly expressing a powerful indictment of cultural expectation. In this way, it is a veiled protest, a hidden and ambivalent unspoken story. The suppressed voice of this yet to be spoken, subjugated story is at once attempting to speak and hide. The struggle is masked, and thus it is easy for therapy to focus on the surface stories of eating and body weight. Yet the unheard voice expressed through women's struggles with the body need to be heard. From a narrative perspective, we need to uncover the alternative suppressed stories partially hidden within struggles with controlling the body and bring forward and nourish them in the creation of new, more helpful stories.

Women's struggles with their bodies tells stories of self-discipline and self-regulation in culture: the ambivalence, contradiction, and impact of the logic of self-management. Eating "disorders" are gendered articulations of women's efforts at self-regulation. According to Bordo (1993),

In advanced consumer capitalism, as Robert Crawford has elegantly argued, an unstable, agonistic construction of personality is produced by the contradictory structure of economic life. On the one hand, as producers of goods and services we must sublimate, delay, repress desires for immediate gratification; we must cultivate the work ethic. On the other hand, as consumers we must display a boundless capacity to capitulate to desire and indulge in impulse; we must hunger for constant and immediate satisfaction. The regulation of desire thus becomes an ongoing problem, as we find ourselves continually besieged by temptation, while socially condemned for overindulgence. (Of course, those who cannot afford to indulge their desires as consumers, teased and frustrated by the culture, face a much harsher dilemma). (p. 199)

Bordo (1993) describes differences in the metaphors of thinness and fatness in our culture. With thinness, needs and desires are contained, while with fatness, disapproval comes largely from the perceived capitulation to desire that fatness communicates. In the case of anorexia, one's life is overtaken by self-denial, self-restraint, and self-deprivation, which appear to mirror the woman's inner life. While thinness is the perfect metaphor of self-restraint, anorexia takes the cultural imperative of self-management too far, exposing the oppressive and controlling ramifications of the cultural demand of self-restraint, self-deprivation, and self-surveillance. These behaviors and cultural metaphors reflect larger cultural discourses of the self. The moral, valued, admired self must be watched, self-policed—the promise of self-surveillance is a well-disciplined, managed, regulated, and normative self and, by extension, a disciplined conforming social body.

With bulimia, women oscillate between self-deprivation and the disciplining of desires and capitulation or surrendering to desires. Unable to sustain a life of such emotional and physical impoverishment and self-denial, a life of such rigid self-management, they sometimes find themselves surrendering, losing control to their desires. The excess of bingeing and the emotional release afforded by purging is at least in part a reaction against, or a resistance to, the demands of excessive self-restraint. Within the cultural logic of self-management, bulimia reveals normative cultural demands: We can have desires as long as we hide, restrict, and manage them.

Bordo (1993) describes the double bind between desire and regulation in the normative way people live their lives in dominant culture:

Conditioned to lose control at the mere sight of desirable products, we can master our desires only by creating rigid defenses against them. The slender body codes the tantalizing ideal of a well-managed self in which all is kept in order despite the contradictions of consumer culture. Thus, whether or not the struggle is played out in terms of food and diet, many of us may find our lives vacillating between a daytime rigidly ruled by the "performance principle" and nights and weekends that capitulate to unconscious "letting go" (food, shopping, liquor, television, and other addictive drugs). In this way, the central contradictions of the system inscribes itself on our bodies, and bulimia emerges as a characteristic modern personality construction. For bulimia precisely and explicitly expresses the extreme development of the hunger for unrestrained consumption (exhibited in the bulimic's uncontrollable food binges) existing in unstable tension along-side the requirement that we sober up, "clean up our act," get back in firm con-trol on Monday morning (the necessity for purge—exhibited in the bulimic's vomiting, compulsive exercise, and laxative purges). (p. 201)

Bordo (1993) argues that how we experience and how we discipline, man-age, and order our bodies reflects the larger tensions of the social body. She suggests that we live in a bulimic culture, in which—as within the bulimic woman—there is an ongoing struggle between desire and discipline. There is a structural paradox for both the culture and the bulimic woman. Dominant culture today is reflected in an unstable personality structure that has diffi-culty finding a balance between the consumer and producer: between surren-dering to desire and pleasure—and ordering, disciplining, controlling, and managing our lives. This social tension is embodied in the bulimic experience; it is embodied in the struggle of the bulimic woman between fulfilling her desires and establishing an adequate sense of control over herself and her life. Fatness, then, symbolically or metaphorically conveys anxieties of the inner self for the world to see. Of crucial significance is the reality that struggling with eating problems and battling their bodies offers many women the possi-bility of a sense of control and mastery over themselves and their lives. As Lawrence (1984) suggests, many women report that control over their bod-ies is the only real form of control they feel they have.

For most women in this culture, regardless of body weight, there is a con-flict between the desire to eat—satisfaction, pleasure, and fulfillment—and the desire to police or discipline their body weight because they fear the social consequences of gaining weight. To gain a sense of control over how they are seen and subsequently treated, women turn the gaze of others upon themselves (Berger, 1972). A woman's body has become her own commod-ity. It is the object with which women bargain in the world. Furthermore, as Orbach (1986) notes, women must be both unique and conform to society as they express themselves through their bodies.

Foucault's (1980b) analysis of the intensification of self-surveillance and control over sexuality is useful for understanding a similar intensification of self-surveillance and control over body size and eating. The increased social imperative to regulate or discipline sexuality or, in this discussion, body size and eating, has the effect of intensifying the desire to surrender control. The imperative to self-regulate, according to Foucault (1980b), "engenders at the same time an intensification of each individual's desire for, in, and over his body" (p. 57). For example, the self-surveillance and self-regulation evident through restricted eating often produces an increased desire for food (Bellar, 1977). The more one thinks about not being able to have food, the more one thinks about having food. In most instances, it would appear that the more self-discipline is exercised, the more desire is intensified. With anorexia, self-discipline appears to become almost absolute, as though it were almost able to eradicate or achieve total control over desire. Yet it may be that desire is only driven further underground, not actually eradicated. The ongoing life of self-denial, restraint, and deprivation hints at how immense the threat of desire is. The threat of eruption then calls for further intensification of self-surveillance and control. The self-restraint of anorexia obscures the desire and the need, but the ferocious and unrelenting display of self-surveillance and self-discipline reveals its unwillingness to simply remain driven underground.

In White's (2001) language, the resurrection of the suppressed voice is a form of social resistance to the gendered performance of the "good woman." The self-regulation or management of the "good woman" requires, in fact, that certain stories be held back, toned down, or made more appropriately feminine. How is a woman to express her desire for more power, control, mastery, and achievement—and also be a "good woman"? How does a woman express her desires or her struggles, when that situates her at the center rather than others? Essentialist constructions of gender minimize women's stories of conflict, anger, desire, dissatisfaction, and aggression. Instead, the "good woman" turns herself toward others' needs and finds her primary satisfaction through doing this. Insofar as she struggles with the world, she turns these struggles inward. The struggles are contained, not permitted to spill over into public view, demonstrating the ultimate compliance to self-management. Through directing the struggle inward to the socially accepted arena of bodily self-management, the struggle has not actually disappeared; it has only become displaced. Such displacement of women's struggles onto the body renders them invisible and controls their social messiness.

Disciplining the Gendered Body

What constitutes the subject's self-discipline is also gendered. What counts as self-management or regulation and the parameters of this are arguably different for men and women. The very fact that 95% of anorexics are women and 80% of bulimics are women suggests that the avenues for self-discipline are gendered (Brown & Jasper, 1993b). One way in which the social body is disciplined is through discourses that interpret and define social problems in individual terms. Since the 1970s, women's struggle for autonomy and a sense of personal adequacy in Western culture has been expressed through a control or management of the body among women who experience anorexia, bulimia, and issues with weight preoccupation. Women's attitudes toward their bodies articulate their uncertainty about how they can achieve a sense of success in society today (Orbach, 1978, 1986). A pioneer in working with women with eating "disorders," Bruch (1978) suggests in *The Golden Cage: The Enigma of Eating Disorders* that women's control over the body and eating expresses the need to establish a sense of mastery, success, or confidence in one area of their lives. The need to control what one eats, regardless of hunger, and the need to control one's weight, regardless of actual body weight, suggests a perceived sense of lack of control of the rest of one's life (Lawrence, 1984). Chernin (1981) writes in *The Obsession: Reflections on the Tyranny of Slenderness* that anorexia nervosa and the "women's reduction movement" reflect the same protests as the women's movement, except the individual's rebellion is "expressed through a veiled and disguised symbolism" (p. 103).

Reflecting on the paradox of self-management in a consumer culture, the anorexic woman must often negate need and rely on self-denial and deprivation. According to Orbach (1986), this is a brutal struggle:

> In each instance of anorexia one can observe the most brutal internal struggle directed at suppression of needs that originate inside the woman. The evidence of need is felt as threatening to a self-image which is based on effacement. If anorexia is always an attempt at negating need, the question is why these women's needs are so fraught and why privation is so highly valued. The answer, I will argue, lies in the particularly heightened sensitivity that these women have absorbed from an early age about the ways in which they are to live *as women*. The individual woman's problem—for which the anorexia has been the solution—is that despite a socialization process designed to suppress her needs, she has continued to feel her own needs and desires intensely. She has not successfully come to terms with negotiating those internal desires either by being able to meet them or by binding them up with ease. Her anorexia is the daily, even hourly, attempt to keep her needs in check, to keep herself and her desires under wraps. In dominating her existence, anorexia negates the force of other needs. In demanding a superhuman submission to denial it provides a self-contained and reliable way of being. . . .
>
> Whenever woman's spirit has been threatened, she has taken the control of her body as an avenue of self-expression. The anorectic refusal of food is only the latest in a series of woman's attempts at self-assertion which at some point have descended directly upon her body. If woman's body is the site of her protest, then equally the body is the ground upon which the attempt for control is fought. (pp. 18–19)

Shifting Performances of Gendered Identity

The self-discipline and denial required by anorexia, bulimia, and weight preoccupation may be a way that women cope with the desperation and uncertainty they feel regarding how they measure up to outer standards at this time in women's history (Brown, 1987a, 1987b; Brown & Forgay, 1987; Brown & Jasper, 1993b; Lawrence, 1979; Rodolico, 1980). The liberation of women from the tyranny of restraint of food and weight involves decoding what eating problems appear to be about and moving beyond the surface, symptoms, or body talk to the underlying construction of meaning. In decoding this phenomenon, Chernin (1985) concludes that the difficulties that women have with food and weight obscure a problem with female identity that has emerged with extending the idea of what it means to be female in our society since the 1970s. Changes in expectations of women's gender performance since this time are fraught with confusion, uncertainty, conflict, and contradiction.

Orbach (1986) describes an eating "disorder" as "a psychological bridging mechanism" (p. 103) between contradictory gender expectations that require women to conform to traditional gender roles, particularly as mothers and wives, while also performing as emancipated women in the public sphere. Both Orbach (1986) and Chernin (1985) describe the current preoccupation women have with weight as being the consequence of a "crisis of identity" from our entry into "masculinist culture." Orbach (1986) suggests that one needs to understand the relationship between "aspects of women's psychology, such as unentitledness, insecurity, shaky boundaries, and outdirectedness, that make them susceptible to seeking validation and safety by acquiring the 'correct body'" (p. 88). Influenced by the work of Orbach (1986), Bordo (1993) states,

> The anorectic embodies, in an extreme and painfully debilitating way, a psychological struggle characteristic of the contemporary situation of women. That situation is one which a constellation of social, economic, and psychological factors have combined to produce a generation of women who feel deeply flawed, ashamed of their needs, and not entitled to exist unless they transform themselves into worthy new selves (read: without need, without want, without body). (p. 47)

Traditional gender scripts based on dualistic constructions of masculinity and femininity no longer coincide with actual expectations and performances of men and women in the public sphere. It is my view that the thin, muscular body ideal today is an expression of both the emancipation and oppression of women, whereby thinness represents increased social equality for women through the image of freedom, action, and independence as well as continued traditional representation of women as vulnerable and dependent. That is, the social image of thinness and women's preoccupation with being thin in contemporary society is an expression of the social position and worth of women. The visible portrayal of cultural change among the relations between men and women in patriarchal society thus communicates the existence of both traditional and contemporary expectations of women. Furthermore, the large-breasted, thin, muscular body ideal today reveals it has been sculpted, worked on, disciplined, and policed.

Weight preoccupation communicates disruptions in traditional notions of women's identities, exposing fragmented and complex gender identities that correspond to women's contradictory social positions. The widespread pervasiveness of weight preoccupation and eating "disorders" is a product of the coincidence of the prevailing thin-body ideal and the fragmented identities of women. Thus, weight preoccupation is a powerful metaphor for the paradoxes of women's social position. The coincidence of the thin, muscular body ideal and the fragmented shifting identities of women today "feed into each other" (Brown, 1987a). Young women especially are often uncertain about who they can be in the world, what they can be, and what they can do as they make sense of what is expected of them. During a time in women's history when women may feel shaky about their ability to take control of their own lives, controlling their bodies offers a form of success and achievement that is widely condoned (Brown & Forgay, 1987). Furthermore, the cultural logic of self-management makes women susceptible to resourcing their own bodies, as a way to achieve this sense of control experienced through control of the body.

Many women diet throughout their lives, repeatedly gaining and losing weight, and it is now well documented that most people who lose weight regain it (Chernin, 1981; Sternhell, 1985). While women report feeling better about themselves when they lose weight, this can be seen as a precarious sense of well-being when one acknowledges the very high "failure rate" of dieting and that ultimately most gain back even more weight than they lose (Chernin, 1981; Dyrenthorth, Wooley, & Wooley, 1980; Orbach, 1978, 1986; Robinson, 1985; Sternhell, 1985). Many women believe that if they lose weight, all their problems will be solved (Millman, 1980; Orbach 1978). People expect to feel more confident, to like themselves better, to be more outgoing, and to be happier and more successful (see Brown, 1987a, p. 9). The cultural inducements for thinness are compelling, and thus most women strive to achieve them. Yet, as Chernin (1981) demonstrates, this "tyranny of slenderness" has a grip on women's bodies and on women's sense of themselves. While women resource themselves through their bodies, seeking greater power and control over their lives, the pernicious and insidious ways that women manage themselves in pursuit of the cultural rewards associated with thinness are illustrative of the normalizing practices of self as disciplinary practices or strategies of cultural power.

Body and Power

In my work with Jasper in *Consuming Passions: Feminist Approaches to Weight Preoccupation and Eating Disorders* (1993a), we asked why thinness has become the dominant cultural ideal or representation at this time in history. We asked, "Why women, why weight, why now?" Bordo (1993) concurs that a sociological analysis of eating problems among women must address the specific social context. We cannot simply suggest women have been indoctrinated by the media in their quest for thinness. Instead, we need to understand how thinness has a particular meaning in this culture, at this time in history, and how that came to be.

Similarly, feminist writers Bordo (1993) and Thompson (1994) urge us to resist focusing only on the issue of appearance, as it can result in overlooking more complicated meaning, such as the "role of the body in the nexus of power relations" (Bordo, 1993). They critique the general tendency of limiting the social analysis of anorexia to the world of aesthetics, the world of the media and fashion. Bordo (1993) believes that the "meaning of the ideal of slenderness" needs to be explored both in the context of women's experiences and "as a cultural formation that expresses ideals, anxieties, and social changes (some related to gender, some not)" (p. 46). The slender body operates as a text that can be read and deconstructed in order to better understand the social context in which eating problems have proliferated. Bordo (as cited in Jacobs, Fox Keller, & Shuttleworth, 1990) wants to understand the "political anatomy" of the slender body:

> Understanding the "political anatomy" (as Foucault would call it) of the slender body requires the interrogation of both "useful" and "intelligible" arenas— interrogation of the practices or "disciplines" of diet and exercise which structures the organization of time, space, and the experience of embodiment for subjects; and, in our image-bedazzled culture, interrogation of the popular representations through which meaning is crystallized, symbolized metaphorically encoded, and transmitted. My overall argument emphasizes the primacy of practice for evaluating the role of bodies in the nexus of power relations. (p. 86)

In "the grip" of cultural practices including relations of power (Foucault, 1980a, p. 155), the body is not stable, constant, asocial, ahistorical, or "natural." According to Bordo (1993), "Our bodies, no less than anything else that is human, are constituted by culture" (p. 142).[3] Foucault is one of the most important contributors to our ability to analyze the relationship between the body, cultural practices, and power. In his studies on sexuality (1980a), madness (1988), and prisons (1995), he illustrates that knowledge is historically constructed and ever shifting and that forms of knowledge correspond to social forms of power, often played out through the body, which constitute humans as both objects and subjects. Transformations in the deployment of sexuality, construction of medicalized notions of madness, and regulation and discipline of the social body are all operations of power. Foucault's (1995) studies center on "power and knowledge relations that invest human bodies and subjugate them by turning them into objects of knowledge" (p. 28). He writes,

> Historians long ago began to write the history of the body. They have studied the body in the field of historical demography or pathology; they have considered it as the seat of needs and appetites, as the locus of physiological processes and metabolisms, as a target for the attacks of germs or viruses; they have shown to what extent historical processes were involved in what might seem to be the purely biological "events" such as the circulation of bacilli, or the extension of the lifespan. But the body is also directly involved in a political field; power relations have an immediate hold upon it; they invest it, mark it, train it, torture it, force it to carry out tasks, to perform ceremonies, to emit signs. (Foucault, 1995, p. 25)

Science, certainly medicine and psychiatry, exercises power in the deployment of knowledge and in the treatment and interpretation of the body. In specialized fields of knowledge, such as eating "disorders," the exercise of power targets the body.

The body has been seen in Western political and social thought through a dualistic framework that bifurcates human life into the world of the body and the material and the world of the mind and the spiritual. Bordo (1993) articulates dimensions of the body as experienced by the anorexic person as reflecting an imagery with a long history in Western culture. She refers to Plato, Augustine, and Descartes, who, like the anorexic woman, see the body as alien or as the "not-self, the not-me," and as "confinement and limitation," a "prison," a "cage," and, last, as the "enemy" (p. 144).

The project of understanding human beings has in large part been an exercise in attempting to gain the greatest degree of control we can over our existence. In this sense, there is a struggle between human bodily or material constraints (i.e., physical effects of aging) and the desire to control or alter these constraints through knowledge, culture, and science (i.e., efforts at slowing down physical effects of aging). In short, nature is, through "science" and culture, to be controlled, disciplined, and overcome. In Bordo's words, our bodies threaten to erupt and disrupt, as they are not entirely controllable. The body is the "locus of all that threatens our attempts at control" (Bordo, 1993, p. 145). The dualism of self and body is evident in our conceptualization of the self as controlled/regulated and the body as being in need of regulation.

The coalescing of the cultural meaning of thinness and of the body with the shifting experiences of women in a patriarchal culture since the 1970s and the psychological sequelae of trauma such as sexual abuse, taken together, may produce in some a significant tension between order and desire in the regulation of self. Women struggle between the need to fulfill subjective desires and the need to fit the social normalization processes of the self. Weight and food are sites for playing out these tensions, especially for women, because of the particular way desire and order are structured in Western advanced-capitalist patriarchal society and the meaning that the body and food have for women.

According to Bordo (1993), women are held responsible for the bodily response of men to them, as women's bodies are seen as speaking "a language of provocation" (p. 6). When women are seen to invite male desire and are subsequently unresponsive, they are seen as teasing or mocking. Women are often blamed for the attacks on their bodies, even seen as "asking for" assaults perpetrated against them. We need to question how the internalization of this discourse impacts on women's sense of their bodies and their power. Further-more, Malson (1997) points out that both women and women's bodies are often constructed as "excess." From an androcentric lens, women may be seen as talking too much and being too emotional or too needy. The message is that women should "tuck themselves in," not take up too much space, and not appear to be uncontained. Black women face the additional coding of being more "bodily."

Encoding the Body: The Embodiment of Race, Class, and Gender

In her discussion on gender and race as the "ampersand problem in feminist thought," Spelman (1988) provides an interesting analysis of *embodiment*. Part of the history of "men's" efforts at controlling nature has been to refute their own embodiment. The dominant and dualistic cultural encoding associates men with mind and women with body. Spelman argues that the "somatophobia" in traditional thought as well as feminist thinking contributes to what Adrienne Rich has previously called "white solipsism" (p. 127). Somatophobia is implicated in racism, sexism, and class prejudice. It is, of course, the marginalized men and women of color, the poor, and White women who are conceptualized as more bodily, more identified with the body. Dominance and superiority, Spelman asserts, have typically been thought to transcend the body. It is, she suggests, problematic when oppressed groups associate their own liberation with freedom from their bodies, as this plays into a framework that accepts the mind/body dualism and values mind over body. Moreover, she notes that the work of the body will have to be done by someone or some group.

> Without bodies, we could not have personal histories. Nor could we be iden-
> tified as woman or man, Black or white. This is not to say that reference to
> publicly observable bodily questions settles the question of whether someone
> is woman, Black or white; nor is it to say that being woman or man, Black or
> white, just means having certain bodily characteristics (that is one reasons
> some Blacks want to capitalize the term; "Black" refers to a cultural identity,
> not simply a skin color). But different meanings are attached to having certain
> characteristics, in different places and at different times and by different
> people, and those differences affect enormously the kinds of lives we lead or
> experiences we have. Women's oppression has been linked to the meanings
> assigned to having a woman's body by male oppressors. Black oppression has
> been linked to the meanings assigned to having a black body by white oppres-
> sors (Note again how insidiously this way of speaking once again leaves
> unmentioned the situation for Black women). We cannot hope to understand
> the meaning of person's experiences, including her experiences of oppression,
> without first thinking of her as embodied, and second thinking about the par-
> ticular meanings assigned to that embodiment. (pp. 129–130)

Drawing upon critiques of previous feminist discourse for the exclusion of adequate discussion of race and class differences among women, the representation of women as passive and lacking agency, and the essentialism of men as aggressive and dominating, Bordo (1993) wisely determines to move beyond the simple oppressor/oppressed model. Furthermore, she concurs with critiques that suggest that simply acknowledging the context of multiple meanings is insufficient. Taking into account the plethora of differences that includes race, class, ethnicity, and sexual orientation makes reading the body very complicated. While acknowledging that readers of the body will assign multiple meanings, Bordo argues we cannot focus at all moments only on the multiple, because to do so is to obscure the homogenizing and normalizing effects of cultural representations.

The Active Subject and the Archeology of Symptoms

Social theorists have endlessly struggled with understanding the relationship between the subject and the social structure, often erring on the side of either subjectivism, with its focus on the individual as a fully free agent, or a rigid social determinism that erases the subject except as product. Bordo (1993) argues that while we can acknowledge the social conditions that produce "psychopathology," in the end, the "symptoms themselves must still be produced (however, unconsciously or inadvertently) by the subject" (p. 177). Indeed, exploring the way the individual has produced symptoms and meanings tells us a story about how power works in everyday life (p. 178). An individual woman has the capacity to both resist and collude with power relations and may well be situated where she does both either consciously or not. When we examine the meaning of the body and eating for the subject, we can "see how the desires and dreams of the subject become implicated in the matrix of power relations" (p. 178). The fantasy is one of power, control, recognition, and approval. While the individual fantasy can exist only in a social context in which it can be meaningful, it is still informative for its "in-itselfness." Hence, we can read the fantasy as conveying an active subject. The subject, however, acts within socially given parameters. The fantasy is not simply an inevitable social product, for it must be meaningful to the subject. For socialization to occur, active participation on the part of the individual is necessary. The conflation of the subject's desires and fantasies with social conditions will shape the archaeology of "symptoms."

Implications for Therapeutic Conversations

Therapeutic conversations with women around a continuum of struggles, including anorexia, bulimia, and weight preoccupation, need to both expose the cultural logic of self-management that influences the development of these problems and not reinvoke or inadvertently champion self-management within the therapeutic work. For example, it is my view that these conversations should not center on the surface stories told about weight and eating, but should instead attempt to uncover their multiple meanings. Externalizing conversations need to unpack pivotal themes such as power, control, and self-discipline and how these are played out through the body. Of importance is the need to explore ways that women feel out of control or powerless in their lives and how they seek to establish a greater sense of power and control through controlling their bodies. For "Genna," issues of self-management are very apparent. Through a brief discussion of Genna's story and her metaphor of the "robot," I will illustrate the need for narrative therapy to consider how cultural requirements of self-discipline are encoded through gendered normalizing practices that center on controlling the body.

Genna is a 24-year-old woman living with a roommate. She is finishing her undergraduate degree. She has been a competitive athlete since adolescence. In her early teens, she was binge eating, but by her late teens, she began to throw up afterward. Recently, she lost quite a bit of weight and attended an inpatient program after her weight plummeted to 80 pounds. She is not interested in the local outpatient program available to her and wishes to stay out of the hospital. She was referred to me in private practice through her doctor. Genna currently weighs 90 pounds, and her health status is stable. She is able to keep her weight at a low, stable, nonfluctuating state. She continues to binge and purge on a regular basis. We have contracted around this, as she needs to have a minimum stable health status to avoid potential hospitalization.

Genna describes herself as a very hard worker, always pushing herself as hard as she can. She takes pride in how hard she can work, how well she does in school, and the sense of control she experiences through this. However, recently she has described this as being like a "robot." She has noticed that the more she pushes herself in terms of restrictive eating and studying, the more she feels like a robot. She had begun to not like feeling like this, observing that when she finds herself in this mental space, she becomes more vulnerable to binge eating.

We are not so much externalizing anorexia or bulimia per se as we are externalizing the "robot." For Genna, we are externalizing the "robot" because this is her stance in the world: "I must be disciplined, I must be controlled." This process enables her to see how this stance not only offers her a sense of greater power and control but also restricts her life. We want to hold onto the tension between the power and control gained and the power and control ultimately lost. Especially at the beginning of this process, I acknowledge both aspects of this tension, but emphasize the power and control gained. This allows her to realize that I see how it makes sense to her. It also involves taking a respectful approach toward the eating problem by acknowledging it as an effort at coping. I do not wish to malign the coping strategy or the need for the coping strategy. Eventually, I want to help bring into higher relief what it is she is coping with. At the same time, we do unpack the effects of self-denial and self-deprivation and how these are taken up as "good things." We are, in effect, constantly involved in exploring the multiple meanings of these descriptions.

For Genna, her perceived success at self-management is measured by her success at self-deprivation and self-control. The harder she works and the less she eats, the more in control she feels. While this is compelling and motivates her to continue to push herself, to continue to act like a robot, without feelings and without needs, it also sets her up for bulimia. Unable to sustain her rigid self-disciplinary practices, she capitulates to desire. The "excess" of restrictive eating is countered with the "excess" of binge eating. Needs and desires are either tightly contained or sprung free, leaving her feeling chaotic, out of control, and unmanageable. Genna's relationship to her needs and her desires arguably reflects a gendered subjectivity. Her shame, guilt, and sense of failure for having needs are evident in both her self-discipline and in her capitulation to desire. Following binge eating, which feels forbidden and disallowed, she compensates by throwing up, or purging. She rids herself of all evidence of her desire and her needs. Returning to restrictive activities and disciplining her body through exercise and controlled eating offers a comfort of constraint, predictability, and control.

Genna is alarmed when asked, "If people were to see you bingeing and purging, what would they learn about you that they don't normally know?" She quickly reveals that they would see that she isn't perfect, always in control, or a "good girl"—that something is wrong and she is struggling, out of control, has needs, and is unhappy. Genna is resourcing her body; she is both seeking a greater sense of power and control over her life and attempting to communicate to the world her ambivalent desire for power and control and what that might cost her.

Many women and girls who struggle with anorexia know that they are not "too fat." What is most important is that they *feel* "too fat."[4] Genna agrees that she "knows" she isn't too fat but that she "feels" too fat. We establish this clearly: "So you 'know' you are not too fat, but you 'feel' too fat. What do you think that might tell us?" Through this distinction, we are beginning to make sense of why she feels fat and what this means to her. We are also establishing that her struggles with anorexia are not a cognitive disorder or a lack of knowledge. Instead, we begin to explore the meaning of the story of "feeling fat" for Genna. This includes exploring the history of this story and what it has meant for Genna over time.

Achieving such thinness requires an extraordinary effort, extraordinary self-surveillance. It is an accomplishment—evidence of being special in some way and that she can do something very well. The control and mastery experienced over her body are experienced as feeling a greater sense of power and control over herself and her life. Yet very often, these experiences are paradoxically fragile. Reading beyond the tremendous commitment to the pursuit of thinness and its rewards, both subjective and social, one often discovers a very vulnerable, uncertain, and fragile individual. It has been my sense as a psychotherapist that the power and control experienced through extreme self-restraint is almost "intoxicating." In the face of overwhelming vulnerability, uncertainty, and fragility, experiences of power and control offer a compelling and understandable alternative.

Genna made it very clear she was not going to give up her anorexia and bulimia until she was emotionally ready. We agreed that I would not ask her to give up these coping strategies, but that we would work at understanding what they mean to her and to see what makes sense about them for her, and that when she was ready, she could begin to look at gradually letting go of this way of coping as she began to develop new stories about herself. Furthermore, we agreed that we would move at a "doable" pace, one that did not exacerbate feeling out of control. This approach reflects the awareness that because giving up anorexic and bulimic behaviors is extraordinarily frightening and difficult, it often helps to emphasize taking very small steps. Consistent with a feminist approach to working with the range of eating problems women experience, this step-by-step approach reflects a harm reduction philosophy (Marlatt, 1998), seeking to reduce harm in a compassionate and pragmatic fashion.[5] This approach starts with what is realistic for a person, emphasizing her own power, safety, and control in the process. Thus, as long as a woman is able to maintain a low, stable weight and a stable physical condition, this work can be done on an outpatient basis. I have found that almost all of the women I have worked with can do this (see also Lawrence, 1984).

Therapeutic strategies that dispossess women and girls of the sense of power and control they achieve through chronic dieting, self-starvation, and even the binge-purge cycle lack compassion and understanding. I have found that by assuring women that I have no desire to take their coping strategies away from them, they are less afraid to begin this work together. Rather than tearing women away from these behaviors, I prefer a slower, gentler, and more humane approach, in which women and girls are encouraged to explore the ways they use their bodies to express their struggles of self in the world. This approach does not exacerbate women's struggles with power and control expressed through regulating the body, and it opens up the possibility of exploring their stories of self-discipline and capitulation to desire. Genna's "robot" metaphor, for example, allowed us to explore her stories of self-discipline and desire. Through unpacking the suppressed stories of women's struggles with their bodies and eating, women are better positioned to address the meaning of these struggles in their lives. Insofar as eating problems are a symbol or metaphor that something is wrong, surely we need to listen to the stories of struggle they ambivalently communicate. Simply trying to control or eradicate behavioral "symptoms" renders invisible the suppressed or subjugated voice and does not engage with or help rewrite the underlying problem story.

Conclusion

I have explored ways women use their bodies as a form of self-regulation or self-discipline, illuminating the tension between the discipline of and capitulation to desire and need in contemporary culture. In "the grip" of cultural practices, including relations of power, women's struggles with eating and body size serve as an example of normalization processes of the self. This analysis concedes that practices of power are often centered in such practices of self-regulation (Bordo, 1993, p. 27), rather than conspiracies of power or coercion, and that therapeutic conversations with women must acknowledge women's agency, choice, and power expressed through eating problems, as well as their struggles for greater power and control. I have argued that women's control of their bodies can be seen as both compliance and resistance to cultural hegemony. As such, the body tells stories of women's struggles between compliance and resistance to gendered subjectivity within a culture logic of self-management.

Notes

1. Parts of this discussion have evolved from graduate research on weight preoccupation (see Brown, 1987a, 2001).

2. I am referring to emotion, need, and desire as socially constructed yet embodied experiences. I am not conceptualizing them in a naturalized or essentialized manner. Furthermore, I am attempting to demonstrate the particular social and historical conditions and discourses that produce psychological distress and which produce socially and subjectively meaningful sites for expressing this distress.

3. The body and eating behavior tend to be naturalized. Not dieting, for example, is presumed to produce one's natural body. The assumption of a "natural body" negates that the body can be known only through social interpretation. It seems to support the belief that the body and eating can exist outside of culture, as is evident in the belief that one should eat only when one is hungry. This belief suggests that eating does not have any meaning above and beyond fueling the body. The body and eating are two areas that are always at once both biological and social (see Brown, 2001). They are, as Malson (1997) suggests, discursive and extradiscursive.

4. While I am aware that feelings and thoughts are interrelated rather than binary oppositions, I am invoking the folk psychology of everyday life (Bruner, 1990; White, 2004). I am holding this binary formulation in tension, knowing that it is limited, but that Genna is likely to understand what I mean.

5. Because eating problems like anorexia and bulimia involve the body and have "real" effects on the body, we must work with both the discursive and extradiscursive (Malson, 1997). I believe that we can work with potential threats to the

Discipline and Desire 129

body and health through a harm reduction philosophy and approach without being inconsistent with feminist and narrative therapeutic conversations. At all moments, I am invested in a nonpathologizing and nonmedicalizing approach to this work that, importantly, emphasizes that women must remain in control of their own bodies and that we have to find ways to make the work feel more emotionally safe (Brown, 1990a, 1990b, 1993a, 1993b, 1993c).

References

Bellar, A. S. (1977). *Fat and thin. A natural history of obesity.* New York: Farrar, Straus and Giroux.

Berger, J. (1972). *Ways of seeing.* London: Penguin Books.

Berger. P., & Luckmann, T. (1967). *The social construction of reality. A treatise in the sociology of knowledge.* New York: Anchor Books.

Bordo, S. (1993). *Unbearable weight: Feminism, Western culture, and the body.* Berkeley: University of California Press.

Brown, C. (1987a). *Feeding into each other: Weight preoccupation and the contradictory expectations of women.* Unpublished master's thesis, University of Manitoba, Department of Sociology, Winnipeg, Canada.

Brown, C. (1987b). *Getting beyond weight: Women helping women. Self-help manual.* Winnipeg, Canada: Women's Health Clinic.

Brown, C. (1990a). *Contracting in feminist therapy for eating "disorders."* Unpublished independent inquiry project, master's of social work. Carleton University, School of Social Work, Ottawa, Canada.

Brown, C. (1990b). The "control paradox": Understanding and working with anorexia and bulimia. *National Eating Disorders Centre Bulletin.* Toronto, Canada.

Brown, C. (1993a). The continuum: Anorexia, bulimia, and weight preoccupation. In C. Brown & K. Jasper (Eds.), *Consuming passions: Feminist approaches to weight preoccupation and eating disorders* (pp. 53–68). Toronto, Canada: Second Story Press.

Brown, C. (1993b). Feminist contracting: Power and empowerment in therapy. In C. Brown & K. Jasper (Eds.), *Consuming passions: Feminist approaches to weight preoccupation and eating disorders* (pp. 176–194). Toronto, Canada: Second Story Press.

Brown, C. (1993c). Feminist therapy: Power, ethics, and control. In C. Brown & K. Jasper (Eds.), *Consuming passions: Feminist approaches to weight preoccupation and eating disorders* (pp. 120–136). Toronto, Canada: Second Story Press.

Brown, C. (2001). *Talking body talk: An analysis of feminist therapy epistemology.* Unpublished doctoral thesis, University of Toronto, Toronto, Canada.

Brown, C., & Forgay, D. (1987, Winter). An uncertain well-being: Weight control and self-control. *Healthsharing,* pp. 11–15.

Brown, C., & Jasper, K. (Eds.). (1993a). *Consuming passions: Feminist approaches to weight preoccupation and eating disorders.* Toronto, Canada: Second Story Press.

Brown, C., & Jasper, K. (1993b). Why weight? Why women? Why now? In
C. Brown & K. Jasper (Eds.), *Consuming passions: Feminist approaches to
weight preoccupation and eating disorders* (pp. 16–35). Toronto, Canada: Second
Story Press.

Bruch, H. (1978). *The golden cage: The enigma of anorexia nervosa.* Cambridge,
MA: Harvard University Press.

Bruner, J. (1990). *Acts of meaning.* Cambridge, MA: Harvard University Press.

Bruner, J. (2002). *Making stories: Law, literature, life.* Cambridge, MA: Harvard
University Press.

Butler, J. (1993). *Bodies that matter: On the discursive limits of "sex."* New York:
Routledge.

Chernin, K. (1981). *The obsession: Reflections of the tyranny of slenderness.*
New York: Harper & Row.

Chernin, K. (1985). *The hungry self: Women, eating, & identity.* New York: Harper
& Row.

Dyrenforth, S., Wooley, O., & Wooley, S. (1980). A woman's body in a man's
world: A review of findings on body image and weight control. In R. Kaplan
(Ed.), *A woman's conflict. The special relationship between women and food*
(pp. 30–57). Englewood Cliffs, NJ: Prentice Hall.

Ewen, S., & Ewen, E. (1982). *Channels of desire: Mass images and the shaping of
American consciousness.* New York: McGraw-Hill.

Foucault, M. (1980a). *The history of sexuality: Vol. 1. An introduction.* New York:
Vintage.

Foucault, M. (1980b). *Power/knowledge: Selected interviews and other writings
1972–1977.* New York: Pantheon Books.

Foucault, M. (1984). *Docile bodies.* In P. Rabinow (Ed.), *The Foucault reader*
(pp. 179–187). New York: Pantheon Books.

Foucault, M. (1988). *Madness and civilization: A history of insanity in the age of
reason.* New York: Vintage Books.

Foucault, M. (1995). (2nd ed.). *Discipline and punish: The birth of the prison.* New
York: Vintage.

Freud, S. (1962). *Civilization and its discontents* (J. Strachey, Ed. and Trans.). New
York: Norton.

Gremillion, H. (2001). Anorexia: A canary in the mine. An anthropological perspective. An interview with Helen Gremillion. In *Working with the stories of women's
lives* (pp. 135–157). Adelaide, Australia: Dulwich Centre Publications.

Gremillion, H. (2003). *Feeding anorexia: Gender and power at a treatment center.*
Durham, NC: Duke University Press.

Grosz, E. (1992). The subject. In E. Wright (Ed.), *Feminism and psychoanlysis:
A critical dictionary* (pp. 409–416). New York: Blackwell.

Jacobs, M., Fox Keller, S., & Shuttleworth, S. (1990). *Body/politics: Women and
the discourse of science.* New York: Routledge.

Lawrence, M. (1979). Anorexia nervosa: The control paradox. *Women's Studies
International, 2,* 93–101.

Lawrence, M. (1984). *The anorexic experience*. London: The Women's Press.

Malson, H. (1997). Anorexic bodies and the discursive production of feminine excess. In J. Ussher (Ed.), *Body talk: The material and discursive regulation of sexuality, madness, and reproduction* (pp. 223–245). New York: Routledge.

Marlatt, G. (1998). Basic principles and strategies of harm reduction. In G. Marlatt (Ed.), *Harm reduction: Pragmatic strategies for managing high risk behaviours* (pp. 49–66). New York: Guilford.

Millman, M. (1980). *Such a pretty face: Being fat in America*. New York: Norton.

Orbach, S. (1978). *Fat is a feminist issue*. New York: Paddington Books.

Orbach, S. (1986). *Hunger strike: The anorectic struggle as a metaphor for our age*. New York: Norton.

Robinson, B. (1985, February). The stigma of obesity: Fat fallacies debunked. *Melpomene Report*, pp. 9–11, 13.

Rodolico, A. (1980). Profile of bulimarexia: Your space, food, and body awareness. *WomanWise, 3*(4), 11.

Spelman, E. (1988). *Inessential woman: Problems of exclusion in feminist thought*. Boston: Beacon Books.

Sternhell, C. (1985, May). We'll always be fat but fat can be fit. *Ms.*, pp. 66, 68, 142–144, 146, 154.

Tanesini, A. (1999). *An introduction to feminist epistemologies*. Malden, MA: Blackwell.

Thompson, B. (1994). *A hunger so wide and so deep. American women speak out on eating problems*. Minneapolis: University of Minnesota Press.

Turner, J. (1978). *The structure of sociological theory*. Homewood, IL: Dorsey Press.

White, M. (1997). *Narrative of therapists' lives*. Adelaide, Australia: Dulwich Centre.

White, M. (2001). Narrative practice and the unpacking of identity conclusions. *Gecko: A Journal of Deconstruction and Narrative Ideas in Therapeutic Practice, 1,* 28–55.

White, M. (2004). *Narrative practice and exotic lives: Resurrecting diversity in everyday life*. Adelaide, Australia: Dulwich Centre.

7

Watching the Other Watch

A Social Location of Problems

Stephen Madigan

Whom do you call bad? Those who always want to put to shame.
What do you consider most humane? To spare someone shame. What
is the seal of liberation? No longer being ashamed in front of oneself.

—Friedrich Nietzsche (1974), Aphorisms 273, 274, 275 (p. 180)

This chapter takes a brief look at the social location, negotiation, and performed response of internalized problem conversations. The social act of us viewing ourselves, referred to in this chapter as *self-surveillance,*[1] is perceived as primary for keeping problem conversations alive. In addition, the relationship of self-surveillance to the perception and experience of being watched/judged by a viewing *audience* (real and imagined) will also be explored. The chapter shows how and within what contexts the relationship between self-surveillance/audience supports internalized problem conversations: how they are created, maintained, and become habit-forming.

The inseparability of self-surveillance/audience will be discussed as a primary discourse of problems. Conversations involving the exploration of self-surveillance/audience are considered an important resource for therapists to explore with clients in therapy and are viewed as discursive sites where problems can be unraveled and change can occur.

Language Traditions Are Hard to Hide

From the cradle, we learn our culture codes through imitation: We copy what we watch and hear. It is ritual observance. We learn from those who learned before, to walk, brush our teeth, ride bicycles, spell words, speak language, and adhere to a culture's ethics and good manners. We fashion our talk and the way we perform and see the world through an internalized fragmented form of karaoke of the dominant other—while they are doing the same. We sing their song of right and wrong and catalogue this in cultural verse.

Our observing practices include partaking in a ritual of ongoing internalized conversations with ourselves (and imagined others) as a way of measuring ourselves against the external world, trying to determine if we fit in and if we are acceptable and wondering if we are "normal" (i.e., normal parent, employee, partner, etc.). The production and reproduction of this dialogue produces a wide variety of both good and bad experience (Bakhtin, 1986; Madigan & Law, 1998). The verdict of this conversation is ever changing, a work in progress.

Internalized problem conversations work alongside a dominant and modernist psychological and scientific framework of how the self and problems are defined and explained. This knowledge is promoted through many discursive venues (institutions) and adheres to both the psychological practice of privatizing and locating problems inside the bodies of the people we see in therapy (Law & Madigan, 1994).

As members of a community of language, we are in constant relationship and interaction with this exterior language. One of the many ways we interact with this language of our culture is within the discursive relationship we have with ourselves. (I heard somewhere recently that scientists were reporting that of the conversations human beings partake in, upward of 90% of these conversations are held within the privacy of themselves.) For example, close your eyes for 30 seconds and allow an internalized conversation of guilt to speak with you.[2] If guilt is not your thing, try choosing another form of common insider talk promoting a less-than-worthy version of yourself. Are you curious at what is being said, how you are being represented, by whom, and with what authority?

These questions promoted my fascination with a poststructural understanding of internalized-problem conversations, which was furthered while I was on a visit with David Epston, in Auckland, New Zealand, in the spring of April 1991. At the time, I was a young Canadian family therapy doctoral student, studying in America and traveling to Australia and New Zealand after being awarded the "Down Under Narrative Therapy Scholarship."[3] On one leg of this trip, I met, lived with, and watched David Epston do therapy, day after day, for a few weeks. One day, he mentioned to me that he had been interviewing young women from around the world who were struggling with disordered eating. He observed that even though their "accents" were very different from one another (due to residing on different continents), their descriptions of the habitual language and practice rituals within the problems of anorexia and bulimia were relationally almost identical.

Slowly, I began to realize, after consulting for a number of years as the film industry's primary psychotherapist and with an "inpatient" adult eating-disorder ward in Vancouver, Canada, that without conversational reflections and an audience to support these reflections, a problem (stemming from self-defeating conversations, cultural expectations, and dominant ideas of personhood, etc.) could, quite simply, not survive. The performance of self-surveillance can be explained as the performance of looking, monitoring, and judging the self[4] (see Foucault, 1965, 1979; Madigan, 1991a, 2003). The monitoring of the self "eavesdropping" on itself is bound together in a dialogic relationship with an active audience discursively positioned elsewhere: our experience of the imagined or recreated thoughts of the other looking, monitoring, and judging us (the "other" includes ourselves looking at ourselves[5]) (Foucault, 1973, 1989; Madigan, 1996, 1999; White, 1995).

When we experience problems within a socially discursive cultural view, we are posed to ask relational questions (e.g., do we or do we not measure up to set social norms/standards of what constitutes the proper person, parent, partner, etc.?). Our internalized conversations with a perceived audience connect and direct us toward what we think the other—who is watching us—thinks about us. The problem conversation is framed within the problem's internalized negative story line about us, as the other, who populates us, views us ("I think that you think that I think that you think that I am a bad employee," and so on). Left unchecked, the internalized discussion provides an important discursive platform for negative ideas about ourselves to ferment and grow.[6] The internalized conversation is also the primary sight for therapeutic conversation as a pathway to change (Madigan, 2003, 2005).

It is through coming to know ourselves and our identities within the discursive framework of dominant cultural norms that we respond to a pressured, pathologized, tortured, and totalized view of ourselves and our relationships (Diamond & Quinby, 1988; Foucault, 1973[7]; White 1992). To build a prejudicial case against a person, self-surveillance and audience come together in a negative supporting way. Imagine the following scenario: You are a social work professional. You have just suffered through a terrible relationship separation. Imagine a robust, internalized discussion taking place about the severed relationship, aimed at indicting you for the problem's allegations against you (cultural blaming conversations of yourself may reproduce a conversation indicting you as a bad parent, poor employee, selfish partner, lousy lover, etc.). In such a scenario, the negative thrust and audience to this internalized story will involve many of the institutions and individuals that populate you. It may involve negative conversations about the deficit you, across the temporal plain, with persons both dead and alive.

At a time of crisis, a negative self-surveillant audience is (re)produced: your children, your ex-partner/wife/husband, your family, friends, colleagues, students, neighbors, your parents and relatives (both dead and alive), the professional community, a religious community, a political community, the legal team, the judge, the banker, the accountant, new associates/colleagues, strangers, future foreign students, the grocer and dry cleaner, the children's teachers, God, et cetera, et cetera. The internalized audience of conversations is brought forth under the problem's influential descriptive frame. Within this discursive context, the negative internalized story being told (reproduced and performed) can be very convincing and assist in the buildup of the problem's injurious speech (Butler, 1997) and subsequent responses.

Now imagine this self-surveillance/audience scenario closer to an example in your own experience. You might be wondering what your colleagues and clients might think about you taking extended holidays, changing careers, getting drunk at the annual party, your stand on American Foreign policy, making money, taking EMDR (eye movement desensitization and reprocessing) training, and so forth. As you reflect on your audience response and *when* the negative imagination takes hold, here is a small sample of questions to consider:

- What/who constitutes an audience to this particular problematized view of yourself?
- Who is the spokesperson? What is this person saying?
- What is the effect of this "saying"?
- What cultural ideas support the saying of this saying?
- Does this audience divide you off from what is considered "normal"?
- Does the audience's conversation influence the opinions you hold of yourself?
- Do these negative imagined accounts that you perceive others hold affect how you perform your life and how you relate to people?
- By what means is the negative audience supported?
- What/who constitutes the "you-supporting" alternative audience?
- If your community of concern were given an opportunity to speak, what would they say about you? Why would they say this?
- How do you account for the difference between "you-supporting" stories and problem stories in the stories they are broadcasting to be true accounts?
- What are the major discursive influences affecting your internal self-surveillance system?

- How did this audience become so powerfully persuasive and beguiling of you?
- How did you respond to the conversation? Is there a history of this response? What are your thoughts on this response? Is this historical response serving your best interests?
- How does self-surveillance/audience respond to a self-supporting response?

Internalized Conversations

It is 7:36 a.m. You examine your body and bank account. You wonder if your point of view will be accepted at work and whether or not your boss would like the color you painted the kitchen (even though she will never be invited to see it). You converse with persons you do not know—a politician, the head of the transit commission—and compare yourself to the made-up story you tell yourself about the stranger you sat next to in the restaurant. Is it snowing outside? You re-remember last night's lovemaking and wonder what your partner is now reliving about you. You hope to arrive at tonight's party with uncommon humor, and feel terrible about what you said to your parents so long ago. We entertain this maze of conversation while taking our morning shower. I would like to say "Don't try this alone," but you will. Listen for it tomorrow—you'll see.

Many clients in therapy confess that internalized-problem conversations are often brutal, shaming, punishing, and guilt ridden. The conversations involve injurious speech acts that reproduce horrible, paralyzing, and long-lasting negative effects on how individuals view themselves (Butler, 1997). Left unchecked, the problem conversation gains support through the many ways that dominant culture supports the noncontextual/nondiscursive views the psychological project has regarding problems. This matchup between dominant culture and dominant psychology helps to secure and promote a one-sided, pathologized view of persons. Institutions of knowledge, in this case family therapy and so forth, collude with these cultural/psychological practices by offering the person specific therapeutic and pharmaceutical devices designed with the intent for the person to be able find a more proper and popular fit within dominant cultural beliefs regarding who he or she should be.

Consequently, the vast majority of people who come to see me in therapy are usually convinced, through a strongly supported cultural/professional-ized belief, that the major source of "their" problem has its origins in some horrid, biological, and/or mystical defect within themselves (Caplan, 1995). People will ponder the mystery and often conclude that they "must have done something terribly wrong to be living a life like this."

A dialogic, relational, cultural, narrative, and textual (re)consideration of what constitutes persons and problems can be helpful (Bruner, 1990; Madigan, 1997, 1999; Madigan & Law, 1998; I. McCarthy, personal communication, 1996; Tamasese & Waldegrave, 1990; Waldegrave, 1996; White & Epston, 1990). This area of study is not concerned with naming, classifying, and holding the body responsible for psychological problems. The focus is on power relations, what happens discursively between persons, and the discourses they shape and are shaped by. This approach to persons and problems moves the professional gaze away from naming the individual as the site of the problem (depressed, obsessed, anorexic, etc.) and toward a broader set of discourses, dominant knowledge, and relations of power (Madigan, 1991a, 1991b; Reynolds, 2002).

The Performance of Community Discourse and Power

During the halcyon days of the beginnings of narrative therapy in Australia and New Zealand (see Epston, 1988; White, 1988; White & Epston, 1990), what seemed to set narrative therapy ideas apart from the dominant psychological project was the articulation of how practices of power/knowledge and discourse[8] shape identity (see Madigan, 1996). David Epston brought this theoretical understanding of discourse into therapy when he puzzled over this question: Who has the storytelling rights to the story being told? (D. Epston, personal communication, 1991). His question speaks to the dialogic interconnectedness of our identity making, the issue of modern power, and the nonneutral bias of the stories we tell and are told about us.

In responding to the question (Who has the storytelling rights to the story being told?) and other questions brought forth by diverse cultural groups and a growing interest in feminism, sexuality, money privilege, and class, efforts were made to locate the "stories" being told in the therapy room within the broader cultural discourses and power relations from which they originated. Michael White insisted that ideas and practices of power and the effects these power relations had on persons and relationships were necessarily integral to a practice of therapy (M. White, personal communication, 1991). In turn, Epston; White; The Family Centre of Wellington, New Zealand; and others began to ask why the professional psychology group was telling "this" particular story of a person or cultural group and not another? Why "this" version of personhood and problems and not an alternative view? These kinds of questions led to a further questioning of the "official" Western psychological and scientific story of the self and, in part, led them toward a thorough questioning of the dominant cultural and modernist strain of psychology and family therapy. The "narrative" practice view[9] developed first by White and Epston (1990) moved forward to challenge the many ways persons were being formally categorized and measured into static, noninteractional, and, more important, nonhistorical forms. Early on, narrative therapy writing and practice invited therapists to turn their attention to the ever-evolving interaction, performance, and textual play of persons' narratives to include the culture and discursive "origin" of problems. This enabled them to move the therapeutic conversation toward bringing forth sites of narrative possibility and resistance designed to unravel any prior, static, finalized interpretations of persons and problems.

Narrative Therapy Understandings

Within narrative therapy, the spoken problem identity is not considered a "fixed state," nor is it located within the body of the person. Instead, the problem identity is viewed within the context of intricate negotiations that take place inside complex fields of power and discourse. Because of this, a narrative therapist[10] attempts to render transparent the status of identity-based politics in the life of the problem and to highlight the effects these discursive practices have had on the person's life and how the person has historically responded (Law & Madigan, 1994; Madigan, 1997; Parker, 1998). Of central importance to those who practice narrative therapy is the bringing forth of re-remembered "alternative" selves (some might say "forgotten" or "unrecognized" selves) that are experienced outside the realm of a specified problem identity (Madigan, 1996). For me, the elegant bit of the narrative interview is when it manages to take a therapeutic position to deconstruct, re-remember, and re-member and build upon these alternative self-meanings (see Madigan, 1999).

Critical social theorist Calhoun (1995) rightly points out that "the fundamental reference of identity is a discourse in social location" (p. 18). Locating problems in the broader social discourse opens up many possibilities for practice.[11] These ideas guide the practice work in the beginning stage of unraveling the particular problem's grip on a person's life. To begin the interview, a therapist proceeds as follows:

- A therapist attempts to help the person name and locate the problem and expand the description to include broader cultural ideas of right and wrong (e.g., who promotes the idea of perfection as a formal inscription of best possible personhood?).
- A therapist questions how the person responds to the problem and how he or she makes sense of this response, and looks for other places of resistance.

- At the same time, the therapist uses language to situate the problem in history and institutional ideas (e.g., what did religion or education and their influence on gender relations have to do with perfection training?).

Once the dialogic apparatus supporting the problem is located and historicized (e.g., where does perfection, fear, negative imagination, etc., come from, and what are they supported through?), we can then begin to construct a *counterview* (Madigan, 2003) of the problem by asking how and through what means these conversations support the life of the identified problem (how perfection training, fear, negative imagination, etc., support disordered eating[12]) (Madigan 2003; Madigan & Epston, 1995).

I propose a therapeutic *counterviewing* position (Madigan, 2003) when interviewing and locating persons and problems. Counterviewing dominant ideas about persons and problems affords a conversational space for re-remembering substitute responses, recalling ways they responded to and resisted the problems, and a rediscovery of alternative ideas and memories regarding who they were, who they are, and who they might become. The counterviewer's intent is to allow for the forgotten/silenced emerging re-remembered[13] story to be told. The therapeutic counterview brings forth a poststructural practice consideration of persons and problems by offering a reexamination of the broader cultural location of problem conversations and the institutions that maintain them (Hoagwood, 1993). The counterview offers up a discursive coproduction of generative possibilities involving an overt appreciation of a person's abilities to respond and resist and stimulates the therapist's imagination to question his or her psychological and family therapy training and ideas (Madigan, 1999; White, 1992).

The counterview acts with purpose and believes that a therapist cannot not take a position. A therapist's overt counterview position involves discussing, deconstructing, questioning, situating, responding, illuminating, exposing, humoring, resisting, and naming the consequences the cultural conversation of person-as-problem has had on the life of the person and problem. The ounterview upholds a therapeutic understanding different from that of the problem's cultural description of the person and in stark contrast to the many professional discourses that have supported a pathologized view of the person.

Self-Surveillance/Audience

An internalized self-surveillance/audience conversation is often described by clients as having a hypnotic-trance quality about it. In a seemingly seamless, deadly, and ongoing conversation, the problem gives the imagined audience the capability to injuriously comment on all aspects of our lives (members of the Vancouver Anti-Anorexia League have reported that while in the depths of their struggles with anorexia, individuals' internalized-problem conversations about their less-than-worthiness rave on upward of 99% of every day; for more on the subject, see Grieves, 1998; Madigan & Epston, 1995). The internalized-problem conversation acts to capture imaginations and hold persons liable for months and years at a time. The long-term impact of these brutal conversations must be exposed, situated, and deconstructed in order for change to occur. A step toward undoing these debilitating internalized conversations is to begin noticing the talk, content, and effects of the dialogue. A few sample questions asked of people, couples, and families troubled by a negative self-surveillance/audience might include the following:

- Why would this injurious conversation want to separate you from your best knowledge of yourself and the persons who love you?
- Do you think the relationship breakup has changed every aspect of who you are as a person?
- Has the breakup somehow turned every single person who once loved you *against you,* including yourself?
- Has the problem created a campaign of gossip about your life?
- Are there any outstanding ideas that you have grown up with concerning relationships that are presently holding you back from a different and perhaps more philosophic/realistic view of your situation?
- Are there any particular popular-psychology knowledges about relationships and gender that seem to be supporting this negative view of yourself?
- Are there any religious views about relationships that seem to be supporting this negative view of yourself?
- If you were alone to speak up for yourself, what might you say on behalf of yourself?

For a problem to survive, it must intertwine itself with the power relations of a dominant dialogic audience of support. Acting through the normalizing gaze (Foucault, 1965), these techniques of power assist us to believe that we know another's negative thoughts about us (back to "I think that you think . . .") without actually ever speaking with them. Questions can begin a process of articulating the exaggerated negative arguments (from the bowels of exaggerated cultural expectations) that the problem relationship is using against the person. Notating the problem's rhetoric, situating this rhetoric within dominant norms, and locating stories of failure within the institutional histories from which they originate can all serve to unnerve and weaken the problem conversation and awaken an alternative response.

Therapists may also want to chart out the problem's unrealistic portrayal of the person's community of persons who love them and whom they love and/or invite these persons into therapy with the client for an up-close counterview. Counterviewing acts serve to contradict the problem audience by bringing forth actual lived accounts from witnesses who have experienced and lived alongside the person in everyday life. To date, the witnessed accounts in favor of the person and against the problem have taken many creative forms, such as letters, letter campaigns, songs, videos, poems, collages, and so forth.

Once a counterview/interview begins a reconstruction of events, it is crucial for the therapist to implement a rich process of reconnection. This may be done alongside a reflecting team of supporters (professional and nonprofessional; see more on this in Madigan, 1992) and through *therapeutic letter-writing campaigns* (see Madigan & Epston, 1995).

Therapeutic Letter-Writing Campaigns

In brief, I developed[14] the therapeutic letter-writing campaigns when I was consulting 2 days a week with an adult inpatient eating-disorder unit in Vancouver, from 1993 to 1998. I created the campaigns in response to the deadly effects anorexia and bulimia were having on the lives and relationships of the people I was encountering on the ward. My attempt was to create a community of concern to help break the problem's isolated view of the person and assist in the re-remembering of unique aspects of a client's life now restrained by the problem. The logic behind the community letter-writing campaign was finding a way to respond to the fact that problems grew stronger the more a person was cut off from alternative and forgotten experiences of themselves and relationships that lived outside of his or her "sick" identity. The obvious direction for me was to include a community of remembering, loving others who held the stories of the client that the problem description had cut them off from.

Members of the family and friends are asked to assist in a re-remembering witnessing process through lettered written accounts outlining their memories of their relationships with the client, separate from the problem's relationship with the client. The letters, by documenting alternative versions, counteract the infirming effects of the problem story. These accounts hold a tremendous potential for the re-storying of persons' lives and relationships (see more on letter-writing campaigns in Madigan, 1999).

Karl's Story

The social work department of a local teaching hospital asked me if I would "see" Karl, a 58-year-old, White, heterosexual, married, middle-class man. Karl was described as "very suicidal and depressed," and, as a consequence, he was labeled *chronic*. The hospital's plan for health had prescribed him antipsychotic, antianxiety, antidepression, and sleep medications, as well as a few rounds of electroconvulsive therapy treatments (ECT) over the previous 6 months and cognitive behavioral groups and individual sessions.

I was informed that Karl was at great risk of taking his own life, that he was unresponsive to "talk" therapy, and that the hospital had done everything they could do on Karl's behalf. Karl had failed the hospital miserably.

Karl was allowed out of hospital on a "pass" so that he and his wife, Cathy, could visit with me in therapy. We had a total of eight visits together over the course of 4 months. On three of those meetings, we were joined by a reflecting team, and on two of those visits, we invited volunteers of the letter-writing campaign to "perform" their written work live, in front of Karl.

The process of reading and witnessing the letters in therapy was as follows:

1. The campaign writers were each asked to read aloud the letter they had written to Karl, in front of Karl, myself, and the other writers of his community and reflecting team.

2. After each writer read, Karl was asked to read the letter back to the writer, so both the writer and Karl could attend to what was being said/written from different positions of speaking/listening.

3. After each letter was read by the writer and Karl, the others in the session who were sitting and listening offered brief reflections of what the letter evoked in their own personal lives.

4. This process continued until all letters were read, reread, and reflected upon.

5. When the reflecting team was present for the sessions, they addressed Karl and his letter-writing community of supporters directly on what the letters had personally stirred up in them, and asked a question related to this stirring.

6. I then followed up the session with a therapeutic letter addressed to everyone who attended the session (including the reflecting team).

During the first interview, I learned from Karl that he was having great difficulty remembering much of his life. The bit of his life Karl could remember was awash in guilt, shame, feelings of "being a jerk," and medical terminology and labels describing and outlining who he was. Karl explained that 1 year prior to our talk, he had been "downsized" from a corporation where he had spent "over half my life." He stated that initially he felt "bitter and angry" on being let go, but now was simply "resigned to the fact that I've wasted my life."

The problem, which he referred to as "depression," had taken over his daily life, from waking to retiring at night. When I inquired further about the grip the problem held over his life, he let me know that "the depression lets me know that life is meaningless and that I am a bum about 90% of my day, and fills 78% of my dreams—7 days a week since I got into the hospital."

I interviewed Karl about the exact wording and themes the depression narrated to him about himself, what it was telling him about the thoughts others were having about him, and what his response to all this had been. I asked Karl (with Cathy's assistance) if he could jot down what the conversation of depression was saying about him throughout the day. An abbreviated version of depression's assault on his personhood included the following:

> You are such a loser. Your children are ashamed of you being in the loony bin. They were right to fire your ass straight out of there, and you should be very surprised that you fooled them for as long as you did. You're nothing but a fraud. What kind of a role model are you to your children? Everyone is better off without your sorry-ass burden. Why couldn't you be like your father who worked hard all his life? Grandfather hates you for not working hard enough. Just kill yourself and get it over with. What a loser!

Karl was living proof that the insider's "talking tour" of the depressed self was as vicious as it was dangerous. Imagine how Karl might be feeling after having to withstand the shock and humiliation of ECT, his "mind-numbing medications," and this all-day/all-night dehumanizing problem chatter. On the surface of what the internalized problem was constructing, there did not appear to be much left of him to defend himself and make a comeback. He was creeping toward death.

Cathy was of the opinion that the effects of his stay on the "mental ward," being on medication, and having been subjected to ECT had contributed to Karl's inability to remember his life in any "positive way." Cathy would bring stories of Karl's life into therapy that lived outside the story depression told; however, at first, Karl would sigh and disagree. In the first session, a (quiet) symmetrical argument between them ensued—"You are worthy/I am not worthy"—and the arguing for depression on Karl's part grew this story thicker.

Cathy stayed the hopeful course and would not give in to the story depression was telling of the "depressed Karl." She was quick to inform me that Karl was well respected by their three children, his friends, former workmates, and community.[15] To not involve myself in the "Is Karl or is Karl not depressed?" debate, I asked Karl if perhaps there were one or two people in his community (audience) who would disagree with the depression's "loser-guy" assessment of him. If this were so, would these people be wrong in their assessment of him being a "good guy"? He puzzled with this question for quite some time, and his response was simple: "Either my pals are crazy about who I am, or the depression and the doctors have it wrong."

My thinking after the third session was to make every attempt to reinvolve Karl with an alternative-relationship context of his community, from which "depression" and "suicidal thoughts" (and other nasty bits of conversation) had separated him. Karl, Cathy, and myself reached an agreement that "depression was a strong adversary" that had made him believe that his community stood alongside the hospital's, Dr. Phil's (a TV behavioral psychologist), and depression's assessment of him. Our thought was to test out this assessment by taking a survey of his friends and family to see what side of the "Is Karl a loser?" argument they would vote for. My hope was that the community response would create an "antidepression team." We agreed to involve the "voice of his community," a community of letter writers he would choose, as a means to counteract the ongoing internal dialogue of failure, shame, hopelessness, and depression that self-surveillance and audience promoted. We collaborated on writing a letter to possible recruits, which Cathy said she would be only too happy to distribute.

Dear friends of Karl and Cathy:

My name is Dr. Stephen Madigan, and I am a family therapist in Vancouver, Canada, working alongside Karl and Cathy. Karl has unfortunately been taken over by incessant and compelling thoughts of himself that he is "a useless human being and not really worth anything to anybody." The problem of depression has also led Karl to believe that you agree with this assessment of him. These depressed ideas about himself have led him toward experiencing a severe sadness about his life—so much so that sometimes the depression has tried to convince Karl that he would be better off dead.

Ever since he lost his job, Karl has been convinced that he is "a worthless person," that he "never did anything worthwhile," and that "everyone thinks he's a lazy bum" (our guess is that maybe lots of other people who unexpectedly lose their jobs after 24 years with the same company might begin to question and eventually turn on themselves as well). This lousy, shortsighted description of Karl is trying hard to help Karl be blind and deaf to all of his qualities, and wants him to turn away from all of the people who love and care about him.

We are writing to ask you to draft a letter in support of Karl and against the depression's version of him. Could you write a little note explaining (a) your life with Karl, (b) what you shared, (c) what he has given you, and (d) what you think your lives will be like together once he kicks this depression and terrible view of himself. Thank you for your help.

Yours in antidepression,

Cathy, Karl, and Stephen

Within 2 weeks, Karl and Cathy were inundated with mail. In the end, more than 40 letters were sent. At first, Karl modestly tucked away the community-of-concern notes, stating that he did "not know quite what to make of all the nice things people were saying." But before long, he was able to share the letters with a few chosen staff members and his visiting family. He then went about the task of diligently writing back to thank all the people who had sent letters. At this time, we arranged for eight letter writers to come and read their letters aloud in therapy. This turned out to be quite a celebration of Karl, and during our second meeting, which had grown to include 11 support persons, we all decided to go for lunch together, with Karl insisting on "grabbing the tab."

With these letters in hand, as well as a much broader and more fuller conversation and opinion of himself, Karl began to give the story of his "anti-depression" team solid consideration. Shortly thereafter, Karl made a unique decision to leave the hospital ward behind—vowing never to go back to that "godforsaken place."

Karl now reports being free of depression. When I ran into him and Cathy at a local market a few months later, he said, with a sly grin, that he was "enjoying life far more now than at that stinking job." Without the recruitment of his community of concern, Karl might never have rebounded to re-remember a healthy version of himself, and his community may have been restricted and restrained in the telling of the wonderful relational Karl they knew. The letter campaign was constructed and viewed not only as ceremonial (re)definition (White, 1995) but also as protest, response, counterview, and counterstruggle.

Conclusion

Without the ongoing relationship to the "other," our "selves" would be invisible, incomprehensible, and unutilizable. The other gives us meaning and a comprehension of ourselves so that we might possibly function in the social world. The knowledge that we have of ourselves appears in and through social practices, namely, interaction, practices, dialogue, and conversation with others' responses. We are not passive; rather, we respond to these interactions and the discourses intent for power. What gets to be said about who we are and with what authority is in constant debate and carried through our language traditions.

Identity, within the context of the institution of modern psychology and psychiatry, might be conceived as who *you* say you are, through what *they* say you can be. Problem conversations are carved out in much the same way, through an ongoing, internalized conversation of what we think we should be and relationally mediated through internalized cultural conversations of what we are not. The entry point of the therapist is one of counterviewing and expanding on the very real and imagined conversations a person brings to therapy regarding who they are, who they have been, and who they might become.

Notes

1. Self-surveillance is also based on the cultural postulation that certain thoughts and actions are dangerous or unwholesome to the constitution of the individual as a subject. From the point of view of the practices of the self, a menace is innocuous unless accompanied by cultural recommendations about the means through which individuals are to confront and subject the problematic part of themselves.

2. This chapter supports a poststructural (Hoagwood, 1993) idea of persons and problems, in which problems and persons are viewed as discursive reproductions coproducing a complex interplay of dominant discourse, cultural ideology, and social intercourse.

3. In 1991, I was selected as the scholarship recipient to travel and study narrative therapy at four different locations in New Zealand and Australia. This included study with David Epston, The Family Centre, Amanda Kamsler, and Michael White. Sallyann Roth of the Family Institute of Cambridge, Massachusetts, was the other person selected for the scholarship.

4. As Foucault (1979) put it, "The disciplinary apparatuses hierarchized the 'good' and 'bad' subjects in relation to one another" (p. 181). This "dividing practice" must not be understood only as something that is imposed from the exterior upon individuals. On the contrary, the classification of each individual along the polarity ranging from normal to abnormal achieves its goal if it is active in the interior of individuals and if it makes them judge and conceive themselves according to this polarity.

5. One central tenet of Foucault's conception of power is that it cannot be located; it is everywhere and therefore also inside us. Power relations produce the subject, or, to be more precise, they instill in individuals a historically determined relation with themselves.

6. Persons like ourselves are systematically and discursively turned from subject into object through agreed-upon discursive practices shaped by a culture's institutional and historically based ideological norms (Diamond & Quinby, 1988; Foucault, 1965, 1979).

7. French philosopher/historian Michel Foucault's (Foucault, 1965, 1971, 1973, 1979) writings on the inseparability of power/knowledge, resistance, discourse, and the three modes of objectification of the subject have been helpful in sorting through my practice ideas regarding internalized conversational habits (see also Madigan, 1992).

8. For the purposes of this chapter, *discourse* will be given a Foucauldian description, simplified to mean "what gets to be said, who gets to say it, and with what authority" (Foucault, 1965; Madigan, 1992).

9. See Jerome Bruner's *Acts of Meaning* (1990) for more on the narrative view of persons and folk psychology.

10. Therapists practice many versions of narrative therapy. I am referring here to the preferred practice of narrative therapy at Yaletown Family Therapy, in Vancouver, Canada, where I work.

11. My therapeutic interviewing would, then, be considered to be under the influence of the first rule of real estate: Location, Location, Location.

12. For an excellent overview of public practice and questions related to disordered eating, see http://www.planet-therapy.com

13. Re-remembering one's past from alternative points of view offers a reconstruction of events and possible liberation. For example, a person traumatized with childhood abuse can be led to re-remember the courage it took him or her to survive and to replace guilt and shame by placing the responsibility of the abuse squarely on the shoulders of the perpetrator and the cultural systems that allows abuse to continue.

14. Therapeutic letter-writing campaigns were born out of my up-close study of White and Epston's (1990) therapy of literary merit, in which they created a process of writing single letters to their clients at session's end. Binding this practice with a tradition of Irish wakes and Mass cards, I extended these practices of the written word to include the person's "community of concern" (for more, see Madigan & Epston, 1995). The client and I would write to members of his or her close community and request that they write letters about the client: who they were, the meaning of their relationship with the client, and what their continuing relationship hopes were. This practice expanded to invite the letter writers into therapy to read their letters aloud in the presence of their friend/client and then to have the friend/client reread the letter back to the person who wrote it. A process of rich redescription is often the result.

15. These people were primarily living in Vancouver, Canada, where my Yaletown Family Therapy office is located and where the therapy took place.

References

Bakhtin, M. M. (1986). *Speech genres and other late essays* (V. McGee, Trans.). Austin: University of Texas Press.

Bruner, J. (1990). *Acts of meaning.* Cambridge, MA: Harvard Press.

Butler, J. (1997). *Excitable speech: A politics of the performance.* New York: Routledge.

Calhoun, C. (1995). *Critical social theory.* Oxford, UK: Blackwell.

Caplan, P. (1995). They say you're crazy: How the world's most powerful psychiatrists decide who's normal. New York: Addison-Wesley.

Diamond, I., & Quinby, L. (1988). *Feminism & Foucault: Reflections on resistance.* Boston: Northeastern University Press.

Epston, D. (1988). *Collected papers.* Adelaide, Australia: Dulwich Centre.

Foucault, M. (1965). *Madness and civilization: A history of insanity in the age of reason.* New York: Random House.

Foucault, M. (1971). Nietzsche, genealogy, history. In D. Bouchard (Eds.), *Language counter-memory, practice: Selected essays and interviews*. Ithaca, NY: Cornell University Press.

Foucault, M. (1973). *The birth of the clinic: An archeology of medical perception*. London: Tavistock.

Foucault, M. (1979). *Discipline and punish: The birth of the prison*. Middlesex, UK: Peregrine Books.

Foucault, M. (1989). *Foucault live: Collected interviews, 1961–1984* (S. Lotringer, Ed.). New York: Semiotext(e).

Grieves, L. (1998). From beginning to start: The Vancouver Anti-Anorexia/ Anti-Bulimia League. In S. Madigan & I. Law (Eds.), *PRAXIS: Situating discourse, feminism, and politics in narrative therapies* (pp. 195–206). Vancouver, Canada: Yaletown Family Therapy Press.

Hoagwood, K. (1993), Poststructuralist historicism and the psychological construction of anxiety disorders. *Journal of Psychology, 127*(1), 105–122.

Law, I., & Madigan, S. (1994). Power and politics in practice. In I. Law & S. Madigan (Eds.), *Dulwich Newsletter* [Special Edition] 2, 4–11.

Madigan, S. (1991a). Discursive restraints in therapist practice. *Dulwich Centre Newsletter, 3*, 13–20.

Madigan, S. (1991b). *Voices of de-mystification: Questions as performative text in therapy practice: A post-structural analysis*. Unpublished doctoral dissertation, NOVA Southeastern University, Family Therapy Department, Ft. Lauderdale, FL.

Madigan, S. (1992). The application of Michael Foucault's philosophy in the problem externalizing discourse of Michael White. *British Journal of Family Therapy, 14*(3), 17–26.

Madigan, S. (1996). The politics of identity: Considering community discourse in the externalizing of internalized discourse. *Journal of Systemic Therapy, 2*, 47–63.

Madigan, S. (1997). Re-considering memory: Re-remembering lost identities back towards re-membered selves. In D. Nylund & C. Smith (Eds.), *Narrative therapy with children* (pp. 338–356). New York: Guilford.

Madigan, S. (1999). Destabilizing chronic identities of depression and retirement. In I. Parker (Ed.), *Deconstructing psychotherapy* (pp. 150–164). London: Sage.

Madigan, S. (2003). Injurious speech: Counterviewing eight conversational habits of highly effective problems. *International Journal of Narrative Therapy and Community Work, 2*, 23–35.

Madigan, S. (2005). Re-writing Tom: Undermining descriptions of chronicity through therapeutic letter writing campaigns. In J. Carlson (Ed.), *My finest hour: Family therapy with the experts* (pp. 66–78). New York: Allyn & Bacon.

Madigan, S., & Epston, D. (1995). From spy-chiatric gaze to communities of concern: From professional monologue to dialogue. In S. Friedman (Ed.), *The reflecting team in action* (pp. 257–277). New York: Guilford.

Madigan, S., & Law, I. (Eds.). (1998). *PRAXIS: Situating discourse, feminism, and politics in narrative therapies*. Vancouver, Canada: Yaletown Family Therapy Press.

Nietzsche, F. (1974). *The gay science* (W. Kaufmann, Trans.). New York: Vintage Books.

Parker, I. (1998). *Social construction, discourse, and realism.* London: Sage.

Reynolds, V. (2002, September). Weaving threads of belonging: Cultural witnessing groups. *Journal of Youth and Childcare,* 12–21.

Tamasese, K., & Waldegrave, C. (1990). Social justice. *Dulwich Centre Newsletter,* 1, 1–11.

Waldegrave, C. (1996). *International narrative ideas and therapeutic practice conference* (Keynote speech). Vancouver, Canada: Yaletown Family Therapy.

White, M. (1988). *Selected papers.* Adelaide, Australia: Dulwich Centre.

White, M. (1992, December). Deconstruction and therapy. *Dulwich Centre Newsletter,* 3, 21–40.

White, M. (1995). *Re-authoring lives: Interviews and essays.* Adelaide, Australia: Dulwich Centre.

White, M., & Epston, D. (1990). *Narrative means to therapeutic ends.* New York: Norton.

8

Internalized Homophobia

Lessons From the Mobius Strip

Glenda M. Russell

F or the past decade or more, I have been thinking about the construct
referred to as *internalized homophobia*. Internalized homophobia typically refers to a process whereby lesbian, gay, bisexual, and transgender
(LGBT) people "internalize" the negative beliefs and feelings held about
LGBT people in North American societies.[1] The term, coined in 1972 by
George Weinberg (1972), is used widely in psychological circles and has also
migrated to nonpsychological venues. It is not uncommon for LGBT people
to call upon the notion of internalized homophobia in personal, social, and
even political settings, and it seems clear that the construct speaks to some
experiences that many LGBT people have had. Indeed, the concept has spoken to me, and I have found it a useful, if also vexing, construct. The persistent recurrence of this latter quality insisted that I examine internalized
homophobia more fully.

In this chapter, I want to describe the evolution of my thinking regarding
the concept of internalized homophobia. In particular, I describe how I have
come to regard the Mobius strip (Grosz, 1994) as an appropriate model for
the relationship between what are usually referred to as *homophobia* and
internalized homophobia. The Mobius strip, which is named after the German
mathematician who described its geometric properties, may be familiar to many
who do not know its name. One can create a Mobius strip using a rectangle

of any flexible material, such as paper. Twist one end of the strip 180° and connect the two ends together. The resulting twisted loop represents a continuous, one-sided surface such that the "inside" and the "outside" flow inextricably into each other; they are inseparable, interdependent, and interdefined. As this chapter will make clear, what has been called homophobia (construed as residing in the world) and what has been called internalized homophobia (construed as residing within individuals) exist in similar relationship to each other such that one cannot be separated from or distinguished from the other.

In keeping with the narrative theme of this book, I will employ a narrative style and some illustrative stories to describe the process by which I came to understand internalized homophobia in this way, exploring the process of my own shifting understanding of internalized homophobia and the evolution of my current thinking. This narrative will be followed by a discussion of pragmatic implications of my current understanding of the topic. Throughout, I will strive to interweave this evolutionary narrative with references to formal work in the field.

By way of prelude, I should mention that my interest in internalized homophobia did not begin with my looking for a critique of the standard approach to the topic; on the contrary, I found the concept of internalized homophobia quite useful. First, it was useful to me as a therapist, particularly in my work with queer clients. I encountered in so many of these clients the burden of internalized homophobia. Sometimes the internalized homophobia was overt, as in the case of a young gay man who had been reared as a Mormon. He had feared that he would die in the aftermath of receiving a non-life-threatening electric shock, a fear we learned was grounded in his own internalized homophobia. His work in therapy led us to understand that he felt as if he had already died when he called himself "gay" and was therefore cast out by his family and by his church. Sometimes the internalized homophobia has appeared in more subtle guises, as in the case of a lesbian client who couldn't understand why her partner was so angry when she was not invited to join other in-laws in the picture taking at a wedding in the client's family. The concept of internalized homophobia was helpful to me as I worked with these and many other clients whose sexual orientations and sexual identities rendered them "different" in the eyes of so many.

In addition, I had found the construct very useful in political contexts. The utility of the internalized homophobia concept became especially apparent to me in 1992, as I watched LGBT clients, friends, coworkers—and, indeed, myself—go through the yearlong campaign in Colorado leading up to the passage of a state constitutional amendment prohibiting legal protections for LGB people who encountered discrimination. The amendment effectively said that discrimination against LGB people was legal and acceptable. I observed LGBT people who had previously felt comfortable with their sexual orientations gradually growing less comfortable, sometimes questioning themselves and the good lives they had created for themselves. In this campaign and its aftermath, I also found the concept useful as a tool in understanding the impact of internalized homophobia at a broader community level. Arguably, no other construct is as adequate as internalized homophobia in accounting for the self-questioning that occurred at the individual level or the lateral hostility (and its variant, lateral suspiciousness) I observed at the level of the LGBT community.

Surely, then, internalized homophobia has been a useful construct, a way to explain important phenomena for which there was no more plausible explanation. Even as I appreciated the value of the concept of internalized homophobia, I occasionally questioned it. I was particularly bothered by the way internalized homophobia was bandied about in the LGBT community; it seemed sometimes to serve as a weapon that LGBT people used against one another. Those times alerted me to the potential for internalized homophobia's serving as a vehicle for pathologizing queer people. My own nagging discomfort with this observation found its validation in a comment made by social psychologist Greg Herek (1997) in a talk at the meeting of the American Psychological Association: Herek expressed concern that LGBT psychology was in danger of replacing the idea of homosexuality as pathology with the idea of internalized homophobia as pathology. Herek's comment spoke directly to the concern I had about internalized homophobia.

Around the same time, I was working with a colleague on a book exploring the more general issue of sexual orientation: What exactly is it, or—even more fundamentally—is it actually an identifiable entity at all (Bohan & Russell, 1999)? These explorations highlighted the tensions between essentialist and social constructionist understandings of sexual orientation, suggesting that although essentialist understandings have often proven strategically useful, they may be problematic in both practical and theoretical ways. Although an elaboration of these issues is beyond the scope of this chapter, suffice it to say that my exploration of these matters initiated my awareness of a need to examine even the most widely accepted concepts in the field of LGB psychology. Among the topics that we did not pursue in any significant way in the book was the issue of internalized homophobia. In one section of the book that discusses the differences between essentialist and social constructionist approaches to therapy with LGB clients, we considered the possible role of internalized homophobia in various client presentations. Our discussions about internalized homophobia suggested a decidedly negative psychological entity residing within the person—an entity that we regarded much like a trait of the person, something that could be observed, measured, and excavated (Bohan & Russell, 1999). As I now reread that passage, I realize that it does not escape the aforementioned concerns raised by Herek (1997): We discussed internalized homophobia as if it were a negative entity infecting the person. We spoke of internalized homophobia in terms not unlike one might speak of a cancer, and we said very little about what might be done with it. In short, our discussion reflected some of the difficulties with the standard understandings of internalized homophobia that I am addressing here. Although in that book, we raised a number of challenges to mainstream considerations of LGBT psychology, in our considerations of internalized homophobia, our critique fell short of what I now believe is necessary.

In recent years, I have had a number of opportunities to explore the concept of internalized homophobia more broadly. Such opportunities have included occasions where I have challenged students in college- and graduate-level classes to engage in a fantasy brainstorm around this question: What would the world be like for people who experienced same-sex attractions if there were no homophobia (or heterosexism, homonegativity, or sexual prejudice[2])? This exercise reveals that many—perhaps most—of our usual notions about the psychological experience of queer people spring from and depend on homophobia/heterosexism/homenegativity/sexual prejudice. It is not uncommon for students to begin this exercise with obvious suggestions: This fantasy world would be devoid of negative attitudes toward LGBT people, of antigay hate crimes, of discrimination, of familial rejection, and the like. More subtle possibilities also emerge: Perhaps there would be no gay bars, no coming out, and no internalized homophobia. The exercise provides a forum for discussions of what is and what is not intrinsic to sexual orientation and sexual identity. Conversely, the exercise enables us to inquire as to the role of sexual prejudice in what we often take to be intrinsic aspects of sexual orientation and sexual identity.

It took several iterations of this exercise for me to fully understand the implication of the observation that in the absence of external homophobia, internalized homophobia would not exist at all. In a sense, this idea seems obvious: If there is no external sexual prejudice, there is nothing to "internalize." At the same time, there seemed to be a more elusive element to this obvious conclusion. In an effort to elucidate the more subtle dimension of the interplay between homophobia in the world and internalized homophobia, I pursued another exercise with students. The setup for the exercise was as follows. In the aftermath of the aforementioned antigay amendment in Colorado in 1992, I had sent out a survey to LGB people in the state in order to explore the impact of antigay campaigns and elections (Russell, 2000). The survey included a series of quantitative questions, followed by an open-ended question at the end. This question asked queer Coloradans to say anything they chose about their responses to this amendment legalizing discrimination against them.

In the exercise I am discussing here, I asked students to look at a single response to this open-ended, "say anything you want" question. The response I examined with students was a comment from a gay man in his 50s, who taught high school in a rural area of the state. What follows is exactly what he wrote on the survey, including the format of his response:

1. I am more cautious when going to a gay bar, day or night;

2. Students in my classroom in high school have asked if I were gay, others accused me of being gay in a negative manner. (In my classes we talked about a "No" vote on [Amendment] Two.);

3. I believe I would hesitate more, since the passage of Amendment Two, to "come out" to someone even though I may have known this person for some time;

4. To be seen in public with a gay male "screamer" would cause me more concern now than before the amendment was passed.

In conducting this exercise, I asked students to examine each statement, numbered by the man himself, and to try to identify indications of external homophobia and internalized homophobia. I acknowledged that given the absence of other information about this man, we were making assumptions based on woefully inadequate information. Without presuming the accuracy of our discussion in describing this man's experience, we were interested in trying to make sense of homophobia in its external and internal manifestations. Although each group that participated in this exercise followed a different course in its deliberations, the following analysis represents observations that often arose during these discussions.

Students commonly agreed that the man's first statement expressing concerns about going to a gay bar may have reflected a realistic concern, since there were reports of increased hate crimes in Colorado in the aftermath of the Amendment 2 election (Robbins, 1993; Spring, 1992; Stepanek, 1992). In addition, we know from other sources that hate crimes against gay men are especially likely to occur near places where gay men are known to congregate (Berrill, 1992), making gay bars potentially dangerous venues. At the same time, negative statements about LGB people had been routine in both the formal campaign and everyday conversations during the preceding months, and it is possible that this man had internalized these negative views enough that he was reluctant to express his sexual orientation socially and perhaps to associate with other gay people, both of which might be construed as suggestions of internalized homophobia. While these latter considerations were often raised, most students opined that the realistic danger this teacher faced was such that his first statement could be understood as an acknowledgment of actual homophobia present in his world rather than as a convincing indication of internalized homophobia.

This man's second statement concerned actual experiences with students in his classes. This statement introduced slightly more ambiguity into the situation. He reported having been approached by students who wondered about his sexual orientation, some of whom "asked" and others of whom "accused." Perhaps his distinction between being asked and being accused reflected identifiable differences in the attitudes with which different students approached him. Alternatively, it is possible that his being asked about his sexual orientation amounted to an accusation, given that the question was directed at a gay man in rural Colorado in the midst of a virulently antigay campaign. We are left to wonder: Did he experience his students' inquiries as accusations because his job could be in danger (homophobia in the world), and/or did he experience them as accusations because he had internalized some of the negative attitudes about LGBT orientations (internalized homophobia)?

This question of where external homophobia "ends" and internalized homophobia "begins" becomes even more salient with the man's third comment. His reluctance to come out, even to someone he had known for a long time, may simply have been a response to the antigay atmosphere in the state. His comment may also have reflected the experience reported by many queer Coloradoans, who were surprised at how many of their acquaintances were willing to vote for an amendment that excluded them from legal protections and were even more surprised by acquaintances who took the campaign as an occasion to participate in antigay rhetoric (Russell, 2000). Each of these responses would represent an acknowledgment of—and even shock at—the homophobia in the world. But this respondent may also have been saying something about how he had been impacted more personally by the campaign and election. Perhaps he was suggesting that he felt worse about himself, less comfortable with his sexual orientation, and therefore less likely to make it known—a discomfort that might convey an internalization of pejorative social judgments.

In the respondent's fourth statement, the delineation of homophobia and internalized homophobia is so ambiguous that even students who had eagerly taken a position on the three earlier statements were reluctant to do so again. This man's caution about being seen in public with a gay male "screamer," someone who appears obviously (i.e., stereotypically) gay, might very possibly reflect a concern that such an association would result in his being viewed as gay. Perhaps he feared that such a conclusion would place him in danger—maybe at risk for gay bashing or maybe in danger of losing his job. This line of reasoning makes some sense, though it also reveals some striking assumptions: that others can accurately know someone's sexual orientation (even that of a "screamer") from his appearance, that being seen with a gay man marks one as inevitably gay, and so on. An alternative possibility is that this man had incorporated widespread and harshly negative judgments about gay people who cannot or do not "pass" for straight. Perhaps antigay rhetoric had found a place in his own thinking, and he had come to dislike or distrust "screamers" himself. In either case, this comment suggests an explanation for the frequent observation that LGBT people under direct attack sometimes display high levels of intragroup hostility.

The boundaries between external homophobia and internalized homophobia grow fuzzier as we move through the four statements. Yet one thing is clear: If we read any of these statements in the absence of an appreciation for the real homophobia that existed in Colorado at the time, these responses seem odd, indeed. At best, this man appears overly cautious—at worst, paranoid. He seems to have isolated himself unnecessarily and was very possibly ashamed both of himself and of other gay men. However, in the context of the antigay sentiment prevalent in the state at the time, his responses seem far less inappropriate; in fact, they are in many ways understandable if not ideal responses. Whether this man's statements reflect internalized homophobia can be accurately understood only by reference to the antigay context in which he found himself.

This exercise quickly taught students to use care in making assumptions about queer people if they did not understand and actively consider their contexts. It further taught us all that understandings of internalized homophobia are dependent on the appreciation of the level of actual homophobia present in the external world at a given time. Indeed, the definitions of external homophobia and internalized homophobia are clearly interdependent; neither makes sense without knowing about the other. Moreover, the exercise suggests the broader postmodern question about the existence of an independent, freestanding self that exists apart from what is usually thought of as one's social context (Gergen, 1994; Sampson, 1993).

It was through experiences such as these that I began to realize that my understanding of (what I had been referring to as) external homophobia and internalized homophobia would benefit from a reunion with the postmodern approaches to sexual orientation that I mentioned earlier. These explorations had made it clear to me that it did not make sense to speak of external homophobia and internalized homophobia as distinct entities. Rather they were both of a piece, both one thing: homophobia (or, if one prefers, heterosexism or homonegativity or sexual prejudice). I began to employ a postmodern analysis in attempting to resolve what now seemed to be a false distinction between homophobia and internalized homophobia.

An Alternative Understanding

One of the basic tenets of postmodern approaches is the inevitable sociality of human experience. From this perspective, human beings do not exist apart from the social world; their entire lives, including their "selves," reside and are defined within their social contexts (Gergen, 1985, 1991, 1994, 2001; Gergen & Gergen, 1988; Harré, 1994; Sampson, 1977, 1985, 1989, 1993; Shotter, 1993). It does not make sense, then, to speak of *internal* and *external* as separate dimensions of experience. The self, usually construed as internal, is created by and within social action; indeed, it exists only as a phenomenon emergent in social interaction. Hence, the self is a shared reality that exists only in interaction.

Within a postmodern perspective, there is no room for internalized homophobia existing as a trait intrinsic to a person. Rather, all people of all sexual orientations reside in a social matrix that is characterized by (among so many things) ambivalent and even hostile attitudes toward any deviation from the heterosexual standard. All people participate in that social matrix; all contribute to it and are, in turn, influenced by it. But even these words are inadequate to describe the seamless, inseparable nature of humans in our social world. The boundaries between (what we usually understand as) the self and the social world are profoundly permeable. And homophobia is simply everywhere in the social world; it could not be "in" any person alone, nor could it exist solely "outside" the person. Homophobia is, in a sense, in the air; persons absorb it; persons express it. As is true with the Mobius strip, it is not possible to define internal or external as distinct entities.

Without wanting or intending to do so, persons in a homophobic society (including people who identify as heterosexual and people who identify as LGBT) learn homophobic attitudes. We take in the cognitive and affective dimensions of anti-LGBT narratives, and we do so as a matter of course. The process of learning homophobia occurs as easily as learning which words go with which colors or which foods are preferred in our culture or what rituals are appropriate for birthdays. Just as easily, people in society participate in the transmission of homophobic narratives, often before they know exactly what they mean. In the process, we contribute to the dissemination and the persistence of the same narratives. We do so through such actions as repeating or failing to question stereotypes, passing on or not interrupting the transmission of "common wisdom" about LGBT people, laughing at jokes about queer people, asserting or disregarding the exercise by others of heterosexual privilege, failing to question homophobic thoughts or feelings, assuming everyone is heterosexual, failing to learn about queer lives or culture, assuming that homophobia is relevant only to LGBT people, and countless other actions. In the vernacular of narrative theory, we absorb, transmit, and, indeed, enact the common narratives about LGBT people. These narratives vary, depending on numerous factors such as one's age, cohort, region of the country, sexual orientation, and so on. These narratives variously hold LGBT people to be disturbed, immoral, laughable, tragic, dangerous, despicable, and, frequently, some admixture of several of these. In more liberal circles, narratives about LGBT people are more likely to contain elements of creativity, suicidality, and the capacity for special friendships (especially with heterosexual women).

The cycle of taking in and promulgating homophobic narratives is as easy and as automatic as inhaling and exhaling; homophobia, like the air, is simultaneously within and without. Homophobia, like air, surrounds us, and its influence cannot be escaped, whether one identifies as lesbian, gay, bisexual, transgender, spectrum, queer, same-gender-loving, heterosexual, some other category, or none of the above, if that is preferable.

As mentioned at the start of this chapter, Grosz (1994) had appealed, in a different context, to a metaphor of the Mobius strip to demonstrate and challenge the mind-body binary. I appreciated Grosz's metaphor and gradually came to view the Mobius strip as an equally apt metaphor for the relationship between what has been called external homophobia and what has been called internalized homophobia. Neither side/aspect of the Mobius strip can be separated from the other, as each drifts immeasurably into the other. Each is given definition by the other; neither exists without the other, and neither can be considered except by reference to the other. Similarly, internalized homophobia and external homophobia are simply different faces of the same phenomenon: ubiquitous homonegative attitudes (narratives). One side, homophobia in the world, depends for its existence on collections of individuals who absorb and express homophobia; internalized homophobia exists only insofar as it is incorporated from and expressed to the larger social world. Any understanding of homophobia requires an appreciation of both aspects of or perspectives on what is actually a unitary phenomenon: that is, a joint understanding of the intractable unity of what has been termed external homophobia and what has been termed internalized homophobia.

As I explored this alternative understanding of homophobia, I came to recognize that even in the absence of a clear articulation of this formulation, I had been using elements of this perspective in my work with clients. (I do not think it is entirely uncommon for therapists to be ahead of their theories.) This framework for considering homophobia has some important advantages over traditional construals of internalized homophobia. First, it normalizes the presence of homophobia: Since everyone participates in homophobia, clients' expressions of it are not extraordinary. This reduces the tendency toward pathologizing that sometimes accompanies therapeutic discussions of internalized homophobia. In addition, by acknowledging homophobia as an inevitable outcome of living in a homophobic society, this approach places an emphasis on the social nature of homophobia rather than portraying it as an individual, intrapsychic trait.

In recognition of the fact that the standard terminology seems inadequate to capture the emergent quality expressed by this model, I have begun using different terms to highlight the social and dynamic quality of (what I had been calling) homophobia; I refer to it instead as *homonegating processes*. This term's plural form implicates the many guises in which homophobia occurs. The term includes a verb form, thus underscoring the dynamic quality of these processes: homonega*ting*. It applies equally well to phenomena that we traditionally think of as within the person and to phenomena that we traditionally think of as outside the person. It sees these phenomena as processes—that is, as enactments—rather than as traits. In addition, it conveys no distinction between an "actual" form and an "internalized" form. The term has the added advantage of applying, in the abstract, equally well to people who identify as lesbian/gay/bisexual/transgender/queer/spectrum/same-gender-loving and people who identify as heterosexual. The term homonegating processes has a final advantage: Because it normalizes one's holding homonegative views, because it locates the problem in the space among people rather than internal to individuals, and because it emphasizes processes or enactments, this construal suggests that remediation can occur through multiple avenues. Certainly, one of these avenues is psychotherapy, but there are other avenues as well.

One of the advantages of this approach is its assumption that all members of a heterosexist society participate in homonegating processes. There is no reason to single out those who identify as lesbian, gay, bisexual, transgender, queer, same-gender-loving, or spectrum from those who identify as heterosexual. Consequently, there is no need for any special inference of pathology for members of any of these groups. In my therapy work, I assume that any client, regardless of sexual orientation, is a candidate for participating in homonegating processes in ways that limit his or her choices in the world.

While this is the case in the abstract, it is also the case that the particulars of a person's sexual orientation and gender identity tend to render the dominant homophobic discourse differentially salient. Persons who self-identify as heterosexual tend to relate to the dominant discourse as a narrative that refers to other people. The homophobic discourse may not be at all personally salient to many, if not most, self-identified heterosexual individuals. On the other hand, for the LGBT person, the dominant discourse, in all its negativity, applies directly and specifically to oneself. At worst, it becomes a statement of what one sees oneself to be. It is difficult—at least as a starting point—for persons who identify as lesbian, gay, bisexual, or transgender to disregard or dismiss this same discourse. For queer people, the dominant discourse tends to be very salient, at least to the degree that their sexual orientations or gender identities are salient to them (Beckstead & Morrow, 2004). I will consider briefly how these variations in salience may play out in psychotherapy, first, for people who identify as lesbian, gay, bisexual, or transgender and then for those who identify as heterosexual.

I have seen a range of variations in how LGBT-identified individuals relate to the dominant narrative about them, with its stark homophobic quality. Some employ a kind of compartmentalization in an effort to maintain some distance between a self-identification as lesbian, gay, bisexual, or transgender and the homonegative narrative depicting those identities. I have encountered this dynamic in any number of clients: in gay men who view their adolescent participation in antigay jokes and even, in a few cases, in overt gay bashing as an effort to keep an emerging gay identity at arm's length; in a heterosexually married woman who insisted to herself that she was "completely heterosexual" even as she engaged in a long-term sexual and romantic relationship with her best woman friend; in several gay men who retrospectively viewed their earlier participation in anonymous gay sex as a means to stay distant from a sense of themselves as having a gay sexual orientation; in a lesbian recovering from active alcohol abuse who came to see her earlier problem drinking as a means to engage sexually with women, something she did not feel comfortable with doing when sober; in a Roman Catholic gay man who endured prolonged periods of self-imposed celibacy, during which he adopted a view of himself as asexual, interrupted by excursions to gay bars only when he traveled to distant cities.

The degree of compartmentalization differs. My clinical experience suggests that a full compartmentalization is difficult to sustain over very long periods of time. However, I have worked with clients who have reported significant levels of compartmentalization that spanned several years. In addition, I wonder if I am likely to see in therapy people who rely foundationally on compartmentalization; my guess is therapy represents the likelihood of serious challenge to such compartmentalization. Still, recent news stories of political figures who have taken long-standing and actively antigay positions while apparently engaging in periodic clandestine homosexual encounters suggest the possibility of long-lived compartmentalization.

I suspect that the more frequent scenario involves a more dynamic give-and-take between the dominant homophobic narrative and one's self-identification as lesbian, gay, bisexual, or transgender. In such cases, people are not able to maintain an ongoing separation of these two inconsistent discourses. Rather than going back and forth between the two incommensurate narratives, as we see in compartmentalization, people are more able to hold greater ongoing awareness of the conflict between the two narratives. They are more likely to have articulated the incommensurate quality of these two discourses, and they typically experience themselves on the horns of a dilemma. In these cases, the work of therapy is to resolve the conflict, to move toward some resolution between the incommensurate narratives. I have seen people come to a variety of resolutions. Sometimes people throw out one or the other narrative. For example, some adherents to traditional religions renounce their self-identification as lesbian, gay, bisexual, or transgender; some other adherents renounce their religious affiliations and, with this, the homophobic elements in their religious narratives; still others manage to reconcile ostensibly incommensurate narratives, changing one or the other or both to smooth over obvious points of dissonance.

Although heterosexual people are not the direct target of dominant homophobic narratives, the salience of such discourse is not uniformly low for all heterosexually identified persons. This salience, where it arises, may take a variety of forms. It may entail a focus on the homophobic narrative with the aim of rejecting the dominant, homonegative narrative and claiming another, more queer-positive narrative; or it may entail an embrace of the dominant narrative with its homonegative meanings. In the former case, the dominant discourse becomes salient as some heterosexual people struggle to change their own narratives and to embrace a more LGBT-positive discourse. In the latter case, the homophobic discourse is very salient as a constitutive element of some heterosexual individuals' personal identities.

Illustrating the former situation (where salience is related to challenging the dominant discourse), I have had many clients who regarded homophobic narratives as basically irrelevant to them until they learned that someone close to them was lesbian, gay, bisexual, or transgender. In the face of this conflict of narratives, they found themselves working to alter their own discourses to accommodate this fact. Several publications are available that contain personal narratives about just such transitions (e.g., Clarke & Vaughn, 2001; DeGeneres, 1999). Other heterosexually identified persons view the dominant homophobic discourse as more or less irrelevant until that position is challenged and the issue made more relevant by an awareness of a conflict between this homonegative discourse and other values that they hold. For example, in some circumstances, heterosexually identified

persons who hold generally liberal values with regard to equal rights may
come to view homophobic discourse not only as salient but also as worthy
of their personal activist attentions (e.g., Castiglione, 1992; Mohr, 1994).

As illustrative of the latter situation (where salience is related to embracing the dominant narrative), some heterosexually identified individuals may
regard the dominant homophobic narrative as personally salient because
of its implications for their own identities. Herek (1992) has suggested that
there are a variety of forms of homophobia, reflecting a variety of motives;
one of these is *ego-defensive homophobia,* which occurs when an individual
embraces homophobic narratives as an affirmation of his or her own distance from any hint of LGBT identity. In this case, expressing an overt
homophobic stance is seen as a means to reduce the anxiety associated with
unconscious conflicts presumably related to sexuality and gender. The whole
notion of ego-defensive homophobia begins to call into question the certainty of one's self-narrative about personal sexual orientation.

In extreme cases, heterosexually identified persons may move into an apparently sudden awareness of the salience of homophobic discourse. A tragic
example of this is evident in the courtroom testimony of one of the young men
who was tried for the murder of a young transgender woman, Gwen Araujo.
The young man testified in court that he was "disgusted" when he found out that
Araujo, with whom he had had anal sex, had male genitalia:

> It's hard to explain. Your whole life you think you're a heterosexual. Then you
> get pleasure from a homosexual [sic]. It disgusted me. . . . I thought it was
> impossible to derive pleasure from a man unless you were gay. I was having
> serious questions about my sexuality. (St. John, 2005)

One cannot judge the degree to which this man's testimony in a murder
trial accurately represents his experience in the actual situation. What is clear
is that the sudden and unexpected salience of the dominant homophobic
narrative is a plausible explanation of (although clearly not an excuse for)
his taking another person's life.

Clearly, the issue of the particular salience of the dominant homophobic
narrative is a critical one. The degree to which the narrative is salient and the
degree of its dissonance with other narratives held by the person are important. In some broad ways, these issues are different for those who identify as
lesbian, gay, bisexual, or transgender (who are the topic of such discourse) and
those who identify as heterosexual (for whom the discourse usually refers to
others). The process of therapy will be influenced by the particular degree and
direction of this salience for each individual. Nonetheless, all clients—indeed,
all people—have some relationship to the dominant homophobic discourse.

Homonegating Processes in Psychotherapy

Whatever the sexual orientation of the client, the application of this postmodern perspective on homophobia, referred to here as homonegating processes, to psychotherapy entails a willingness by the therapist to broach the political as well as the personal. A therapist who tries to confine the therapeutic discourse to the purely personal aspects of homonegating processes will be in the position of trying to isolate one side of the Mobius strip, an impossible task. Thus, the sociopolitical elements as well as the personal experience of homonegating processes are not only fair game but also essential elements of therapeutic approaches to this topic.

When I work with homonegating processes in therapy, I often normalize them by asserting that homophobia (the term I am more likely to use with clients) is pervasive in the culture and, therefore, no one is immune from it. We all have grown up breathing it in and sending it forth. There was (typically) no intentionality in that—only inevitability. Acknowledging that reality and nurturing the awareness of homophobia can mean that one has the power to interrupt its processes. With some clients who remain embarrassed about their own participation (past or present) in homophobia, I suggest that one of the privileges of the therapeutic process is the opportunity to hold ourselves accountable by changing what we enact rather than by engaging in self-punishment for what we have learned.

As in most good therapy, the content of the discussion about homonegating processes is built upon clients' own experiences and how they make sense of them. We go where the homonegating processes take us, and that can be virtually anywhere. There is no set pattern for our explorations (see, e.g., Freedman & Combs, 1996; McNamee & Gergen, 1992; White, 1991), though the discussion often begins in one of two major ways: Either the client brings up the issue or I do.

Client-Initiated Explorations

In the first case, a client notices and raises something—a belief, an assumption, an act—that she views as reflecting one or more of the homophobic narratives. Sometimes clients raise such issues sheepishly, opening an opportunity for me to speak briefly about homophobia's pervasiveness and the inevitability of our participating in it. If a client has raised the issue himself, I ask him to explore what he knows or thinks about the matter, where he learned it, perhaps what the fit is between his thoughts and his feelings on the matter. My stance during this sort of discussion is very much in keeping with my usual stance in psychotherapy: I am curious as I ask questions that might lead both the client and me to some understanding of the homonegating processes he has identified (see Andersen, 1990; Cecchin, 1987; Freedman & Combs, 1996).

My questions sometimes focus on the client's more private experiences: what her secret beliefs and ambivalences about nonheterosexual orientations might be and how she understands these beliefs. Sometimes my questions focus more on public matters—certainly on where and how she learned such narratives, paying particular attention to the affective as well as the cognitive lessons to which she has been exposed. In true hermeneutic fashion, we wonder as much about what was not said regarding queer orientations as what was said regarding them. I invite other public matters into the therapy session as well; I am interested in the client's understandings of how he participates in the transmission of homophobia, to himself and to others. I am curious as to how the material experiences of his life promote the homophobia and what experiences serve to interrupt it. I am as curious about how the client interrupts homophobic narratives in her public world as I am about how she interrupts them in her more private spaces. The questions move seamlessly from the external to the internal.

An Illustrative Case

By way of illustration, I offer my work with a heterosexually identified client, a woman in her mid-40s. She had initially sought therapy for the purpose of exploring her sense that she had "dead-ended" in her work as a high-level administrator. These explorations were interrupted when the client, I will call her "Jane," learned that her godson and favorite nephew, a college-age man, was gay. Jane revealed this news to me with obvious discomfort. She loved her nephew and had always felt close to and supportive of him. Both Jane and her nephew lived in a liberal world that encouraged tolerance (if not always acceptance) of LGBT people, and she also held political beliefs very much in support of queer rights. Thus, her reactions about her nephew's news caught her by surprise. She felt vaguely sad and disoriented, but her feelings matched neither her cognitive reaction nor what she expected of herself. She was unsure exactly what her reservations were. Intellectually, she supported her nephew in everything he did, just as she supported gay rights. Emotionally, she felt queasy at the thought of this favorite nephew's newly announced gay orientation.

Our first order of business was to discuss Jane's reluctance to acknowledge the negative elements of her response to her nephew's disclosure. She did not wish to see herself as a person who did not accept her nephew or LGBT people in general. I suggested that, like all of us, she had grown up in a homophobic world and that she had inevitably incorporated negative narratives, with both cognitive and affective elements, about nonheterosexual orientations. I also suggested that her nephew's coming out represented an opportunity for Jane to examine the homophobic narratives that she had learned but she could take advantage of this opportunity only if she allowed herself to look clearly at them. Therapy was not an occasion for being politically correct, I suggested, but rather an occasion for examining the subtle lessons we all learn from living in a homophobic world.

Once Jane gave herself permission to examine her homophobic narratives, she took little time in finding several important threads. One thread went to stories she had heard as a child, stories about a man who lived in her hometown. Jane's parents and neighbors sometimes made pointed references to the man. Sometimes they laughed about him; sometimes they lowered their voices when they mentioned him. She recalled the words "different" and "delicate" being used in reference to this man. Jane did not remember ever hearing anyone refer to the man as "gay" (or homosexual), but she gradually realized that he was gay. She also could not remember being warned to avoid this man. The feeling that came through about him was one of "differentness" and "pity," and these were prominent images in how Jane had responded to her nephew's coming out.

Another narrative thread that Jane noticed in her reaction to her nephew involved her religious upbringing. She continued to be a member of the liberal Christian church that she had attended as a child. Her church was generally accepting of LGBT people, although she did not actually know any LGBT members of her congregation. She could recall no single instance of a sermon for or against homosexuality at any time. This led us to discuss how the absence of the topic in church carried its own message. Queer orientations and identity were invisible, and Jane wondered if she hadn't understood this invisibility to mean they were unmentionable. It seemed clear that the silence on the matter at church paralleled the whispered references about the gay man in her town. We also discussed how the absence of gay men in her current social network repeated the same theme: There are these men out there, but I do not know them. I feel vaguely sad about them now, just as I did as a child when I heard about the gay man in town.

As Jane sat with and explored these threads, she could understand the ease with which she had developed uncomfortable feelings about gay men. She could see clear parallels between the feelings she had had in response to her earliest lessons about gay men and her contemporaneous feelings about her nephew's coming out. She also acknowledged that she wanted to change the narratives she employed, not only at the overt level but at more subtle levels as well. We talked at length about ways she could do that. The possibilities were broad and included talking with her nephew about his life, learning more about gay culture generally, engaging in some political work on gay issues, and discussing the issue with a friend whose son was gay and with whom Jane had never pursued the topic. As Jane delved into these topics more extensively, she raised the issue of her heterosexuality—how she had never considered it something to look at or even acknowledge. Jane was not questioning her sexual orientation; rather, she began to think about herself as a heterosexual, as someone with access to the privileges and safety associated with being a member of the sexual majority. Here, some sadness about her nephew resurfaced; she was aware of what privileges were denied him by virtue of his sexual orientation. I wondered with Jane if she had run into the old pity again. She said no, and made this distinction: Her sadness for her nephew was based on constraints imposed on his life solely because of social attitudes. Her former feelings of pity, on the other hand, had been based on rumor, gossip, and innuendo. Her present sadness was counterbalanced by knowing her nephew as a human being and by her nephew's and her own hopefulness that social attitudes were changing.

Therapist-Initiated Explorations

There is the second, more subtle way that discussions of homophobia might begin in therapeutic sessions, a situation in which I am considerably more tentative about raising the issue. In this case, I bring up the possibility that something the client believes or has said or done suggests some negative feelings about queer orientations. I offer this possibility with the same openness and curiosity described above, but my tentativeness is decidedly greater. My language is typically marked by a combination of curiosity and uncertainty: "I wonder if. . . . " or "I almost hear in your statement. . . . " and similar invitations for the client to consider the possibility that some heretofore unnoticed homophobia is floating about. Sometimes clients take me up on the invitation; sometimes they do not. In the latter case, I almost always drop the matter. I am certain that my tentativeness and willingness to withdraw occasionally result in forfeiting the possibility of elucidating homonegating processes with the client. It is a choice I make for several reasons. First, if this issue is that far from the client's concerns, there is little likelihood that my pushing it will change its salience. Indeed, I worry that my pushing it could reduce the likelihood that the client will examine the issue at some point. I also believe—and my clinical experience provides considerable support for this belief—that clients often return at a later time to issues that were raised too early or were raised in the context of more pressing concerns. Ultimately, I am tentative because while the therapy is created by both the client and me, it needs to serve the client first of all.

When the client does follow up on the invitation to explore homophobia, the ensuing conversation looks much like the one that occurs when the client raises the possibility of homophobia, which I described in the case above. Again, we work together to understand homophobia from both sides of the Mobius strip.

One way of thinking about therapeutic work on homophobia is to conceptualize it as two intertwined processes. The first process involves creating a coherent story about the homophobia, its origins, and its manifestations. The second process involves deconstructing the story and constructing other possibilities for how a person wants to see himself or herself (see, e.g., Freedman & Combs, 1996; White 1991). Of necessity, conversations about both of these issues frequently involve references to political realities. The self and the social exist not as separate entities, but as the two sides of the Mobius strip, inevitably bound together in reciprocal interdependence. This mutuality carries significant implications not only for how homonegating processes are understood in therapy but also for how homonegating processes are addressed outside of the therapy hour. Because personal and sociopolitical domains are neither separate nor separable, therapy guided by this perspective invites clients to participate in social and political activities that challenge homophobia. Healing at the individual level often springs from and also generates change at a community level (Russell, 2000; Russell & Bohan, in press-a; Russell & Richards, 2003). In fact, this approach has much in common with liberation psychology and its emphasis on the importance of providing a macrosociological understanding of the forces that frame the internalization of negative attitudes (e.g., Martín-Baró, 1994; Prilleltensky, 1994; Russell & Bohan, in press-b). The more one knows about how homonegating processes operate in the broader world, the better one understands the very particular ways that these processes impact oneself.

Interrupting Homonegating Processes

When homonegating processes emerge as a focus in psychotherapy, I view them as one aspect of a dominant discourse in the broader world. In this case, the discourse makes reference to nonheterosexual orientations and/or nonnormative gender expressions. This discourse has traditionally and pervasively been characterized by negative attitudes toward any but a very circumscribed set of heterosexual and gender-normative expressions. All else, including positive representations of queer and gender-defying expressions, might be thought of as belonging to an alternative or marginalized discourse. The dominant discourse has traditionally been "granted the status of truth, the agreed-upon frameworks of language and meaning" (Marecek, 1999, p. 161). Marginalized discourses "refuse or challenge" the usual view.

Psychotherapy that is sensitive to these issues allows for direct inquiry into the client's relationship to the dominant discourse: Is it appropriate, acceptable, working for them, helpful, and so on? At the same time, therapy affords clients the opportunity to construct (with therapists as their coauthors) alternative discourses. Therapy provides what McCorkle (1998) has called the "critical space" in which such alternative understandings may be generated. Clients and therapists create these alternative discourses using essentially the same tools they have used to construct more traditional meanings of sexual orientation and gender identity (Hollander, 2002). Clients and therapists work together to question and deconstruct old understandings and to try out new ones. The new understandings are scrutinized in much the same way as the traditional frameworks: Are they appropriate, acceptable, working for the client, useful to the client, and so on? These explorations may involve any number of therapeutic techniques, including those that fall into the province generally considered as narrative therapy. However, any specific technique is less important than the overarching approach: a conversation in which traditional narratives are confronted and new narratives may be developed and enacted.

If therapy is to be more than a safe space for generating ideas with little impact on clients' lives, it is imperative that therapists and clients focus some of their attention on how new understandings can be enacted in the world that clients inhabit beyond the therapy room. It is important that clients consider how to live out the new understandings, try them on in different relationships and different settings, and enact them not just in their own heads, but in social and political spheres as well. To that end, therapy must address where the new understandings will go, how they will be lived out, how they can change the world, and how ignoring them can contribute to the status quo. Clearly, this is not a one-time discussion, but a reiterative conversation that takes place many times, with different points of focus and with changing emphasis as therapy progresses. Conversely, the therapy conversation is informed and enriched by clients' efforts to enact new understandings in extratherapy spheres. In the process, the so-called internal and external dimensions of the Mobius strip are addressed simultaneously, even as a given therapeutic conversation might highlight one side or the other.

The Role of Client and Therapist Sexual Orientation

Thus far, I have described this approach without reference to the sexual orientation or sexual identity of the therapist. As with clients, I assume that therapists of any sexual orientation, including myself and therapists I supervise, may be enacting homonegating processes in the practice of psychotherapy; indeed, an awareness of the impact of these processes is crucial to supervision as well as to therapy (Russell & Greenhouse, 1997). My guiding principle in deciding to invite consideration of these topics is the best interests of the client. I am willing to raise the issue, just as I am willing to raise questions about participation in other forms of social oppression that may be limiting to a client and/or to a therapist I supervise. At the same time, I am aware that there are certainly times when clients or therapists are impeded far more by other factors than by their participation in oppressive attitudes and behaviors.

Besides differences rooted in sexual orientation, we can expect that other variables influence how clients relate to homonegating processes. We might anticipate gender differences in the ways homonegative attitudes would be experienced, as well as variations related to the client's and therapist's race/ ethnicity, family background, class, geographic locale, and other matters that influence people's relationships to themselves and others. Events that influence societal levels of overt and subtle forms of homophobia would also be expected to exert varying influences on both clients and therapists; prominent political campaigns or widespread media coverage of debates about LGBT issues, for instance, might heighten the salience of these concerns. The therapist would additionally need to consider the potential interaction between his or her own sexual orientation (whatever it is) and clients' work, including questions regarding the disclosure of consistencies or differences between a therapist's and a client's sexual orientation (see, for example, Russell, 2006). It is neither possible nor necessary to understand how each of these differences might impact a particular client's experience of homonegativity. Instead, we can use these variations in identity experience as sensitizing devices (Gergen, 1973), rough guideposts to help us notice and inquire about issues that might be relevant to clients' or therapists' explorations of homonegating processes.

There is nothing of a new therapeutic technique in this approach. Rather, it offers an alternative way to understand homophobia, a phenomenon that has traditionally been construed as having identifiably distinct external and internal manifestations and that might be more accurately and fruitfully understood in a more dynamic and complex way. This alternative perspective, in turn, suggests a new story line for therapy, one that addresses homonegativity not as a trait of individuals, but as a process of social exchange, both within and outside the therapy hour. The resulting suggestions for psychotherapy practice simply bring this new understanding to familiar techniques: the usual attention to what clients say (and what they do not say) and a willingness to acknowledge and talk both about what happens when the world at large accompanies our clients to their therapeutic sessions and what happens when clients take lessons from their therapy and enact them in their larger social and political worlds.

Notes

1. The term *internalized homophobia* has been used particularly in reference to lesbians and gay men, sometimes encompassing bisexuals as well. Other terms, *biphobia* and *transphobia,* have been coined to refer to the unique aspects of negative attitudes toward bisexual and transgender people, respectively. In this chapter, I mean to employ the term internalized homophobia in its broadest sense, with implications for all who identify as other than heterosexual.

2. I use all of these terms to refer to negative attitudes toward LGBT people and their relationships. Each term connotes a somewhat different perspective on these attitudes.

References

Anderson, H. (1990). Then and now: A journey from "knowing" to "not knowing." *Contemporary Family Therapy, 12,* 193–197.

Beckstead, A. L., & Morrow, S. L. (2004). Mormon clients' experiences of conversion therapy: The need for a new treatment approach. *Counseling Psychologist, 32,* 651–690.

Berrill, K. T. (1992). Anti-gay violence and victimization in the United States: An overview. In G. M. Herek & K. T. Berrill (Eds.), *Hate crimes: Confronting violence against lesbians and gay men* (pp. 19–40). London: Sage.

Bohan, J. S., & Russell, G. M. (1999). *Conversations about psychology and sexual orientation.* New York: New York University Press.

Castiglione, J. (1992). *The straight person's guide to gay people's anguish.* Salt Lake City, UT: Northwest.

Cecchin, G. (1987). Hypothesizing, circularity, and neutrality revisited: An invitation to curiosity. *Family Practice, 26,* 405–413.

Clarke, P., & Vaughn, E. (2001). *Keep singing.* Los Angeles: Alyson.

DeGeneres, B. (1999). *Love, Ellen: A mother/daughter journey.* New York: Rob Weisbach.

Freedman, J., & Combs, G. (1996). *Narrative therapy: The social construction of preferred realities.* New York: Norton.

Gergen, K. J. (1973). Social psychology as history. *Journal of Personality and Social Psychology, 26,* 309–320.

Gergen, K. J. (1985). The social constructionist movement in modern psychology. *American Psychologist, 40,* 266–227.

Gergen, K. J. (1991). *The saturated self.* New York: Basic Books.

Gergen, K. J. (1994). *Realities and relationships: Soundings in social constructionism.* London: Sage.

Gergen, K. J. (2001). *Social construction in context.* London: Sage.

Gergen, K. J., & Gergen, M. M. (1988). Narrative and the self as relationship. *Advances in Experimental Social Psychology, 21,* 17–56.

Grosz, E. (1994). *Volatile bodies: Toward a corporeal feminism.* Bloomington: University of Indiana Press.

Harré, R. (1984). *Personal being: A theory for individual psychology.* Cambridge, MA: Harvard University Press.

Herek, G. M. (1992). Psychological heterosexism and anti-gay violence: The social psychology of bigotry and bashing. In G. M. Herek & K. T. Berrill (Eds.), *Hate crimes: Confronting violence against lesbians and gay men* (pp. 149–169). Newbury Park, CA: Sage.

Herek, G. M. (1997, August 15). *Sexual orientation and public policy.* Paper presented for Distinguished Contribution to Psychology in the Public Interest at the convention of the American Psychological Association, Chicago.

Hollander, J. A. (2002). Resisting vulnerability: The social reconstruction of gender in interaction. *Social Problems, 48,* 474–496.

Marecek, J. (1999). Trauma talk in feminist clinical practice. In S. Lamb (Ed.), *New versions of victims: Feminists struggle with the concept* (pp. 158–182). New York: New York University Press.

Martín-Baró, I. (1994). *Writings for a liberation psychology.* Cambridge, MA: Harvard University Press.

McCorkle, J. A. (1998). Going to the crackhouse: Critical space as a form of resistance in total institutions and everyday life. *Symbolic Interaction, 21,* 227–252.

McNamee, S., & Gergen, K. J. (Eds.). (1992). *Therapy as social construction.* London: Sage.

Mohr, R. D. (1994). *A more perfect union: Why straight America must stand up for gay rights.* Boston: Beacon.

Prilleltensky, I. (1994). *The morals and politics of psychology: Psychological discourse and the status quo.* Albany: State University of New York Press.

Robbins, L. (1993, March 12). Study: Hate crimes rise 129 percent. *Daily Camera* [Boulder, CO].

Russell, G. M. (2000). *Voted out: The psychological consequences of anti-gay politics.* New York: New York University Press.

Russell, G. M. (2006). Different ways of knowing: The complexity of therapist disclosure. *Journal of Gay and Lesbian Psychotherapy, 12*(10), 79–94.

Russell, G. M., & Bohan, J. S. (in press-a). The case of internalized homophobia: Theory and/as action. *Theory and Psychology.*

Russell, G. M., & Bohan, J. S. (in press-b). Liberating psychotherapy: Liberation psychology and psychotherapy with LGBT clients. *Journal of Gay and Lesbian Psychotherapy.*

Russell, G. M., & Greenhouse, E. (1997). Homophobia in the supervisory relationship: An invisible intruder. *Psychoanalytic Review, 84,* 127–142.

Russell, G. M., & Richards, J. A. (2003). Stressor and resilience factors for lesbians, gay men, and bisexuals confronting antigay politics. *American Journal of Community Psychology, 31,* 313–328.

Sampson, E. E. (1977). Psychology and the American ideal. *Journal of Personality and Social Psychology, 35,* 767–782.

Sampson, E. E. (1985). The decentralization of identity: Toward a revised concept of the personal and social order. *American Psychologist, 40,* 1203, 1211.

Sampson, E. E. (1989). The challenge of social change for psychology: Globalization and psychology's theory of the person. *American Psychologist, 44,* 914–921.

Sampson, E. E. (1993). *Celebrating the other: A dialogic account of human nature.* Boulder, CO: Westview Press.

Shotter, J. (1993). *Conversational realities.* London: Sage.

Spring, T. (1992, December 14). Hate crimes on rise. *Colorado Daily* [Boulder, CO].

Stepanek, M. (1992, December 23). Gay-bashing on rise in Colorado. *San Francisco Examiner,* p. A9.

St. John, K. (2005, July 26). Accused killer was "disgusted" that transgender teen was male [sic]. *San Francisco Chronicle.* Retrieved July 26, 2005, from http://www.sfgate.com

Weinberg, G. (1972). *Society and the healthy homosexual.* New York: St. Martin's Press.

White, M. (1991). Deconstruction and therapy. *Dulwich Centre Newsletter, 3,* 21–40.

PART III

Challenging Essentialism

9

Dethroning the Suppressed Voice

Unpacking Experience as Story

Catrina Brown

I n this chapter, I will problematize the conceptualization of experience as it is often taken up in modernist therapeutic practices. Doing so will include taking apart routinized assumptions in practice that naturalize emotions and that privilege, authorize, and decontextualize clients' experiences, separating them from their social construction. Drawing on the work of Joan Scott (1992) and Dorothy Smith (1990, 1999), experience is interrogated, as is subsequently the privileging of the suppressed voice in therapeutic practice. Within this work, experience is an interpretation that needs interpretation (Scott, 1992). It is argued that the suppressed or disqualified voice is located within dominant social stories—it does not escape the social—and thus it must, like all other stories, be unpacked. If we wish to move beyond the limitations of subjectivism in which the individual is seen to be independent of the social world, experience must be taken up in narrative work as fully social.

Narrative therapy emphasizes the resurrection of the suppressed voice, bringing into view disqualified knowledge (White, 2001). Externalizing internalized dominant discourse often allows for suppressed or subjugated knowledge to emerge. However, along with White (1997, 2001), I will argue that resurrecting the suppressed voice is not the discovery of the real, unencumbered self. As such, it should not be privileged as natural or as providing an authoritative foundation. Suppressed stories or subjugated stories are not inherently more true than those that reflect dominant knowledge. All aspects of stories require unpacking for individuals to determine a preferred way of being in the world. While narrative therapy encourages individuals to embrace a preferred identity, we need to remember such preferences do not exist outside the influence of culture. As such, choice exists within the opportunities and constraints of culture and cannot be individualized (Butler, 1993; Foucault, 1991, 1995). It is not, therefore, only the harmful or negative stories that narrative therapy must take apart. White (1997, 2001) reminds us of the importance of unpacking both positive and negative accounts of identity, as neither are evidence of the "real self." Both the dominant and subjugated knowledge within experience stories are socially constructed, and, indeed, the existence of one story tends to rely upon the existence of the other (Foucault, 1980). Thus, while clients' preferred realities are privileged in reconstructing or re-authoring identities, these preferred realities should not be naturalized any more than unhelpful stories should. I will argue in this chapter that therapeutic reflexivity must extend beyond the resurrection of the suppressed voice in order to dethrone the suppressed voice itself from naturalized positions that privilege it as self-legitimizing. Postmodern narrative therapy will then need to hold on to the tension between accepting and rejecting aspects of experience (Brown, 1994, 2001, 2003).

The Social Construction of Experience

Experience is grounded in existing stories, both reproducing and challenging them. We make sense of our experiences through the stories that we tell about them (Anderson, 1997; White & Epston, 1990). According to Anderson (1997), "Through conversations we form and reform our life experiences and events; we create and recreate our meanings and understandings; and we construct and reconstruct our realities and our selves" (p. xvii). In Gergen's (1985) elaboration of a social constructionist approach to psychological inquiry, he states, "What we take to be experience of the world does not in itself dictate the terms by which the world is understood" (p. 266). Furthermore, "The terms in which the world is understood are social artifacts, products of historically situated interchanges among people" (p. 267), and "descriptions and explanations of the world themselves constitute forms of social action. As such, they are intertwined with the full range of other human activities" (p. 268).

Like Scott (1992), Geertz (1986) examines the making of experience, observing that while we are often not quite satisfied with the conceptualization and deployment of experience, we cannot really do without it. Geertz observes that while accounts or stories of experience often become problematically "encoded statements of social facts" (p. 376), they need instead to "transcend our deep grained assumption that signs are one thing and experiences are another" (p. 380). From this view, it is not just language and stories that are socially constructed, but experience itself.

Postmodernism offers a constructionist formulation of experience and of our representation or story telling about experience. From this lens, we make sense of our experiences through the use of stories: We language our experience into being. The symbolic universe allows for the organization of meaning within culture such that it is taken for granted in everyday life. Within this process, individuals come to see themselves as subjects in nature rather than social constructions (Mead, 1977). Members of society imagine themselves belonging to an inherently meaningful, stable, and fixed environment, which was there before birth and which will continue after death (Berger & Luckmann, 1967). The symbolic universe of language is presumed to actually represent social life rather than create it. It is a simulacrum, appearing to be one thing while doing another. For Gergen (1999), "Language is not a picture of the real" (p. 226). While language makes shared meaning possible, people can see only what language and concepts allow them to see. All stories about social life and subjective experience involve interpretation and reflect the social processes of meaning making. There can be no experience outside the stories we tell. The subjective acknowledgment or recognition of perceptions, events, images, memories, and emotions all involve interpretation and the cultural and historical assignation of meaning. Meaning is not inherent in these subjective moments. It is not independent of social life.

Problematizing the Authority of Experience

Modernist therapeutic practices are often predicated upon valuing, validating, and legitimating experience. This approach ascribes a truth value to experience, and the subsequent privileging of experience often prohibits challenging "first-voice" stories. There are two major problems with this conceptualization of experience. If, on the one hand, experience is taken at face value and validated, it is often problematically essentialized, dehistoricized, universalized, and authorized. Within this approach, experience is taken at face value, treated as uncontestable and authoritative knowledge. If on the other hand, one attempts to re-story experience, this involves decentering and delegitimizing the client's "expert" or authoritative voice. This competing stance on the authority of experience suggests that, on the one hand, experience ought to be taken at face value and, on the other, it ought not. I suggest that deautho-rizing or challenging the inherent authority of clients' experiences is a move-ment away from problematic conceptualizing of experience as essential or natural. I concur with other critics of essentialism that experience is something we need to explain.

We know from the wisdom of Scott (1992) that experience is not itself explanatory—it is not self-evident. Therapy is nothing if not a site for the deconstruction of experience and, specifically, the meaning of life experi-ences. For Scott (1992), experience is "at once already an interpretation and in need of interpretation" (p. 38):

> What counts as experience is neither self-evident nor straightforward; it is always contested, always therefore political. The study of experience, there-fore, must call into question its originary status in historical explanation. This will happen when historians take as their project [not] the reproduction and transmission of knowledge said to be arrived at through experience, but the analysis of the production of that knowledge itself. (p. 38)

We need to attend to the paradoxes of experience in which experience is both an obstacle to and a necessary aspect of how we can "know" the world (Haug, 1992). Experience should be the beginning rather than the end point of social inquiry (Scott, 1992). As experience is "ideologically cast" (Fuss, 1989, p. 114), we need to be concerned with how experience is socially orga-nized (Haug, 1992; Scott, 1992; Smith 1987, 1990, 1999).

From a postmodern lens, "'experience,' interpreted as a function of the modernist unitary subject, cannot provide a direct and uncontaminated access to reality since it is already discursively determined" (Smith, 1999, p. 101). According to Haug (1992), human beings cannot give objective accounts of themselves; rather, they subjectively construct and transform them:

> Individuals turn and twist, change and falsify, repress and forget events, pur-suing, what is in fact no more than an ideological construction of individual-ity, giving oneself an identity of the present to which the "facts" of the past are subordinated. (p. 9)

Arguably, when we do not question or unpack these stories, we reproduce as unchallenged the existing story. As such, the discourses and social rela-tions of oppression and domination may simply be reified. For example, if we legitimate or validate, leaving intact a battered woman's claim that she caused the violence against her, we reify not only her self-blame but also social relations of domination. Or, in another instance, should a 65-pound woman who struggles with anorexia say she is too fat, we are unlikely to accept this description. To accept these two narratives at face value, as inherently authoritative and self-legitimizing, may actually constitute oppressive practice. In contrast to modernist practices of naturalizing experience and thereby authorizing clients' interpretations of events in their lives, the postmodern influence on narrative therapy recognizes that as experience stories are socially constructed, they cannot be inherently authoritative or self-legitimizing. From a postmodern narrative view, these experience stories include both subjugated and dominant knowledge. As the self-stories clients bring to therapy are often oppressive and harmful, we cannot leave experience intact. In narrative processes of deconstructing and reconstructing stories of the self, we destabilize both experience and the self. Following Bourdieu (as cited in White, 1992), in unpacking the everyday, taken-for-granted aspects of reality, we "exoticize the domestic" (p. 122).

Essentializing Experience:
The Fiction of the Transcendental Subject

For Jerome Bruner (2002), the "self" is always also the "other" (p. 66). There is no self outside the social: The self is fully social (Smith, 1999). There is no transcendental subject, no escaping the social world. As such, there can be no autonomous, fixed, given, essential self. Within postmodernism, this has been referred to as the "death of self" (Zweig, 1995) or, as Gergen (1991) describes, "the self under siege." In a postmodern era, "selves as possessors of real and identifiable characteristics—such as rationality, emotion, inspiration, and will—are dismantled" (Gergen, 1991, p. 7). Gergen asks, "What is it about our characterization of self—the ways in which we make ourselves intelligible to each other—that is so critical to our lives?" (p. 4). Despite this desire, Gergen describes the "eroding of the identifiable self" in a postmodern era:

> In the postmodern world we become increasingly aware that the objects about which we speak are not so much "in the world" as they are products of perspective. Thus, processes such as emotion and reason cease to be real and significant essences of persons; rather, in the light of pluralism we perceive them to be imposters, the outcome of ours ways of conceptualizing them. Under postmodern conditions, persons exist in a state of continuous construction and reconstruction; it is a world where anything goes that can be negotiated. Each reality of self gives way to reflexive questioning, irony, and ultimately the playful probing of yet another reality. The center fails to hold. (p. 7)

If there can be no "true" story or no "true self" and all stories and constructions of self are discursive, then we must seriously question our well-intended desire to privilege the suppressed voice in such a way that it is treated as truth. To *essentialize* experience refers to naturalizing it or treating it as a fixed, or given, element of a "real" or natural self. Essentializing experience takes it out of its social and historical context. It is, then, problematically treated as though it were unquestionable truth: It is given the authority to represent truth. *Essentialism* is defined by Diana Fuss (1989) as follows:

> Essentialism is most commonly understood as a belief in the real, true essence of things, the invariable and fixed properties which define the "whatness" of a given entity. In feminist theory, the idea that men and women, for example, are identified as such on the basis of transhistorical, eternal, immutable essences has been unequivocally rejected by many anti-essentialist poststructuralist feminists concerned with resisting any attempts to naturalize human nature. (p. xi)

According to Smith (1999), "Experience, as it is spoken, is always social and always bears its social organization" (p. 96). Rather than taking it at face value, the construction of experiences is explored as a way to politicize and change the limits of essentialism (Fuss, 1989, p. 119).

People make sense of their lives through developing accounts of themselves and their worlds. They organize and give meaning to their experiences through the storying of experience. Stories do not represent or mirror reality; they are constitutive, shaping our lives and relationships. These stories are constructed through culturally available discourses, which themselves organize and reify power. Individual experience is, then, always more than subjective, as it is never outside cultural discourse and social relations. In this way, there is no singular author of experience.

Smith (1999) describes "subjectivism" as a process of writing out the social whereby implicitly or explicitly, the individual becomes the transcendental subject. This approach suggests individuals exist independently of the social world. Discursive accounts formulate experience as individual and subjective, as outside social construction. In this process, we lose the history of its construction; we lose how it was put together and how it was socially organized. Individualized or subjectivist approaches to experience are decontextualized, dehistoricized, and depoliticized. As such, experience and often identity is naturalized or essentialized. This stands in contrast to the postmodern view that all social life is inseparable from the meaning-making processes. From this view, meaning is always multiple, political, and contestable.

In an unquestioned celebration and honoring of individualism, it is often asserted that it is impossible to experience another person's experience. Kapferer

(1986) problematizes the subjectivism within this common belief, suggesting that "whatever uniqueness there might be in my experience is generalized and lost in a set of culturally constituted constructs, concepts, or typifications" (p. 190). The "retreat into subjectivism" suggests that "the meaning and the nature of experience are simply the sum total of individual interpretive response" (p. 192). What is left out of this essentialist construction is how interactive, social, and historical forces shape the creation, interpretation, and performance of meaning.

According to Alcoff (1988), essentialist interpretations of identity obscure social mechanisms of power. Women, for example, may invoke their experiences "as women" in an effort to revalidate undervalued female attributes yet essentialize women in the process. Particular formulations of feminist theory have relied on essentialist notions of women in this process. This is similar to therapeutic questions about how to position experience, as it is often thought that one is advancing an emancipatory psychological agenda through validating experience and that freeing individuals from oppressive constraints will enable the discovery of the real self. In both instances of essentialism, the self is turned back upon itself. Alcoff suggests,

> The mechanism of power referred to here is the construction of the subject by a discourse which weaves knowledge and power into a coercive structure that "forces the individual back on himself and ties him to his own identity in a constraining way." On this view, essentialist formulations of womanhood, even when made by feminists, "tie" the individual to her identity as a woman and thus cannot represent a solution to sexism. (p. 415)

Narrative therapy explores how people's experiences have been organized through investigating how they have storied them. By holding on to the story metaphor of experience, we are reminded that stories of experience are socially constructed rather than natural or private (White, 1989a, 1989b, 1989c). This is important because the degree to which stories are essentialist is often seen as a measure of their ability to be progressive or their capacity to enable social change.

White (2001) critiques naturalistic accounts of life and identity in his work:

> Another misunderstanding concerns the alternative knowledges and practices of living that are identified in re-authoring conversations. These are often taken to be the "true" knowledges and the "genuine" or "authentic" practices of life, that are considered to be "intrinsic" or "unconscious" in nature. However, I have never considered this to be the case. Rather, I have always assumed these knowledges and practices, that shape other ways of going through life, to be the products of history and culture. (p. 36)

Although I argue that experience is socially and historically shaped, I reject social determinism, as it reduces individuals to social products, disallowing human agency and power. White (2004) describes this as "indeterminancy within determinancy," and in doing so, he is recognizing the complex interplay between individuals and culture: "People do not passively reproduce these cultural knowledges and practices" (p. 101). People are active, not simply puppets, in their interpretations and performances of social life.

Unpacking Experience: Moving Past Surface Stories Toward Thick Description

There is a striking paradox in inflating the authority of experience as a source of knowledge and truth when, typically, people seek therapy in order to make better sense of their experiences. Rarely is experience straightforward. Most of us go through the world living with endless contradictions and conflicts. No story encompasses the richness of human experience, and stories center on selective aspects (White & Epston, 1990). Humans do not produce objective accounts of themselves; they subjectively construct and transform experience to make life less contradictory (Haug, 1992). The task in narrative therapy should be to avoid rather than produce the "authority of experience." Instead, the story needs to be unpacked with the client, with the aim of producing alternative narratives: stories with preferred outcomes for the client.

Practitioners necessarily interpret their clients' interpretations, but not necessarily reflexively. Rather than accepting "surface" realities or thin descriptions, we need to seek out thick descriptions (White, 2001). While avoiding the surface/depth metaphor that White (1997) critiques for its reliance on the idea that the therapist can help discover the deeper "truths" underlying people's problems, reading behind the surface telling of stories not only acknowledges the complexity of people's lives but also recognizes that such stories are often embedded in dominant cultural stories. For example, when the woman who weighs 65 pounds reports that she is too fat, we are unlikely to simply accept this account. Initially, her story may appear to not make sense. The predominant binary imperative requires that we either accept this story as is or replace it with a better one. However, we can help produce a thicker description by resisting her surface telling of the story, as well as making sense of it. Without dismissing, minimizing, or pathologizing her story, we can unpack, make sense of, and challenge it. It is the responsibility of therapy to explore alternative meanings to this narrative, and despite the client's skeletal bravado, the practitioner might look past the surface story to consider whether she might also feel scared, fragile, unsafe, disconnected from others, alone, powerless, and out of control. In externalizing her story, we may also see a gendered performance of subjectivity, whereby her body becomes both a site of resistance and compliance. In other words, women perform and encode their behaviors as appropriately female within the cultural terms in which gender is constructed. This means that gender is not simply determined by society, it is performed and enacted, taken up as meaningful by women in their lives as women. Thus, the female encoded body itself becomes a site to express aspects of gendered experience. While she may comply, at least in part, with gender expectations through policing her body, so too does she seek control and power and thus resist limiting gender constructions through controlling her body. The practitioner is, then, positioned to explore alternative and less evident stories her self-starvation may reveal about her experience of herself in the world.

The multiple and even contradictory meanings clients attach to their experiences may not be immediately apparent to them. A complexity not present at the surface telling of the story will be revealed through questioning stories as they unfold. We cannot simply affirm clients' stories. They cannot be treated as authoritative in therapy, for the narratives people tell about their lives are socially constructed or constituted and, as such, embody social relations of power. Experience is often deployed discursively in an attempt to understand people's stories without unpacking how experience itself has been organized and constructed. Within a postmodern sensibility, experience can remain both centered and deconstructed. Thus, while people's stories of their experiences stay at the center of therapeutic work, they are not left intact. As it is clear that we cannot do without the concept of experience in therapy, our attention needs to focus on how it is put together and socially organized, especially if we are committed to anti-oppression and social justice (White, 1994). Such a commitment relies upon contextualizing rather than individualizing experience. From this stance, the process of accepting, rejecting, and subsequently re-storying aspects of experience is political.

Typically, clients seek help with problems or difficulties in their lives because they feel stuck, trapped, or problem saturated. We cannot assume that they have an analysis of their situations, that they are not trapped in unhelpful dominant narratives, or that they are yet able to move beyond existing, often unhelpful methods of coping. Through therapeutic conversations, the therapist and client will unpack and make sense of experience. Within narrative therapy, they will "re-story" the client's narrative together.

When we are transported by the need to elevate the voice of experience, believing this to be a political act, we often abandon the discursive and material conditions of experience and reduce them to a subjectivist frame. Valorizing subjectivity and experience does not necessitate decontextualizing, depoliticizing, or essentializing them.

Re-Storying Dominant Discourse:
Cocreating Alternative Stories

We can continue to critique and reject objectified accounts that abstract, silence, pathologize, and disembody experiences without compensatory elevation and subsequent authorization of experience in our therapeutic conversations. Experience has been privileged as truth, granting it the authority to challenge dominant social ideology and its corresponding experts. Experience has been used as a corrective to exclusion, domination, and conservative discourse. However, while dominant knowledge or truth claims have excluded subjugated knowledge, we cannot simply accept subjugated knowledge as uncontestable truth. In therapy, we need to recognize the diversity of experiences and encourage subjugated stories, while not being afraid to work with clients in externalizing them. If therapy is to attend to the contradictions and gaps in experience stories, we must both accept and reject elements of experience. We need to problematize the therapeutic imperative to validate and legitimate experience, as well as the claim that clients are their own best experts. I suggest, instead, that we value clients' experience and knowledge without essentializing or authorizing them. From a postmodern stance, I advocate embracing the tension between legitimating and challenging experience, while acknowledging that both the client and therapist bring wisdom to the work.

Madigan (1998), a narrative therapist, suggests that therapists help to create new interpretations of and responses to problems. Often the interpretation that people bring to therapy reinforces existing relations of power and dominant discourses of meaning. I have given two examples of dominant discourses that are often internalized: women blaming themselves for being battered and women's experience of themselves as fat and the concurrent desire to lose weight. Madigan writes,

> In other words, different stories about the subject can emerge which highlight preferred outcomes. A counterpractice can be viewed as those actions which invite an alternative description; such descriptions differ from those dominant descriptions the individual and others have previously described regarding a particular event. These new descriptions of the subject in relation to the problem story are in a sense countercultural; they often act to help the client break free of limiting cultural descriptions. (p. 33)

Madigan (1998) and Adams-Westcot, Dafforn, and Stern (1993) do not authorize clients' experiences, but instead recognize the social construction of narratives and the need to unpack them. In not overvalorizing stories of experience, they recognize the oppressive content that often shapes people's stories. They view therapy as a place to unpack the story told and help create new stories that move past replicating original problematic experiences.

White, like other narrative theorists, underscores the importance of unpacking dominant stories (Adams-Westcot et al., 1993; Hare-Mustin, 1994). He cautions practitioners from taking up the suppressed story at face value as though it were more true, genuine, or authentic. Alternative stories are created in therapy and often encourage voicing suppressed or previously untold stories. This process of re-authoring is often seen as "liberatory" (White, 2001, p. 36). The re-authored story may then be viewed as the "freeing of people to live a life that is more accurately a reflection of their 'true nature,' or their 'essential humanness,' and of their 'authenticity'" (p. 36). White suggests we cannot take up any story at face value: We cannot idealize, authorize, or privilege the subjugated voice. Within humanist and modernist interpretations, re-authored stories are often separated from power and from their social construction. If we accept these stories at face value without deconstruction, we unwittingly accept the discursive constitution of the story, and this may inadvertently reproduce oppressive and dominant stories of power. How we approach the suppressed voice is critical to producing alternative, nonoppressive stories. The search for the "real self," to create one's "own story," reveals slippage into essentialist notions of self. As there is no real, fixed self, there can be no real story to discover outside social discourse.

Therapy is a process of exploring the meaning of experience. The therapist helps the client, often through the process of reframing or re-storying, to produce new meanings, interpretations, frameworks and narratives. I have argued that re-storying in the therapeutic process conflicts with the authority of experience and the presumption of expert knowledge in discursive approaches to therapy. Whether anti-oppression based or expert medical model based, the therapist, in fact, helps facilitates new understandings. Narrative therapy that emphasizes the dialogue between the practitioner and the client and highlights their joint work in exploring unhelpful narratives and creating new stories moves away from limiting binary constructions of knowledge and power. This approach moves away from formulations that problematically claim clients as the "experts" or authorities on their experiences and that too often rely heavily on inadequately unpacked or thin accounts of experience.

Resurrecting and Dethroning the Suppressed Voice: The Fiction of the Real Discoverable Self

Constructing stories of preferred realities will involve a tension between accepting and rejecting aspects of experience. The idea of dethroning the suppressed voice does not negate the importance of making the suppressed voice visible, but rather challenges slippage into the essentialism and naturalizing of experience and, subsequently, its subjectivist deployment. The narrative deconstruction process reveals the influence of dominant discourse on people's lives and uncovers that which has often been subsequently obscured. Very often marginalized, silenced, or obscured accounts offer a challenge to taken-for-granted dominant discourse. Even still, it cannot be privileged as though it represents uncontestable authoritative truth. I want to avoid setting up an oppositional structure between dominant and subjugated knowledge and, instead, propose that a significant tension exists between recognizing suppressed stories and proceeding to deconstruct them in narrative therapy. For these reasons, I advocate both resurrecting and dethroning the suppressed voice. Thus, while it is an important ingredient in shaping new stories, or new realities, it is not in itself outside social and political relations of power and domination. Elevating or privileging the suppressed voice as though it has somehow escaped the social unwittingly relinquishes it to the depoliticized limitations of subjectivism.

Foucault (1980) reminds us that the silent is not separate from the spoken and the known is not separate from the unknown. Self-stories that emerge are a composite of the spoken and the unspoken. In unpacking the dominant unhelpful stories clients tell, many narrative practitioners are sensitive to exploring the ways such stories are put together. Therapists explore how people are recruited into unhelfpul stories and the sequence of events over time that provide support for such stories. As there is significant interest in moving away from unhelpful stories, they are often thoroughly interrogated. Furthermore, in a move away from the idea of emancipatory psychologies in pursuit of the real discoverable self, White (2004) advises therapists to not view narrative deconstruction as a mechanism for liberating the "real self":

> It is in the context of these misunderstandings that narrative practices are portrayed as "liberatory" practices that are considered to be freeing of people to live a life that is more accurately a reflection of their "true nature," or their "essential humanness," and of their "authenticity." I believe that this humanist take on narrative therapy is quite understandable, because, in contemporary Western culture, humanist discourses have become pervasive in the shaping of our taken-for-granted understandings of most expressions of life. These understandings provide naturalistic accounts of life and identity. In them, identity is taken to be the product of nature, of human nature; a nature made up of "essences" or "elements" that are to be found at the center of who one is. According to this take on life and identity, the problems that people experience are the outcome of forces that are oppressive of, repressive of, or distorting of the essences or elements of human nature. The solution to people's problems

that is proposed by these naturalistic notions is to identify, to challenge, and to throw off these oppressive, repressive and distorting forces so that people might have the opportunity to become more truly who they really are, so that they might be free to live a life that is a more accurate reflection of their human nature. (p. 129)

White's problematization of naturalizing identity suggests that therapists may have difficulty abandoning the foundational modernist belief that the discovery of truth brings freedom, or emancipation. Often therapists separate out those aspects of experience or identity conclusions they choose to uphold as truth and, by extension, as potentially liberating, and those that are seen as false and, by extension, oppressive. From this approach, experiences become divided into representations of truth and representations of fiction. Those deemed positive or helpful are more likely to be defined as truth compared with those considered negative or unhelpful. Yet White (2001) points out despite the preference for one story over the other, neither escapes social construction. All such accounts are discursive. What is not seen is that it is possible to advance a preferred position or story without naturalizing or essentializing it. The therapist and client can work together on re-authoring a more positive identity without resorting to the claim they are discovering the real self. The realization that all experiences are storied interpretations of lived events challenges the authorizing and privileging of all experience and, subsequently, results in dethroning the suppressed voice. Seeking a thicker description of people's stories means including that which has been disqualified, marginalized, or suppressed, but that does not mean that inclusion necessarily needs to be either privileged or naturalized. The tension between resurrecting and dethroning the suppressed voice is at the heart of this work.

The Social Construction of Emotional Life

Emotional experience is particularly difficult to make sense of, for it requires the acknowledgment of discursive, extradiscursive ("real" effects are not simply discursive; i.e., poverty is more than discursive because it has material effects), and embodied qualities (Ussher, 1997). The embodied "in-itselfness" of emotion can provide an entry point into exploring meaning, rather than being evidence of the discovery of the real self. Just as with experience, we cannot write out emotion or stories of emotion. Instead, we need to expose how they are not inevitable or universal, but private, subjective human qualities existing outside human constructions of meaning. Emotions are culturally encoded and embodied responses to lived events, which, in turn, shape lived events. Elaborating upon cultural variation in what counts as emotional life,

Gergen (1991) points out that we learn acceptable responses to others' emotions and acceptable ways of expressing our own emotions. He provides the example of how we know it is okay to be angry if someone steps on our foot, but not if someone steps on our shadow. The danger in therapy is that emotions have authority; they rule. As such, emotional experience gets taken up as inherently self-legitimizing or uncontestable. Yet just because one feels something to be true does not make it so. Experience is conflated with truth when one invokes experience itself as the evidence of truth. We hear people contest and support others' ideas through statements beginning with "Based on my experience. . . ." However, just because one claims something to be true doesn't make it so.

Experiences of emotion and need are both discursive and embodied. There is an inseparability of lived events, interpretations of them, and emotional responses. We make sense of events in our lives and our emotional responses to them through the stories we tell. Emotional responses are, indeed, part of the story we tell about life events. They are often used to justify and shape particular interpretations. Although reason and emotion form a dominant oppositional construction within Western culture, they are inseparable from each other. They are often seen as opposites of each other, rather than one and the same thing. Just as one needs the idea of "inside" to talk about "outside," reason and emotion are confluent. What we call "emotion" informs reason, and what we call "reason" informs emotion. They each help us to make sense of the other.

Similar to the naturalizing of experience, the naturalizing of emotion results in taking up emotion as self-legitimatizing and uncontestable. Need, like emotion and experience, is also taken up as self-legitimizing and authoritative and therefore not to be contested. For example, when clients declare their needs to their partners in therapeutic conversation, the conversation is often closed down rather than opened up, as claims of need are often privileged. When assertions of need are made, it is often presumed that we must assist the individual in meeting this need. The idea that need is immediately and unequivocally self-legitimizing or uncontestable deserves further scrutiny. For example, when individuals seeking therapy claim they need to abstain from alcohol if treatment for alcohol use problems is to be successful, the need asserted is unlikely to be separate from the dominant social discourse on addiction, which maintains that abstinence is a treatment requirement.

Recognizing that emotional experience and need are socially constructed and performed means unpacking them to explore what they have come to mean. Choice, responsibility, and agency can be emphasized in reference to subjective emotional realities. Rather than avoiding emotion talk in an effort to not give it too much credence or from the fear of essentializing subjective life, it is possible to explore emotion talk as a significant ingredient in the social construction of the stories people tell about their experiences. Emotions cannot be written out of narrative therapy simply because they are socially constructed. They have "real" effects and cannot be ignored. However, in narrative therapy, we are left wondering how we can talk and make sense of emotional life and not reduce it to either essentialism or nominalism (i.e., social constructionism).

Emotional life is both discursive (i.e., a socially constructed and socially meaningful sign or signifier) and extradiscursive (i.e., more than a sign, embodied with actual effects). Yet despite its subjective embodiment, emotion is never reducible to a private internal subjective world. Emotion is at once internal and external, private and fully social. The binary formulations of internal/external, private/social, mind/body, and emotion/thought are all evident in modernist construction of experience and its twin components, emotion and need. There is no doubt that particular emotional worlds, emotional realities, or subjectivities correspond to, without being reduced to, particular subject positions such as race, class, or gender within culture. Concepts such as experience, emotion, and need have been pivotal not only to narrative therapy but also to informing the structure of storytelling itself. As a modernist formulation of these concepts is often invoked without questioning, it becomes clear that reflexivity about these concepts is critical to a postmodern approach to narrative therapy. Regardless of the blend of discursive and extradiscursive within people's experience stories, therapeutic conversations can only ever really attend to the meanings attached to experience. In therapy, we need to explore what experiences, needs, and emotions mean and how they came to mean what they do within the larger context of people's lives. However, in the process of such inquiry, I argue that it is useful to adopt a "both/and" stance of accepting and rejecting these categories. If they are only destabilized, one will not have a focus of inquiry. Rather, they can be treated as stable starting points, while proceeding to destabilize them.

In a similar kind of struggle, feminist poststructural theorists have grappled with how to have a politics of gender without essentializing or fixing the category of women. Butler (1992, 1993), Riley (1988, 1992), and Alcoff (1988) all argue against simply embracing the paradox of essentialism and nominalism, whereby sex difference is either emphasized (essentialism) or denied (nominalism). Alcoff (1988) argues for a third possibility, the idea of "positionality," as a way out of this bind. From this stance, identity is recognized as a point of departure, but also as a construction (p. 432). The emotional world of the subject can perhaps be dealt with in a similar way. Experience, emotion, and need can be treated as points of departure, while also being seen as social and historical constructions. Following this view,

Gergen (1999) does not recommend giving up psychological discourses, only that we reflexively acknowledge their limitations and explore alternative formulations. Although we may understand that "the vocabulary of mental life" is socially constructed, a larger concern, as Gergen suggests, involves the "consequences in cultural life of placing such terms in motion" (p. 235). However, as we struggle to reconcile these aspects of subjectivity from a postmodern view, we cannot simply censor them out. And in our desire to de-essentialize them, we cannot disembody them. White (2004) borrows Bruner's (1990) description of folk psychology as a bridge for negotiating the social construction of emotional life and as a way to engage with these culturally normative constructions within therapeutic conversations themselves. Folk psychology, Bruner (1990) suggests, is the way in which culture interprets "how humans tick" and the everyday, normative, or taken-for-granted truths about the human mind (p. 35).

Conclusion

I have explored the problem of essentializing and naturalizing experience. I have argued that we need to ensure that the social is written into clients' stories of their experiences. Subjectivism produces the transcendental subject, the subject that "just is" and exists uninfluenced by social and historical forces. Subjectivism has a conservatizing effect, leaving intact dominant discourse and social relations of power that are embedded in stories of experience. Through a postmodern lens, experience cannot be conflated with truth or treated as though it were authoritative, self-legitimizing, and thus uncontestable. Rather, stories of experience are interpretative, political, and contestable. Like all stories, they are multiple, fluid, changing, contradictory, and full of gaps: They are, like all stories, imperfect.

In narrative therapy, clients' problem stories and negative identity conclusions are re-storied. From a postmodern perspective, all stories reflect subjugated and dominant knowledge, and, subsequently, both are unpacked within therapeutic conversations. I suggest that while narrative therapy resurrects the suppressed voice, the suppressed voice must also be dethroned from essentialist, authoritative, and privileged positions. While bringing the suppressed voice or disqualified knowledge into view presents the possibility of alternative stories, they are not inherently truer stories. A therapeutic process that seeks thick rather than thin descriptions seeks to uncover the suppressed voice because it is obscured, not because it is truer. This means that the story told is richer and thicker, allowing consideration of multiple interpretations for the creation of alternative stories. Postmodern narrative therapy needs to reflexively avoid slippage into essentializing the resurrected voice as though it represented the true self. When experience is unpacked and understood to be a story, or interpretation, the suppressed voice is dethroned. We cannot take up stories of experience as "truth," but as stories that emerge within culture. The suppressed voice, while important and valued, cannot be privileged as beyond inquiry.

References

Adams-Westcot, J., Dafforn, T., & Sterne, P. (1993). Escaping victim life stories and co-constructing personal agency. In S. Gilligan & R. Price (Eds.), *Therapeutic conversations* (pp. 258–276). New York: Norton.

Alcoff, L. (1988). Cultural feminism versus post-structuralism: The identity crisis in feminist theory. *Signs: Journal of Women in Culture and Society, 13*(3), 405–436.

Anderson, H. (1997). *Conversation, language, and possibilities: A postmodern approach to therapy.* New York: Basic books.

Berger. P., & Luckmann, T. (1967). *The social construction of reality: A treatise in the sociology of knowledge.* New York: Anchor Books.

Brown, C. (1994). Feminist postmodernism and the challenge of diversity. In A. Chambon & A. Irving (Eds.), *Essays on postmodernism and social work* (pp. 35–48). Toronto, Canada: Canadian Scholar's Press.

Brown, C. (2001). *Talking body talk: An analysis of feminist therapy epistemology.* Unpublished doctoral thesis, University of Toronto, Canada.

Brown, C. (2003). Narrative therapy: Reifying or challenging dominant discourse. In W. Shera (Ed.), *Emerging perspectives on anti-oppressive practice* (pp. 223–245). Toronto, Canada: Canadian Scholar's Press.

Bruner, J. (1990). *Acts of meaning.* Cambridge, MA: Harvard University Press.

Bruner, J. (2002). *Making stories: Law, literature, life.* Cambridge, MA: Harvard University Press.

Butler, J. (1992). Contingent foundations: Feminism and the question of postmodernism. In J. Butler & J. Scott (Eds.), *Feminists theorize the political* (pp. 3–21). New York: Routledge.

Butler, J. (1993). *Bodies that matter: On the discursive limits of "sex."* New York: Routledge.

Foucault, M. (1980). *The history of sexuality: Vol. 1. An introduction.* New York: Vintage.

Foucault, M. (1991). Politics and the study of discourse. In G. Burchell, C. Gorden, & P. Miller (Eds.), *The Foucault effect, studies in governmentality* (pp. 53–72). London: Harverster.

Foucault, M. (1995). Strategies of power. In W. Anderson (Ed.), *The truth about the truth: De-confusing and re-constructing the postmodern world* (pp. 40–45). New York: Tarcher/Putnam.

194   Challenging Essentialism

Fuss, D. (1989). *Essentially speaking: Feminism, nature, and difference.* New York: Routledge.

Geertz, C. (1986). Making experiences, authoring selves. In V. W. Turner & E. Bruner (Eds.), *The anthropology of experience* (pp. 373–380). Chicago: University of Illinois Press.

Gergen, K. (1985). The social constructionist movement in modern psychology. *American Psychologist, 40*(3), 266–275.

Gergen, K. (1991). *The saturated self: Dilemmas of identity in contemporary life.* New York: Basic Books.

Gergen, K. (1999). *An invitation to social construction.* Thousand Oaks, CA: Sage.

Hare-Mustin, R. (1994, March). Discourses in the mirrored room: A postmodern analysis of therapy. *Family Processes, 33,* 19–35.

Haug, F. (1992). *"Learning from experience": A feminist epistemology.* Unpublished paper presented at the Ontario Institute for Studies in Education, Toronto, Canada.

Kapferer, B. (1986). Performance and the structuring of meaning and experience. In V. W. Turner & E. Bruner (Eds.), *The anthropology of experience* (pp. 188–203). Chicago: University of Illinois Press.

Madigan, S. (1998). Practice interpretations of Michel Foucault: Situating problem externalizing discourse. In S. Madigan & I. Law (Eds.), *PRAXIS: Situating discourse, feminism, and politics in narrative therapies* (pp. 15–34). Vancouver, Canada: Cardigan Press.

Mead, G. (1977). *On social psychology.* Chicago: University of Chicago Press.

Riley, D. (1988). *"Am I that name?" Feminism and the category of "women" in history.* Minneapolis: University of Minnesota.

Riley, D. (1992). A short history of some preoccupations. In J. Butler & J. Scott (Eds.), *Feminists theorize the political* (pp. 121–129). New York: Routledge.

Scott, J. (1992). Experience. In J. Butler & J. Scott (Eds.), *Feminists theorize the political* (pp. 22–40). New York: Routledge.

Smith, D. (1987). *The everyday world as problematic. A feminist sociology.* Toronto, Canada: University of Toronto Press.

Smith, D. (1990). *The conceptual practices of power. A feminist sociology of knowledge.* Toronto, Canada: University of Toronto Press.

Smith, D. (1999). *Writing the social: Critique, theory, and investigations.* Toronto, Canada: University of Toronto Press.

Ussher, J. (1997). *Body talk: The material and discursive regulation of sexuality, madness, and reproduction.* New York: Routledge.

White, M. (1989a). Narrative therapy: What sort of internalizing conversations? *Dulwich Centre Newsletter, 1,* 1–5.

White, M. (1989b, October). Therapy in the world of experience. *Dulwich Centre Newsletter, 1,* 4–6.

White, M. (1989c, October). The world of experience and meaning. *Dulwich Centre Newsletter, 1,* 1–2.

White, M. (1992). Deconstruction and therapy. In E. Epston & M. White (Eds.), *Experience, contradiction, narrative, and imagination: Selected papers of David Epston and Michael White 1989–1991* (pp. 109–151). Adelaide, Australia: Dulwich Centre.

White, M. (1997). *Narratives of therapists lives.* Adelaide, Australia: Dulwich Centre.

White, M. (2001). Narrative practice and the unpacking of identity conclusions. *Gecko: A Journal of Deconstruction and Narrative Ideas in Therapeutic Practice, 1,* 28–55.

White, M. (2004). *Narrative practice and exotic lives: Resurrecting diversity in everyday life.* Adelaide, Australia: Dulwich Centre.

White, M., & Epston, D. (1990). *Narrative means to therapeutic ends.* New York: Norton.

Zweig, C. (1995). The death of the self in a postmodern world. In W. T. Anderson (Ed.), *The truth about the truth: De-confusing and Re-constructing the postmodern world* (pp. 145–150). New York: Penguin Putnam.

10

Conversations With Men About Women's Violence

Ending Men's Violence by Challenging Gender Essentialism

Tod Augusta-Scott

D ominant approaches to domestic violence (Adams & Cayouette, 2002; Dobash, Dobash, Wilson, & Daly, 1992; Pence, 2002; Pence & Paymar, 1993) are very helpful in focusing the field on both men's responsibility and the significant influence the dominant-gender stories have on men's choices to abuse their partners. Within this dominant approach, battering is explained by the power and control story that states that men want, use, and get power and control through abusing their female partners (Pence & Paymar, 1993). While the power and control story is very important in my conversations with men, I have begun to notice other stories that are also important in ending men's violence (Augusta-Scott, 2003). Previously, I relied exclusively on the power and control story to explain battering. This grand narrative disqualified alternative stories influencing people's decisions to perpetrate abuse in relationships.

The dominant domestic violence approach and the power and control story are influenced by gender essentialism. Essentialist ideas about gender maintain that men are abusive and women are not and that women are victims and men are not (Brown, 2001; Fuss, 1989; Segal, 1990). This formulation of gender significantly informed my early training in work with men who abused their partners (Pence & Paymar, 1993). Any attempts men made to talk about their own experiences of being abused were thought of as attempts to avoid responsibility and were interrupted immediately. Furthermore, if a women's aggressive behavior was acknowledged, it was defined solely as self-defense, not abuse (e.g., Hamberger & Potente, 1994).

As I was introduced to postmodernism, I began to challenge my faith in grand narratives that purported to explain everything about a subject (Lyotard, 1984). Narrative therapy helped me appreciate the multiple and often contradictory stories that are important to acknowledge in my efforts to end men's violence against women. One of these stories that had previously been smothered by the grand narrative of the power and control story is that some of the men's partners perpetrated abuse themselves.

I began acknowledging women's abusive behavior once I had conversations with women and listened to their accounts of their own behavior. Gender essentialism had previously influenced my practice by leading me to believe women were not strong or powerful enough to hurt men. When I began to have conversations with partners, women directly challenged this gender essentialism. Women resisted me essentializing them as powerless victims and, in turn, defining all their aggressive behavior as "self-defense." Women acknowledged being abused and held their male partners responsible for their choices. At the same time, these women expressed shame over perpetrating abuse against their partners that involved a range of abusive behavior. Many expressed remorse for shaming their male partners because they did not live up to traditional male gender expectations, such as earning enough money. In a more extreme situation, a woman showed up in my office unannounced. She was distraught. She had just left her partner in his house after having used an ax to chop up his front porch. While she had been abused, she did not define or want to define her behavior as self-defense.

These clinical observations of women's abusive behavior are also supported by a growing body of research on heterosexual relationships (Johnson, 1995; Johnson & Ferraro, 2000; Pearson, 1997; Segal, 1990) and same-sex relationships (Renzetti & Miley, 1996; Ristock, 2002). Acknowledging women's violence does not necessitate concluding that women and men perpetrate abuse equally, in terms of the degree, frequency, or effects of the abuse. I am also not suggesting that all men's partners whom I work with perpetrate abuse. Often men alone perpetrate abuse in relationships; sometimes women and men abuse each other; and occasionally, only women perpetrate abuse. My thesis is, simply, for men who abuse and are abused by their partners, it is often helpful to talk about both of these experiences in our efforts to stop men's violence against women.

By acknowledging women's abusive behavior in conversations with men, I am not creating a narrative of systemic causality, blaming his abusive behavior on hers. He needs to stop his abuse even if she does not. In my earlier work, I was concerned that acknowledging women's abuse might mitigate men's responsibility for having used abusive behavior. Now I can acknowledge how both women and men are responsible for their choices. As I moved away from dichotomous thinking (Derrida, 1980, 1998), I was able to acknowledge both women's and men's power and powerlessness, their experiences of perpetrating abuse and being victimized by abuse, and their responsibility for their own choices. Recognizing this complexity has helped me hear men's stories differently and assisted in the rewriting of identity stories for men that move them past the gender essentializing and totalizing stories of them.

Rather than excusing men's abusive behavior, acknowledging is helpful in assisting men to take responsibility to stop their abuse. In this chapter, I demonstrate how inviting men to talk of their partners' abusive behavior can challenge excuses and justifications for perpetrating abusive behavior, challenge gender essentialism, and create conversations with men that are fair to both men and their partners.

Studying Excuses and Justifications

Sometimes men blame their abuse on their partners' behavior. When this happens, I invite men to study how these excuses and justifications support their choice to abuse. In the past, I interrupted men and redirected them to look at their own behavior. This response, ironically, often thwarted exploration of the excuses and justifications. Now, when a man is blaming his abuse on his partner, I write down the excuse on a big notepad (i.e., a large white board) in full view of him and invite him to become curious about the idea and to study it. The big notepad serves to externalize these ideas (White & Epston, 1990) by actually putting the problem or the ideas outside of the man; this way, the conversation focuses on the ideas rather than on the man. This process allows me to collaborate with the man against the ideas and practices, rather than opposing him.

Men often justify the abuse and their expectations of their partners and themselves by invoking naturalistic accounts of gender (e.g., "Boys will be boys"; "You know how women are"). Traditional gender expectations often lead men to excessively rely and depend on their partners emotionally and socially in relationships (Jenkins, 1990). This traditional gender story often leads men (and women) to expect women to be peacekeepers and nurturers. As a result, when men use abusive behavior, they often blame their partners for not having solved the conflict, not making everyone feel better, or not keeping the peace (Jenkins, 1990). I find it helpful to disrupt this gender essentialism by inquiring about where men have learned these ideas about women and men:

- When did you learn the idea that all women are nurturing?
- What do women and men learn from society about women and men's responsibilities in a relationship?
- If a man were influenced by these ideas, how might these ideas affect the trust, caring, and respect in his relationship over time?

Often the responses to these questions lead to an exploration of the social expectations of women and men in relationships. Men are also invited to explore the effects of justifying and excusing their abuse by blaming it on their partners. By studying the effects of this idea, men often become critical of it. The following questions help facilitate this exploration:

- How strong has the influence this idea—that your partner is to blame for your choices to abuse—been on your life?
- Where have you let this idea lead you?
- What has this idea blinded you from seeing about your partner and her feelings and intentions?
- What effect does the idea (that a man's partner is to blame for his violence) have on a relationship over time?
- How has this idea stopped you from building the relationship you prefer? (Jenkins, 1998)

Men distance themselves from the idea that "she's to blame" when they explore the influence this idea has on their choices. I also ask externalizing questions that highlight how the idea that his partner is to blame for his abusive behavior restrains him from taking responsibility for his behavior:

- If a man wanted to stop his abuse but thought that his partner was to blame for it, would he try to control himself or try to control her?
- Would the idea that his partner is to blame increase or decrease the abusive and controlling behavior over time? (Jenkins, 1998)

To continue to focus the man on his responsibility for his choices and move him away from blaming and relying on his partner to stop his violence, I ask the following questions:

- How have these ideas led you to see your problem with control as your partner's problem?
- How has this idea prevented you from taking control of yourself?
- Who has worked harder to stop your abuse and prevent violence, you or your partner? (Jenkins, 1998)

Typically, men themselves begin to resist the idea that their abusive behavior is their partners' fault. Toward this end, I ask men directly, "Whose job is it to stop your violence?" (Jenkins, 1998). When I ask this question, most men will say it is their job. Within this context, I can invite men to reflect on how they may have previously relied on their partners to take responsibility to stop their own violence:

- Who has been studying your violence and its effects the most up until now, you or your partner?
- Who needs to be studying how you work yourself up to abuse?
- Who needs to be thinking about the effects of the abuse?
- What would happen if you continued to rely on your partner to do your work for you?
- Could you handle a relationship in which you control your own violence, or do you need your partner to try to control it for you by keeping her quiet or "walking on eggshells" around you?
- Do you want to take action to put the brakes on yourself, or would you rather leave it to your partner to continue to try to stop the abuse for you? (Jenkins, 1998)

At the same time I explore men's efforts to provide excuses or justifications for their abusive behavior, I might ask men to talk about what a partner would have to do to take responsibility for her own abusive behavior. As a man talks (indignantly) about his partner's abusive behavior, I often invite him to develop a definition of *responsibility* using his partner as an example. Through this process of defining and exploring women's behavior, men are often able to articulate what the woman would have to do to take responsibility for her own choices to perpetrate abuse. I ask the following questions:

- Who is responsible for stopping your partner's abusive behavior?
- What would happen if she blamed you for her choices to use abuse in the relationship?
- What would it mean if your partner could slow down and think about the effects of her behavior on you?

Once the man has established this definition of responsibility, I invite him to apply it to himself and ask him what he would have to do to take responsibility. I am then able to ask him, "Who is responsible for stopping your abusive behavior?" Most men do not argue for a double standard, one definition of responsibility for her and another for him. Most men conclude that they both have to take responsibility, and, toward this end, men often affirm their commitment to take responsibility, whether their partners do or not.

Sometimes men are influenced by the idea that "I can't change if she won't change." To guard against this idea, I ask men the following questions:

- If your partner is being unreasonable or abusive, how can you respond to her to get closer to the relationship you want?
- Are you saying that even if your partner is not taking responsibility and is yelling at you that you still value taking responsibility?
- If she decides to go down the path of "disrespect," are you saying that you still want to go down your own path of "respect" rather than follow her down the path of "disrespect"?

The idea "I can't change if she won't change" leads men to believe that to stop their own abusive behavior, their partners would have to stop their unreasonable or even abusive behavior. When men make this statement, they are often (erroneously) equating responsibility for making a relationship work with responsibility for stopping abuse, and I invite men to distinguish between the two. I often agree with men's statement: "It takes two" to make a relationship work, and both partners are responsible for contributing to the relationship in respectful ways. But if he doesn't stop his abuse, the relationship will not work. If she doesn't stop her abuse, the relationship will not work. I invite men to consider that while it takes two to make a relationship work, it takes only him to stop his own abusive behavior.

Gender

To acknowledge women's abusive behavior, I had to change how I think about gender. While previously, I believed gender was socially constructed, my practice often essentialized gender as fixed, static, and immutable (de Lauretis, 1985, 1990). Rather than viewing women and men as being biologically determined, I viewed them as socially determined (Brown, 2001). I began to question the gender essentialism influencing my work when I realized how my use of the power and control story as a grand narrative to explain men's violence actually replicated traditional gender ideas: Men are powerful perpetrators, and women are powerless victims (Augusta-Scott, 2003).

In an effort to resist gender essentialism, I now find it helpful to think of gender as *stories* that are told about women and men. Thinking of gender as stories also allows me to recognize that people are more complex and contradictory than the traditional gender stories suggest. When I talk of "women" and "men," I am not talking about how women and men *are*, but rather the *stories* that are told about how women and men are. For example, there are many ways men are nurturing and caring that do not get "storied" into the world. By thinking of gender as story, I am able to move away from the essentializing and universalizing of women and men.

While gender stories do not fully *determine* women and men, they powerfully *influence* people's choices and behavior. This distinction allows me to explore with women and men how they participate in, are influenced by, and resist the gender stories. I also find it helpful to understand gender as a *performance* (Butler, 1990; 2004; Halberstam, 1998). Thinking of gender as a practice challenges the patriarchal idea that masculinity and femininity are fixed, natural, immutable biological identities. Noticing how "masculinity," for example, is a practice or performance allows me to notice how both women and men practice behavior that is constructed as "dominant masculinity." For example, by thinking of gender as a performance, I can notice how women practice "dominant masculinity" as they perpetrate abusive behavior.

The dominant domestic violence approach reproduces gender stories and presumes a totalizing, monolithic, or universal influence of these stories on women and men. In contrast, I now notice that gender stories influence these relationships in multiple ways. For example, the gender stories influence men's choices to perpetrate abuse to establish power and control over their partners (Pence & Paymar, 1993). At the same time, by promoting the idea that women are primarily weak, powerless, and peaceful, these gender stories also render invisible women's power and perpetration of abuse. By acknowledging the multiple influences of gender stories, the process of inviting men to take responsibility to stop their abusive behavior has become increasingly nuanced.

Creating Respect by Challenging Gender Essentialism

For therapeutic conversations to move men toward respectful relationships with others required that I ensured that my conversations with men were fair and respectful (Jenkins, 1998). For my conversations to be effective in addressing men's disrespectful practices, I needed to also examine my behavior toward them. If I wished to have men commit to stand against their own perpetrations of injustice, I had to make a similar commitment. I am reminded of Gandhi's famous words, "Be the change you wish to see in the world."

Creating antiessentialist conversations often involves allowing men to talk about their experiences of being hurt. By essentializing men as tough and strong, I interrupted and disqualified men's emotional accounts of being hurt by their partners. By interrupting men's accounts of being abused by their partners, I not only precluded studying possible justifications and excuses of their violence but also negated men's emotional experiences of being abused. I replicated dominant masculinity by negating men's experiences of pain through challenging and confronting men in an oppositional manner. Not only were men well accustomed to these practices of dominant masculinity, this approach did not offer men alternative ways of relating to others.

Now, rather than interrupt men, I challenge the gender essentialism that influenced my practice by attending to the emotional experience of men who are being hurt by their partners. Challenging the influence of gender essentialism on my practice is important in creating conversations with men that are fair for both men and their partners. Ensuring that the conversations are respectful has been helpful in moving men toward taking responsibility to stop their abuse. Men challenge traditional masculinity by talking about their experiences of being hurt, particularly by women. Through sharing their vulnerabilities and caring for other men in the context of a therapeutic group, men reveal alternative ways of being. Furthermore, by experiencing caring relationships, men can recreate these caring practices with their partners. Rather than engaging in oppositional confrontation, I now challenge men by emphasizing safety and respect (Augusta-Scott, 2003). As a result of feeling safe and respected, men are often able to face the behaviors they are ashamed of and feel most vulnerable discussing for the first time.

The gender essentialism informing my practice created unfair inconsistencies in my conversations with men. Essentialist constructions of men as tough and women as weak define abuse as serious only when women, not men, are abused. For example, I often emphasize how emotional abuse is as serious as physical abuse.[1] If a man reports that *he* used emotional abuse against his partner, I invite him to consider the seriousness of this abuse. In my previous practices, however, if a man reported that *she* used emotional abuse against him, I minimized the seriousness of emotional abuse. I minimized it by automatically defining her behavior as "self-defense" and redirecting him to refocus on his responsibility for hurting her. The implicit message men received was that emotional abuse is serious only when he, not the woman, perpetrates it. Furthermore, I emphasized that he take responsibility for how he was hurting her but demonstrated no concern about her taking responsibility for hurting him. Men experienced this inconsistency as confusing and unfair. As a result, men often resisted this unfairness, which made having conversations about the seriousness of their own behavior more difficult.

When I challenge gender essentialism and listen to men's experiences of being hurt, they are generally more ready to take responsibility for their own abuse and acknowledge its effects on their partners. For example, prior to being referred to have conversations with me, many men have experienced protection agencies negating their partners' abusive behavior. One man early in a group process exclaimed, "I know what I did was wrong, but I just want to hear someone acknowledge that my wife abused me too." Within a narrative approach, his partner's abuse was acknowledged, and he then began to focus on his own abusive behavior. In contrast, with the dominant discursive approach, I would have shut this conversation down and simply redirected the man to focus on his own behavior.

The dominant approach in domestic violence work assumes that if men talk about their partners' behavior, they are avoiding responsibility by justifying and excusing their own abusive behavior (Pence & Paymar, 1993). There are, however, many times when a man talks about his partner's responsibility for her abusive behavior and is not avoiding responsibility by blaming her. Men often acknowledge both their own and their partners' responsibility for perpetrating abuse at the same time. Many men talk about their experiences of injustice, including their partners' perpetrating abuse, while not excusing or justifying their own abuse or avoiding responsibility. Many men are able to acknowledge their experiences of being hurt while still acknowledging their responsibility for hurting others.

Political Positioning

To acknowledge women's abusive behavior, I also had to change how I communicate my politics in these conversations with women and men. My central political beliefs in this work are that men's violence toward women is oppressive; men's violence is strongly influenced by sexism; and men need to take full responsibility for their abusive behavior (Pence & Paymar, 1993). I try to communicate my politics in conversations through my questions and curiosity rather than imposing my politics on the men or pretending to be neutral. While I invite clients to share their particular experiences, values, and politics with me, I recognize that we both have only partial knowledge and that the ideas put forth are all reflexively shared, valued, and deconstructed. Through these conversations, I reflexively question my own politics and practices in a manner similar to that which I am inviting men to do.

Imposition

In my past work, I communicated my politics by imposing them on men in a challenging and confrontational manner. In accordance with the dominant approach to working with domestic violence, I previously adopted the traditional expert stance in conversations with men. I assumed the role of unilaterally defining the "facts" in a situation: whom to believe and not to believe, and what is true or false.[2] Adopting the expert position led me to take on an interrogative, policing detective role in therapeutic conversations with men. This detective or policing position—Do I believe him or not?—led me to focus on myself rather than what might be helpful for the man and his partner. For example, if I started to believe the man, I became afraid that I was being manipulated, duped, and outwitted in the conversation. Alternatively, by believing him, I feared I would be disappointed if the man perpetrated abuse again. To avoid the emotional risks involved in believing men, I simply assumed the men were dishonest, and I did not believe them. Furthermore, when I did not believe men's stories, I precluded the exploration of their partners' abusive behavior from our conversations.

Contrary to my intentions, the effect of policing men's honesty increased their denial of the abuse and minimization of the seriousness of it. My policing of men implicitly supported the totalizing story that men are dishonest, which they, in turn, often performed for me. Policing men was a way for me to take responsibility for how honest men were with me. By my not policing men and, instead, being curious about their ideas, they get the implicit message that they can be honest if they choose. The result is that most men begin to take responsibility themselves for being honest in the conversation. Early in the conversations, while I am caring of them, they often realize I am not invested in whether or not they are honest. If they choose to be dishonest, they realize I will not be disappointed, hurt, or angry. As a result, men often realize that the only people who will be hurt or "fooled" in the conversation by their dishonesty are themselves. Many men reveal to me in the first conversation, "I might as well be honest with you because if I'm not, I'm only hurting myself." As a result, men are forthcoming with the accounts of their own abuse and their partners, accounts that are often confirmed by their partners.

I have been able to have conversations with men about their partners' abusive behavior by not imposing my politics and adopting the traditional "expert role." I am no longer caught in my emotional dilemma of deciding whether or not to believe a man when listening to his experience of his partner's abusive behavior. Instead, I focus on how I might be helpful to him and his partner. This approach allows me to be curious about the contradictions and complexities involved in a man's and woman's experiences of each other's abuse. When I hear them both talk of their own perpetration of abuse, I hear their conflicting experiences and accounts of the relationship. I am often in conversations with a woman and man both individually and together. I listen to both in a manner that is attentive to their emotional experiences, while not expressing doubts or taking a stand on the "truth" of the story—not seeking to believe or not believe the person's story. While I have my own interpretation of the situation, I try to remain open to the ambiguity of these conversations, and I can help the couple share their stories and thoughts. I rely on the couple's capacity to make wise decisions as the process moves along. As well, I focus on safety and how they could be best protected (Goldner, 1999; Reichelt, Tjersland, Gulbrandsen, Jensen, & Mossige, 2004).

In situations that involve the criminal justice system or child protection, I am expected to impose my evaluation of a man's level of risk to others and offer a traditional "expert" opinion. For example, when a man has been removed from his home, I am often required to have an opinion about whether or not he is ready to return home. When men argue that they are ready to return home, I am faced with deciding whether or not I agree with them. This responsibility to the court and the larger community is important. There are collaborative ways of dealing with issues of "policing," such as being initially clear with men about the limitations of confidentiality, collaboratively talking about evaluation criteria, and so forth. However, sometimes collaboration is unsuccessful, and I am required to offer an assessment that conflicts with a man's assessment of himself. When I am (necessarily) responsible to impose this "expert position," this practice does strain the therapeutic relationship and, in turn, hinders efforts to stop his abuse. This tension is but one example of the dilemmas faced in this work.

Neutrality

Although I try not to impose my politics on men as I listen to their experiences of their partners' abusive behavior, I do not believe it is possible to adopt a "neutral stance" that is often articulated in the theorizing of family therapy (Minuchin, 1974). I am also not suggesting that therapists try and embrace a "not-knowing stance," as espoused by various relativist postmodern therapists (e.g., Anderson, 1997). These positions cannot account for the therapist's power and seem to reflect modernist ideals about the possibility of being objective or value free (Brown, 2003). The fiction of "objectivity" and "neutrality" does not acknowledge the institutional and relational power the therapist inevitably has in shaping these collaborative therapeutic conversations (Brown, 2001; White, 1992). I want to be reflexively focused on how my questions and responses are shaped by my own meaning system and politics and how I, in turn, shape the men's responses by the questions I ask them. I have an agenda behind the questions I choose to ask them. For example, my agenda in having them talk of their partners' abusive behavior is both to acknowledge their hurt and to stop their abusive behavior.

I practice a collaborative approach with people (White, 1995) that helps to challenge the traditional expert authority of the therapist. Often, however, therapists seek to challenge the traditional expert authority and power of the therapist by asserting that the therapist is an expert on process rather than content and should thereby adopt a "not-knowing stance" (Anderson, 1997). I find this manner of challenging the traditional expert authority often leads therapists to deny the knowledge and power they have and thereby not take responsibility for it.

Conclusion

The dominant domestic violence discourse resists having conversations with men about their experiences of their partners' abusive behavior. In part, this reflects the gender essentialism that continues to influence the field of domestic violence. When these conversations surface, however, I find that men take more responsibility to stop their own abusive behavior and build respectful relationships. These conversations allow men to challenge their excuses and justifications for abusing their partners. They also help resist gender essentialism, whereby men are totalized to a one-dimensional identity as "perpetrators" and women are reduced to a one-dimensional identity as "victims." My challenging of gender essentialism has created conversations that are more reflective and empathetic to both women and men, moving from confrontational to invitational practices and from centering only on my ideas to collaborating with members of both sexes. I have also changed how I communicate my feminist politics. By using questions and curiosity unexpectedly, accessing men's stories of women's abusive behavior has become an important component within conversations to end men's violence against women.

Notes

1. Initially, I did not make distinctions among the various types of abuse and their severity. I did not realize that emotional abuse may be as serious, more serious, or less serious than physical abuse. I never wanted to consider that occasionally emotional abuse is not as serious as physical abuse, for fear of minimizing the seriousness

of the emotional abuse. Now, I realize the importance of noticing differences in the severity of abuse and different levels of risk in order to respond to a family's particular circumstances in a helpful manner (Johnson & Farraro, 2000).

2. My coworkers and I took this approach with women as well. For example, while our rhetoric was to respect women's choices, often the practice was to tell them what was "really" happening in their relationships, drawing on the power and control story of the dominant domestic violence approach (Pence & Paymar, 1993).

References

Adams, D., & Cayouette, S. (2002). Emerge: A group education model for abusers. In E. Aldarondo & F. Mederos (Eds.), *Programs for men who batter: Intervention and prevention strategies in a diverse society* (pp. 3-1–3-16). Kingston, NJ: Civic Research Institute.

Anderson, H. (1997). *Conversation, language, and possibilities: A postmodern approach to therapy*. New York: Basic Books.

Augusta-Scott, T. (2003). Dichotomies in the power and control story: Exploring multiple stories about men who choose abuse in intimate relationships. In *Responding to violence: Collection of papers on working with violence and abuse* (pp. 203–224). Adelaide, Australia: Dulwich Centre.

Brown, C. (2001). *Talking body talk: An analysis of feminist therapy epistemology.* Unpublished doctorate thesis, Dalhousie University, Halifax, Canada.

Brown, C. (2003). Narrative therapy: Reifying or challenging dominant discourse. In W. Shera (Ed.), *Emerging perspectives on anti-oppressive practice* (pp. 223–245). Toronto: Canadian Scholars' Press.

Butler, J. (1990). *Gender trouble: Feminism and the subversion of identity.* New York: Routledge.

Butler, J. (2004). *Undoing gender.* New York: Routledge.

de Lauretis, T. (1985). The essence of the triangle or, taking the risk of essentialism seriously: Feminist theory in Italy, the U.S., and Britain. *Difference: A Journal of Feminist Cultural Studies, 1*(2), 3–37.

de Lauretis, T. (1990). Upping the anti in feminist theory. In M. Hirsch & E. Fox Keller (Eds.), *Conflicts in feminism* (pp. 255–270). New York: Routledge.

Derrida, J. (1980). *Writing and difference* (A. Bass, Trans.). Chicago: University of Chicago Press.

Derrida, J. (1998). *Of grammatology* (G. Spivak. Trans.). Baltimore, MD: Johns Hopkins University Press.

Dobash, R., Dobash, E., Wilson, M., & Daly, M. (1992). The myth of sexual symmetry in martial violence. *Social Problems, 39*, 71–91.

Fuss, D. (1989). *Essentially speaking: Feminism, nature, and difference.* New York: Routledge.

Goldner, V. (1999). Morality and multiplicity: Perspectives on the treatment of violence in intimate life. *Journal of Marital and Family Therapy, 25*(3), 325–336.

210   Challenging Essentialism

Halberstam, J. (1998). *Female masculinity.* Durham, NC: Duke University Press.

Hamberger, K., & Potente, T. (1994). Counseling heterosexual women arrested for domestic violence: Implications for theory and practice. *Violence and Victims, 9*(2), 125–137.

Jenkins, A. (1990). *Invitations to responsibility: The therapeutic engagement of men who are violent and abusive.* Adelaide, Australia: Dulwich Centre.

Jenkins, A. (1998, May). Facing shame without shaming: The therapeutic engagement of men who have enacted violence. *Therapeutic Conversations, 4.* Toronto, Canada: Yaletown Family Therapy Conference.

Johnson, M. (1995). Patriarchal terrorism and common couple violence: Two forms of violence against women. *Journal of Marriage and the Family, 57,* 283–294.

Johnson, M., & Ferraro, K. (2000). Research on domestic violence in the 1990s: Making distinctions. *Journal of Marriage and the Family, 62,* 948–963.

Lyotard, J.-F. (1984). *The postmodern condition: A report on knowledge* (G. Bennington & B. Massumi, Trans.). Minneapolis: University of Minnesota Press.

Minuchin, S. (1974). *Families and family therapy.* Cambridge, MA: Harvard University Press.

Pearson, P. (1997). *When she was bad: Violent women and the myth of innocence.* Toronto, Canada: Random House.

Pence, E. (2002). The Duluth domestic abuse intervention project. In E. Aldarondo & F. Mederos (Eds.), *Programs for men who batter: Intervention and prevention strategies in a diverse society* (pp. 6-2 – 6-4) Kingston, NJ: Civic Research Institute.

Pence, E., & Paymar, M. (1993). *Education groups for men who batter: The Duluth model.* New York: Springer.

Reichelt, S., Tjersland, O., Gulbrandsen, W., Jensen, T., & Mossige, S. (2004). From the system of sexual abuse to the system of suspicion. *Journal of Systemic Therapies, 23*(1), 67–82.

Renzetti, C., & Miley, C. (1996). *Violence in gay and lesbian domestic partnerships.* New York: Haworth Press.

Ristock, J. (2002). *No more secrets: Violence in lesbian relationships.* New York: Routledge.

Segal, L. (1990). *Slow motion: Changing masculinities, changing men.* London: Virago Press.

White, M. (1992). Deconstruction and therapy. In D. Epston & M. White (Eds.), *Experience, contradiction, narrative, and imagination: Selected papers of David Epston and Michael White, 1989–1991* (pp. 109–151). Adelaide, Australia: Dulwich Centre.

White, M. (1995). *Re-authoring lives: Interviews & essays.* Adelaide, Australia: Dulwich Centre.

White, M., & Epston, D. (1990). *Narrative means to therapeutic ends.* New York: Norton.

11

Challenging Essentialist Anti-Oppressive Discourse

Uniting Against Racism and Sexism

Tod Augusta-Scott

I have been challenging issues of racism and sexism for more than a decade, since I began counseling men who abuse their female partners.[1] During that time, I have worked with Black and White men[2] in therapy groups and conducted various antiracism and antisexism workshops in the community. My practice has been significantly influenced by Black women writers who see value in addressing issues of racism and sexism at the same time (Hill Collins, 1990, 1998, 2000; hooks, 1984, 1995, 2004; Jordan, 1998a, 1998b; Lorde, 1984; Richie, 2005). I have also been inspired by those in African American communities who work in the domestic violence field to develop helpful ways of working with people as both oppressed and oppressor, victim and perpetrator (Donnelly, Smith, & Williams, 2002; Oliver, 2002; Williams, 1992, 1994, 1998; Williams & Donnelly, 1997). There have also been significant contributions to this literature from members of the Hispanic (Hernandez, 2002; Perilla & Perez, 2002), Native (Wood, 1992), and Asian communities (Almeida & Dolan-Delvecchio, 1999). I have, however, limited the scope of this chapter to focusing on participating in and resisting racism as it relates primarily to relations between Black and White people.

I am a White man, and I attend public gatherings designed to resist racism and sexism. Often the participation of men at gatherings to address sexism and the participation of White people at gatherings to address racism is lacking. Previously, at gatherings to address sexism, I often asked despairingly, "Where are the men?" I concluded that the *only* reason more men did not attend was because of their sexism. Similarly, I concluded that the *only* reason more White people did not attend events designed to address racism was because of their racism. Since I have increasingly engaged in reflexive practice, however, I have begun to question how the employment of an essentialist anti-oppressive discourse might also contribute to the alienation of some men and White people who would otherwise join us. Feminist bell hooks (1984) also has concerns with anti-oppressive discourse: "So far, [the] contemporary feminist movement has been primarily generated by the efforts of women—men have rarely participated. This lack of participation is not solely a consequence of anti-feminism" (p. 67). In addition to fostering more conversations with men and White people to address social injustices, I am also interested in having more conversations with women and Black people who might also join us at these gatherings but presently do not because they find the current essentialist anti-oppressive discourse unhelpful.

In this chapter, I will share the processes I find helpful in conducting therapy groups with Black and White men and public workshops with women and men to address issues of racism and sexism. The disruption of racism and sexism through public workshops and therapy groups involves deconstructing essentialist anti-oppressive discourse (e.g., Bell, 1992; Cose, 1993, 1997; McIntosh, 1998; Tatum, 1997; West, 1993; Wiley, 1993). This dominant discourse often essentializes people from different social locations *only* as different and renders similarities invisible. Challenging this essentialist discourse involves being able to explore the differences *and* similarities among people from different social locations. Along with noticing differences, this process involves acknowledging *shared* values people hold for resisting injustice and fostering respect in their relationships. Then, within this context, people are invited to explore their *shared* oppressive practices that lead them away from these values. Exploring the similarities among the Black and White men in groups, for example, disrupts racism by not essentializing Black and White men *only* as different from each other. Furthermore, these men are invited to explore their *shared* oppressive practices; that is, they are invited to examine how their abusive behavior is often an expression of racism and sexism. Men are then asked to explore the costs of these oppressive practices and how they hinder their ability to establish and maintain loving, caring relationships. This reflexive process often serves to motivate and inspire individuals to change their behavior.

Furthermore, the process of confronting social injustice in groups with people from different social locations also involves creating a context in which people can experience shame, anger, and pride. This context is achieved by inviting people to critically explore their experiences rather than confronting and challenging people in an oppositional manner. The current essentialist anti-oppressive discourse encourages confrontational practices that further strain relationships between women and men as well as Black and White people (Lasch-Quinn, 2001). Specifically, this discourse often creates division among those who are committed to addressing social injustices of racism and sexism.

Preferences

In workshops designed to end racism and sexism among people from various social locations, I find it helpful to have people initially define the qualities and values they prefer in relationships (Hill Collins, 2000). In response to this inquiry, people often state their desires to have relationships based on kindness, fairness, equality, and respect. People also identify a desire to take a stand against injustice and prejudice. Once people's preferences are acknowledged, they are often willing to explore how some of their practices may lead them away from their desired relationships, values, and preferences. This process also reveals the shared values people from various social locations have for justice and respectful, caring relationships. Similarly, Martin Luther King Jr. gathered Black and White people before the Lincoln Monument in Washington, D.C., and appealed to their shared values as represented in the *Declaration of Independence* (see King, 1986). He appealed to people to notice these common values when he wrote, "Within the White majority there exists a substantial group who cherish democratic principles above privilege and who have demonstrated a will to fight side by side with the Negro against injustice" (King, 1967, p. 59).

For various reasons, I had resisted acknowledging possible commonalities between those in dominant and subordinate groups. Specifically, I resisted noticing the possibility that people in dominant and subordinate social groups may share similar values in their desire to challenge social injustices. Dichotomous thinking led me to believe people want either respect and equality *or* power and control. By moving away from dichotomous thinking, I have been able to acknowledge, for example, that men I work with often want both power and control as well as equality and respect in their relationships. I am now able to acknowledge contradictions that often exist in people's desires and intentions (Augusta-Scott, 2003).

I also resisted noticing commonalities among people from different social locations because of how anti-oppressive discourse essentializes gender and race. Specifically, anti-oppressive discourse essentializes women and men *only* as different and Black and White people *only* as different. Anti-oppressive discourse often essentializes those who are oppressed as powerless victims without agency and those who oppress as powerful perpetrators. Identity is defined in dichotomous, essentialist terms: People are either Black or White, female or male, powerful or powerless, oppressors or oppressed, or victims or perpetrators (Augusta-Scott, 2005; hooks, 1984; McWhorter, 2000; Segal, 1990; Steele, 1990). For example, when working with men who abused their female partners, I often essentialized men according to the traditional gender ideas: that men are tough and strong and want only power and control in their relationships while women are only weak and nurturing (Pence & Paymar, 1993). Rather than promoting these traditional gender stories about women and men, for example, I am now attentive to the tensions and dilemmas of trying to name injustices of sexism without reconstituting the very gender categories that are creating the injustices. By constructing only differences among social groups, essentialist anti-oppressive discourse renders invisible possible commonalities among people from different social locations.

Acknowledging commonalities among those in subordinate and dominant social groups is also difficult because dichotomous thinking leads people to believe that people are either similar or different. As a result, people often acknowledge commonalities by denying differences among various social groups. People often universalize the experiences of those in dominant social groups (e.g., "We're all the same," "I don't see skin color," etc.). Differences among social groups are important to acknowledge, in part because they are often sources of injustice as well as pride. For example, for Black men I work with, their skin color is often both a source of pride and a source of injustice as a result of racism. Conversations with Black and White men benefit from having these differences acknowledged.

This dichotomous framework, however, often leads people to believe that acknowledging commonalities automatically means denying differences and thus denying injustices. By moving away from this dichotomous framework, people from various social locations are able to notice both their differences and similarities. In this context, acknowledging commonalities does not mean denying, eradicating, or denigrating differences. While focusing on difference helps to make visible injustices based on difference, focusing only on difference reifies social categories of difference and hinders efforts to unite people against racism and sexism.

Although there are differences between the ways in which identity is constructed in oppressive and anti-oppressive discourses, there are also some troubling similarities. In racist and sexist discourses, "Black" is devalued, and "White" is valued; women are devalued, and men are valued. Anti-oppressive discourse replicates dichotomous thinking by simply inverting this value system: Black people are valued, and White people are devalued; women are valued, and men are devalued. Hooks (1984) makes a similar observation about the women's movement: "In fact, even that statement 'men are the enemy' was basically an inversion of the male supremacist doctrine that 'women are the enemy'—the old Adam and Eve version of reality" (p. 76).

Feminist Lynn Segal (1990) emphasizes the importance of moving away from essentialist notions of identity in order to notice potential commonalities across traditional social categories. Segal sees the necessity to reconstruct identities,

> Without the need for binary opposition in which some of us, or maybe all of us, are burdened with the role of representing somebody else's Other. A vision of radical equality, without hierarchical ordering . . . must always be the basis of any progressive restructuring of diversity and difference. (p. 201)

Hooks (1995) also supports such efforts to resist essentialism in order to address racism. She states,

> Postmodern critiques of essentialism which challenge notions of universality and static over determined identity within mass culture and mass consciousness can open up new possibilities for the construction of self and the assertion of agency. . . . Abandoning essentialist notions would be a serious challenge to racism. (pp. 121–122)

I find that noticing differences and similarities among women and men as well as Black and White people disrupts the gender and race essentialism that hinders progress to address sexism and racism.

Oppressive Practices

Due to the dichotomous framework of an anti-oppressive discourse, people's experiences of victimization and powerlessness are emphasized at the expense of their agency and power (McWhorter, 2000; Steele, 1990, 1999). Furthermore, essentializing race and gender in a manner that renders invisible the agency of those who are oppressed makes it more difficult for those in marginalized groups to take responsibility for exercising the personal agency they have to improve their relationships. For example, anti-oppressive discourse leads some Black men I work with to acknowledge their own victimization and powerlessness while not noticing how they are oppressing their female partners. In my practice, the work is further complicated by the fact that many Black men I am in conversation with abuse White female partners. Consequently, when a Black man I work with identifies himself only as an oppressed victim, he is unlikely to acknowledge his agency and responsibility for participating in his oppressive practices toward his partner. By inviting men to move away from the dichotomous framework of thinking of themselves as either oppressed or oppressors, they are better able to conceptualize their victimization from racism while, at the same time, acknowledging their oppressive practices through sexism. When men are able to entertain the complexities of having both responsibility and agency to stop their oppressive practices, they are more successful in creating the quality of relationships they prefer.

To facilitate people in acknowledging their experiences of victimization and their oppressive practices, I use lines of inquiry developed by Alan Jenkins (1998a, 1998b, 2005b, 2006b):

- What is it like to take responsibility for hurting/oppressing others when you have been so hurt/oppressed yourself?
- What is it like to take responsibility for hurting/oppressing others when no one is taking responsibility for how you are being hurt/oppressed?

This line of questioning helps to reveal the complexities of people's experiences. To consider only how men oppress others without acknowledging how they are being oppressed creates an injustice for them. Alternatively, to acknowledge only how men have been oppressed and not how they oppress others creates an injustice for their partners. Previously, in therapeutic conversations, I was concerned that acknowledging the agency of Black men I counseled might mitigate White people's responsibility for their racist practices. This concern stems from the dichotomous thinking I have invoked by employing anti-oppressive discourse that defines people as either victim or perpetrators, when it is more helpful to focus on both. Regretfully, to focus on the agency of those in subordinate groups in order to change their lives or address their own oppressive practices often results in accusations that one is "blaming the victim" (Steele, 1990).

I find it is helpful to identify commonalities between people's participation in and resistance to oppressive practices. When people recognize their participation in and resistance to oppressive practices, this can become a source of connection between them. I ask Black and White men to study how they engage in oppressive practices toward their partners. As well, Black men are invited to articulate their resistance to oppressive practices due to racism, which also enhances the discussions. In one conversation with a White man, he told me about his adopted younger sister who was Black. He shared with me the hardship experienced by both his younger sister and his family as a result of the racism they faced in their predominantly White community. He spoke of his history of violence at school, defending and protecting his adopted sister from others' cruelty and racist practices. These often complex and contradictory conversations, in which people identify how they both resist and participate in oppressive practices, often support connections among Black and White men in groups. Furthermore, I have witnessed how sharing these stories and supporting each other strengthens their commitment and resolve to end their oppressive practices toward their female partners and others.

Often men in these groups do not have supportive relationships with other men. After attending a 20-week therapy group for abusing his partner, one Black man reported that he was very pleased to have a chance for the first time to forge supportive and caring relationships with men and, in particular, with White men. Notably, their point of connection was their shameful participation in and prideful resistance to oppressive practices. By resisting essentialism through acknowledging similarities and differences in people's experiences of resisting and participating in oppressive practices, people are often more willing to work together from various social locations to address injustices.

Noticing the oppressive practices of both Black men and White women, for example, disrupts essentializing oppressive practices as "being White" or "being men." By essentializing White women as powerless victims, for example, gender essentialism renders invisible their oppressive practices as they relate to racism, classism, and homophobia as well as the abuse they may perpetrate against men (hooks, 1995). Specifically, within the domestic violence movement, there has been a history of essentializing men as violent and women as peaceful, thereby rendering invisible women's violence (Pearson, 1997).

Essentializing Black people as powerless victims similarly renders invisible Black people's oppressive practices as they relate to sexism, classism, and homophobia. Furthermore, this discourse often fails to problematize the situation when Black people act disrespectfully toward White people, especially when such disrespect is excused because the recipients are White (Lasch-Quinn, 2001; Lynch, 2002). As well, there is a maxim of anti-oppressive discourse that "people who are Black can't be racist." While it may be helpful to reserve the term *racism* to refer to the specific practices of White people, this maxim is often erroneously conflated with the idea that people who are Black do not engage in oppressive practices. By challenging the essentialism of anti-oppressive discourse, all people are better able to take responsibility for their oppressive practices.

Shame, Anger, and Pride

In therapeutic groups or workshops, I find it helpful to create a context in which people can feel shame, anger, and pride when addressing racism and sexism.[3] It is useful to create a respectful context in which people can experience shame for engaging in oppressive practices. Creating this context is more attainable when people's expressions of shame are honored as evidence of their preferences not to engage in racist and sexist practices (Jenkins, 1998a, 1998b, 2005a, 2006a). I often ask questions such as the following:

- What does it say about you that you feel ashamed over your oppressive practices?
- What would it say about your values if you did not feel ashamed?

I ignored men's shame for many years, in part because I negated possible contradictions between the types of relationships men desire and the painful relationships they experienced because of their oppressive practices (Augusta-Scott, 2003). However, hooks (1984) notes, in the case of men and sexism, that men's pain over the outcome of their oppressive practices can be acknowledged while still recognizing their responsibility (p. 73). Furthermore, acknowledging men's shame over abusing their partners develops men's motivation to change (Augusta-Scott, 2003; hooks, 1984). When Black and White men notice their participation in oppressive practices, they are less likely to adopt an unhelpful self-righteous anger over experiencing oppression that, in turn, renders invisible their own participation in oppressive practices.

At the same time, while inviting people to feel shame for participating in oppressive practices, it is also helpful to invite them to experience anger over social injustice. By acknowledging anger, people are able to avoid becoming self-absorbed in their own shame for participating in racism. Regretfully, anti-oppressive discourse restrains White people from feeling and expressing their anger over racism. Dichotomous thinking leads people to believe people must feel *either* shame *or* anger. By expressing anger, those in the dominant group are suspected of taking the focus off of their shame for participating in oppressive practices. Psychologists Grier and Cobbs (1968) validate the importance of Black people's anger over racism: "No matter what repressive measures are invoked against Blacks, they will never swallow their rage and go back to blind hopelessness" (p. 179). Along with Black people, White people also need to be invited to "never swallow their rage" in response to racism. Similarly, hooks (1984) writes,

After hundreds of years of anti-racist struggle, more than ever before non-White people are currently calling attention to the primary role White people must play in anti-racist struggle. The same is true of the struggle to eradicate sexism—men have a primary role to play. (p. 81)

People are often better able to address social injustices when they can feel pride about resisting racist and sexist practices. For example, Black men I work with often feel shame about abusing their female partners, feel anger over racism and sexism, and feel pride for stopping their own abusive behavior. In this way, the process of addressing social injustice can be a journey of both self-respect and respect for others (Jenkins, 1998a, 1998b).

Studying Effects

In addressing racism and sexism, it is often helpful for people to study the effects of their oppressive practices toward others. After people identify the types of relationships they prefer, I invite them to study the effects of their oppressive practices on their relationships. Through studying these effects, people can see how their oppressive practices lead them away from their values and the quality of relationship they prefer.

Often it is helpful for men to study their own experiences of oppressive practices (due to racism, poverty, and homophobia) to better appreciate the effects of their own (sexist) oppressive practices on their partners. Previously, influenced by the perpetrator/victim binary, I resisted having conversations with men about their experiences of injustice because I was concerned these experiences might excuse men's responsibility for perpetrating abuse (Augusta-Scott, 2003). In retrospect, I recognize how the story that essentialized men as powerful and in control created a lot of dissonance for many men. Negating their experiences of injustice along with the story that they were gaining power and control was particularly unfair for many Black men I worked with who were marginalized by both poverty and racism. By moving away from dichotomous thinking, I have been able to acknowledge men's experiences of power and powerlessness while still appreciating that they are responsible for their behavior.

Rather than learning about the effects of oppressive practices by reflecting upon one's own life, "sensitivity training" workshops are often designed to simulate experiences of racism or sexism through subjecting participants to oppressive practices so they can experience what they put others through (for example, the "Brown Eyes" workshop, as described by Lasch-Quinn, 2001). Reflecting essentialist notions, the intent of such workshops is to provide men or White people with an experience of oppression, which will make them more empathic and lead them to stop their own oppressive practices. Often these exercises give the implicit message that only White participants or male participants engage in oppressive practices. Furthermore, the exercise ignores that most men have already had experiences of oppression, which they can draw upon to better understand other people's experiences. When I initially worked with men in groups, we simulated role-plays with them that were guided by similar ideas. Unfortunately, these workshops often further strain relations between Black and White people, as well as women and men, by fostering antagonism between facilitators and participants and among participants.

Those in the dominant groups need to study their own experiences but also need to participate in dialogue with those in subordinate groups to appreciate similarities and differences in their specific experiences. When these dialogues occur, people come to appreciate differences in people's experiences of oppressive practices based on issues of race, gender, and sexual orientation. They also see how these differences relate to the social and historical contexts of people's experience of oppression. For example, I invite Black and White men to study their partners' experiences of oppression within their relationships as well as within the larger social and historical contexts of gender and racial oppression.

Essentialist anti-oppressive discourse often thwarts people from different social locations in sharing their different experiences and helping each other. The self-help therapy movement has had numerous influences on anti-oppressive discourse (Lasch-Quinn, 2001). One influence has been the idea that only people with similar experiences can help each other. Within anti-oppressive discourse, there is a hopelessness that closes down possibilities that people from different social locations can help each other to address issues of social injustice. When we occupy different social locations, differences are often thought to preclude the possibility of helping each other. This idea is often implicitly inferred by the maxim "You don't know what it is like to be Black." This discourse leads some men to be initially disappointed that I do not have the experiences of substance misuse or family violence. They assume these differences mean I cannot help them. In keeping with this idea, anti-oppressive discourse promotes the idea that only those from the same social location can help each other. This way of thinking leads to the assumption that only women can effectively counsel women and only Black people can help others who are Black. At the same time, while I often have a different social location and different experiences from those with whom I am working, sometimes I find it helpful to self-disclose similarities between my experience and theirs. For example, while not having misused alcohol, participated in family violence, or lived in poverty, I find it helpful to share with Black and White men the ways I connect with them in both participating in and resisting oppressive practices.

Invitational Approach

I was initially expected to address issues of sexism with men who abused their female partners by confronting and challenging them in an oppositional manner (Hardy & Laszloffy, 1998; Pence & Paymar, 1993). These practices were often informed by totalizing narratives of men wanting only power and control in their relationships. Ironically, these confrontational practices recreated similar practices with men that I was trying get them to disrupt with their female partners (Augusta-Scott, 2003). I also used these confrontational practices in anti-oppressive workshops, classes, and public forms. When men or White people resisted these confrontational, disrespectful practices by becoming angry or defensive, I would simply define their behavior as evidence of their racism or sexism.

Confronting both Black and White men about their sexism in this way was unhelpful. Rather than facilitate an exploration of their oppressive practices for which they felt ashamed and vulnerable, confronting them in an oppositional manner created defensiveness and closed down this exploration. My colleagues who are women or Black also used these practices. Some of these same colleagues have since expressed regret for adopting both an unreflexive anger and a feeling of entitlement to direct this anger at men or White people who were participating in workshops. I am reminded of Audre Lorde's (1984) words, "The master's tools will never dismantle the master's house" (p. 110). Because of the influence of dominant masculinity on the lives of men I work with, they are accustomed to these confrontational practices. In retrospect, I realize people benefit from witnessing and experiencing alternative ways of being, as modeled by facilitators of therapy groups or workshops. When facilitators provide respect and safety through an invitational approach, they create a context for people to explore their own oppressive practices as well as alternative practices that support respect and equality (Jenkins, 1990, 1996, 2005b, 2006b).

While I am suggesting that an invitational approach is most helpful in the context of group therapy or workshops to address oppressive practices, I am not suggesting that legal and administrative authorities should adopt an invitational approach. People who attend therapy groups or workshops designed to address racism and sexism often need to be mandated by the larger community through legal sanctions or employers. Within this mandated context, however, rather than using oppositional practices to address racism and sexism,

I find it more helpful to engage people with invitational practices. Communities and institutions need to clearly communicate to their citizens and workers that racist and sexist behavior will not be tolerated. Furthermore, communities also have a responsibility to create contexts in which respectful conversations can happen to help people resist oppressive practices.

Conclusion

In this chapter, I have shared the processes I find helpful in addressing issues of racism and sexism. This process of addressing social injustices involves moving away from dichotomous thinking as well as race and gender essentialism. Along with noticing differences among people, this process is also facilitated by noticing commonalities among people in how they both resist and participate in oppressive practices. People are invited to explore the effects of these oppressive practices to develop their motivation to change. This process is attentive to the importance of attending to people's shame, anger, and pride in addressing social injustices. I also find it helpful to be attentive to not re-creating oppressive, oppositional practices in my efforts to address them in therapy groups and workshops. I have found the result of these efforts helpful in creating conversations that foster positive relationships and unite people from different social locations against racism and sexism.

Notes

1. I have also been addressing issues of class and homophobia. As Audre Lorde (1984), Cornell West (1993), Patricia Hill Collins (2000), bell hooks (1984), June Jordon (1998a), and others identify, racism, sexism, class, and homophobia are intimately linked. I share the opinion that to unravel one, people must work to unravel them all. Exploring these connections among a group of Black and White men surviving on low incomes and working to end their violence toward their partners is often very powerful. Along with the ideas presented in this chapter, I also invoke conversations about homophobia and poverty. I have not included the work of addressing homophobia and poverty in this chapter because of the limited space available.

2. I am using the term *Black* to refer to Afro-American and Afro-Canadians and the term *White* to refer to Euro-American and Euro-Canadians. I appreciate the possible difficulties with these categories (see Patterson, 1998) and use them for their ease and because they continued to be invoked by both Black and White people. Through this chapter, I want to disrupt fixed identity categories such as *Black people* and *White people* and recognize the complexity and diversity that these categories often render invisible. At the same time, I will invoke these categories as a means of articulating the current injustices that stem from them.

3. While referring to these emotions, contrary to modernist therapeutic discourse, I am not essentializing them or attempting to render invisible the social context in which they are constituted. Rather, I want to acknowledge that *emotion* is an idea and that what we learn to feel about various situations as well as how people communicate and express emotion are socially constructed.

References

Almeida, R., & Dolan-Delvecchio, K. (1999). Addressing culture in batterers' intervention: The Asian Indian community as an illustrative example. *Violence Against Women, 5,* 854–682.

Augusta-Scott, C. (2005). *Scripted ways of talking about race: Moving beyond race essentialism towards reconciliation.* Unpublished doctoral thesis, University of South Australia, Adelaide, Australia.

Augusta-Scott, T. (2003). Dichotomies in the power and control story: Exploring multiple stories about men who choose abuse in relationships. In *Responding to violence: Collection of papers on working with violence and abuse.* (pp. 203–224). Adelaide, Australia: Dulwich Centre.

Bell, D. (1992). *Faces at the bottom of the well.* New York: Basic Books.

Cose, E. (1993). *The rage of a privileged class.* New York: HarperCollins.

Cose, E. (1997). *Color-blind: Seeing beyond race in a race-obsessed world.* New York: HarperCollins.

Donnelly, D., Smith, L., & Williams, O. (2002). The batterer education program for Incarcerated African-American men, 1997–2000. In E. Aldarondo & F. Mederos (Eds.), *Programs for men who batter: Intervention and prevention strategies in a diverse society* (pp. 13-1 – 13-18). Kingston, NJ: Civic Research Institute.

Grier, W., & Cobbs, P. (1968). *Black rage.* New York: Bantam Books.

Hardy, K., & Laszloffy, T. (1998). The dynamics of a pro-racist ideology: Implications for family therapists. In M. McGoldrick (Ed.), *Re-visioning family therapy: Race, culture, and gender in clinical practice* (pp. 18–128). New York: Guilford.

Hernandez, A. R. (2002). CECEVIM–Stopping male violence in the Latino home. In E. Alarondo & F. Mederos (Eds.), *Programs for men who batter: Intervention and prevention strategies in a diverse society* (pp. 12-1 – 12-30). Kingston, NJ: Civic Research Institute.

Hill Collins, P. (1990). *Black feminist thought: Knowledge, consciousness, and the politics of empowerment.* London: Routledge.

Hill Collins, P. (1998). What's going on? Black feminism through and the politics of postmodernism. In *Fighting words: Black women and the search for justice* (pp. 124–154). Minneapolis: University of Minnesota Press.

Hill Collins, P. (2000). Toward a new vision: Race, class, and gender as categories of analysis and connection. In M. Adams, W. Blumenfeld, R. Castaneda, H. Hackman, M. Peters, & X. Zuniga (Eds.), *Readings for diversity and social justice: An anthology on racism, anti-Semitisim, sexism, heterosexism, ableism, and classism* (pp. 457–462). New York: Routledge.

hooks, b. (1984). Men: Comrades in struggle. In *Feminist theory: From margin to center* (pp. 67–81). Boston: South End Press.

hooks, b. (1995). Postmodern Blackness. In W. Anderson (Ed.), *The truth about the truth: De-confusing and re-constructing the postmodern world* (pp. 117–124). New York: Penguin Putnam.

hooks, b. (2004). *We real cool: Black men and masculinity*. New York: Routledge.

Jenkins, A. (1990). *Invitations to responsibility: The therapeutic engagement of men who are violent and abusive*. Adelaide, Australia: Dulwich Centre.

Jenkins, A. (1996). Moving towards respect: A quest for balance. In C. McLean, M. Carey, & C. White (Eds.), *Men's ways of being* (pp. 117–133). Boulder, CO: Westview Press.

Jenkins, A. (1998a, May). Facing shame without shaming: The therapeutic engagement of men who have enacted violence. *Therapeutic Conversations, 4*. Toronto, Canada: Yaletown Family Therapy Conference.

Jenkins, A. (1998b). Invitations to responsibility: Engaging adolescents and young men who have sexually abused. In W. Marshall, Y. Fernandez, S. Hudson, & T. Ward (Eds.), *Sourcebook of treatment programs with sexual offenders* (pp. 163–189). New York: Plenum.

Jenkins, A. (2005a). Knocking on shame's door: Facing shame without shaming disadvantaged young people who have abused. In M. C. Calder (Ed.), *Children and young people who sexually abuse: New theory, research, and practice developments* (pp. 114–127). London: Russell House.

Jenkins, A. (2005b). Making it fair: Respectful and just intervention with disadvantaged young people who have abused. In M. C. Calder (Ed.), *Children and young people who sexually abuse: New theory, research, and practice developments* (pp. 98–113). London: Russell House.

Jenkins, A. (2006a). Discovering integrity: Working with shame without shaming young people who have abused. In R. Longo & D. Prescott (Eds.), *Current perspectives: Working with sexually aggressive youth and youth with sexual behavior problems* (pp. 419–442). Holyoke, MA: NEARI Press.

Jenkins, A. (2006b). The politics of intervention: Fairness and ethics. In R. Longo & D. Prescott (Eds.), *Current perspectives: Working with sexually aggressive youth and youth with sexual behavior problems* (pp. 143–165). Holyoke, MA: NEARI Press.

Jordan, J. (1998a). A new politics of sexuality. In M. Andersen & P. Hill Collins (Eds.), *Race, class, and gender: An anthology* (pp. 437–441). London: Wadsworth.

Jordan, J. (1998b). Report from the Bahamas. In M. Andersen & P. Hill Collins (Eds.), *Race, class, and gender: An anthology* (pp. 34–42). London: Wadsworth.

King, M. L. (1967). The Black Power movement. In *Where do we go from here: Chaos or community?* (pp. 27–77). New York: Harper & Row.

King, M. L. (1986). I have a dream. In J. Washington (Ed.), *Testament of hope: The writings and speeches of Martin Luther King Jr.* (pp. 217–220). New York: HarperCollins.

Lasch-Quinn, E. (2001). *Race experts: How racial etiquette, sensitivity training, and new age therapy hijacked the civil rights revolution.* New York: Bowman & Littlefield.

Lorde, A. (1984). *Sister outsider: Essays & speeches.* Freedom, CA: Crossing Press.

Lynch, F. (2002). *The diversity machine: The dive to change the "White male workplace."* New Brunswick, NJ: Transaction Publishers.

McIntosh, P. (1998). White privilege: Unpacking the invisible knapsack. In M. McGoldrick (Ed.), *Re-visioning family therapy: Race, culture, and gender in clinical practice* (pp. 147–152). New York: Guilford.

McWhorter, J. (2000). *Losing the race: Self-sabotage in Black America.* New York: Free Press.

Oliver, W. (2002). Preventing domestic violence in the African-American community. *Violence Against Women, 6,* 533–549.

Patterson, O. (1998). *Rituals of blood: Consequences of slavery in two American centuries.* New York: Basic Civitas Books.

Pearson, P. (1997). *When she was bad: Violent women & the myth of innocence.* Toronto, Canada: Random House.

Pence, E., & Paymar, M. (1993). *Education groups for men who batter: The Duluth model.* New York: Springer.

Perilla, J., & Perez, F. (2002). A program for immigrant Latino men who batter within the context of a comprehensive family intervention. In E. Alarondo & F. Mederos (Eds.), *Programs for men who batter: Intervention and prevention strategies in a diverse society* (pp. 11-1 – 11-31). Kingston, NJ: Civic Research Institute.

Richie, B. (2005). A Black feminist reflection on the antiviolence movement. In N. Sokoloff & C. Pratt (Eds.), *Domestic violence at the margins: Readings on race, class, gender, and culture* (pp. 50–55). Brunswick, NJ: Rutgers University Press.

Segal, L. (1990). *Slow motion: Changing masculinities, changing men.* London: Virago Press.

Steele, S. (1990). *The content of our character: A new vision of race in America.* New York: St. Martin's Press.

Steele, S. (1999). *A dream deferred: The second betrayal of Black freedom in America.* New York: HarperCollins.

Tatum, B. D. (1997). *Why are all the Black kids sitting together in the cafeteria? And other conversations about race.* New York: Basic Books.

West, C. (1993). *Race matters.* Boston: Beacon Press.

West, C. (1998). Race matters. In M. Andersen & P. Hill Collins (Eds.), *Race, class and gender: An anthology* (pp. 120–125). New York: Wadsworth.

Wiley, R. (1993). *What Black people should do now.* New York: Ballantine Books.

Williams, O. (1992). Ethnically sensitive practice to enhance treatment and participation of African-American men who batter. *Families in Society: Journal of Contemporary Human Services, 73,* 588–595.

Williams, O. (1994). Group work with African-American men who batter: Toward more ethnically sensitive practice. *Journal of Comparative Family Studies, 25,* 91–103.

Williams, O. (1998). African-American men who batter: Treatment considerations and community response. In R. Staples (Ed.), *The Black family: Essays and studies*. Belmont, CA: Wadsworth.

Williams, O., & Donnelly, D. (1997). *The batterer education curriculum for incarcerated African-American men*. Decatur, GA: DeKalb County Jail.

Wood, B. (1992). *A change of season: A training manual for counselors working with Aboriginal men who abuse their partners/spouses*. Vancouver, Canada: Bruce Wood and the Squamish Nation Publishing.

PART IV

Re-Authoring
Preferred Identities

12

Movement of Identities

A Map for Therapeutic
Conversations About Trauma

Jim Duvall and Laura Béres

T his chapter begins with an exploration of our philosophical positioning
as narrative therapists and then presents a map for guiding therapeutic
conversations toward the development of preferred story lines. We present
these ideas in relation to our work with people who have experienced the
trauma of sexual abuse. We begin by reviewing three aspects related to our
philosophical position: the need for people to talk about, or give voice to,
their traumas; ideas about how memories and hope are both situated in the
present; and the need to be aware of how "unknowable" another's experience can be. This philosophical position colors all that we do in our work
with people who have experienced trauma and so also influences our stance
when using a conversational map. The conversational map is made up of five
key elements: points of stories, backstory, pivotal events, evaluating effects,
and summary. A case example is presented to demonstrate the utility of this
conversational map in therapeutic practice. This case example illustrates
how narrative ideas and practices can be applied to the specific stories of survivors. As therapists, we adopt an open and curious stance in relation to the
details of the person's story. We also maintain an active position to structuring a story that will allow the person to access what was previously invisible to that individual in his or her own story.

Our work was initially influenced by writers such as Bass and Davis (1988), Sgroi (1982, 1988), and Herman (1981, 1992). These writers highlighted the power dynamics that are often present within parent-child relationships and male-female relationships, which encouraged practitioners to move away from the possibility of victim blaming. These feminist approaches not only positioned past abuse within a context of privilege and oppression but also confronted the ongoing pressures and constraints that survivors and therapists experience throughout the process of recounting memories and seeking change. These approaches were crucial in "raising consciousness" in both the counseling and public spheres, and they also spurred anger in those recovering from and working with memories of childhood sexual abuse.

Our work continued to be informed and influenced by Dolan's (1991) approach to working with people who have experienced childhood sexual abuse. She was able to present an approach that acknowledged the hurt brought about by their memories of abuse, while at the same time moving toward ways of living that reflect their preferred identities. This is one of the tensions we recognize in working with people overcoming the effects of trauma. It is important to politicize the context in which abuse often takes place and move away from individualizing and pathologizing practices, while also helping to create preferred identities and ways of being in the world. The creation of preferred identities will involve a tension between recognizing individuals' victimization and their power and agency. We therefore believe it is most useful to develop practices that acknowledge pain and anger and move toward alternative possibilities.

What we offer here is a detailed description of our underlying philosophy of working with people who have experienced trauma, prior to offering a map for therapeutic conversations. Although our practice was initially influenced by feminist theorists, our philosophical position has also been influenced by psychoanalytic thought, Jewish ethics, and, most particularly, social constructionist and postmodern concepts. Our philosophical positioning influences our therapeutic conversations and assists us in maintaining a focus on both the political and emotional aspects of trauma to create a movement toward preferred identities.

Philosophical Position

Giving Voice to Trauma

In the romantic epic *Gerusalemme Liberata,* Tancred mistakes his disguised lover, Clorinda, as someone else and kills her. After her burial, he staggers into a magical forest, slashing with his sword. He gashes a tree, which begins to bleed. He then hears the voice of Clorinda, whose soul has been imprisoned in the tree. She tells him that he has wounded her again. This epic is retold by Freud to illustrate how trauma can be unwittingly repeated (Caruth, 1996). Caruth elaborates on this theme in her book *Unclaimed Experience: Trauma, Narrative, and History*. Psychoanalysis and literature are both interested in the "juxtaposition of the unknowing, injurious repetition and the witness of the crying voice" (p. 3). She writes,

> The wound of the mind—the breech in the mind's experience of time, self, and the world—is not, like the wound of the body, a simple and bearable event, but rather an event that, like Tancred's first infliction of a mortal wound on the disguised Clorinda in the duel, is experienced too soon, too unexpectedly, to be fully known and is therefore not available to consciousness until it imposes itself again, repeatedly, in the nightmares and repetitive actions of the survivor. (Caruth, 1996, p. 4)

This is similar to our experiences working with people who have survived sexual abuse as children and who were thus unable to make sense of the abuse. People who request counseling may, in fact, describe a history of repeated abuse throughout their lives, and so a great deal of the intervention often has to do with a philosophical stance that provides the time and space for people to give voice to the trauma that was not previously understood or "knowable." Often children will either blame themselves for the abuse or else truly not understand what is happening to them. They may be confused by the manner in which the body responds and have no way to make sense of that. If a child was preverbal when the abuse occurred, the adult may have difficulty finding a method of expressing memories, because the experience was not processed by words as a child. And, of course, others may have dissociated from some experiences. The notion of providing the space for the "voice" of the person is the first of three important aspects of our philosophical positioning when in conversation with someone who has experienced trauma.

Situating Memories and Hope in the Present

The second aspect of our philosophical position concerns how we take up notions of time. In *Present Hope: Philosophy, Architecture, Judaism* (1997), Benjamin discusses ways in which to engage with the collective and historic trauma of the Holocaust. Benjamin asks,

> What does memory know? The language of knowledge will always reach a limit. However, this limit is not located within the realm of the purely epistemological; in other words it does not pertain exclusively to what can be known. Rather,

it is the limit established and thus delimited by the work of representation, since any epistemic claim will always be enacted within the general problematic of representation. It does not just always have to appear as representation. Rather, it is *constrained* to appear as one. (What is opened here is the complex and ultimately conflictual relationship between epistemology and judgement.) The question—the question of knowing what took place—therefore concerns the representation of what is known. Representation presents the known. Fiction's parasitism, a self-given site, is included therein. The situation is more complex since the connection of representation and knowledge has already been and will already have been reworked by memory. (p. 57)

Healing work will have more to do with tracing the movement of interpretations of the abuse and the implications of that on the ever-fluid and changing identity than with attempting to find an absolute or objective truth outside of interpretation and context. What is remembered cannot be spoken of without representation. Individuals cannot communicate the meaning of their memories without representing those memories through language. It is useful that Benjamin reminds us that words and stories, as forms of representation, are only ever partial. As such, aspects of experiences and memories—images and sensations—will always fall outside any representation of them. Furthermore, Benjamin (1997) suggests,

> Indeed, the inability of classical epistemology to deal with memory because of the former's failure to take up and thus to re-present the ineliminable link between memory and repetition—a link opening the move from memory to remembrance—will need to be noted. Initially as memory, the work of remembrance operates as the already present mediator of the present. Even though it cannot be reduced to it, the mediation involves memory. Here, memory comprises that which, in part, gives the present itself. Furthermore, it will be the work of memory in the present, working to maintain the present that will inscribe hope. However, rather than providing an opening to the future and thus only ever being of the future, hope will form an integral part of the present's constitution. (p. 57)

Benjamin thus places memory, representation, and hope in the present. Although hope is generally thought of as being about the future and memories are generally thought of being about the past, both hope and memories are represented in the present. When working with someone who has experienced sexual abuse, it is useful to keep in mind that how someone speaks of memories of the past and hopes for the future can tell us more about the person's present situation and meaning-making activities than some objective knowable/verifiable truth.

The Limitations of Knowing

The third philosophical position we advance in therapeutic conversations relates to the limits of what we can "know" as therapists. If we think about working with Holocaust survivors, for example, we can perhaps see that there are limits to empathy. We cannot know what it was like to live in a ghetto or camp if we have not experienced it. We may think we can imagine what it was like, but there will be limits to our imagination, and so we perhaps are called to move "beyond empathy."[1] Godzich (1986) describes Levinas's stance regarding situations beyond our own experiences, which has greatly influenced our belief in the need to let go of what we "know" and of our certainty in order to experience another person's story, whether it is a story of historical trauma or childhood sexual trauma. Levinas, a Jewish philosopher who writes about ethics, suggests that we attempt to let go of our certainties and our "knowledge" in order to engage in an ethical interaction with the "Other," so that we can be fully present and open to new ways of knowing and understanding the stories of those people. This stance contributes to a sense of curiosity and tentativeness, which are needed in collaborative work. Here, we are describing this part of our philosophical position as an ethical stance, just as White (1995) talks about an ethical position that has to do with "values with a small 'v'— not those that propose, or are based on, some universal notion of the good, and not those that establish some normalising judgement of persons" (p. 58).

The idea that memories and meanings change over time also relates to the idea of identities being fluid and pluralistic rather than fixed, static, and singular and therefore knowable in some fixed and final manner (White, 1995). Thinking about identity as fluid allows for the possibility for movement from an identity that focuses only on being victimized by the trauma to one that includes having survived and resisted it. People can move their identities from defining themselves only in relation to the traumatic experience to having identities that also involve other elements of their lives. This philosophical stance creates a platform for an ethical position for us as therapists, moving away from pathologizing interactions toward a context that makes it more possible for people to experience themselves as being able to overcome the effects of trauma.

Narrative therapy, with its postmodern and social constructionist underpinnings and temporal diversity (ability to discuss the past, present, or future, privileging the person's preferred focus) is particularly fitting for providing people with experiences in which they can give voice to their traumas, evaluate their interpretations, reconsider their identity conclusions, and re-author their lives from victimhood to survival and beyond. Although these ideas can be used in connection with collective historic trauma, the trauma of war, accidents, rape, wife assault, and others, we are interested in discussing our use of narrative approaches in working with adults who have survived child-hood sexual abuse.

In the therapeutic conversation, both the person seeking consultation and therapist are active interpretative subjects (Anderson, 1997; Duvall & Beier, 1995; Freedman & Combs, 1996; Ricoeur, 1991; White, 1995). As this is a postmodern approach, we work from the position that there is no absolute truth to be discovered, but rather multiple interpretations and multiple "truths." The conversations are collaborative (Anderson, 1997). The therapist and the client have access to (i.e., know) only partial truths or only one type of interpretation initially, and through therapeutic conversations, the client may come to know more about memories that had previously been "unknow-able." As White (1995) suggests, externalizing conversations contribute to the politicizing of representations, so we would also be informed by the need to assist the person in moving away from any self-blame stories. Traumatic memories expressed in the present are partial memories, more often exclud-ing a person's response to the trauma and the aftermath of its effects. Therefore, there will be multiple truths and multiple retellings, and what is most important is the giving of voice to the present wound, to what is cur-rently known, so that hope can be reclaimed and that which had previously been silenced can be further accessed.

Recovery from trauma does not come about merely by "giving voice to the wound," but through the therapeutic conversations, which access differ-ing meanings and knowledge about the wound, opening up possibilities for movement toward preferences. To reiterate, this philosophical position that we take in our work informs our interactions and our way of being in rela-tion to people who come to speak of their experiences of abuse, and we have found that it is also helpful to have a map as a guide for the types of con-versations we believe are useful.

The Conversational Map

As therapists, we guide our interactions with a *conversational map,* which invites people to give voice to their experiences through the process of devel-oping and discussing the story line. People experiencing the effects of trauma and abuse often arrive at therapy with a significant sense of despair. As stated previously, therapy runs the risk of reinjuring and exacerbating their despair. Through the therapeutic conversation, this map provides a structure for therapists to introduce scaffolding to the person's story, helping him or her to move from the despair inherent in the knowable and taken-for-granted dominant story to the hope that is inherent in what is possible to know in the emergent alternate story. The chasm that exists between the known and the taken for granted and what is possible to know is what Vygotsky (1978) refers to as the "zone of proximal development." As therapists, we play a critical role and have a responsibility to provide the scaffolding, through such maps and therapeutic questions, in order to provide the incremental and progressive steps needed to move from the knowable to what is possible to know (Vygotsky, 1978; White, 2005). This movement is the result of social collaboration and of the therapist taking responsibility to scaffold that learning space so that people can experience a distancing from the immediacy of their experiences.

Conversational maps capture significance and meaning in people's stories, inviting them to make distinctions between similarities and differences. As people move away from taken-for-granted understandings of the experiences of their lives, they arrive at intentional understandings of what is important to them. Like the scaffolding around a building while it is being built or repaired, which is removed after the building is completed, this conversational map provides a framework for a process, which is no longer required once the process is over.

The map includes five primary elements of inquiry. We refer to the first element as the *points of stories*. This element addresses what the person thinks is most important to talk about. The person may say, "I really want to feel better about myself." This introduces a purpose to the therapeutic conversation. As the conversation continues, the point of the story may change, and the therapist constantly checks with the person to ensure that the conversation focuses on what is most important for that person to talk about. The second element is the *backstory*, which establishes a context for the person's story in his or her relationships with others, within a temporal landscape. *Pivotal events*, the third element of inquiry, represent those significant events in people's lives that strongly influence their sense of identity and the overall development of meaning in their story. Fourth is the *evaluation of effects*, which invites people to explore and evaluate the effects of the problem story and their achievements in standing up to it. And fifth, the *summary*, helps to bring coherence to the therapeutic conversation and provides a bridge toward a future and receiving context.

This conversational map is based on the notion that people's lives are multistoried experiences. Not only are these stories constitutive of people's lives, they also express their lives through these stories. Their story lines are gateways to their abilities and preferences (White & Epston, 1990, pp. 15–17). However, this is not an "anything-goes" process; simply listening to people's stories may not help them re-author their lives toward more preferred ways of being. In addition, all stories are not equal, and some things are more important to talk about than others. The map helps us facilitate conversations that provide the opportunity for people to connect with and engage in telling the story that is most important to them. Participating in the telling and retelling of a person's stories helps to bring life and significance to them, making it possible for individuals to re-author their lives to preferred ways of being in the world (Bruner, 1986; White & Epston, 1990).

People who have experienced trauma in their childhoods as a result of being sexually abused sometimes surrender to a pervasive cynicism, resulting in a pessimistic outlook on life. Their stories are darkened by a foreshortened sense of future (Dolan, 1991), and they are frozen in a reduced sense of identity defined by victimhood, obscuring alternative possibilities for who they might be (Eron & Lund, 1996; White; 2003b). The effects of the abuse may have entered various domains of their lives, making it difficult for them to sustain meaningful relationships with significant partners, to maintain employment, or to parent their children. In addition, they often experience a dampened satisfaction from the simple pleasures of everyday life. However, people's lives are uniquely storied, including their own particular responses to their traumas, their own meanings, and their own interpretations, all of which influence their beliefs about what is possible and what they give value to. Their lives are storied from the complex web of experiences based in the events of their past and present relationships over the landscape of time, forming themes that contribute to the shaping of their identities. The following represents an example of one person's experience of trauma and the effects of its aftermath.

Susan's Story

Susan,[2] a 38 year-old woman, married, with a 9-year-old daughter, had as a young adolescent girl, been sexually abused by her father and was subsequently raped by a number of men. In the years following these events, Susan constantly battled the effects of depression and despair. Over the next 16 years, she was admitted to the hospital on numerous occasions for attempting to commit suicide. Susan had been attending sessions with a psychiatrist on a regular basis for over 14 years. Her last attempt at suicide had occurred just the week before the session described below. She had seen a flyer for our counseling program while she was confined to the psychiatric ward of the local hospital. Susan asked a nurse if she would accompany her to a counseling session if she could arrange an appointment. She told the nurse that she wanted to "try something different."

Susan arrived at the appointment with her nurse the following week. She entered the room with her head down, barely making eye contact, the clear blue plastic identification bracelet from the hospital on her right wrist. The nurse sat at the opposite end of the couch from Susan. The therapist began by eliciting what was important for Susan to talk about at this time.

Point of the Story: Identifying Preferred Identity

As the therapeutic conversation began, the therapist assumed a curious, decentered position and invited Susan to bring forth the point(s) of the story with which she most strongly connected. The point of the story is like an abstract that briefly describes the story. It is a forward reference that announces the story. As the therapeutic conversation continues, it is important to periodically summarize what is being said and remain congruent with the point of the story, as it may change as the conversation develops. When the therapist does not pay close attention for an invitation to listen to what is important for the person to talk about, the process runs the risk of becoming an imposition by the therapist. This map for story line is not a linear, fact-finding assessment process meant to gain information for the therapist, but rather a conversational meaning generating process that occurs between the therapist and the person seeking consultation.

Therapist: Susan, I understand that it was your decision to make this appointment. Can you tell me what you were hoping for?

Susan: What was I hoping for? I really want to feel better about myself. The ripple effects of the traumatic things that have happened to me over the years seem to be too big for me to handle on my own. I'm always in and out of crises. What I have been doing isn't working, so I wondered if maybe talking to someone else might help.

Therapist: Are you saying that these traumas have challenged how you might have seen yourself from the time before they happened? Do you see yourself differently than before all the traumas happened?

Susan: Oh . . . very much different now than before . . . until I was 10 years old, before the abuse started with my father, I was OK. I wish I could go back to what life was like then. The world seemed like a better place to live.

Therapist: Is it like you would like to see yourself the way you did then, and feel better in that way?

Susan: Yes.

When people have been disconnected from their preferred identities, their sense of purpose gets lost and they derive less satisfaction from the ordinary, everyday details of life. Susan recounted an experience of stumbling through life from "crisis to crisis," longing to "feel better" and become connected with a preferred identity. This preferred identity might be related to how she experienced herself before the trauma, or it may be more fluid and represent more of a "becoming" identity.

Backstory: The Temporal Landscape

Backstory is the element of story line that elicits a backdrop, a social context that provides an intelligible frame from which the storyline unfolds. People's lives are situated in social and cultural contexts that shape their beliefs and actions. Understanding unfolds from these social and cultural contexts and the relationships that exist between people. Therefore, understanding becomes a process of deconstruction and coconstruction of meaning and intention between people. To take alternate action, nonproductive beliefs are called into question, and preferred beliefs and actions are made more visible. In developing a backstory, therapists invite people to orient to a time on the temporal landscape that is meaningful to them. This frame of intelligibility brings coherence to their stories. The backstory elicits past events that often contain rich interactions. These interactions contain the influence, effects, and voices of others.

By asking Susan about herself before the abuse, the therapist was privileging the parts of Susan's identity that had been partially eclipsed by her victimhood. This did not mean that space would not be given to her pain, but it presupposed that there was more to Susan than just her stories of abuse. It also invited her to look at herself as a person within a temporal landscape, rather than as a fixed identity trapped in the present. Susan happened to remember a time before the trauma, whereas many people do not. In these cases, we invite them to remember feeling and being a different way than they are now, which may highlight for people the fluid nature of identity and that they are not "fixed" in their current sense of themselves as only "a victim." Susan harkened to a past time.

Therapist: Can you tell me a little bit about that person? Who was she? Can you introduce me to the Susan back then?

Susan: (Looks up, laughs, more animated) She was a really cool kid. You would have liked to meet her. She had lots of friends and lots of energy. Although she was just a kid, she was very organized.

She was smart and beautiful and knew how to take care of herself and give to herself.

Therapist: So, if you were feeling more like this cool person, with lots of energy, lots of friends, organized, smart, beautiful, and knew more about how to give to yourself, then you would be feeling more like how you would prefer to be in the world?

As Susan described her preferred identity, there was immediacy in her response as she became more engaged in the telling. She richly described various characteristics that brought meaning to her life. This experience was like adding vivid color to a black-and-white painting. The therapist continued to develop the backstory by contrasting the past with the present.

Susan: Oh, yeah.

Therapist: So, how is it different now? What's troubling you about the way you experience yourself now?

Susan: I've become sort of a recluse. I've isolated myself from pretty much everything. I don't go out much. I don't answer the phone half the time. I'm getting to where I don't want anyone in my space that's going to upset me, judge me, or criticize me. Although, I get along with people most of the time, I feel like they don't understand me.

Therapist: So, you have become more isolated from other people and have the experience of feeling misunderstood by them?

Susan: Yes, I need to take care of myself and figure out how to give to myself again.

Therapist: You want to be able to give to yourself again? How do you imagine that happening?

Susan: Well . . . (looking up, pausing), there would be lot's of love, understanding, and empathy. I'm not much for sympathy. I need empathy. That was quite often missed. Well . . . it was missed in my life.

Therapist: And empathy for you means . . . ?

Susan: Understanding, sharing, allowing, not being judged. To be allowed to feel my emotions. When I am upset and I feel like crying, for others to recognize that is what I need to do. For them to realize that although they are not "there," they can empathize with me that I am having those emotions. I empathize with others, why can't they do that with me?

Therapist: Are you saying that you want to be more in touch with your emotions, and acknowledge them, and that you want to be more empathic with yourself?

Susan: Yes.

Therapist: Do I also understand you to say that you have been giving to others, but you haven't experienced people being understanding of you since you were 10 years old?

Susan: That's right, not from 10 on. From 10 on I have been in another world. There has been a big hole, a big vacuum, a tremendous emptiness. I love my daughter, I have an excellent husband who has been behind me throughout our marriage . . . but I can't seem to give to myself.

Through continuing to describe her backstory, Susan articulated what it was that she needed from the therapist and others in her life. These preferences represented some of the main points of her story and what was important for her to address in the therapeutic conversation. She called it "empathy," or wanting to be understood. She said she did not want sympathy, but she wanted to "be allowed to have her emotions." The therapist made space in the conversation for Susan to express her voice and articulate her preferences. Susan gave voice to the wound, and the therapist was able to resonate with her pain and the effects of her memories. This was not done in a way that retraumatized her, but rather in a way that acknowledged that by Susan giving voice to the effects of the trauma, she was expressing those things that were important to her in her life (e.g., "to be allowed to have her emotions"). This could be done even though the therapist began by inquiring about her identity prior to the abuse.

This inquiry began early on in the therapeutic conversation by assuming the stance White (2003b) refers to as "double listening." The therapist accomplishes this through attending to people's backstories, allowing them to voice the pain and what they have done to stand up to trauma in their responses to it, thereby revealing "signs for what the person continues to give value to in life despite all that they have been through" (White, 2003b, p. 51). However, those things that people give value to are often overshadowed by the effects of the aftermath of the trauma. The therapist continued to invite Susan to develop her backstory by thickening the details and meaning of her backstory.

Therapist: You get along okay with others, but you're not being who you want to be.

Susan: I hate who I am and the person I have become. I hate when I wake up in the morning and say to myself, "Damn it, it's another day out there and I've got to put on this front." I can't do it anymore. I've lost that strength to fake it anymore. I feel like I have to put on a smile when I feel like smashing this table (looks at coffee table).

Therapist: So, what do you want in place of feeling like you have to fake it, putting on a mask, acting like things are better than they are? What would be more in line with who you want to be?

Susan: It's so hard. There is so much self-hatred, loneliness, the big void, the anger. . . .

That Susan was able to talk about the person she had become gave her hope as she began to realize that identity is fluid rather than fixed and she could continue to shape her identity to a more preferred way of being in the world (Eron & Lund, 1996; Freedman & Combs, 1996; White & Epston, 1990).

As Susan had been dislocated from those things in her life that brought meaning and significance, the subsequent experience of loneliness and desolation contributed to her shame. Therefore, to find opportunities to hear about what was important and of value to Susan, it was essential that the therapist hear about her responses to the effects of the trauma. This would provide gateways to connect with her preferred identity. The therapist continued to develop her backstory by extending her sense of her identity across time.

Therapist: It's hard. I wonder, that given how hard it is, how you have been able to sustain the effort to want to give more to your self? Susan, as you are able to give to yourself more how do you imagine your life being different?

Susan: Well . . . (long pause), I think I'll be more true to myself. I think I'll realize that I need to accept myself as I am, with limitations. I think I would be aware that I am a good person and I can be a good person. People tell me I'm a good person all the time, but it's not something I feel. Somewhere along the line, I've lost hope that life will ever be fulfilling for me. I want to be a whole person and stop living in the shadows.

Therapist: Any ideas about what you will retain from your previous life that will help you along on this journey of learning to give to yourself?

Once again, the therapist reached into the past, presupposing that there were knowledges and abilities that Susan had been distracted from that might prove useful to her as she made plans for the future. This had the effect of expanding her sense of identity across the temporal landscape (Bruner, 1986). The therapist then explored her backstory by helping mark differences in how she presently saw herself and then considered what actions she might take to support these new realizations.

Susan: I don't know. I truly believed that if I killed myself last week, it could have been better for people around me in the long run. Pain subsides. They would get over it eventually. This is better than a lifetime of ups and downs and me without the hope or possibility that things will ever get better for me.

Therapist: So you want to like yourself and feel like you are a good person?

Susan: And allowing myself my emotions. . . .

Therapist: Oh, all right. So, is this a new stage in this process?

Susan: Yeah . . . to allow myself to say yes, I feel depressed, or I feel like crying. But, right now I bottle it up and then I start the pacing and then I start the anger. . . .

Therapist: It almost sounds like a different kind of allowing. What are the signs that you would be doing this "allowing"?

Susan: I'd just "let it be there," just let it be there. Let the memories come to the surface and just let it be there and feel it. My hope is that once I'm able to do that, then I think maybe everything else can be finally put to rest. It's not something I'm ever going to forget, but it will be put to rest, and the anger will subside. Then I can have everyday "normal" ups and downs.

Therapist: You said that you will be putting things to rest.

Susan: I need to just be able to talk about the rapes on my own terms and put it to rest. I need to be in a safe place. I want to say to people, "Yes, it was horrible, but I survived it and I'm going to live. I'm going to live!" Then it's put to rest. Those things never go away. But, then they are not going to be in control of me. I'll be in control. It won't be overwhelming.

Therapist: So, when it's not put to rest, these memories and feelings are controlling you? They are walled off and. . . .

Susan: Yes, then it's out of control and overwhelming, controlling me. When it's at rest I'll, feel it in a controlled manner and be able to manage it. That's what I'm hoping to achieve, that's the point I want to get to.

Therapist: And as you put some of these things to rest, how do you imagine you experiencing yourself differently?

Traumatic memories invaded the present state of Susan's everyday life. This reduced her ability to make sense of her life in the present and evaluate the effects of her experiences. This could create a sense of her being dislocated from her identity over the landscape of time (Bruner, 1986). She expressed a beginning reevaluation of the effects of the traumatic memories and a desire to control them by putting them to rest, rather than the memories controlling her. As she continued to get more in touch with being "in control," a pivotal event was evoked.

Pivotal Events

Events in a sequence, strung out over time, are essential in order to form themes and an overarching plot to a story (White & Epston, 1990). People often choose to privilege some events over others. These events are particularly significant or pivotal in their lives. We want to collaborate with people to select those pivotal events that are strongly influencing and shaping of their beliefs and identity conclusions. Often pivotal events are more emotionally loaded and provide people with a heightened state of arousal and connection to them. These events provide fertile ground for the reinterpretation and re-authoring of people's stories.

In unpacking these events, the therapist is careful to engage in externalizing conversations regarding the problem (White & Epston, 1990). The therapist also notices people's achievements in standing up to the problem. In a sense, the therapist is helping people to break their engrossment in the "spell" of the problem, making it more difficult for them to automatically reproduce it.

Events that fall outside their problematic view have generally gone unnoticed and have been unknown. In these cases, therapists help people notice incidences and evidence of achievement and action that are in contrast with their problematic, saturated view.

The recounting of an event provided rich experience and fertile ground for Susan's recovery through more realizations and reevaluations of her response to the ongoing effects of her father's abuse of her.

Susan: I'll be more true to myself, honest with myself. . . . (pausing, looking off) Actually, there was one time when I thought I was the most true to myself. This was the time when I finally dealt with the control my father once had over me. More than what he did to me, it was amazing the control he had over me. Whenever I was around him I would be very nervous and edgy. There came a point where something took place, and the tables turned. All of a sudden he no longer had control over me. I realized that I don't love him, but I don't hate him.

Susan had given a clue that she was about to describe a pivotal event, something she had forgotten that was significant, a unique outcome representing a time that she was able to respond differently to the effects of her father's abuse.

Therapist: What happened that the table turned?

Susan: It was a strange turn of events. We were having a party at my brother's house. I went into the spare bedroom to get a sweater from the closet. My father followed me into the room and closed the door, saying that he wanted to talk to me. I could tell he had been drinking, and there was a strong smell of alcohol on his breath. He turned the lights off and tried to put his arms around me. I thought to myself, "What the hell do you think you're doing?" Then, I pushed him out of the way, turned the lights back on, and opened the door. I then turned and walked right up to him, put one hand on his throat and put my finger in his face. I yelled at him, "Do not come near me again, and do not come near my daughter!" Suddenly, I realized that I was choking him pretty hard with my left hand. When I turned around, my brother, mother, and other family members were standing at the door looking at me with disbelief. Yet I had no real hatred at the time I was doing it. I was just doing it. Then I said to him, "You have no control over me anymore, it's gone."

This pivotal event provided a realization for Susan that she could stand up to her father and could take control of those things that were important to her in her life and more in line with her preferred identity.

Evaluating Effects

Similar to Michael White's statement-of-position maps (White, 2003a), this process invited Susan to evaluate the effects of this pivotal event when "the tables turned." People are asked to judge the effects of the event themselves. These evaluations mark what stands out in this story. They amplify what is remarkable about this story and why it is worth telling. This posture creates more possibilities for collaboration, which is the spirit of this work: collaboration, cooperation, and affiliation. The therapist facilitated the process of exploring and evaluating effects and finally expressed curiosity regarding what Susan's actions in this pivotal event said about her as a person and her preferences.

Therapist: It's almost like you choked the life out of the control.

Susan: Yes, I took his control away. I realized I now had the control. It wasn't through the "violence." It was just that here was this man who had intimidated me all my life. I was scared of him. I never wanted to upset him. I remembered the massive abusive things he had done to me and my mother.

Therapist: You realized that you had control. The voice that you had been hearing and the practice that you had been given was don't do anything to make him angry, walk around on eggshells, and don't try to ever seize control of the situations.

Susan: Pretty much.

Therapist: Was there something different about you that enabled that to happen?

Susan: I don't know

Therapist: Susan, I wonder, I don't know, I'm just speculating here, was there a long trail of small little pieces that maybe led to this event that seemed instantaneous?

Susan: Yeah, now that you mention it. There were little battles that we would have. Yes, I think over time, I started thinking about how I would allow them to influence me and what I would accept. I mean, they are my parents, I'm not theirs. I gave up the hope that they would ever change.

Therapist   Are you saying that you finally came to the point where you said, "This is what I can accept"?

Susan: Yes, I knew my life was going down the tubes. I decided to start taking control of those little things that I knew I could control.

Susan was now talking about what was previously neglected and so unknowable to her from a position of victim. She previously thought she had no power, no control, and no ability to take back control in her life. The health professionals Susan had already seen were immersed in the dominant therapeutic discourse. This discourse led them to respond to her suicide attempts and pain as a victim of trauma, and, in doing so, they contributed to the totalization of her sense of identity as a victim and rendered these other ways of understanding herself invisible and unknowable. Being invited into a space to look back over her story of both resistance and pain, Susan had the opportunity to become aware of and evaluate previously neglected areas of experience.

Evaluating this pivotal event provided the possibility for reinterpretation of the effects of the trauma and the realization for Susan that she had control over her father. This realization reconnected her to a preferred identity and a sense of what she valued in her life. This reconnection with an aspect of preferred identity made it possible for her to consider moving forward in her life.

The Summary

The summary of the therapeutic conversation, or of the entire therapeutic process, captures the primary elements of the conversation and punctuates the achievements of the person seeking consultation. The summary may contain acknowledgments, inspirations, and statements about the effects of the achievements on other people involved.

The summary is not meant to be a proclamation of truth from the therapist. It is tentative and open to being questioned or reshaped. People are encouraged to correct or adjust our summaries so that they best fit their experiences of the process. In this way, the meaning contained in the summary is mutually generated and can provide a bridge for next steps.

The therapist provided a summary of his conversation with Susan thus far and then explored future territories with her.

Therapist: Susan, we have talked about a number of things in our time together today. You came to today's session saying that you wanted try something different and to feel better about yourself. You then described many of your experiences of responding to the effects of the abuse. You said that you want to be able to give to yourself, allow the emotions, and feel more like how you prefer to be in the world. Then you described a powerful event, where you took back control of your life from your father and how that has led you to come to understand what you can accept from your parents. Is this your understanding of our conversation so far? If it's not, I just want you to give me your understanding.

Susan: Actually, that pretty much sums it up.

Therapist: All right, then, given what we have talked about, what ideas do you have about continuing this process that you have started? You know, when you look out over the next month or two.

This part of the therapeutic conversation helped to make visible and sustain the work done so far between the therapist and Susan and then led the conversation toward possible next steps for action. Susan's problem-saturated view of her sense of identity had led her to negative conclusions about her abilities, which provided a receiving context for her experience that supported stories of "lack of control," "self-hatred," or other impoverished views. The therapist then worked with Susan to build a new receiving context for her experience that would make the association with her impoverished views harder to accomplish and the interpretation of meaning more supportive of preferred identity conclusions.

As Susan expressed her desires for the reconnection to her relationship to herself, her husband, her daughter, and others in her life, she built a receiving context. This receiving context provided a new frame of intelligibility that would contribute meaning and value for Susan to sustain a coherent sense of identity over time. The reconnection to desires, purposes, and values that were important to her helped her begin to form increasingly rich preferred identity conclusions.

Susan: Well (stares down at the floor), I think if I can get the thought of death off my mind. If I can look out the window and start to see some of the beauty, instead of all the negative. If I can share some of the responsibility with my husband. I just realized as I am saying this that he has already begun doing that. If I can regain the closeness with my husband and my daughter that I once had, and if I can learn to stop taking care of everybody else. Man, I didn't know I knew all this. I think these are signs that may give me some hope.

Therapist: Looking out the window and seeing the beauty. . . .

Susan: Yeah . . . not just, it's there, it's a sunny day, but really seeing it and feeling it. It's a good day to get out there. I think I can use the strength that has kept me alive so far. I'm a strong-willed person.

Here is another example of how much Susan already knew but that was not immediately accessible to her. The therapist's position as someone comfortable with ambiguities, uncertainties, and tentativeness provided a context in which Susan was able to have realizations and experience movement in identity. She did not have to present herself as a fixed identity with a fixed history, but was able to explore both the known and unknown and open up space for new ways of being.

Conclusion

It is important to us in our work with people who have experienced trauma to be, first and foremost, aware of how crucial the philosophical stance of the therapist is, because it colors the therapeutic conversation with the person who survived sexual abuse. With that in mind, we have described our philosophical stance as well as a conversational map that can guide interactions. The philosophical stance involves a recognition of the importance of creating the space for "giving voice to the trauma," a recognition of the limits of what can be known and understood, and an awareness of how memory and hope are situated in the present and speak to current meaning-making behaviors.

We have also introduced a map for organizing conversations that help to carefully scaffold people's experience toward what is possible to know. This map of the conversation involves eliciting the *points of their stories* and what is most important for them to talk about by creating a context for therapeutic inquiry situated on the temporal landscape through the development of their *backstories;* by making space for people's voices through unpacking *pivotal events* as meaning-rich platforms contributing to the development of alternate and preferred stories; by exploring and *evaluating* the effects of trauma, its aftermath, people's response to it, and what they hold as important in their lives; and by offering a *summary* that helps to bridge the person's sense of identity to a future and receiving context. We have proposed that memories are only partial expressions of the past in the present, leaving many knowledges, abilities, possibilities, and hope yet to be acknowledged and created.

Notes

1. Roger I. Simon taught a doctoral level course entitled "Beyond Empathy" at the Ontario Institute for Studies in Education at the University of Toronto, and we credit him for this term.
2. "Susan" is a pseudonym.

References

Anderson, H. (1997). *Conversation, language, and possibilities: A postmodern approach to therapy.* New York: Basic Books.

Bass, E., & Davis, L. (1988). *The courage to heal: A guide for women survivors of child abuse.* New York: Harper & Row.

Benjamin, A. (1997). *Present hope: Philosophy, architecture, Judaism.* New York: Routledge.

Bruner, J. (1986). *Actual minds, possible worlds.* Cambridge, MA: Harvard University Press.

Caruth, C. (1996). *Unclaimed experience: Trauma, narrative, and history.* Baltimore, MD: Johns Hopkins University Press

Dolan, Y. M. (1991). *Resolving sexual abuse: Solution focused therapy and Eriksonian hypnosis for adult survivors.* New York: Norton.

Duvall, J. D., & Beier, J. M. (1995). Passion, commitment, and common sense: A unique discussion with Insoo Kim Berg and Michael White. *Journal of Systemic Therapies, 14,* 57–80.

Eron, J. B., & Lund, T.W. (1996). *Narrative solutions in brief therapy.* New York: Guilford.

Freedman, J., & Combs, G. (1996). *Narrative therapy: The social construction of preferred realities.* New York: Norton.

Godzich, W. (1986). Foreword. In M. de Certeau, *Heterologies: Discourse on the other.* Minneapolis: University of Minnesota Press.

Herman, J. L. (1981). *Father-daughter incest.* Cambridge, MA: Harvard University Press.

Herman, J. (1992). *Trauma and recovery.* New York: Basic Books.

Ricoeur, P. (1991). *From text to action: Essays in hermeneutics* (K. Blamey & J. B. Thompson, Trans.). Evanston, IL: Northwestern University Press.

Sgroi, S. M. (Ed.). (1982). *Handbook of clinical intervention in child-sexual abuse.* Lexington, MA: Lexington Books.

Sgroi, S. M. (Ed.). (1988). *Vulnerable populations: Evaluation and treatment of sexually abused children and adult survivors*. Lexington, MA: Lexington Books.

Vygotsky, L. S. (1978). *Mind in society: The development of higher psychological processes* (M. Cole, V. John-Steiner, S. Scribner, & E. Souberman, Eds.). Cambridge, MA: Harvard University Press.

White, M. (1995). *Re-authoring lives*. Adelaide, Australia: Dulwich Centre.

White, M. (2003a). *Statement of position maps 1 & 2, therapeutic posture, re-authoring conversations, re-membering conversations, definitional ceremony and outsider witness responses, attending to the consequences of trauma, distinctions between traditional power and modern power, addressing personal failure*. Adelaide, Australia: Dulwich Centre. Available at Dulwich Centre Web site, http://www.dulwichcentre.com.au/

White, M. (2003b). Working with people who are suffering the consequences of multiple trauma: A narrative perspective. *International Journal of Narrative Therapy and Community Work, 1*, 45–76.

White, M. (2005, April). *Mapping narrative conversations*. A Five-Day Intensive sponsored by Brief Therapy Training Centres-International, the Hincks-Dellcrest Institute, Toronto, Canada.

White, M., & Epston, D. (1990). *Narrative means to therapeutic ends*. New York: Norton.

13

Letters From Prison

Re-Authoring Identity With Men Who Have Perpetrated Sexual Violence

Tod Augusta-Scott

Joshua is currently in prison for sexually assaulting his daughter over a 3-year period. Joshua is in his early 40s, and his daughter was age 11 when the abuse began. I had conversations with Joshua for 18 months prior to his being sentenced to 4 years in prison.[1] Since he has been in prison, Joshua and I have corresponded through letters. In this chapter, I share Joshua's letters, in which he reflects upon our conversations. The conversations have focused on re-authoring his identity in a manner that allows him to take greater responsibility for his abuse and to foster respectful, caring relationships.

Joshua had lived on a low income and has an eighth-grade education. Previous to his latest conviction, he had a history of imprisonment and counseling related to lighting fires, stealing, alcoholism, and sexually abusing his 14-year-old niece. Partly because of Joshua's work at making amends and taking responsibility (Jenkins, Joy, & Hall, 2003), his wife and their four children, including the daughter he sexually abused (who is now 16), have chosen to reestablish varying degrees of relationships with him. Joshua's family has chosen to reestablish relationships with him not because of feeling pressured or obligated to forgive or forget his actions, of which they have done neither. While expressing their anger, outrage, and disgust, the family continues to love Joshua.

When I first met Joshua, he believed that he was "bad," "disgusting," and "dirty." He felt ashamed about himself and reported feeling this way for a long time. Furthermore, Joshua believed that his identity was fixed, static, and therefore unchangeable. He felt he had no choice over who he was or how he acted. He reported that he acted in destructive ways simply because this is the way he was: essentially "bad," "disgusting," and "dirty." These negative identity conclusions supported Joshua's continuing destructive behavior. White (2004) indicates that our lives are constituted through stories. While we live and construct stories about ourselves, these stories also live and construct us (Bruner, 2002; White, 1995). Change was made more difficult by Joshua's identity being further totalized by labels such as "abuser" and "sex offender."

In this chapter, I illustrate some of the processes of inviting Joshua to re-author his identity to help him take responsibility and make amends for sexually abusing his daughter. This process has involved him naming his preferred identity, which has been supported by noticing the various times in his life—the unique outcomes—when he acted according to his preferred values and commitments. Furthermore, re-authoring has involved noticing the traumatic experiences in his life in which he was recruited into a negative story about himself. This negative story has contributed to and reinforced his destructive behavior. The re-authoring process has also involved Joshua facing shame both for perpetrating sexual abuse and for the other self-centered destructive ways he used to avoid shame.

Through Joshua's letters to me, I also share Joshua's attempts at making amends that have, in turn, created an audience for his re-authored identity. This process of re-authoring identity has helped create a context in which Joshua can continue the work of making amends to his wife and his children.

Preferred Identity

Re-authoring identity with a postmodern sensibility amplifies the fluid, changeable nature of identity. Through this lens, the process of re-authoring identity focuses on people's agency, preferences, and values in relationships rather than a fixed, unchangeable essence. In my first conversation with Joshua, we began to create alternative possibilities of who he might be, and can be, by my asking him what was important to him in relationships. I asked him what his values were and what kinds of relationships he would prefer to have with his wife and children. Joshua began to talk about what he wanted for his wife and children in terms of their safety, respect, and being cared for. Like many men, Joshua was surprised to identify what is really important to him, that is, what his values are. Many men I work with have not considered their preferences for loving, caring, respectful relationships. Often the influences of dominant-gender stories preclude men I talk with from focusing on their relationships in a nurturing manner because to do so is considered "women's work."

The re-authoring identity process explored various times in Joshua's life when he lived these values and preferences (White, 1995). Joshua identified times when he *acted* contrary to the problem-saturated story about himself, times when his preferences for justice and fairness, for example, were evident (Jenkins, 1998a, 2005; White, 1995). These events, or unique outcomes, contradicted the problem-saturated story of his identity, in which he perceived himself as being without agency and unable to change. (Although Joshua and I focused on re-authoring his identity through exploring both "unique outcomes" and painful events in his life that recruited him into negative identity conclusions about himself, this chapter primarily focuses on the latter.)

Identifying his preferences and values, his preferred identity, has allowed Joshua to confront his own abusive behavior on the basis of his own values and ethics. As a result, the process of taking responsibility for his sexual abuse of his daughter, ending it, and making amends can be a journey of self-respect and integrity (Jenkins, 1998b, 2006). Rather than continuing to perform his former identity story about himself, now Joshua increasingly performs his preferred, alternative-identity story. The process of Joshua's naming his preferences allows me to join with him against his perpetration of violence and the ideas that support it, rather than adopting a position of being against him.

An important part of the re-authoring process involves moving away from dichotomous thinking. Previously, I believed men wanted either power and control in their relationships or respectful relationships (Augusta-Scott, 2003). I thought men either perpetrated abuse or acted respectfully. By moving away from dichotomous thinking, I have been able to notice that men often want both power and control and loving, nurturing relationships. While men perpetrate abuse in their families, they often also want to be caring, respectful fathers. By moving away from dichotomous thinking and acknowledging the contractions in people's lives, I now notice how people's practices often contradict their preferred values and preferences.[2]

Recruitment Into Negative Identity Conclusions

Joshua's choices to sexually abuse his daughter were influenced by his acting out negative identity conclusions and his preoccupation with avoiding, numbing, or soothing his own shame and pain. The following narrative of Joshua's life focuses on those experiences in which he was recruited into negative identity conclusions about himself (i.e., that he is "bad," "disgusting," and "dirty"). These identity conclusions support his sexual abuse of his daughter. By identifying the experiences in Joshua's life in which he *learned* these negative identity conclusions about himself, he has been able to recognize that his identity is not innate, natural, and static but, rather, fluid and changeable. As a result, Joshua has been able to challenge these identity conclusions and move closer to his preferences for fairness and justice.

Talking about Joshua's past experiences of victimization and injustice does not create excuses, justify, or mitigate Joshua's responsibility for choosing to sexually abuse his daughter. Joshua's own childhood abuse did not *cause* him to sexually abuse others. Most people who are sexually abused do not abuse others. The meaning Joshua made of his having been abused, however, informed his choices to sexually abuse. Through being sexually abused, Joshua was recruited into believing that he was "dirty," "bad," and "disgusting," and, therefore, he acted accordingly. As a result, investigating this meaning he made about himself for having been sexually abused is important to interrupting Joshua's perpetration of sexual abuse.

Previously, dichotomous thinking led me to believe I needed to work with a man as either a perpetrator or a victim. Furthermore, to acknowledge he was a victim in any way meant that somehow he was no longer responsible for his actions. By moving away from dichotomous thinking, I have been able to work with Joshua as someone who is both powerful and powerless, who has both perpetrated abuse and been abused, and who is still responsible for his actions (Augusta-Scott, 2003).

Initially, when I invited Joshua to talk about his past, he resisted, reporting that other counselors had also asked him about his history. He was reluctant to talk about his abusive experiences because he did not want to make excuses for his abuse and he did not see any connection between his own abuse and his abuse of his daughter. Joshua also avoided talking about being abused because he thought these experiences reinforced negative identity conclusions about himself (i.e., that he is "bad," "disgusting," and "dirty"). Conversations about Joshua's past started only after he began to study the effects of sexual abuse on his daughter.[3] As he studied his daughter's experience, he began to remember his own experiences of childhood sexual abuse. For the first 10 years of his life, Joshua was regularly sexually assaulted and terrorized by his older brothers and their friends. Each day, he would run to and from school, hiding along the way in an effort to avoid his brothers and their friends. He blamed himself for the abuse and concluded that he was "bad," "dirty," and "disgusting" and that there was something wrong with him. Joshua felt guilty and ashamed. He reported feeling alone, hurt, scared, and isolated throughout this time period. He also stated much of his childhood was spent "pretending" that he was all right.

As we continued to study the effects abuse had had on him, Joshua was mortified as he began to acknowledge that perhaps his daughter might also feel responsible, bad, dirty, and disgusting because of his sexual abuse of her. In studying the effects of his abuse on his daughter, Joshua firmly believed that it was he, not his daughter, who was completely to blame and responsible for the abuse. By remembering his past, he began to wonder if perhaps he also had not been responsible for the abuse that had happened to him. Rather than continuing to blame himself, he started to think that perhaps those who abused him in childhood had been completely responsible for abusing him, just as he had been for abusing his daughter.

In addition, by identifying how he had been recruited into thinking of himself as "bad" and "disgusting," Joshua was able to challenge the idea that his identity was fixed and static. He began to realize that he had learned these negative identity conclusions about himself; they were not natural or innate. He began to realize he had choices about how he acted and who he wanted to be. He could chose to live according to his preferred values and practices rather than believing his participation in destructive behavior was inevitable. Joshua expressed relief that he was not fated to live his life repeating the destructive behaviors that confirmed the painful negative identity conclusions about himself.

Joshua's negative identity conclusions had been reinforced as he continued to experience traumatic experiences and to use destructive behavior to cope with these experiences. For example, at the age of 10, Joshua's father moved himself and his family to another community but did not include Joshua's older brother. Joshua described his father as the only person with whom he was close. He reported that his life got better in the absence of his brother and he did not have to pretend and lie to himself that everything was okay. By this time, Joshua was 16, and his father had been suffering from diabetes for a number of years. One day, Joshua's father requested that he help bring buckets of water to the neighbors. After Joshua refused, his father began to lift the buckets of water himself and had a heart attack in the driveway. Joshua went to the driveway and held his father in his arms as he died. He blamed himself for not helping his father, reporting, "I killed my father." From this experience, Joshua concluded he was bad, and he felt ashamed and guilty. The meaning Joshua made of his father's death supported the narrative about himself that he was "bad," "disgusting," and "dirty."

Having lost his father, the only person with whom he was close, Joshua's feelings of "overwhelming loneliness, fear, and desperation" returned. He was then sent back to live with the older brother who had previously sexually assaulted him. At this point, centered on his own pain, Joshua began to make himself feel better by drinking, stealing, lighting fires, and sexually assaulting his niece. Joshua performed the negative identity conclusions through acting out these destructive, self-centered behaviors. These behaviors, in turn, confirmed the negative identity.

Upon leaving prison at age 28 for stealing and lighting fires, Joshua reported feeling better for the next 10 years, no longer "pretending" and instead being honest with himself and others. He then experienced another traumatic event when working with a close friend on a road construction crew. Joshua was responsible for safety on the work site and was advised of the dangers of the steamroller to the work crew. Shortly after, Joshua witnessed his friend being crushed by the steamroller. As with his father, Joshua remembers holding his friend's dead body in his arms. Joshua blamed himself for his friend's death, which reinforced the negative identity conclusions he held about himself. He interpreted this event as more evidence that he was "bad" and was again flooded with feelings of guilt, shame, and overwhelming loneliness, as he had experienced in childhood. He began to have nightmares of his experiences of childhood sexual abuse and began thinking of suicide. To avoid his shame over his identity, which he felt he could not change, Joshua again began to abuse drugs and alcohol.

Shortly after his friend's tragic death, Joshua's daughter was diagnosed with diabetes. Because he assumed his daughter had genetically inherited her diabetes from him, Joshua also blamed himself for her diabetes. The meaning Joshua attached to this experience reinforced his negative identity conclusions about himself. His feelings of overwhelming loneliness, isolation, and fear were further intensified because he thought his daughter was going to die and leave him, as his father had. Joshua continued "pretending" everything was okay, lying to himself and others. At this time, he increased his misuse of alcohol and drugs to make himself feel better; eventually, he began to sexually abuse his daughter.

Preoccupation With Self:
Studying Justifications and Excuses

Part of Joshua taking responsibility for sexually abusing his daughter has involved acknowledging how he was preoccupied with his own pain and the irresponsible manner he used to cope with his painful feelings. This process has involved studying and confronting the ideas and excuses Joshua had used to justify abusing his daughter. Through clearly identifying these justifications and excuses, he has been better able to interrupt and challenge them. Joshua had told himself he was comforting his daughter so that she would not feel empty and alone as he did. In the moments leading up to the abuse, along with telling himself he was doing it for her benefit, he had also told himself that she liked it. He had chosen to interpret the positive attention his daughter sought from him or gave him as evidence that she liked his sexual attention. Joshua has realized he had taught his daughter that she had to be sexual in order to get her father's attention. In our conversations, he has also spent many sessions exploring how he had ignored his daughter's resistance to the abuse (e.g., she would not look at him, etc.) and how he had pressured her not to tell anyone. Joshua identified the ways he had tricked, manipulated, and silenced his daughter and how he justified these actions to himself.

Joshua reported that part of his sexual abuse of his daughter was related to his inability to maintain a sexual relationship with an adult, that is, his wife. He felt inadequate about himself and believed he was unable to emotionally negotiate an adult sexual relationship with his wife and turned to his daughter instead. At times, when he was abusing his daughter, Joshua called her "Sue" rather than "Susan" as he usually did. Upon studying this distinction, Joshua identified that when he called her "Sue," he was able to pretend he was having sex with an adult rather than his daughter "Susan." Joshua reported that this pretending made the sexual abuse seem momentarily okay.

Reflecting back on our conversations, Joshua wrote a letter about the painful effects others' violence had had on him and the destructive ways he used to soothe, numb, and avoid his own pain:

> But the biggest problem I had was that deep sense of loneliness, guilt, shame, feeling lost, hurting inside all the time, and I didn't know why I was hurting. And I would drink and do other things I shouldn't, to make myself feel good. But was I ever fooling myself. Those so-called good feelings were for short times only, and I always felt worse after. It's the same as the sexual abuse on Susan. It made me feel good because I thought she felt good by me doing that to her. But after I abused her I felt worse. I believe the drinking, setting of fires (for my own selfish need for attention), and the sexual abuse I did was all a phony way to make me feel good.

In this letter, Joshua identified his preoccupation with his own pain and his attempts to make himself feel better. In another letter, Joshua reflected on the process of studying the "triggers" and self-centered justifications that led to sexually assaulting his daughter. By identifying the "warning signs" and excuses, Joshua began to interrupt and challenge the ideas and not escalate toward abuse. Joshua wrote,

> I am the person I want to be now. But the trick is to stay that person. I know there's a lot of different triggers that might send me back into that bad person way. But I know what those triggers are now, so hopefully I can see it coming. I know that I take traumatic events in my life way too hard and see them

different and worse than other people do. But the biggest thing that is helping me change is that fact that I have and am dealing with my childhood with you, Tod. I have never told anyone about my childhood. Only you know and now [my wife] Mary. But I won't keep it a secret anymore. I have been and will continue to look at my whole life and sort through all the painful things in my life. Because I believe that's a key to getting better.

Joshua named the importance of studying his childhood to notice how he was recruited into the negative identity conclusions that influenced his choices to enact sexual abuse and other irresponsible behavior. Rather than running from the pain and trauma, Joshua was facing it and finding responsible ways to attend to the effects of the abuse on himself. He also identified the importance of continuing to study and monitor his thoughts, feelings, and the possible "triggers" that may lead to abuse, so that he could interrupt his escalation toward abuse.

Re-Authoring Identity Through Facing Shame

In the context of work with violence, re-authoring identity often involves exploring the meaning men make of the shame they experience for perpetrating abuse. Often men see their shame as evidence of negative identity conclusions they hold about themselves. Alternatively, in the process of re-authoring identity, men are invited to consider how shame over their actions may be considered evidence of their values and preferences in relationships. Men can see their shame as evidence that they prefer to stand against abuse and build respectful, caring relationships. Rather than associating his shame with a fixed identity, a self that he thinks cannot be changed, through the process of re-authoring identity, a man associates the shame with his behavior. He considers how his actions may have been a mistake rather than defining himself as a mistake. The shame he feels about his behavior is defined as evidence of his values and preferences not to participate in such irresponsible behavior.[4]

In this work, the process of re-authoring identity involves asking a man what his experience of shame might say about his values or what is important to him. Alan Jenkins (1998a, 2005) developed lines of inquiry to help facilitate this process:

- What would it say about you if you could tell me about the abuse and not feel low and ashamed?
- What does it say about you that you do feel low and ashamed?

Often in response to these questions men begin to identify their experiences of shame as evidence of their values and preferences for love and respect over violence. Constructing their shame as evidence of their desire for loving relationships gives men permission to feel shame and, in turn, creates the opportunity to study and stop the abuse.

This inquiry constructs the path of stopping the abuse as one of integrity that will lead to self-respect. When men face their violence through facing their shame, they are able to build self-respect (Jenkins, 1998b, 2006). Some lines of inquiry that help facilitate this process are as follows (Jenkins, 1998a):

- Does it take more courage to face up to the abuse (as you are doing here) or to run from it, make excuses for it, and blame others?
- Do you think facing up to your abuse makes you stronger or weaker over time?
- Would you respect yourself more for facing up or for avoiding the abuse and just leaving it to others to think about?

The process of Joshua facing his violence and shame has helped re-author an identity he prefers. Other lines of inquiry that serve to amplify Joshua's sense of integrity for taking the path of facing and stopping the abuse are as follows:

- What might your willingness to stop the abuse mean to your children?
- What difference will it make to be taking the time to stop and think about what you have put them through?
- What difference would it have made if your father would have done for you what you are now doing for your children?
- What difference will facing the abuse make to your partner (Jenkins, 1998a)?

Through these questions, men often feel shame and grief about having perpetrated abuse, and, at the same time, they feel a sense of integrity for acknowledging these feelings and their commitment to stopping the abuse.

In one of his letters to me, Joshua wrote about his shame over sexually abusing his daughter as being evidence of his preference to be a caring, respectful father:

> That makes me feel even more guilty. But those feelings are what tell me where my true values are. So feeling guilty and ashamed for the pain I caused my daughter and wife and others is what I would call healthy guilt and shame. It's not at all like the guilt and shame I felt as a kid when I was going through different kinds of abuse. Those feelings as a child were misplaced or phony. I think they were meant for my brothers and their friends, and other people in the community.

SOURCE: Quotes from Jenkins, 1998, from "Facing the shame with shaming: The therapeutic engagement of men who have enacted violence" in *Therepeutic Conversations*, 4 May. Reprinted with permission from Alan Jenkins.

He explained that the shame and guilt he felt as a kid needed to be accepted by those who abused him, "my brothers and their friends, and other people in the community." Men are invited to attribute responsibility for the abuse to the person who perpetrated the abuse rather than the person who is victimized by it. As mentioned earlier, Joshua realized that in the same way his daughter was not responsible for the sexual violence he had done to her, he had not been responsible for the sexual violence done to him. Through this process, Joshua was also able to identify that he had not been responsible for his father's or his friend's death or his daughter's diabetes, as the problem-saturated story about himself had led him to believe. At the same time, Joshua identified the importance of his accepting the shame for abusing his daughter. He has been better able to take responsibility and face his shame when it is defined as evidence of his preferred identity (Jenkins, 1998a, 2005).

Encouraging men to take responsibility and face their shame about their abusive behavior without changing the meaning they make of this shame is unhelpful. Again, initially, men often define their shame as evidence of negative identity conclusions about themselves (i.e., that they are "bad"). The negative fixed identity conclusions support men's choices to perpetrate sexual abuse. Without changing the meaning of the shame, the process of acknowledging their violence and shame can inadvertently reinforce the negative identity conclusions, which subsequently support the continuation of the sexual abuse.

The shame Joshua feels and accepts now reflects his taking responsibility for sexually assaulting his daughter. Through the process of re-authoring his identity, he now associates his shame with his actions as opposed to a fixed negative identity. The meaning he makes of his shame no longer supports the negative identity conclusions that render invisible his ability to change. Joshua also defines his shame as evidence of his preferences for actions that support caring, respectful relationships.

More recently, Joshua has begun to have conversations with others who are in prison for perpetrating sexual abuse. He has begun helping them define their shame in reference to their behavior and as a reflection of their preferences for fair and respectful relationships. Joshua wrote,

> One guy said there is no hope for him because he has hurt so many people and done so many bad things. He said when he looks back he hurts so bad for what he has done. I tell him *that* is his hope, having those hurting feelings. That's where the changes can really take place. And I explain to him that is his conscience and empathy.

The idea is not to lessen men's feelings of shame. Rather, the re-authoring of identity both amplifies and honors men's experiences of shame. The process is not one of "forgive and forget"; rather, it is one of remembering and living with the shame of having sexually abused one's daughter. Joshua recognizes that re-authoring his identity does not serve to mitigate his responsibility for, or the seriousness of, the pain and suffering he has caused others through sexually assaulting his daughter. He remains connected to the shame of sexually abusing his daughter. The re-authoring of his identity has made it possible for him to confront the story of himself that supported his abusive behavior. Joshua wrote,

> Tod, do you remember when I used to say to myself, "I'm bad," "I am evil," "I am no good for anyone or anything"? Well I realized I was right, but only at certain times. There's no denying I was all those things. But I also realize I was a real Dad to my children at times too and I was a good person at times toward other people. And I was a good husband to my wife at times too. So I asked myself which of the two different types of personality do I want. . . . Well, of course, I want to be the good person. But to really be a true good person, I believe I have to deal with that bad person that was in me. I know our talks have helped me see that I wasn't always bad and that I can change my bad ways into good ways. I have been doing a lot of thinking about who I am and who I want to be.

Joshua demonstrates that while he is constructing a preferred identity story about himself, his life remains multistoried. His preferred story of himself does not negate or dismiss his history of destructive behavior and the traumatic effects it has had and continues to have on others.[5] Rather than distancing him from the seriousness of his abusive behavior, Joshua demonstrates how connecting with his preferred values and identity increases his capacity to take responsibility. He now draws on his own ethics and values to tolerate his experience of shame and confront his irresponsible behavior. Joshua is able to move away from a problem-saturated narrative about himself and entertain other possibilities of who he can be.

Restitution

Through establishing his preferred identity and his ability to face his violence and shame, Joshua is able to both stop the abuse and work on addressing the effects the abuse has had and may have on others. Joshua is able to study himself and hear directly from his partner and children about the effects of his choices on them.

Over the last 2½ years, Joshua has worked to address the effects of perpetrating sexual abuse on his family. Rather than focus only on his own experience, *restitution* involves Joshua investing in understanding his daughter and others' experiences of his perpetration of sexual abuse. This process of making amends involves accepting the shame and responsibility for such actions. He has committed to studying others' experiences of his sexual abuse of his daughter. He has engaged in numerous conversations with his family in which they express their pain, anger, and disappointment. Through these conversations, Joshua listens and works to take full responsibility for the effects of his actions on all of them.

Restitution shifts the focus from Joshua's own pain or from making hollow promises and apologies, such as those that he has previously made. Restitution does not require a response of forgiveness from those who have been victimized. There is also no expectation that engaging in restitution carries any sense of entitlement for reconciliation. If the abused person wants to have contact, he or she is entitled to determine the level of reconnection (Jenkins et al., 2003). Joshua is extending himself without expecting any form of acceptance or pardon in return. He invests in making amends with the knowledge that his behavior can never be undone or forgotten (Jenkins et al., 2003).

Joshua eventually decided that he wanted to make restitution to the larger community. As a result, he initiated a conversation with myself and the sexual assault worker at the local sexual assault center. Joshua's intention was to give back to the community by helping those who work with people hurt by abuse. He wanted to give people trying to help a greater understanding of those who are perpetrating sexual abuse. Furthermore, toward this end, Joshua recently acted as a consultant for three university students conducting research on clinical interventions for those who have perpetrated sexual abuse. In addition, Joshua was willing to be interviewed by men in front of a local transition house worker. The sexual assault worker, transition house worker, and the students reported being struck by the honesty and courage Joshua demonstrated in confronting what he had done to his daughter. They also spoke of finding the conversations very hopeful.

Along with working to make restitution with his family and professionals in his immediate community, Joshua has continued to repair the effects of what he has done to the community in other ways. Joshua is now listening to many other men who are in prison for their sexually abusive behavior. In an effort to stop abuse, he now devotes many hours of his day trying to be helpful to others who have perpetrated sexual abuse. Joshua shared his conversations with a man who is also in prison for sexual assault:

> He said in group that he didn't like what he saw in his past actions. In fact, he became very depressed about them. So I asked him today about them and why he felt so bad. He said he couldn't believe the things he did and he hated himself. He said he felt so guilty and ashamed. So much so that he wanted to die. So I told him I felt the same way last summer. Then I said, "You should feel good about feeling so bad."

He said, "What are you crazy!"

I said, "No, but think about it—if you have those feelings, then that means you care, that means that you are human, that means you have started to heal."

So after a while he came back to me and said, "I thought about what you said, and I see what you mean." He said, "I feel pretty good. I'm not a monster. I *can* be a good person."

I said, "Yes you can." And he opened up and told me everything about his case and stopped a few times to cry. It was so emotional, Tod. I wish you were there. We talked for about 3 hours—I should say, he talked. It was the best thing ever to see. And I just got done talking to him this afternoon, and he is real happy, and he feels real good about himself. It is the most amazing thing to see someone take such deep negative feelings and emotions and turn them into good ones. He keeps thanking me and says he sees things so different now. He wants me to go walking with him tonight and meet some other guys that are in for the same thing we are.

Having the opportunity to help others move away from abuse resonates with Joshua's preference to stand against injustice. Joshua provides these men with a platform with which they can begin the process of taking responsibility and making amends. Joshua continued,

I must say, Tod, I feel great about myself, and I think I am doing good things, helping kids read, getting more education, and being a friend to these guys and helping them see what they are capable of. And that all comes from you passing it on to me. And I feel great to pass it on to others. You showed me the good in me, and now I have a chance to show other guys the good in them. And I know for a fact these guys can do good things and maybe have no more victims.

There are other guys I talk to also, and two of these guys want me to move into their [prison] house. They said I understand them better than they do themselves. When I talk to these guys, we talk about everything, they tell me things they can't tell other people. I have built a trust with each and every one of these guys. They cry, they even hug me. I love being there for them, they need someone who has been there and understands them. I am so amazed how many of them open up to me, and only me. I know they feel so comfortable with me and they know I truly care (and I do care, Tod). . . . I thought that was great. I feel I am doing some very important things here, Tod and it is helping me in return. Well I must go for now Tod, take care. Joshua.

Through helping other men in prison take responsibility for their sexual abuse, Joshua is practicing a different way of being in the world. Rather than "pretending," he practices being honest with himself and others, taking responsibility, and facing his shame and embarrassment. Joshua is not overconfident about the changes he is making. He is humble about these changes. It is not surprising that Joshua may be the "only" person some men have initially talked with, given these are sexual offenses being disclosed in the context of prison. He has not lost sight of his personal journey by becoming overzealous or evangelistic toward others as though he has it "all figured out." As the effects of Joshua's behavior will not be forgotten, he does not forget or cast off his shame for perpetrating sexual abuse. Joshua manages his shame through a reclaiming of his integrity through respectful and responsible actions over time (Jenkins et al., 2003).

Joshua remains vigilant in taking responsibility for monitoring his thoughts and feelings every day. Previously, to cope with the stress and shame of going to prison for 4 years, he would have "pretended" everything was okay, lying to himself and others and escaping his feelings through abusing alcohol and sexual abuse. Today, he respects himself for facing his stress and shame rather than avoiding and running from these feelings. He accepts his prison term as part of his larger project to take responsibility and accepts the consequences for his actions.

Audience

Through the process of creating possibilities for restitution, Joshua has been able to perform and circulate his preferred identity with others. The sexual assault worker, the students, the transition house worker, and those in prison with Joshua have all become part of an audience for the changes he is making. The feedback from this audience supports and strengthens Joshua's commitment to his re-authored identity, which continues the life-long journey of accepting the shame and responsibility for having sexually abused his daughter (White, 1995). The audience's circulation of this re-authored story about Joshua and the audience's belief and trust in his re-authored identity help Joshua sustain the changes he is making over time.

Unexpectedly, I recently received a letter from a man in prison whom I do not know. The person is part of Joshua's audience, a witness to Joshua's attempts at restitution. The letter was written by Kirk, one of the men Joshua is talking with in prison who also sexually abused one of his children. He wrote,

> I know that Joshua has told you about our conversations. You are very correct in assuming that they are unique. With any other person, I'd be beaten by now. Joshua has helped me understand how wrong I've been in what I did. . . .

He has convinced me that he actually cares about what happens to me. He says I have also helped him with his guilt and that makes me feel useful for the first time in years. . . . He has also given me an important goal. And that is to ensure I never ever have another victim. I wish Joshua was on staff here. I believe he could help many others, people like me who know in their hearts, who are sure they are wrong in what they've done.

With Kirk's permission, I shared this letter with Joshua, and he reported that he felt supported and amplified in his commitment to living his values. Joshua stated feeling that this re-authored identity gets stronger as more people recognize and appreciate it.

Conclusion

In this chapter, I have illustrated the importance to Joshua of re-authoring his identity and taking responsibility for having sexually abused his daughter. The process of re-authoring has involved Joshua naming his preferred identity and identifying the history of events that might support such identity conclusions about himself. Joshua also identified how he was recruited into a negative identity story about himself. Furthermore, he noticed the way he had acted out this negative story about himself and had attempted to sooth his hame and guilt through self-centered, destructive behavior. For Joshua, re-authoring his identity also involved facing shame and taking responsibility for perpetrating sexual abuse. As a result of re-authoring his identity and studying the effects of violence, Joshua has created a platform for hearing his partner's and his children's experiences of his actions. He is in a position where he can begin the process of making amends to his family and the larger community. In turn, as reflected in Joshua's letters from prison, an audience is developing that supports his efforts to live according to his preferred identity.

Notes

1. The name "Joshua" is a pseudonym, as are all the case names used in the chapter. The stories and letters used in this chapter are all used with the informed consent of those involved.

2. Re-authoring does not simply create new positive identity conclusions, which rely upon essentialist, humanist notions such as a person's "fundamental goodness" or "true self" (White, 2004).

3. For various reasons, men often deny and minimize the seriousness of the effects of their violence on others. Men's motivation for stopping their violence is

significantly increased when they are invited to *acknowledge the effects* of their violence on what and who is important to them. Along with abusing others, most men I work with have been abused themselves. Many men who deny and minimize the seriousness of the effects their violence on others also deny and minimize the effects of others' violence on themselves. Working to interrupt the violence involves encouraging men to appreciate the experience of being victimized by violence through studying the effects of violence upon both themselves and others. In the context of studying men's values and preferences, inviting men to study the effects of violence on themselves and others increases their motivation and capacity to take responsibility for responding to these effects.

Inviting men to take responsibility for responding to the effects of their violence on others involves men considering unhelpful and helpful responses to the effects of violence. Many men respond to the violence inflicted on them by denying and avoiding it. Rather than face these traumatic experiences, many men respond to the effects by trying to soothe, numb, and comfort themselves through drugs, alcohol, gambling, and sexual abuse. (In the beginning of my conversations with Joshua, he was aware of trying to avoid and soothe his painful feelings but was unclear about the traumatic experiences that the feelings were associated with. In one conversation, Joshua reported that he had recently confided in his sister that he thought he had been sexually abused as a child. His sister confirmed that he had been). When men become self-absorbed with their own pain, they remain unaware of others' experiences. Men are invited to face rather than avoid their traumatic experiences. As men find more helpful ways of responding to their own pain, they also find helpful ways of responding to the pain they have caused others.

Previously, in accordance with the dominant domestic violence approach (Pence & Paymar, 1993), I restricted the study of the effects of abuse to include only the effects on those whom men had hurt. The process of studying the effects of men's violence on others became much more profound when I also invited men to study the effects of violence on themselves. When men study others experiences of violence, they often gain insight into their own experiences of violence. Conversely, as men study their own experiences of violence, they gain a greater understanding of others' experiences. Men's experiences are often both similar to and different from experiences of those they have hurt. The process of studying the effects eventually involves hearing directly from those they have hurt.

4. Many have contributed to these distinctions about shame. Some popular authors are Bradshaw (1988), Brown (2004), Gilligan (1997), and Luskin (2003).

5. Again, re-authoring does not simply create new positive identity conclusions that rely upon essentialist, humanist notions such as a person's "fundamental goodness" or "true self" (White, 2004).

References

Augusta-Scott, T. (2003). Dichotomies in the power and control story: Exploring multiple stories about men who choose abuse in intimate relationships. In

Responding to violence: Collection of papers on working with violence and abuse (pp. 203–224). Adelaide, Australia: Dulwich Centre.

Bradshaw, J. (1988). *Healing the shame that binds you*. Deerfield Beach, FL: Health Communications.

Brown, B. (2004). *Women & shame: Reaching out, speaking truths, and building connection*. New York: 3C Press.

Bruner, J. (2002). *Making stories. Law, literature, life*. Cambridge, MA: Harvard University Press.

Gilligan, J. (1997). *Violence: Reflections on a national epidemic*. New York: Vintage.

Jenkins, A. (1998a, May). Facing shame without shaming: The therapeutic engagement of men who have enacted violence. *Therapeutic Conversations, 4*. Toronto, Canada: Yaletown Family Therapy Conference.

Jenkins, A. (1998b). Invitations to responsibility: Engaging adolescents and young men who have sexually abused. In W. Marshall, Y. Fernandez, S. Hudson, & T. Ward (Eds.), *Sourcebook of treatment programs with sexual offenders* (pp.163–189). New York: Plenum.

Jenkins, A. (2005). Knocking on shame's door: Facing shame without shaming disadvantaged young people who have abused. In M. C. Calder (Ed.), *Children and young people who sexually abuse: New theory, research and practice developments* (pp. 114–127). London: Russell House.

Jenkins, A. (2006). Discovering integrity: Working with shame without shaming young people who have abused. In R. Longo & D. Prescott (Eds.), *Current perspectives: Working with sexually aggressive youth and youth with sexual behavior problems* (pp. 419–442). Holyoke, MA: NEARI Press.

Jenkins, A., Joy, M., & Hall, R. (2003). Forgiveness and child sexual abuse: A matrix of meanings. In *Responding to violence: Collection of papers on working with violence and abuse* (pp. 35–70). Adelaide, Australia: Dulwich Centre.

Luskin, F. (2003). *Forgive for good*. San Francisco: Harper.

Pence, E., & Paymar, M. (1993). *Education groups for men who batter: The Duluth model*. New York: Springer.

White, M. (1995). The narrative perspective in therapy. In *Re-authoring lives: Interviews & essays* (pp. 11–40). Adelaide, Australia: Dulwich Center.

White, M. (2004). Narrative practice and the unpacking of identity conclusions. In *Narrative practice and exotic lives: Resurrecting diversity in everyday life* (pp. 119–147). Adelaide, Australia: Dulwich Center.

14

Talking Body Talk

Merging Feminist and Narrative Approaches to Practice

Catrina Brown

Taken together, feminist and narrative therapies enable moving beyond pathologizing approaches to eating "disorders" through an emphasis on listening to the gendered stories that women's bodies tell. The continuum of struggles women experience with eating and their bodies make sense when we situate their stories within the culturally available meanings and discourses that make them possible. Specifically, in this chapter, I present a blend of feminist and narrative therapy that acknowledges ways that women resource or use their bodies as forms of both compliance and resistance to dominant cultural ideas, including those of feminine subjectivity.

Dominant cultural ideas of gender are inseparable from both experiences and performances of the gendered self. Through controlling and regulating the body, women can comply to cultural dictates to constrain, discipline, and regulate themselves; at the same time, controlling the body is meaningful to women as a means of establishing a sense of control and power. Women's struggles with eating and their bodies is a form of agency, an effort at having greater control over their lives. While not speaking out or protesting directly, talking through the body conforms with gender expectations of the "good woman." *Body talk* refers to the culturally specific ways that women speak or communicate through their bodies. Body talk begins to speak the unspoken, or *yet to be spoken*, through weight preoccupation struggles. It has begun to draw attention to women's struggles at a cultural level and to make them visible. Body talk resists the cultural idea of the "good woman" through the very expression of struggle. Yet body talk stories often reveal a struggle between conforming to and resisting dominant gender scripts. Through body talk, women can speak without fully owning, being accountable for, or being prepared to deal with the social ramifications of their talk. It thus allows women to simultaneously *speak and hide* from speaking. In this way, speaking and hiding are metaphors for women's ambivalence about speaking out directly for themselves, given gender scripts that reward constraint in feminine performance. In short, body talk disrupts the social expectations of gender performance, which require women to yield to the needs and demands of others at the expense of themselves and, above all, to avoid conflict or the appearance of being difficult or confrontational. This dominant gender social script of the "good woman" often results in the suppression of alternative stories, especially those that emphasize her needs, pain, or anger. A feminist narrative approach to body talk will resurrect these alternative stories so that women can speak rather than hide the counterstories of their lives.

I explore ways the body is within "the grip" of cultural practices and, subsequently, the narrative process of externalizing the gendered performance of self. Through struggles with eating and the body, women participate in normalization processes of self. Women's socially constructed gendered performance of self involves self-surveillance and self-regulation; it is here that body talk allows for both social conformance and resistance. Weight preoccupation issues, including anorexia nervosa and bulimia, provide symbolic cues of subjective struggles and are an entry point to further uncover the meanings they hold. I argue in this chapter that body talk needs to be unpacked to uncover the yet to be spoken stories of these struggles. Furthermore, I suggest that the voicing and hearing of these stories may make this specific body talk unnecessary.

Blending feminist and narrative approaches will involve not only formulating feminist therapy through a postmodern lens but also situating gender stories within narrative work. As a critical response to the dominance of androcentric theory and practice in the provision of social services to women, feminist therapy has sought to validate women's experiences and to empower women. Today, postmodern feminism addresses the limitations of preserving a unified and essentialized feminine subject sometimes advanced in modernist feminism. This chapter weaves together feminist and narrative therapies through a postmodern lens that recognizes the social construction of women's experiences, challenges gender essentialism, and abandons a modernist deployment of knowledge and power. In addition, the postmodern merging of feminist and narrative therapy approaches to women's body talk challenges dominant social narratives that contribute to women's struggles with their bodies and eating. Blending feminist and narrative therapy will center on rewriting women's stories to escape limiting cultural meanings and descriptions and draw upon the strengths of feminist and narrative approaches (Adams-Westcot, Dafforn, & Sterne, 1993). Merging feminist and narrative approaches enables an analysis and practice with women that does not lose sight of the construction and performance of gendered subjectivities through culturally available discourses and the socially constructed storytelling that women do through their body talk.

In this chapter, I highlight the importance of an externalization process in which the problem of weight preoccupation is taken beyond the individual and located within cultural practices and discourses. This externalization process further recognizes (a) the meaningful avenue that weight preoccupation offers women for attaining a sense of power and control that is often perceived to be missing from their lives and (b) the need to move past surface descriptions that focus on weight and eating to the formation of thicker descriptions that acknowledge and honor women's emotional needs and desires that otherwise feel forbidden.[1] My approach to listening to women's body talk emphasizes the importance of escaping cultural descriptions of women as victims and thus not overemphasizing conformity and compliance in the externalization process at the expense of acknowledging women's agency and resistance. I critique existing strategies within narrative therapy that attempt to acknowledge women's agency and power through resisting anorexia and bulimia but fail to also acknowledge and thus render invisible women's resistance *through* anorexia and bulimia.

A feminist narrative strategy implies a positioned stance, as feminism does not claim to be neutral, but rather explicitly interested in disrupting the construction, performance, and internalized devaluation of gendered subjectivities within patriarchal social relations. As such, the externalization process will reflect the therapist's understanding of eating problems within a gendered social context. Just as there is no neutral telling or hearing of a story, there is no neutral, singular, or correct externalizing of "the problem" (White, 1994). For me, externalizing women's body talk seeks out the suppressed voice, women's disqualified experiences and knowledge that have been rendered silent and unspeakable. In resurrecting the suppressed or subjugated stories expressed through body talk, I attend to the multiple points of ambivalence and uncertainty in women's stories about their bodies and about themselves. In doing so, I attend to the ambivalence and uncertainty women often have with discovering and exercising their own voices. Uncovering, strengthening, and thickening women's unspoken stories about their desires, their feelings about themselves and others, their capacity to deal with conflict and unhappiness, and their anxiety and perceived lack of control over their lives reveals that body talk expresses so much more than the desire to be thin.

The Emergence of Feminist Approaches to Eating "Disorders"

Since the late 1970s, feminist or women-centered approaches to understanding women's problems with eating and the body have emphasized women's experiences, revealing the ways they make sense. Such understandings of the continuum of weight preoccupation and eating "disorders" among women avoid individualizing and pathologizing women's experiences. Early feminist writing by Susie Orbach (1978) in her well-known book *Fat Is a Feminist Issue;* Kim Chernin's (1981) *The Obsession: Reflections of the Tyranny of Slenderness;* Marcia Millman's (1980) *Such a Pretty Face: Being Fat in America;* and later, Naomi Wolf's (1990) *Beauty Myth,* to name but a few, challenged the hegemonic thin ideal and drew our attention to the deleterious impact of this ideal on women's body image and sense of self. The title of Orbach's (1986) *Hunger Strike: The Anorectic Struggle as a Metaphor for Our Age* reveals the idea that struggle with the body is a metaphor for women's struggles in the world. More recently, Gremillion's (2001, 2003) work suggests that women resource their bodies:

> In fairly recent history, women have been encouraged to resource their own bodies, to take that task on themselves. Again, the dominant idea now is that you "make yourself," you shape your own body, and you use your body as a resource. Women and girls are now resourcing their own bodies in ways that draw upon the same traditions of thought that place nature as an object that exists outside of us. (p. 142)

Many of these feminist writers established the groundwork for the understanding that women's struggles with eating and their bodies exist within a cultural context. From here, we are able to recognize that the body talks. The body is a "medium of culture" (Bordo, 1993, p. 165). It is "a powerful symbolic form, a surface on which the central rules, hierarchies, and even metaphysical commitments of culture are inscribed and thus reinforced through the concrete language of the body" (Bordo, 1993, p. 165).

By the early 1990s, a fairly extensive feminist critique of the cultural pressure to be thin had been amassed; however, this cultural critique had rarely translated into feminist clinical practice. Three feminist collections, however, emerged almost simultaneously: the Canadian volume *Consuming Passions: Feminist Approaches to Weight Preoccupation and Eating Disorders* (Brown & Jasper, 1993a); the American *Feminist Perspectives on Eating Disorders* (Fallon, Katzman, & Wooley, 1994); and the British *Eating Problems: A Feminist Psychoanalytic Treatment Model* (Bloom, Gitter, Gutwill, Kogel, & Zaphiropoulos, 1994). Along with others, these three compilations represented both feminist scholarship and feminist-based practice that evolved in response to dominant medicalizing and pathologizing approaches to eating "disorders." The feminist works published in the 1990s built upon the previous decade of feminist clinical practice and advocacy.[2]

Identifying the constructive aspects of restrictive eating, bingeing, and purging helps take eating problems out of the realm of "disorder" and into the realm of coping mechanisms. Portraying them as individual "disorders" rather than as responses to psychosocial distress is part of the historical tendency to mislabel the results of social injustices as individual pathologies. It is for this reason that many feminist theorists are uncomfortable with using the term "disorder" in relation to women's eating patterns, particularly since, for many women, bingeing, purging, and dieting begin as creative coping mechanisms. Indeed, it is often the circumstances and contexts in which they emerge that we need to problematize (Brown, 1993c; Thompson, 1994).[3]

These feminist voices on eating "disorders" and weight preoccupation problems among women have challenged many of the myths within dominant discourse about beauty, the body, health, and eating behavior.[4] They have protested against the "tyranny of slenderness," the stigma and cultural hatred against fatness, and the pathologization of women who adopt more extreme behaviors and stances around eating and the body. Feminist critique has observed the paradox of pathologizing anorexic and bulimic women as diseased, while the vast majority of women in our culture were applauded for their investments in the everyday cultural practices of oscillating self-restraint and excess (Bordo, 1993) related to weight preoccupation and efforts at weight loss, despite the fact that they are often extreme and involve unhealthy weight loss strategies (Brown, 1993a). Although most women were influenced by cultural discourses that associated thinness with power, control, success, and a sense of well-being, practices of power exercised by the helping professionals, such as labeling and pathologizing, served as dividing practices that separated "normal behaviour" from "abnormal behaviour" (Foucault, 1980a, 1980b). The dividing practice of separating anorexia and bulimia from most women's experiences of their bodies reflected a dehistoricizing and decontextualizing of weight preoccupation practices that reinforced a focus on individual pathology separate from cultural meaning.[5] Feminist voices have attempted to make sense of women's struggles with eating and their bodies as cultural articulations rather than as individual diseases, disorders, or deficits.

Despite this effort, it was barely recognized that these problems are gendered within the mainstream or among large, hospital-based eating "disorder" programs that had begun to spring up across North America and Britain in most large centers. While some feminists have emphasized the importance of adopting a nonmanagement focus and empowered-based approach that emphasizes women's right to control their own bodies, very few feminist programs grounded in a feminist, empowerment, and non-disease-based framework have been developed in North America (for an example of a feminist program, see Brown, 1987b; Brown & Forgay, 1987; Brown & Zimberg, 1993).

Feminist critics took exception to early hospital-based treatment approaches rooted largely in behavioral strategies or behavior modification. Legitimized by the medical model and reflecting the anxiety and concern that women and girls might die, early interventions were often drastic and coercive. Lawrence (1984) highlights the way these practices took control away from women who already had only the most fragile sense of control. Indeed, such practices exacerbate the problem when women feel their last vestige of control is being threatened (Brown, 1993c; Brown & Forgay, 1987; Lawrence, 1984). If the problems of anorexia and bulimia are a response to feeling out of control of one's life, deliberately taking control away from women through practices that included forced bed rest, hospitalization, refeeding, and the relentless gaze of supervision was likely to exacerbate the problem (Lawrence, 1984; Lawrence & Lowenstein, 1979).

While treatment strategies today are less coercive than in their early development, the ongoing behavioral focus is often at the expense of uncovering the meaning of the behaviors themselves. Furthermore, the focus is still on managing body weight and food intake, which often simply reifies women's existing preoccupation with these issues. Gremillion (2001) notes that "while the goal here is to 'undo anorexia,' these foci in treatment deploy the same kind of logic that makes anorexia possible" (p. 143). Referring to this logic, she states, "Both construct the body as an object and a thing that needs to be resourced to create a self of a particular kind" (p. 142). The cultural logic of self-management dominates both the treatment approach and women's overinvestment in controlling their eating and their bodies.

I have found it is more helpful to shift the focus away from the preoccupation on body weight and eating behavior and to focus instead on how these preoccupations distract women from both the sources and the existence of their struggles.

Body as Metaphor

The body as a physical object plays a central part in connecting shared social and individual levels of experience (Berger & Luckmann, 1967). It is an instrument of nonverbal and symbolic communication that mediates social life. Polthemus (1978) therefore argues that body image is molded in our interactions with others within our culture. Women have often invested much of their sense of self in their appearance. It has been the case in Western society that men are "supposed to transcend their bodies and turn their energies toward the world. . . . Women on the other hand are given approval for continuing and even increasing their investments in their bodies" (Polthemus, 1978, p. 120).

According to Polthemus (1978), the thin body ideal has become so widely accepted that it is forgotten that other societies and periods of history have held different ideals. Women's position in society has been expressed through the kind of body fashionable in a given period. Most societies create a uniform body ideal for women, which is often difficult or painful to attain but represents the woman's moral and social status.

Feminists seem to agree that weight preoccupation, eating "disorders," and the thin ideal are metaphors.[6] While a range of perspectives have emerged about the cultural meaning of the thin body ideal today, I concur with Orbach's view (1986) presented in *Hunger Strike: The Anorectic Struggle as a Metaphor for Our Age*. For her, the coexisting image and value of thinness are an expression of both the emancipation and oppression of women. Rather than totalizing women as victims of culture or as oppressed, this "both/and" position allows space to recognize both women's emancipation and their oppression. This perspective further enables a theoretical approach to clinical practice and the externalization of eating "disorders" in narrative therapy that honors women's agency and power, while not minimizing the impact of oppressive social discourses and social relations. The thin and increasingly muscular and fit body ideal that emerged in the 1980s represented the paradoxical realities of women's lives and, indeed, both women's emancipation and continued oppression (Brown, 1987a; Orbach, 1986).[7] Drawing upon the work of Orbach (1986), Bordo (1993) states,

The anorectic embodies, in an extreme and painfully debilitating way, a psychological struggle characteristic of the contemporary situation of women. That situation is one in which a constellation of social, economic, and psychological factors have combined to produce a generation of women who feel deeply flawed, ashamed of their needs, and not entitled to exist unless they transform themselves into worthy new selves (read: without need, without want, without body). (p. 47)

Thinness can thus represent increased social equality for women through the image of freedom, mobility, and independence as well as a continuation of the traditional representation of women as vulnerable, small, and dependent (Hollander, 1980). I suggest that the contradictory story of thinness metaphorically represents women's contradictory social realities and social expectations (Brown, 1987a; Brown & Forgay, 1987; Brown & Jasper, 1993b). It is an image that contains at once the conditions of liberation alongside the maintenance of patriarchy and the oppression of women. Thinness, then, is a complex and contradictory feminine image of vulnerability, dependency, self-denial, and weakness alongside self-management, independence, freedom, mobility, strength, and sexuality separated from reproductive function and its associated rounded body.

Bordo (1993) offers a significant contribution to understanding the weight preoccupation issues among women today in *Unbearable Weight: Feminism, Western Culture, and the Body*. Like Thompson (1994), Bordo critiques the general tendency to limit social analysis of anorexia to the world of aesthetics, the world of the media and fashion.[8] She believes that the "meaning of the ideal of slenderness" needs to be explored both in the context of women's experiences and "as a cultural formation that expresses ideals, anxieties, and social changes (some related to gender, some not)" (p. 46). Hosking (2001) supports this argument through her account of her experiences with bulimia:

To sum up my experience as simply about wanting to be thin, wanting to be attractive to men, a hopeless, pointless, time-wasting write off is to discount and dishonour my life. Bulimia was a strategy for coping, a strategy that enabled me to continue public life as normal, to maintain the facade of a capable young woman, to keep the nice and normal separate from the messy and wild. Bulimia was a search for myself, a grappling with my identity as a woman, a frustrated attempt to express the profound. I fight not to feel ashamed of those desperate years. Through them I feel I have gained a greater knowledge about life. (pp. 163–164)

Along with Thompson (1994) and Bordo (1993), Malson (1997) acknowledges the need to recognize the social pressure to be thin, without reducing sociocultural analysis to this domain. Recognizing the wider cultural significance captures the multiple and, indeed, often contradictory meanings of women's struggles with food and the body. Malson builds upon feminist interpretations of "anorexia," advancing the idea that anorexia reflects cultural concerns with "feminine excess" and the need to regulate the unruliness of women's embodiment. Within the Western Cartesian body/mind dualism, in which mind is identified with self, Malson (1997) believes that "thinness is valued here because it signifies the mind's triumph over the body and its desires"(p. 235). Experiences of the body can be understood only within culturally available meanings. Abandoning the tendency to naturalize the body, this discussion of women's struggles with eating and body size serves as an example of how women participate in normalization processes of self.

Body Talk

Recognizing that the body tells stories of women's struggles of self in culture shapes my approach to externalizing eating "disorder" stories. I acknowledge both the compliance and resistance to cultural ideas in the gendered performance of self in my interpretation of the meaning of body talk. It is my view that feminist narrative therapy will not only recognize women's struggles revealed through body talk but also help to resurrect the subjugated knowledges or stories ambivalently expressed through body talk. Body talk is a gendered performance that serves as an entry point to discover the hidden struggles of self within the social context of who women believe they should be and how they should be seen as they perform femininity within the dominant culture (Butler, 1993). Gendered subjectivities are constructed and internalized; they come into existence through their very performance. Butler recognizes that the performativity of gender involves disciplining gendered subjectivities through regulating norms. Thus, gender performance is not simply about choice or "free play," as it "cannot be understood outside of a process of iterability, a regularized and constrained repetition of norms" (Butler, 1993, p. 95). Body talk is one way that women's gendered subjectivies are disciplined and constituted. Body talk tells stories about gender performance through the body.

The body is itself discursively and extradiscursively constructed. Ussher (1997) advances this material-discursive approach, "the view that we need to move away from the binary divide between the material and discursive analyses of the body, towards a position which allows us to recognize the interaction and interrelationship between the two" (p. 1). Malson's (1997) analysis also reflects a material-discursive approach to "women's bodies," arguing that "anorexic bodies are always-already located within multiple systems of significations and power relations" (p. 225). The meanings of anorexic bodies are constituted in multiple discourses, from Malson's perspective, but not separate from their extradiscursive material reality. Malson suggests that analysis of anorexia most often focuses only on the discursive aspects of the anorexic body, negating the actual "physicality of the body" (p. 225). For Malson, "analyses of 'anorexia' must seek to engage with both the discursive and the extra-discursive of 'anorexic' bodies" (p. 225).

While the emergence, experience, and meaning of "anorexia," "bulimia," and women's preoccupation with weight must be situated as discursive cultural practices, the material effects on the body cannot be ignored. However, although the body is physical, constrained by its material reality, its meaning can be understood only within its sociocultural discursive context. Nonetheless, therapeutic conversations must contend with the embodied effects of self-starvation, bingeing, and purging as discursive and extradiscursive.

The dominant cultural story of psychological identity ties individual value and self-esteem to the power associated with self-denial, self-restraint, and self-control. The capacity for such self-regulation is often interpreted and experienced within the larger dominant culture as being strong, capable, and in control. On the one hand, women today expect that they should be strong, capable, and in control, yet on the other, this experience of themselves is often very difficult to attain. Taken together, these cultural stories make it possible for women today to use their bodies to speak to themselves and the world about their struggles to achieve a positive sense of their own worth and value. Using the body as a means to accomplish a sense of themselves as strong, capable, and in control works within the complexity of cultural stories about the meaning of fatness/thinness and the importance of self-surveillance, ensuring that the "private does not erupt into the public" (Hosking, 2001, p. 162). By watching themselves being watched, women attempt to gain some control over the process (Berger, 1972). Self-surveillance provides some assurance about being seen in the best possible light and to, subsequently, promise the satisfaction of social approval and reward.

Making Sense of Body Talk:
Blending Feminist and Narrative Approaches

Feminist therapy brings a politicized understanding of women's body struggles as gendered struggles through the language of metaphor. Narrative therapy provides a postmodern edge to this interpretation, arguing that we live storied lives (White, 1995; White & Epston, 1990). The notion that we live storied lives allows us to see the social construction of the stories we live, and thus the possibility for alternative story lines and re-authored, nonessentialized identities. Blending feminist and narrative approaches offers a gendered politicized narrative conversation which focuses on making sense of women's body talk, rather than pathologizing women's experiences. Therapists do not need to engage in struggles over who shall control feeding the body or what size it should be: It should be assumed that women and girls must maintain power and control over their own bodies (Bordo, 1993; Brown, 1987b; Brown, 1993a, 1993c; Brown & Forgay, 1987; Brown & Jasper, 1993a; Brown & Zimberg, 1993; Lawrence, 1984). Externalizing body talk makes sense of women's experiences by adopting a "both/and" position, offering a cultural contextualization of these struggles without totalizing women as cultural products.

A feminist postmodern sensibility informs my endeavor to unpack the creation and performance of gendered subjectivities through women's body talk (Butler, 1993). The notion of body talk, then, implies both metaphor and story. It also suggests that women can tell stories about their lives and their struggles through their bodies. Body talk is active, not passive. It is at all moments socially and historically located and is thus never a story that women make up all by themselves. The body is a text, whereby body talk is never innocent and never simply subjective. Thus, not only do women's body talk stories make sense, they have an implicit agenda, to message or language struggle. My feminist narrative approach is respectful of these messages, of these voices, at the same time that it unpacks and explores these stories. In the process of making sense of women's body talk, the stance my feminist narrative approach adopts will negotiate the tensions between respecting and valuing women's experiences of struggle, while, importantly, not essentializing them. These struggles, then, are at all moments seen as reflections of culture. The meaning that women attach to their stories can unfold only through social process of interaction and meaning making (Berger & Luckmann, 1967; Bruner, 2002; Mead, 1977).

Drawing upon White (2001), we cannot simply tell and retell stories; we must unpack them and rewrite more helpful stories. As a feminist narrative therapist, I am positioned in my desire to avoid reproducing dominant social stories. Through the narrative process of externalization, I seek to help women uncover their disqualified or suppressed voices and to explore the ways that their body talk may communicate both conformance and resistance to gendered subjectivities. We might ask, what suppressed or subjugated story is the body telling? What does her problem reveal to her and others about herself that is not usually known?

Often, women are afraid of their own voices and the possible consequences of them. There is a gendered context that requires women and girls to not complain, to act satisfied, and to be happy and content. This makes it difficult to find space for the discontented or uncertain voice: It is driven underground, suppressed. Women and girls become very skilled at convincing themselves and others that all is well, when this is too often not the case. Externalizing conversations can help women and girls see that they can move beyond internalized stories of the "good girl" or the "good woman" and the expectation that any performance of self that causes conflict or distress in others is unacceptable.

We can respectfully uncover the unheard stories together in this work and their meaningful connections to eating "disorders" and weight preoccupation issues. In an environment that is safe and noncoercive, we can encourage emotional work and coexisting behavioral changes at a realistic and doable pace. If we respect that symptoms of eating problems are meaningful clues to women's and girls' subjugated emotional stories, we can begin to unpack their displaced meaning. Giving space to these stories, making them visible, and hearing them are likely to make body talk of eating "disorders" and weight preoccupation unnecessary. Focusing on changing behavior without making space for unheard stories is likely to entrench the need for such body talk. Body talk communicates that which is yet to be spoken, and yet to be heard.

Externalizing Body Talk

Making sense of women's body talk involves in narrative terms a process of externalization. Consistent with feminist approaches to therapy, this means acknowledging that the "problem is the problem," not the woman herself. Furthermore, in situating the problem outside of the individual, we can explore the social context in which it occurs. Stories of starvation, of feeling fat, of binge eating or purging are all meaningful cues to women's and girls' struggles about how they experience themselves and how they are seen to experience themselves in the world. In therapeutic conversations, the exploration of such behaviors is a search for meaning. Drawing on anthropologist Geertz (1973), "Behaviour must be attended to, and with some exactness, because it is through the flow of behaviour—or more precisely, social action—that cultural forms find articulation" (p. 17).

Unfortunately, within narrative therapy, the efforts at externalizing eating "disorders" have often resulted in objectifying anorexia or bulimia as an enemy that has taken hold of women. What is missed in this external-ized conceptualization is how women's body talk is an effort at agency and how these struggles are an effort to say what cannot easily be said or acknowledged directly. In seeking a thick description, I wish to go beyond the surface or apparent meaning of the body talk story. When externaliz-ing practices stay within the surface meaning—the distraction of the anorexia or bulimia—the complex and multiple layers of storytelling remain invisible. I suggest that the task of rendering women's struggles vis-ible is at the heart of this work. If externalizing is reductive or participates in further silencing the suppressed voices of women's struggles, through for instance, totalizing women's body talk as a product of dominant media images of thinness, women's agency or active voices remain suppressed. Externalizing conversations that totalize women as victims of anorexia, bulimia, and culture fail to see how women actively resource or use their bodies to talk (Gremillion, 2001, 2003), not simply as victims, but as efforts to establish some sense of power and control over their lives (C. Brown, 1989, 1990b, 1993a, 1993b, 1993c; Lawrence, 1979, 1984).

We live in a culture in which women's attitudes around weight and food reflect a coalescing of the social pressures to be thin, the cultural logic of self-management, and conflict with the performance of socially constructed gendered subjectivities. Geertz (1973) suggests that "social actions are com-ments on more than themselves" (p. 23), and this is clearly so for women's attitudes and behaviors that center on attaining thinness. This focus on thin-ness comments not just on culture but also on women's relationship to cul-ture. Thus, for Geertz, these are symbolic and meaningful actions, not simply individual actions. Geertz's (1973) anthropological perspective may foster therapeutic conversations by providing a "vocabulary" for interpreting self-stories and ensuring thick descriptions in the therapeutic externalization process. For Geertz, this involves a double task:

> Setting down the meaning particular social actions have for the actors whose actions they are, and stating, as explicitly as we can manage, what the knowl-edge thus attained demonstrates about the society in which it is found and, beyond that, about social life as such. Our double task is to uncover the con-ceptual structures that inform our subjects' acts, the "said" of social discourse . . . that is, about the role of culture in human life. (p. 29)

This double task of interpreting social actions such as self-starvation, weight preoccupation, bingeing, purging, and physical exercise regimes thus involves people's own interpretations and the meanings they attach to these behaviors as well as a therapeutic uncovering of the cultural shaping of such interpretations. This is, in fact, the purpose of externalization within narrative therapy. The separation of the problem from the individual is a search for the way the story has been organized or put together over time and has become meaningful to people within the larger social context of their lives. Through externalizing a dominant problem story, we begin to pull apart the story and make space for alternative stories to emerge.

Externalization will necessarily rely upon the worldviews of the therapist and the client. My approach to the externalization of eating "disorders" reflects an analysis of women's struggles with the body and eating in which women are viewed as active subjects. From a feminist approach, it is crucial that women not be rendered as victims and that we acknowledge their agency. Thick descriptions that seek out the meaning of women's relationships to eating and their bodies within our cultural obsession with thinness and self-control lead us toward interpretations and stories that do not totalize women as victims of cultural forces.

Like Bordo (1993), I see women's struggles with their bodies and eating as a cultural articulation. Thus, the focus on these behaviors alone can offer only a thin description. Seeking a thicker description of these behaviors as cultural articulations may enable the narrative externalization process to notice how controlling the body is a viable arena for controlling and regulating oneself, especially when other aspects of women's lives feel unmanageable (Brown, 1993a, 1993c; Lawrence, 1984).

Problematizing Externalizing Strategies

For over a decade, feminist theorists and clinicians have emphasized the importance of acknowledging the power and agency of women's struggles with their bodies. Orbach (1986) describes the protest women speak through their bodies. Like Bordo (1993) and Gremillion (2001, 2003), I suggest that women resource the body in the social process of creating and performing the self. Influenced by the work of Foucault (1980a, 1980b) and Bordo (1993), I argue that women use their bodies as a form of self-regulation, struggling between wishing to control or discipline their bodies and their desires and wishing to satisfy them. Women's active use of the body languages this struggle, one that is situated within the context of gender, power, and cultural practices. As I have argued, we cannot, therefore, reduce eating problems to an "appearance-based disorder" (Bordo, 1993; Brown & Jasper, 1993b; Thompson, 1994). It is much more complex than this. Externalization should be a process that helps to resurrect the suppressed voice encoded in body talk.

Although Epston, Morris, and Maisel (1998); Nyland (2002); and White (1991, 2004a, 2004b) are committed to challenging oppression in their work, ironically, in their externalizing conversations, they construct women as victims of the cultural pressure to be thin. All are determined to situate women's struggles with anorexia and bulimia within a gendered social context. All wish to encourage women to claim power back over their lives by fighting back against or resisting the power of anorexia and bulimia. White (1991) observes,

> Just consider the practices of self-subjugation that persons with anorexia nervosa are recruited into: the rigorous and meticulous self-surveillance, the various self-punishments of the body for its transgressions, the perpetual exile, the precise self-documentation, and so on. It is significant that it has mostly been women who have suffered from anorexia nervosa, and I think that this says a lot about how this modern system of power has been taken up in the domain of gender politics. (p. 45)

While I agree with White's (1997) description, I am concerned about what he and others leave out. There is little doubt that eating "disorders" among women serve as some of the most poignant examples of Foucault's (1980a, 1980b) notion that through processes of subjectification, normalization practices of self, and self-surveillance, individuals as "docile bodies" are vehicles of social power. Yet, I accept Foucault's model of power, because it isn't based on the notion of power as repression, but allows for both constraint and resistance. Similarly, White (2004a) argues for "indeterminancy within determinacy," which emphasizes individual agency, choice, and power, while also acknowledging the context of social constraint in people's lives. However, the externalizing processes in narrative therapy for eating "disorders" would benefit from a greater focus on women's agency and power.

Self-surveillance has been totalized as a negative force of power. Krusky (2002) states, "When we shift the Panopticon gaze out of our practices, when we live and practice in ways that defy the strategies of self-surveillance, we become architects of a different discourse" (p. 74). From this view, strategies of self-surveillance are only repressive. Narrative therapists often externalize the self-surveillance specified through eating "disorders" through a focus on resisting anorexia or bulimia. I argue, however, that self-surveillance specified through eating "disorders" is not so absolute that there is no space for resistance or counterdiscourse within the deployment of self-surveillance itself. Indeed, self-surveillance through policing the body paradoxically offers a socially sanctioned site for simultaneous protest or resistance.

Anti-anorexia leagues have become popular in narrative therapy, with an emphasis on demonstrating that women are seduced by anorexia: They are its victims (Grieves, 1998).[9] The externalization practices of these "leagues" do not acknowledge the complex ways in which women seek to establish a sense of mastery, control, and power through the extreme self-discipline practices of anorexia. Simply taking a stance against anorexia, being anti-anorexia, renders invisible important content of women's struggles and their efforts to talk through the body. Anorexia is arguably as much a friend as it is an enemy. It is both well intended and problematic. When anorexia is formulated or totalized as something bad, we negate the ways that it is creative and helpful to women. Overprescribing to an approach centered on fighting against anorexia and bulimia is a prescription against listening to anorexia and bulimia. As such, therapeutic conversations that adopt the anti-anorexia approach are in some sense adopting a stance that further shuts down the yet to be spoken, embodied in the highly disciplined normalizing practices of self. When the yet to be spoken shifts into the *beginning to be spoken,* it is often fragile, delicate, and cautious. In this initial surfacing of a woman's distress, struggle, and conflict, we can begin to see ways in which she wishes to create a new story of self that suits her better as well as her ambivalence about continuing to perform a story of self that no longer does.[10]

Instead of exploring what meaning the eating problem may have for a woman—how she may use it to cope or how she may find it helpful, as well as ways it may be unhelpful—the "anti-anorexia" or anti-bulimia approach is set up to focus on how it does not work for her. Thus, any meaning anorexia and bulimia may have for women is invalidated and minimized as evidence of the individual having been tricked or duped by the power of the eating "disorder." In my view, it is far more helpful to adopt a more textured appreciation, one that recognizes that women create these approaches to coping within the context of existing social discourses and social relations as well as become constrained by them. It is profoundly discrediting of women's intelligence, agency, and power to assume they have simply been constrained. In my work with women over many years, and in my own history of struggle, I have never seen women only be constrained or victimized by eating problems.

Like White (1991, 2004b), Epston et al.'s (1998) focus on eating "disorders" as oppressive fails to recognize their coexisting expression of resistance. In addition, however, Epston et al. use violent language that totalizes the power that eating disorders have over women: Women are "murdered," "tortured," or "tricked." Within this approach, the "good intentions" that women have in using eating "disorders" are framed as anorexia tricking or outwitting them, which, again, renders invisible how eating "disorders" are often meaningful or make sense for women. For instance, in *Biting the Hand that Starves You,* Maisel, Epston, and Bordon (2004) state, "Almost all of a/b's [anorexia's and bulimia's] tactics of imprisonment can be subsumed under a perverse appeal to a perverted morality" (p. 31). Furthermore, they describe the "camouflage" of eating "disorders" in this way:

Contending with a/b means having to prepare for a prolonged struggle with a relentless and diabolically clever adversary. After glimpsing the deceptiveness and wickedness of a/b, one is not free to simply turn one's back on it and walk away. Little Red Riding Hood, after discovering the deception she had fallen prey to, still had to contend with the wolf. A/b is like the wolf who disguises himself as a loving benefactor. But unlike the wolf in the Little Red Riding Hood story, a/b is capable of shifting its shape and disguising its identity endlessly: in a blink of an eye, the wolf can cloak itself in sheep's clothing or appear as inviting as a cuddly teddy bear. Much of a/b's power is connected to this astonishing capacity for camouflage and deception. (p. 38)

Further illustration of this externalizing approach is revealed by Epston et al. (1998), who state in one therapeutic conversation about anorexia, "Why does it want to murder you? Why doesn't it want you to protest? Why doesn't it want you to put up any resistance? Why does it want you to go to your death like a sheep?" (p. 154). What is so evidently missed here is that anorexia *is protest*: It is not just compliance. So committed is this approach to rescuing women from their compliance, their victimhood, it negates the complex, multiple, and contradictory stories of anorexic body talk. As Connie Hosking (2001) says, this kind of interpretation dishonors what is profound about the struggle, about the efforts at voicing one's struggles, one's protests. One needs to ask, what is the effect of therapy continuing to construct women only as victims, as compliant sheep? What is the effect of not hearing women's protests? What is the effect of reinscribing essentialized gendered subjectivity as weak, helpless, and compliant? Like Hosking, I have no interest in providing a testimonial, but my interest in working with women, in hearing their voices, arises from my own struggles. I resist, as I have always resisted, any characterization of myself or women in general only as powerless victims. I would "counter-translate" (Maisel et al., 2004) the essentialist story of women in these externalization practices.

Other narrative practitioners invoke the same binary that formulates women as victims, tricked by their eating "disorders." Courtney and Williams (2000) describe their work facilitating support groups for women with eating "disorders" using a narrative approach, and they reveal that women are invited to explore all the ways that their eating "disorders" don't work for them, rather than encouraging a "both/and" approach that looks at what is also working about the eating problem. This is true for Kraner and Ingram's (1998) group, helping women to reclaim their lives from anorexia. Like Epston et al. (1998), they use externalizing language such as the "monster," which plays tricks, imprisons, makes promises, and controls. I don't refute the value in exploring the power that eating "disorders" often have over women's lives, but the one-sidedness of this approach is reductive, overlooking a thicker, richer description that allows women with eating "disorders" some degree of dignity and of agency. Erased is the usefulness, the creativity, the resistance, the ways that eating "disorders" are not simply monsters or murderers, but make sense in women's lives.

Externalizing conversations need to explore the ways in which women express their power and agency, not just their powerlessness. When women receive the message that they are victims of culture or victims of eating "disorders" without agency or power, their existing struggles with gendered subjectivity, with their power and agency as women, are only reaffirmed. In overprescribing to this story of women in the process of externalization, competing stories that may be meaningful to women are obscured. Furthermore, when the measure of well-being and power is conflated with abandoning the eating "disorder," the power exercised through the eating "disorder" itself is problematically negated (Bordo, 1993; Brown & Jasper, 1993b; Gremillion, 2001, 2003; Orbach, 1986).

Gremillion (2003) suggests that externalizing conversations help to challenge the totalizing descriptions of "anorexic" identity and that they help to "personify 'anorexia' as an agent with its own motives and purposes, a linguistic move that allows therapists and clients to speak about anorexia's negative effects without requiring clients to indict themselves for their anorexic actions" (p. 197). While I agree this is the intent, there is, nonetheless, an indictment of the self. The "anti-anorexia" or "anti-bulimia" approach to externalization reflects a deterministic stance whereby women are constructed as products of cultural forces. Many women would experience the idea that they are simply victims or products of cultural forces as an indictment of themselves as weak, passive, and undiscerning. If eating "disorders" express deeply "personal and private" unspoken messages about living in the world, condemnation of eating disorders is condemnation of the self. No doubt, internalized dominant discourse on gender, on weight, and on self-management all need to be externalized in therapy. Yet drawing on Foucault (1980a, 1980b), both constraint and agency need to be recognized in this externalizing work.

Gremillion (2003) views agency as central to practices of externalization:

> The point of engaging in "externalizing conversations" with clients is to create a discursive space to name, unpack, and detail the relational and ideational contexts of problems so that clients can imagine and experience a sense of active agency, rather than passengerhood or inevitability, in connection to these problems. (p. 201)

While I agree entirely with Gremillion's emphasis on agency, the current approaches to externalization limit their focus on agency to the resisting of anorexia and bulimia, without acknowledging the resistance and agency of body talk.

In addition to the problem of reinscribing essentialist notions of femininity—as weak, passive victims—is the inadvertent pathologization of women's experiences when the therapeutic focus centers on what does not make sense about anorexia and bulimia. In tandem, essentialism and pathologization have the effect of disqualifying stories about how controlling the body makes sense for women and, subsequently, how this is evidence of women's agency. Oddly reminiscent of traditional cognitive and behavioral strategies is the attempt to make women see how and why this body talk is "bad for them." Externalizing conversations are set up to show women how they are being tricked and manipulated by eating "disorders." This language makes women turn their gaze upon themselves, not only as products of culture, but as products of the eating "disorder." The eating "disorder" "confuses you" and "confounds you," in the words of Epston et al. (1998). From a feminist perspective, it is curious that efforts to help women deal with these struggles reduce women to pawns in anorexia's or bulimia's game. Where are women as active, engaged, embodied subjects in such formulations? How does this advance women as individuals or collectively? What discourses does this form of externalizing lean on and subsequently reinforce?

Externalizing the Suppressed Voice, Moving Past Thin Descriptions

I have observed that women who struggle with anorexia are ambivalent about taking up space, being large, and being visible. To me, this ambivalence often reflects doubt and fear about the risk involved in expressing their own needs, desires, and power. Most often, a part of the woman wishes to take this risk, and another part desperately fears doing so, for fear of upsetting others. This is a powerful metaphor for women struggling with anorexia: the fear of taking up space. One woman I worked with described herself as a "waste of space." Women describe anxiety and fear that their own self-doubts about being entitled to take up space will be confirmed by others' reactions. Instead of communicating these kinds of struggles of self in a direct fashion, it is far more emotionally safe to let the body talk. When people who are important in the life of a woman struggling with anorexia demand of her to give up her eating "disorder," it places her in an excruciating bind. It is like asking a parent to choose the life of one child over another or asking a person to cut off a limb in order to survive.

This bind in many ways captures the heart of the struggle: A woman must choose between what feels like "the only thing that she has that is just hers" and complying with others' desires in order to satisfy them and avoid further conflict. This dilemma mirrors her ambivalence with the gender script she has often complied with throughout her life. Reflecting this ambivalence, she wishes the impossible: that she could resolve the dilemma by being able to simultaneously satisfy both others' demands and her own desires. She wishes she could simply comply with the demand that she give up the eating "disorder," but she finds she just cannot. The demand is experienced as too much self-sacrifice, something, ironically, that anorexia both resists and reflects. When others demand that she renounce the eating "disorder," a woman feels she is being asked to choose between her own fragile sense of self-preservation and survival and continuing to please others at her own expense.

I sometimes use a visualization exercise that allows women to explore how they feel trapped or stuck in their lives by looking at what works and doesn't work for them about the trap (Hutchinson, 1985). In this visualization, women imagine themselves in a trap that they have designed and can therefore escape when they are ready. They are able to image how they built the trap, what it feels like to be inside the trap, and what it feels like when they attempt to leave, and they can then explore what feelings emerge after escaping. One woman described being caught in a very large hunting trap with large teeth. She was able to successfully escape, but she had to rip her leg off in the process. This is an illustrative metaphor of what women report feeling when being asked to be "anti-anorexia," to give it up; they often feel as if they are being asked to give up or destroy part of themselves. They are, in fact, being asked to give up the suppressed voice, the yet to be spoken, before it has a chance to become spoken. When, instead, we explore what stories anorexia tells or what stories it helps women tell, this honors and gives space to their struggles, rather than shutting them down. This visualization exercise is a way for women to explore both what works and what does not work for them about their eating problems. Often women describe feeling very safe inside their traps and deeply ambivalent and afraid to leave them. We draw connections between these traps they have created as a way to cope and the ways they experience their eating problems. Women report the ways that eating "disorders" limit their lives, but at the same time they often can't imagine living without them.

Clearly, eating "disorders" are only superficially about being thin or conforming to this idealized representation of self. Eating "disorders" are "both/and" practices of self-attempting to "have one's cake and eat it too." In short, eating "disorders" resist constraining and limiting performances of the feminine gendered self—this is the struggle. Simultaneously, they conform and resist without overtly disrupting a gendered performance of self. They achieve this by appearing only to conform, while actually also resisting. Eating "disorders" are a way for women to simultaneously *speak* and *hide from speaking*. The struggle is masked and hidden. Efforts to simply eradicate or manage symptoms keep this struggle masked and hidden and thus render invisible the suppressed voice. When we move past constructing women as simply victims of anorexia, we allow for the interpretation of the body as an arena of both conformity and resistance—a site for control and power. The story of externalization that constructs women as victims, tricked by anorexia or bulimia, doesn't allow for this recognition, and, critically, it therefore does not enable the rewriting of unhelpful, limiting, constricting, or oppressive problem stories of self. My observation is that the unheard voice must be heard or the body will continue to talk. The body will continue to represent the unspoken, and the unspoken, hidden struggle will become more entrenched. Externalizing approaches that totalize women as being without power or agency may contribute to the exacerbation and entrenchment of the eating "disorder."

Talking Body Talk: Resourcing the Body as Voice

Sarah was a 20-year-old woman living at home with her parents. She had attended community college and hoped to attend university in the fall to study theater. She worked retail in a women's clothing store but was otherwise very socially isolated. She attended a residential program out of the province when she felt her bulimia had gotten too out of control and learned some behavioral strategies for slowing down the desire to binge and purge. She was not interested in local outpatient or inpatient programs available to her. She was referred to me in private practice through her doctor. At that time, Sarah was 120 pounds, which she felt was too fat. She binged and purged several times a day. I noticed that when I asked her to elaborate upon a story she was telling or when I attempted to explore what something meant, Sarah almost always said, "I don't know." She had recently broken up with a boyfriend who had been emotionally restrictive and controlling. She reported that she did not feel loved and that she felt invisible in her own life. Almost all of her close relationships were conflicted for her because she had so much difficulty expressing what she actually felt to others, for fear of disapproval. Although her parents had been pressuring and policing her to stop her bulimic behavior, she emphatically stated to me, "I am not giving it up to make them happy." This became an important entry point for us to talk about how her bulimia was a form of resistance, especially as this may have been one of only a few times in her life (a unique outcome or stalled initiative) that she chose to do something she wanted to do when it was likely to upset someone else.

In our work together, I drew her attention to how often she said "I don't know" when asked a question, without giving herself time to think about it. I told her that I had a feeling that she probably could know if she gave herself permission to explore her thoughts and feelings. I shared with her that I wondered if she might be ambivalent, even scared, of listening to or expressing her own voice. This very quickly became an entry point for us to explore the extent to which she recognized and exercised her own voice and to begin to explore how she resourced her body as her voice. When Sarah said, " I don't know," I slowed down the conversation and encouraged her to notice how she had attempted to stop the conversation from proceeding, to explore what was hard or scary about expressing herself.[11] By the time we had ended our work together, Sarah no longer said "I don't know" in therapy. Instead of masking, she had begun to claim her voice.

Sarah's story is illustrative of a tension between compliance and resistance to the performance of gendered subjectivity. She feared being too aggressive, loud, or disagreeable or being thought of as selfish. Yet complying with this expectation left her feeling dissatisfied with her relationships and with how powerless she felt over her life. She wanted to feel more powerful and more in control of her life, but to achieve this, she had to resist or reject the gendered performance of self she had internalized. Sarah described her bulimia as "the only thing I have that is for me."

Through the narrative process of externalization, I encouraged the resurrection of Sarah's suppressed voice. In doing so, we explored what story the eating "disorder" told that Sarah herself was not yet comfortable saying more directly. I explored with Sarah the difference between believing that she was fat and feeling that she was fat. Sarah told me that she "knew" she was not too fat, but that she "felt" too fat. This was an initial way to shift our focus away from weight and eating onto the *meaning* or story of her weight and eating behavior for her. Through exploring her weight history and body image, times she felt thinner or fatter, and the meanings associated with this for her, we further opened up the idea that it is the meaning of fatness and thinness that is critical, not the actual weight. Through connecting the story of her weight with her difficulty expressing her struggles, we began to make a connection between her weight, bingeing, purging, and her lack of voice. We explored how she learned what it meant to be a "good girl" and her history of conforming to and resisting this idea. In this re-authoring of gendered identity, we explored the limitations of these expectations and what she wanted that was different.

My approach to externalizing Sarah's struggle is not to externalize the bulimia so much as to externalize the unspoken narrative threads that have produced this kind of body talk. With Sarah, we began by externalizing "I don't know" and moved into externalizing her expectations of herself as a young woman. From there, we moved into externalizing the relationship between being afraid of her own voice and her internalized gender performance. We made sense of how she was afraid of her voice and began to work on her being less afraid of it. In therapy, she began to explore what would happen when she said what she thought and expressed what had previously been unexpressible. She was invited to abandon her notions of being a "good girl" when we were engaged in therapeutic conversations. We explored what "worked" and "did not work" for her in keeping her voice suppressed. We agreed that our efforts would focus on resurrecting her suppressed voice, the yet to be spoken. We unpacked her bulimic behavior, its history of development, its influence on her life, and her influence over it. We explored what kind of life she wanted, what kind of relationships. She replaced the story that she had, to control her thoughts or feelings or "suck it up" when she was upset, with the importance of expressing herself. In addition, she began to develop a better sense of the kinds of relationships she might be able to have if she abandoned some of her previous internalized dominant stories of appropriate gender performance. This meant acknowledging that she preferred to be in relationships in which she didn't make herself disappear and in which, subsequently, there was greater intimacy. Throughout this externalization process, Sarah's power, choice, and agency were emphasized. I did not help to create an externalization of her story that was anti-bulimic; instead, we explored the many layers in her story of bulimia, looking at how it had come to make sense in her life and how it was now making less sense. We explored her ambivalence about the bulimia.

There were several important elements to my work with Sarah that I introduced at the onset to set the stage for our work together. I began by telling Sarah that I wasn't going to engage in power struggles about her weight and eating—that she was in charge of this. I explained that we would not focus too much on weight and eating, but more on exploring the meaning they had for her. I suggested that eating "disorders" make sense and that we needed to figure out what her eating "disorder" was saying. I also made my stance very clear: I told her that I didn't believe she was cognitively impaired (she had been told she was and was concerned with this) or that she has a disease. I was not trying to convince her that her bulimic behavior was bad or to educate her on its negative effects on her life. Reflecting my feminist approach, I emphasized the importance of her being in control of or in charge of what happened to her body. Part of adopting a nonpathologizing approach included the recognition that she was responsible for taking care of her health status. My approach to externalizing conversations stressed that her bulimic behavior made sense in the context of her life.

There are many competing and contradictory stories that need to be explored in the process of externalization. My focus is on helping women to re-author their gender identities and rewrite stories that work better for them. Together, Sarah and I explored the story lines "I don't know" and "I am not giving it up to make them happy," discovering that they reflected conformance and resistance to gendered subjectivity, which was articulated through her body struggles. We shifted the focus from the surface story in attempting to make sense of her bulimia and toward resurrecting her suppressed or hidden voice. Although we explored many aspects of her experience, I have focused here upon externalizing "I don't know" and "I'm not giving it up to make them happy."

Through Sarah's story, we can see the ways in which she used or resourced her "bulimia" as a way to deal with struggles in the gendered performance of self. She struggled with internalized dominant stories about what it means to be a "good girl" and, in particular, the requirement that she should not have needs or desires or be oppositional in relation to others. These gendered demands often resulted in her sense of being invisible, unworthy, unloved, and desperately lost when it came to the direction she wanted her life to take. For so long, she had disqualified her own sense of what she wanted that she no longer knew what she wanted. She had been so busy trying to please other people that she had stopped listening to her own voice and to what she needed and wanted. Indeed, she appeared to have been afraid of her own voice.

Conclusion

A merging of feminist and narrative approaches can help women recognize how they resource their bodies to express their struggles. As women attempt to control their bodies as a mechanism for achieving greater control in their lives, it is important to not reinscribe culturally limited stories of women as victims. Externalizing approaches that construct women as victims of anorexia and bulimia fail to recognize that these eating problems are forms of resistance. If these forms of resistance are shut down or controlled during the externalization process, a woman's suppressed voice is only further disqualified. It is important to unpack ways in which body talk expresses both conformance and resistance to gendered subjectivity. Totalizing women's troubles with eating "disorders" and weight preoccupation as products of an oppressive culture strips women of their power and agency. Externalizing that focuses only on women's powerlessness, without also acknowledging women's power, strength, and agency, dishonors and trivializes not only the eating "disorders," but women themselves. Re-authoring gendered identities within feminist narrative therapy requires deconstructing the subjugated problem stories. Until unheard stories of struggle and resistance are heard, the body will continue to talk.

Notes

1. I refer to *needs, emotions,* and *desires* in this chapter as fully social and embodied, not as fixed, natural, or essential. The chapter attempts to articulate the specific way that women resource their bodies in the performance of gendered subjectivity to reconcile conflicts between their internal lives and the social expectations of them. I am, furthermore, not suggesting that by resurrecting the suppressed voice of body talk that women will discover or satisfy their real selves. I adopt the view that the self is a fully social construct that takes particular forms relative to the social and historical contexts of its creation. The self is both a creator of and created by social life.

2. Other contributions to feminist therapy in this field include Bergner, Remer, & Whetsell (1985); C. Brown (1987b, 1900a, 1990b); L. Brown (1985a, 1985b, 1989); Hutchinson, 1985; Kano, 1985; Kearney-Cooke (Kearney-Cooke, 1988, 1991; Kearney-Cooke & Striegel-Moore, 1994); Lawrence (Dana & Lawrence, 1988; Lawrence, 1984, 1987; Lawrence & Dana, 1990); Root (1988, 1991); Root & Fallon (1988, 1989); Steiner-Adair (1991); Wooley (1991, 1994); Wooley & Kearney-Cooke (1986); Wooley & Wooley (1980, 1984, 1986a, 1986b, n.d.); Wooley, Wooley, & Dyrenforth (1979a, 1979b).

3. Within this dominant discourse, the social context that makes eating problems a viable and common response to women's distress is either minimized as being one variable among many that "determine" eating "disorders" or rendered completely invisible. In contrast, feminist interpretations of women's body struggles acknowledge their experiences of trauma, the particular historical epoch in which eating "disorders" have proliferated, the changing and contradictory social roles of women, the social pressure to be thin, and the meaning of the body for women in advanced Western capitalist societies. Women's particular social locations with respect to class, race, ethnic, and sexual preference are also considered important social contexts in shaping the likelihood for developing eating "disorders" (Bellar, 1977; Brand, Rothblum, & Solomon, 1992; Dolan, 1991; Epel, Spanakos, Kasl-Godley, & Brownell, 1996; Grange, Telch, & Agras, 1997; Hefferman, 1996; Hsu, 1987; Rand & Kuldau, 1992; Rosen et al., 1988).

Postmodern and anti-oppressive models of practice inquiry urge us to recognize differences among women's experiences. As a feminist inquiry, this project does refer to a generalized "woman," while acknowledging that women's experiences of their bodies and eating are not universal. The meaning that women attach to their bodies and eating behavior is significantly shaped by social location, despite the homogenizing impact of body ideals. Through epidemiological studies, we can see that the meaning and experience of the body is always socially mediated.

Unlike most of the feminist writers to date, Thompson (1994) articulates the experiences of women of color with eating and body image problems in North America. Hers is one of few comprehensive examination of this issue, making visible the relationship women of color have to their bodies and eating. Thompson views eating problems as a survival mechanism or strategy to "injustices including racism, sexism, homophobia, classism, the stress of acculturation, and emotional, physical, and sexual abuse" (p. 2). In addition, she argues, like many feminists, that women and girls use their bodies to speak of atrocities and trauma, including histories of sexual abuse.

4. There are many discourses at work in this therapeutic field that may remain problematically intact (see Bellar, 1977; Brown & Jasper, 1993a; Dyrenforth, Wooley, & Wooley, 1980; Keys, Brozek, Henschel, Mickelson, & Taylor, 1950). For example, so entrenched is the value of thinness, it may not be questioned. Largely unsubstantiated assumptions about health, eating, and the body are often take up as truth. For example, it is often assumed that fat is unhealthy, that all people want to be thin, that all people can be thin, that fat people eat more than thin people, and that fat people have psychological problems (Brown & Jasper, 1993a). In addition, it is often presumed that there is a natural body—a universally preferred, healthy, and attractive body. This assumption makes no room for differences in human body types, cultural preferences, or changing body ideals over time. The body itself is naturalized, treated as though it could be understood outside of the cultural meanings that are attached to it. Similarly, eating itself is often naturalized, whereby it is assumed that there are inherently healthy food choices and patterns of eating. Once again, not only does this negate differences across cultures and time, it presumes we can produce an objective account of this independent of cultural meaning and value.

5. Even the development of criteria for eating "disorders" in the *Diagnostic and Statistical Manual of Mental Disorders (DSM)*—a dividing practice, separating the normal weight-preoccupied individual from the abnormal—has kept evolving, adding important new attitudinal and behavioral distinctions. The "fine-tuning" of such categorical markers reflects a means to determine the differences between women, when, in fact, many "normal" or average women would meet significant aspects of the *DSM* criteria. The *DSM,* then, became a socially sanctioned and legitimized mechanism for drawing a line in the sand, differentiating those with socially condoned weight obsession from those marked with problematic and pathological obsession. That said, fear of being fat, preoccupation with dieting and weight loss regardless of body size, and "distorted body image," all signs of eating "disorders," were, and are, common, everyday behaviors among most women in North American culture (Garner, Olmstead, & Garfinkle, 1983; Garner, Olmstead, Polivy, & Garfinkle, 1984).

6. While some feminists (Seid, 1989; Wolf, 1990) characterize women's preoccupation with weight as a "being at war with their bodies," others, such as Chernin (1981), argue that the thin ideal represents women's continued oppression, requiring women to police their bodies and deny their appetites; and yet others, such as Hollander (1980) and Cauwells (1983), suggest thinness represents increased equality through a nonreproductive image of freedom, mobility, and independence.

7. Parts of this chapter draw on *Feeding Into Each Other: Weight Preoccupation and the Contradictory Expectations of Women* (Brown, 1987a), my unpublished master's thesis in sociology at University of Manitoba.

8. One problem with the media's pressure to be thin as an explanation of women's experiences with their bodies and weight is that it doesn't explore why thinness as a metaphor might have meaning for our culture and for women specifically. Thinness as an ideal must offer something to women for it to have taken hold as it has. There can be little doubt that women absorb and internalize the ideal of thinness through myriad messages and experiences that stigmatize against fatness. They often report positive consequences, including significant social approval for losing weight and women's conversations with each other that reify the value and cultural meaning of thinness. Furthermore, the medical profession, a powerful and authoritative body, rearticulates the message that "fat is bad" and "thin is good" on a regular basis in their demands that patients lose weight and their often unfounded assumption that fat is unhealthy. Legitimized by their social status as "knowers," medical doctors and even nutritionists perpetuate many socially constructed myths about fat and eating as members of this culture who also have internalized the dominant stories about weight (Thille, 2004). As such, the veneer of social assumptions obstructs practices that were are both helpful and healthy. Making sense of understanding women's weight preoccupation must go beyond seeing women as victims of social pressure (from media, the medical profession, family, and friends) to exploring how women might meaningfully seek power and express resistance through the culturally encoded thin body ideal and the ways that the associated actions for attaining thinness become gendered practices of self-restraint. This feminist narrative approach allows for stories to surface that acknowledge both women's power and powerlessness.

9. The "anti" leagues are not the only way that one can become involved in educating people about weight and shape issues or challenging the pressure to be thin and dieting behaviors. Over the past 30 years, many different organizations have emerged, including the National Eating Disorders Information Center (Bear & Gayle, 1993); Hersize: A Weight Prejudice Action Group (Jasper, 1993); and the Eating Disorders Awareness Group in Toronto. Many organizations have come and gone over time. I started a program "Getting Beyond Weight" at the Women's Health Clinic in Winnipeg during the 1980s, and it approached the continuum of weight preoccupation issues among women in a nonmedicalizing, nonpathologizing, and socially contextualized manner (see Brown, 1987a; Brown & Forgay, 1987; Brown & Zimberg 1993). We were, in fact, externalizing eating "disorders" before narrative therapy emerged on the scene. In the process of externalizing eating "disorders," we never had to resort to constructing women as passive victims who were being tortured, murdered, or imprisoned by the problem. We deliberately sought to demystify eating problems to look at what made sense about them in the context of women's lives. While contemporary narrative externalizing strategies to eating "disorders" are well intended, they are reminiscent of traditional psychiatric approaches that abstract, objectify, and pathologize women's experiences. Within these traditional approaches, women's experiences were either invisible or they were something to put under the expert's gaze.

10. The anti-anorexia and anti-bulimia approach that some narrative therapists adopt is deeply problematic. In a discussion of White's work (1991, 2004b), well-known solution-focused therapist de Shazer (1993) highlights significant critiques of his approach to anorexia after viewing a videotape:

> I find it surprising and interesting that White seems to use "unique outcomes" as a tool in the battle against the power of anorexia. . . . what establishes the equation "unique outcomes equals anti-anorexia." This sets up "pro-anorexia vs. anti-anorexia," which leaves the focus precisely on "anorexia." That is, the "anorexia" is still the focal point of life and thus "anorexia" has lost none of its "Power to oppress." In fact, it now has two ways to "oppress the victim" (including the whole family), i.e., "pro-" and "anti-" ways. His behavior during the session indicates that he thinks that he has the better way. He introduces his "code book". . . . in short, his language is used rather than the client's language. . . . He confirms for them that anorexia is powerful and it needs continued "anti" practices to keep it in its place, i.e., under control. It is not a "both/and" practice, but an "either/or" practice: Something is either "pro-anorexia" *or* it is "anti-anorexia." (pp. 117–118)

De Shazer draws an analogy with disease-based treatment of "alcoholism," where the person is often storied as being under the control of alcohol. Dominant social discourses on alcohol use problems reify and totalize individuals as "alcoholics" through the idea that the individual has no control over alcohol—that it has control over them. As such, "alcoholics are fated to always be alcoholics," who must therefore abstain for life from alcohol use. Similar to the externalizing language of eating "disorders," traditional views of "addiction" describe individuals as being tricked or manipulated by their substance problems. Within this view, individuals' agency has been rendered invisible. Most often the problem becomes individualized, so that the social context and meaning of the problem remain unexamined. In contrast, within narrative approaches to eating "disorders," the problems are contextualized. However, when the context becomes deterministic or totalizing, individuals are left with no agency. Rather than being products of biology, they are now products of culture.

11. By referring to 'expressing herself' I am not referring to an essentialist notion of 'inner life' or of the self; rather, I view her subjective emotional experiences as inseparable from cultural discourse and context. I am relying on the notion of folk psychology, the language commonly used to understand sentient life (White, 2004a). Furthermore, I do not intend to invoke an absolute binary here between internal and external life, as they too are inseparable.

References

Adams-Westcot, J., Dafforn, T., & Sterne, P. (1993). Escaping victim life stories and co-constructing personal agency. In S. Gilligan, & R. Price (Eds.), *Therapeutic conversations* (pp. 258–276). New York: Norton.

Bear, M., & Gayle, A. (1993). The National Eating Disorders Information Program. In C. Brown & K. Jasper (Eds.), *Consuming passions: Feminist approaches to weight preoccupation and eating disorders* (pp. 409–420). Toronto, Canada: Second Story Press.

Bellar, A. (1977). *Fat and thin: A natural history of obesity.* New York: Farrar, Straus and Giroux.

Berger, J. (1972). *Ways of seeing.* London: Penguin Books.

Berger, P., & Luckmann, T. (1967). *The social construction of reality: A treatise in the sociology of knowledge.* New York: Anchor Books.

Bergner, M., Remer, P., & Whetsell, C. (1985). Transforming women's body image: A feminist counselling approach. *Women and Therapy, 4*(3), 25–38.

Bloom, C., Gitter, A., Gutwill, S., Kogel, L., & Zaphiropoulos, L. (1994). *Eating problems: A feminist psychoanalytic treatment model.* New York: Basic Books.

Bordo, S. (1993). *Unbearable weight: Feminism, Western culture, and the body.* Berkeley: University of California Press.

Brand, P., Rothblum, E., & Solomon, L. (1992). A comparison of lesbians, gay men, and heterosexuals on weight and restrained eating. *International Journal of Eating Disorders, 11*(3), 253–259.

Brown, C. (1987a). *Feeding into each other: Weight preoccupation and the contradictory expectations of women.* Unpublished master's thesis, University of Manitoba, Department of Sociology, Winnipeg, Canada.

Brown, C. (1987b). *Getting beyond weight: Women helping women. Self-help manual.* Winnipeg, Canada: Women's Health Clinic.

Brown, C. (1989, Summer). Review of "Never Too Thin," by Eva Szekely. *Fireweed, 29,* 123–127.

Brown, C. (1990a). *Contracting in feminist therapy for eating "disorders."* Unpublished independent inquiry project, master's of social work. Carleton University, School of Social Work. Ottawa, Canada.

Brown, C. (1990b). The "control paradox": Understanding and working with anorexia and bulimia. *National Eating Disorders Centre Bulletin.* Toronto, Canada.

Brown, C. (1993a). The continuum: Anorexia, bulimia, and weight preoccupation. In C. Brown & K. Jasper (Eds.), *Consuming passions: Feminist approaches to weight preoccupation and eating disorders* (pp. 53–68). Toronto, Canada: Second Story Press.

Brown, C. (1993b). Feminist contracting. Power and empowerment in therapy. In C. Brown & K. Jasper (Eds.), *Consuming passions: Feminist approaches to weight preoccupation and eating disorders* (pp. 176–194). Toronto, Canada: Second Story Press.

Brown, C. (1993c). Feminist therapy: Power, ethics, and control. In C. Brown & K. Jasper (Eds.), *Consuming passions: Feminist approaches to weight preoccupation and eating disorders* (pp. 120–136). Toronto, Canada: Second Story Press.

Brown, C., & Forgay, D. (1987, Winter). An uncertain well-being: Weight control and self control. *Healthsharing,* pp. 11–15.

Brown, C., & Jasper, K. (1993a). *Consuming passions: Feminist approaches to weight preoccupation and eating disorders.* Toronto, Canada: Second Story Press.

Brown, C., & Jasper, K. (1993b). Why weight? Why women? Why now? In C. Brown & K. Jasper (Eds.), *Consuming passions: Feminist approaches to weight preoccupation and eating disorders* (pp. 16–35). Toronto, Canada: Second Story Press.

Brown, C., & Zimberg, R. (1993). "Getting Beyond Weight": Women's Health Clinic Weight Preoccupation Program. In C. Brown & K. Jasper (Eds.), *Consuming passions: Feminist approaches to weight preoccupation and eating disorders* (pp. 400–408). Toronto, Canada: Second Story Press.

Brown, L. (1985a). Power, responsibility, boundaries: Ethical issues for the lesbian feminist therapist. *Lesbian Ethics, 1,* 30–45.

Brown, L. (1985b). Women, weight, and power: Feminist theoretical and therapeutic issues. *Women and Therapy, 4*(1), 61–71.

Brown, L. (1989). Fat-oppressive attitudes and the feminist therapist: Directions for change. *Women and Therapy, 8*(3), 19–29.

Bruner, J. (2002). *Making stories. Law, literature, life.* Cambridge, MA: Harvard University Press.

Butler, J. (1993). *Bodies that matter: On the discursive limits of "sex."* New York: Routledge.

Cauwells, J. (1983). *Bulimia: The bing-epurge compulsion.* New York: Doubleday.

Chernin, K. (1981). *The obsession: Reflections of the tyranny of slenderness.* New York: Harper & Row.

Courtney, J., & Williams, L. (2000). Linking lives: Working with women experiencing eating problems. *Gecko: A Journal of Deconstruction and Narrative Ideas in Therapeutic Practice, 2,* 17–38.

Dana, M., & Lawrence, M. (1988). *Women's secret disorder: A new understanding of bulimia.* Toronto, Canada: Grafton Books.

de Shazer, S. (1993). Commentary: De Shazer and White: Vive la difference. In S. Gilligan & R. Price (Eds.), *Therapeutic conversations* (pp. 112–120). New York: Norton.

Dolan, B. (1991). Cross-cultural aspects of anorexia nervosa and bulimia: A review. *International Journal of Eating Disorders, 10*(1), 67–78.

Dyrenforth, S., Wooley. O., & Wooley, S. (1980). A woman's body in a man's world: A review of findings on body image and weight control. In R. Kaplan (Eds.), *A woman's conflict. The special relationship between women and food* (pp. 30–57). Englewood Cliffs, NJ: Prentice Hall.

Epel, E., Spanakos, A., Kasl-Godley, J., & Brownell, K. (1996). Body shape ideals across gender, sexua lorientation, socio-economic status, race, and age in personal advertisements. *International Journal of Eating Disorders, 19*(3), 265–273.

Epston, D., Morris, F., & Maisel, R. (1998). A narrative approach to so-called anorexia/bulimia. In D. Epston (Ed.), *Catching up with David Epston: A collection of narrative practice-based papers published between 1991–1996* (pp. 149–174). Adeldaide, Australia: Dulwich Centre.

Fallon, P., Katzman, M., & Wooley, S. (1994). *Feminist perspectives on eating disorders.* New York: Guilford.

Foucault, M. (1980a). *The history of sexuality: Vol. 1. An introduction.* New York: Vintage.

Foucault, M. (1980b). *Power/knowledge: Selected interviews and other writings 1972–1977.* New York: Pantheon.

Garner, D., Olmstead, M., & Garfinkle, P. (1983). Does anorexia nervosa occur on a continuum? *International Journal of Eating Disorders, 2*(4), 11–20.

Garner, D., Olmstead, M., Polivy, J., & Garfinkle, P. (1984). Comparison between weight-preoccupied women and anorexia nervosa. *Psychosomatic Medicine, 46*(3), 255–266.

Geertz, C. (1973). *Thick description: Toward an interpretive theory of culture.* New York: Basic Books.

Grange, D., Telch, C., & Agras, W. (1997). Eating and general psychopathology in a sample of Caucasian and ethnic minority subjects. *International Journal of Eating Disorders, 21,* 285–293.

Gremillion, H. (2001). Anorexia: A canary in the mine. An anthropological perspective. An interview with Helen Gremillion. In *Working with the stories of women's lives* (pp. 135–157). Adelaide, Australia: Dulwich Centre.

Gremillion, H. (2003). *Feeding anorexia. Gender and power at a treatment center.* Durham, NC: Duke University Press.

Grieves, L. (1998). From beginning to start. The Vancouver Anti-Anorexia/Anti-Bulimia League. In S. Madigan & I. Law (Eds.), *PRAXIS: Situating discourse, feminism, and politics in narrative therapies* (pp. 197–205). Vancouver, Canada: Cardigan Press.

Hefferman, K.(1996). Eating disorders and weight concern among lesbians. *International Journal of Eating Disorders, 19*(2), 127–138.

Hollander, A. (1980). *Seeing through clothes. Fashioning ourselves an intriguing new look at image making.* New York: Viking Press.

Hosking, C. (2001). My body will not be excluded. In *Working with stories of women's lives* (pp. 159–164). Adelaide, Australia: Dulwich Centre.

Hsu, G. (1987). Are the eating disorders becoming more common in Blacks? *International Journal of Eating Disorders, 6*(1), 113–124.

Hutchinson, M. (1985). *Transforming body image: Learning to love the body you have.* New York: The Crossing Press.

Jasper, K. (1993). Hersize: A Weight-Prejudice Action Group. In C. Brown & K. Jasper (Eds.), *Consuming passions: Feminist approaches to weight preoccupation and eating disorders* (421–428). Toronto, Canada: Second Story Press.

Kano, S. (1985). *Making peace with food: A step-by-step guide to freedom from diet/weight control.* Danbury, CT: Amity.

Kearney-Cooke, A. (1988). Group therapy of sexual abuse among women with eating disorders. *Women & Therapy, 7*(1), 5–21.

Kearney-Cooke, A. (1991). The role of the therapist in the treatment of eating disorders: A feminist psychodynamic approach. In C. Johnson (Ed.), *Psychodynamic treatment of anorexia nervosa and bulimia* (pp. 295–320). New York: Guilford.

Kearney-Cooke, A., & Striegel-Moore, R. (1994). Treatment of childhood sexual abuse in anorexia and bulimia nervosa: A feminist psychodynamic approach. *International Journal of Eating Disorders, 15*(4), 305–319.

Keys, A., Brozek, J., Henschel, A., Mickelson, O., & Taylor, H. (1950). *The biology of human starvation* (Vol. 1.). Minneapolis: University of Minnesota Press.

Kraner, M., & Ingram, K. (1998). Busting out-busting free. A group program for young women wanting to reclaim their lives from anorexia nervosa. In C. White & D. Denborough (Eds.), *Introducing narrative therapy: A collection of practice-based writings* (pp. 91–115). Adelaide, Australia: Dulwich Centre.

Krusky, M. (2002). Women and thinness: The watch on the eve of the feast. Therapy with families experiencing troubled eating. *Journal of Systemic Therapies, 21*(1), 58–76.

Lawrence, M. (1979). Anorexia nervosa: The control paradox. *Women's Studies International, 2,* 93–101.

Lawrence, M. (1984). *The anorexic experience.* London: The Women's Press.

Lawrence, M. (Ed.). (1987). *Fed up and hungry: Women, oppression, and food.* London: The Women's Press.

Lawrence, M., & Dana, M. (1990). *Fighting food: Coping with eating disorders.* London: Penguin Books.

Lawrence, M., & Lowenstein, C. (1979, June). Self starvation. *Sparerib, 83,* 41–43.

Maisel, R., Epston, D., & Borden, A. (2004). *Biting the hand that starves you: Inspiring resistance to anorexia and bulimia.* New York: Norton.

Malson, H. (1997). Anorexic bodies and the discursive production of feminine excess. In J. Ussher (Ed.), *Body talk: The material and discursive regulation of sexuality, madness, and reproduction* (pp. 223–245). New York: Routledge.

Mead, G. (1977). *On social psychology.* Chicago: University of Chicago Press.

Millman, M. (1980). *Such a pretty face: Being fat in America.* New York: Norton.

Nyland, D. (2002). Poetic means to anti-anorexic ends. *Journal of Systemic Therapies, 21*(4), 18–34.

Orbach, S. (1978). *Fat is a feminist issue.* New York: Paddington Books.

Orbach, S. (1986). *Hunger strike: The anorectic struggle as a metaphor for our age.* New York: Norton.

Polthemus, T. (1978). *Social aspects of the human body.* New York: Penguin Books.

Rand, C., & Kuldau, J. (1992). Epidemiology of bulimia and symptoms in a general population: Sex, age, race, and socioeconomic status. *International Journal of Eating Disorders, 11*(1), 37–44.

Root, M. (1988). Treatment failures: A role of sexual victimization in women's addictive behavior. *American Journal of Orthopsychiatry, 59*(4), 542–549.

Root, M. (1991). Persistent, disordered eating as a gender specific, post-traumatic stress response to sexual assault. *Psychotherapy, 28*(1), 96–102.

Root, M., & Fallon, P. (1988). The incidence of victimization experiences in a bulimic sample. *Journal of Interpersonal Violence, 3*(2), 161–173.

Root, M., & Fallon, P. (1989). Treating the victimized bulimic. The functions of binge-purge. *Journal of International Violence, 4*(1), 90–100.

Rosen, L. W., Shafer, C. L., Drummer, G. M., Cross, L. K., Deuman, G. W., & Malmberg, S. R. (1988). Prevalence of pathogenic weight-control behaviors among Native American women and girls. *International Journal of Eating Disorders, 7*(6), 807–811.

Seid, R. P. (1989). *Never too thin: Why women are at war with their bodies.* New York: Prentice Hall.

Steiner-Adair, C. (1991). New maps of development, New models of therapy: The psychology of women and the treatment of eating disorders In C. Johnson (Ed.), *Psychodynamic treatment of anorexia nervosa and bulimia* (pp. 225–244). New York: Guilford.

Thille, P. (2004). *Women-centred sensitive guidelines for weight issues: A proactive primary prevention approach.* Unpublished master's thesis, Dalhousie University, Halifax, Canada.

Thompson, B. (1994). *A hunger so wide and so deep: American women speak out on eating problems.* Minneapolis: University of Minnesota Press.

Ussher, J. (1997). *Body talk: The material and discursive regulation of sexuality, madness, and reproduction.* New York: Routledge.

White, M. (1991). Deconstruction and therapy. *Dulwich Centre Newsletter, 3,* 21–40.

White, M. (1994). *The politics of therapy: Putting to rest the illusion of neutrality.* Adelaide, Australia: Dulwich Centre.

White, M. (1995). *Re-authoring lives: Interviews & essays.* Adelaide, Australia: Dulwich Centre.

White, M. (1997). *Narrative of therapists' lives.* Adelaide, Australia: Dulwich Centre.

White, M. (2001). Narrative practice and the unpacking of identity conclusions. *Gecko: A Journal of Deconstruction and Narrative Ideas in Therapeutic Practice, 1,* 28–55.

White, M. (2004a). *Narrative practice and exotic lives: Resurrecting diversity in everyday life.* Adelaide, Australia: Dulwich Centre.

White, M. (2004b, March 8–9). *Narrative therapy: New modalities of practice* (Workshop). Truro, Canada.

White, M., & Epston D. (1990). *Narrative means to therapeutic ends.* New York: Norton.

Wolf, N. (1990). *The beauty myth.* New York: Vintage Books.

Wooley, S. (1991). Uses of countertransference in the treatment of eating disorders: A gender perspective. In C. Johnson (Ed.), *Psychodynamic treatment of anorexia nervosa and bulimia* (pp. 245–294). New York: Guilford.

Wooley, S. (1994). Sexual abuse and eating disorders: The concealed debate. In P. Fallon, M. Katzman, & S. Wooley (Eds.), *Feminist perspectives on eating disorders* (pp. 171–211). New York: Guilford.

Wooley, S., & Kearney-Cooke, A. (1986). Intensive treatment of bulimia and body image disturbances. In. K. Brownell & J. Foreyt (Eds.), *Handbook of eating disorders: Physiology, psychology, and treatment of obesity, anorexia, and bulimia.* New York: Basic Books.

Wooley, S., & Wooley, O. (1980). Eating disorders: Obesity and anorexia. In A. Brodsky & R. Hare-Mustin (Eds.), *Women and psychotherapy: An assessment of research and practice* (pp. 135–158). New York: Guilford.

Wooley, S., & Wooley, O. (1984). Should obesity be treated at all? In A. Stunkard, & E. Stellar (Eds.), *Eating and its disorders* (pp. 186–192). New York: Raven Books.

Wooley, S., & Wooley, O. (1986a, October). Ambitious bulimics: Thinness mania. *American Health*, 68–74.

Wooley, S., & Wooley, O. (1986b). Editorial: The Beverly Hills eating disorder: The mass marketing of anorexia nervosa. *International Journal of Eating Disorders, 1*(3), 57–69.

Wooley, S., & Wooley, O. (n.d.). *Women and weight: Toward a redefinition of the therapeutic task.* Unpublished paper, University of Cincinnati, Department of Psychiatry, College of Medicine, Cincinnati, OH.

Wooley, O., Wooley, S., & Dyrenforth, S. (1979a). Obesity and women II: A neglected feminist topic. *Women's Studies International Quarterly, 2,* 81–92.

Wooley. S., Wooley, O., & Dyrenforth, S. (1979b). Theoretical, practical, and social issues in behavioral treatments of obesity. *Journal of Applied Behavior Analysis, 1*(12), 3–25.

Index

Miley, C., 198
Miller, L. J., 25, 33
Miller, S., xxxix, 65
Millman, M., 119, 272
Minuchin, S., 81, 207
Mobius strip, xxvii, 151–152, 158,
   159, 164, 168, 169
Mohr, R. D., 163
Molnar, A., xiii, xxxix
Monk, G., xiii
Moore, D., 44
Morris, F., 282
Morrow, S. L., 161
Mosher, L. R., 66
Mossige, S., 207
Musto, D. F., 60

National Institute of Mental Health
   (NIMH), 56n 7
Negative identities, 178, 192,
   252, 253–256
   behaviors and, 255–256
   shame and, 258–261, 260
   See also Identities
Nemeroff, C. B., 23
Neutrality, xi, 6
   men's violence and, 207–208
   non-neutral and, 11–12
Nietzsche, F., 133, 149
Not-knowing stance, 7–9
Nyland, D., 282

O'Hanlon, W., 82
Olivardia, R., 56n 4
Oliver, W., 211
Olmstead, M., 294
Oppression:
   dichotomous framework and, 216
   experiences and, 180, 183, 185
   homosexuals and, 170
   identities and, 189
   men's violence and, 205
   power and, 13, 14–15, 18, 105
   re-storying and, 187
   sexism and, 219–221. See also
      Sexism; Sexual abuse
   women and, 118–119,
      275–276, 276

women's bodies and, 110, 123
   See also Anti-oppressive discourses
Orbach, S., 115, 117, 118, 119, 272,
   275, 282, 286

Pain:
   re-authoring identities and, 261
   sexual abuse and, 253, 255, 256,
      262
   substance misuse and, 33, 38, 63,
      65, 67, 69, 72
Pare, D., xxiii
Parents:
   medications and, 94, 95
   narrative psychiatry and, 79, 80,
      81, 83–84, 85, 86, 87, 88,
      91–92, 97–98
   victim blaming and, 230
   See also Families
Parker, I., 139
Parry, A., xiii, 11
Parry, T., 82
Patterson, O., 222n 2
Paymar, M., 197, 198, 203, 205,
   209, 214, 221, 266n 2
Payne, M., xiv
Pearson, P., 198, 217
Peele, S., 60, 61
Peller, J., 11
Pence, E., 197, 198, 203, 205, 209,
   214, 221, 266
Perez, F., 211
Perilla, J., 211
Personality traits, 43–44
Phillips, K. A., xiv, 56, 56n 4
Phillips, M., xiv
Pinhas, L., 41
Politics, 14
   diseases and, 72
   eating disorders and, 48–51, 55
   experiences and, 17, 192
   gender and, 191
   homosexuals and, 161, 167,
      168, 170
   men's violence and, 207–208
   narrative psychiatry and, 78
   substance misuse and, 62, 63,
      64, 65, 72

self and, 17, 158
self-discipline and, xxvi,
    105–109, 112
women's bodies and, 110, 115–116,
    122, 275
See also Western culture
Solomon, L., 293
Spanakos, A., 293n 3
Spelman, E., 122, 123
Spiegel, A., 61
Spring, T., 155
St. John, K., 163
Stanley, L., 11
Statement-of-position, xxxiii, 245
Steele, S., 214, 215, 216
Steiger, H., 56n 5
Steiner-Adair, C., 293n 2
Stepanek, M., 155
Sterne, P., 271
Sternhell, C., 119
Stoppard, J. M., xxii, 23, 24, 25, 27,
    31, 32, 33, 34
Storytelling rights, 138
Stress:
    narrative psychiatry and, 91, 98
    schools and, 95
    women's depression and, 31–32
Striegel-Moore, R., 293n 2
Strong, T., xiii
Stuckless, N., 41
Sturdivant, S., 24
Suberri, K., 92
Substance misuse, xxviii, 59–60, 70
    adolescents and, 62, 66
    alcoholism and, xviii, 60, 63,
        251, 296
    diseases and, 60–63, 61, 63, 68, 72
    harm reduction and, 63–66, 72,
        127, 129
    identities and, 69, 71
    pain and, 33, 38, 63, 65, 67, 69, 72
    psychological pain and, 63
    re-authoring and, 72
    tobacco and, 71
    treatment of, 60–63
    See also Drugs
Suicide:
    identities and, 256
    sexual abuse and, 246

Sullivan, P. F., 43
Summaries, 107, 246–248, 249
Sunderland, J., 31
Szasz, T., 60

Tamasese, K., 67, 138
Tanesini, A., xxi, 5, 109
Tantleff-Dunn, S., 48
Tatum, B. D., xxx, 212
Taylor, H., 294n 4
Telch, C., 293n 3
Therapeutic conversations,
    124–127, 128
Therapeutic letter-writing, 142–146
Thille, P., 295, 295n 8
Thompson, B., 120, 273, 276,
    282, 294n 3
Thompson, J. K., 40, 48
Thomson, G., 66
Tiggemann, M., 41
Tjersland, O., 207
Tomm, K., 81, 82
Toner, B., 41
Tozzi, F., 56n 6
Training, 85, 89, 93
Transgender. *See* Lesbian, Gay,
    Bisexual, And Transgender
    (LGBT)
Trauma:
    conversational maps and, xxxvi,
        229, 234–236, 248
    cynicism and, 236
    identities and, 232
    letting go and, 233
    limitations of knowing and,
        233–234
    memories and, 231–232, 233,
        243, 249
    narrative psychiatry and, 83, 87
    pivotal events and, 243–245
    preferred identities and, 138, 178,
        237–239, 241, 242, 247
    self-blame and, 234
    sexual abuse and, xxxvi, 230,
        231, 246
    voice and, 231, 233, 240, 248
Treasure, J. T., 46, 49, 50
Truth, xv, xviii, xxix, 19
    clients as experts and, 9

tricking, 285, 287, 289
violence and, xxix
voices and, 279–280, 281
women's abusive behaviors and,
    198–199
Women's bodies:
control and, 110, 111–113, 115,
    117, 119, 125, 126–127, 128,
    185. *See also* Control
culture and, 106, 111, 113, 120,
    121, 128, 185
depression and, 25, 28, 30, 34,
    40–41
eating disorders and, 274. *See also*
    Eating disorders
environments and, 48
exhaustion and, 25, 28, 30,
    31, 32, 34
harm reduction and, 127
identities and, 118
inward struggle and, 116
power and, 120–122, 124, 126
race and, 122–123, 294n 3
resistance and, 111, 289, 292
self-discipline and, 105
society and, 275
values and, 278
weight loss and, 119, 270, 271,
    274–275, 278, 280, 292
See also Controlling women's
    bodies; Self-discipline
Women's depression, 23–34
abuse and, 24, 34

blame and, 31
bodies and, 25, 28, 30, 34, 40–41.
    See also Women's bodies
caring and, 31–33
culture and, 25–28, 30, 31, 34
identities and, 26–27, 30, 31–33
material-discursive approach to,
    xxii, xxiii, 25–30, 33, 34
media and, 31
medicalized approach to, 24
recovery and, 28–30
stress and, 31–32
understanding, 25–28
violence and, 24, 34
Wonderlich, S., 43
Wood, B., 211
Woodside, D. B., 42, 43, 46
Wooley, O., 119, 294n 4, 393n 1
Wooley. S., 119, 273, 294n 4, 393n 1
Worell, J., 24
Workshops:
invitational approaches and, 221
sexism and, 212–213, 218,
    219–220, 221, 222
Wylie, M. S., 61

Yardley, L., 25

Zaphiropoulos, L., 273
Zimberg, R., 274, 279, 295
Zimmerman, xiii
Zimmerman, J. L., xiii
Zweig, C., 181

About the Editors

Catrina Brown, MA, MSW, PhD, is an assistant professor at the School of Social Work at Dalhousie University, in Halifax, cross-appointed to Gender and Women's Studies and Nursing. Social Work and cross-appointed to Gender and women's Studies and Nursing at Dalhousie University, Halifax, Canada. She is also a feminist psychotherapist in private practice, with a focus on eating "disorders." She is the coeditor of *Consuming Passions: Feminist Approaches to Eating Disorders and Weight Preoccupation*. She conducts research in the area of women, eating "disorders," body image, trauma and sexual abuse, depression, and alcohol use problems.

Tod Augusta-Scott, MSW, is the program coordinator at Bridges, a domestic violence counseling, research, and training institute in Truro, Nova Scotia, Canada. He has taught at the School of Social Work at Dalhousie University, Halifax, Canada. He works as a consultant on issues of domestic violence for both government and nongovernment organizations. He is currently a member of the editorial board for *Canadian Social Work*. He publishes and presents his work internationally. His practice focuses primarily on issues of violence, sexual abuse, sexism, racism, and homophobia.

About the Contributors

Laura Béres, MSW, RSW, PhD, is an assistant professor at the School of Social Work at King's University College at the University of Western Ontario. The majority of her direct practice experience has been with adults who have experienced childhood sexual abuse and with women who have experienced abuse from their partners. She has also been involved in facilitating groups for men who have perpetrated abusive behavior. She is involved in research with the Hincks-Dellcrest Gail Appel Institute and the University of Toronto, examining narrative therapy and training, and with Catholic Family Services of Toronto, examining narrative approaches to working with men who have perpetrated abusive behavior.

Normand Carrey, MD, is a child and adolescent psychiatrist at the Department of Psychiatry, Dalhousie University, in Halifax, Canada. He is responsible for the family therapy training of psychiatry residents. He also teaches the History of Psychiatry and Reciprocal Influences of Psychiatry and Culture. He is a member of the International Resilience Project and clinical director of the Children's Response Program, a residential program for children. His research interests include developmental psychopharmacology and neuroimaging of severe disruptive behavior. In his spare time, he writes poetry, film reviews, and short stories. He is also a musician.

James Duvall, MEd, RSW, is the Director of Brief Therapy Training Centres-International™ (a division of The Hincks-Dellcrest Institute), Director of Training at The Hincks-Dellcrest Institute, and previous clinical director of a children's mental health center. In collaboration with the University of Toronto, Faculty of Social Work, he serves as co-investigator in a research project that focuses on narrative ideas and practices in training and therapy. He serves on the editorial advisory board of the *Journal of Systemic Therapies*. He consults and trains with various organizations internationally.

Karin Jasper, PhD, MEd, is Clinical Specialist with the Day Program for Eating Disorders at the Hospital for Sick Children in Toronto. She teaches a course on feminist issues in counseling and psychotherapy at the Ontario Institute for Studies in Education/University of Toronto (O.I.S.E./UT) and is coeditor with Catrina Brown of *Consuming Passions: Feminist Approaches to Weight Preoccupation and Eating Disorders.* She is currently occupied with developing the program at Sick Kids, using narrative and feminist practice to negotiate the tensions between teens' developing autonomy and the oppressive "authority" of the eating disorders in teens' lives.

Michelle Lafrance, PhD, is an assistant professor of psychology at St. Thomas University, in Fredericton, Canada. She has recently completed her PhD in clinical psychology at the University of New Brunswick, where she carried out research for her doctoral dissertation on women's recovery from depression. Her research interests are in the area of women's health and wellness.

Stephen Madigan, MSW, MSc, PhD, opened Yaletown Family Therapy in Vancouver (http://www.yaletownfamilytherapy.com) as the first narrative therapy clinic and training facility in the Northern Hemisphere. He is a cofounder of the narrative and therapy professionally accredited CE Web site (http://www.planet-therapy.com) and sponsors the annual Therapeutic Conversations Conference (http://www.therapeuticconversations.com). He is the father of amazing 10-year-old twin daughters, Hannah and Tessa Madigan.

Glenda M. Russell, PhD, is a psychologist who has worked as a therapist, teacher, researcher, organizational consultant, and activist. She serves as clinical director at New Leaf: Services for Our Community, a not-for-profit, multipurpose counseling center for the lesbian, gay, bisexual, and transgender community in San Francisco, and as senior research associate for the Institute for Gay and Lesbian Strategic Studies in Amherst, Massachusetts. She is the author of *Voted Out: The Psychological Consequences of Anti-Gay Politics* and, with Janis Bohan, *Conversations About Psychology and Sexual Orientation,* as well as numerous journal articles and book chapters.

Colin James Sanders, MA, lives in Vancouver, British Columbia. Colin teaches at and supervises the internship clinic for City University and is a therapist with the Employee and Family Assistance Program of Vancouver Coastal Health. He holds an MA in cultural anthropology and is interested in the ways in which theological, philosophical, and literary themes and ideas may be utilized to therapeutic benefit.

Janet Stoppard, PhD, is a professor of psychology at the University of New Brunswick, in Fredericton, Canada. She has worked as a clinical psychologist and has published widely on women, mental health, and depression. She is the author of *Understanding Depression: Feminist Social Constructionist Approaches* (2000) and the editor (with Linda McMullen) of *Situating Sadness: Women and Depression in Social Context* (2003).